Neural Computation and Self-Organizing Maps

An Introduction

Helge Ritter
University of Bielefeld, Germany

Thomas Martinetz
University of Illinois-Beckman Institute

Klaus Schulten
University of Illinois-Beckman Institute

Translated by Daniel Barsky, Marcus Tesch, and Ronald Kates

ADDISON-WESLEY PUBLISHING COMPANY

Reading, Massachusetts • Menlo Park, California • New York
Don Mills, Ontario • Wokingham, England • Amsterdam • Bonn
Sydney • Singapore • Tokyo • Madrid • San Juan • Milan • Paris

The Beckman Institute at the University of Illinois at Urbana-Champaign, where this book originated, has been made possible through the generosity of Arnold and Mabel Beckman. The authors have benefitted immensely from the privilege of working in this beautiful and stimulating place. We dedicate this book with gratitude to Arnold and Mabel Beckman whose lives have enriched and inspired so many.

Library of Congress Cataloging-in-Publication Data

Ritter, Helge.
Neural computation and self-organizing maps: an introduction / Helge Ritter, Thomas Martinetz, Klaus Schulten.
p. cm.
Also appeared in German under title: Neuronale Netze.
Includes bibliographical references and index.
1. Neural networks (Computer science) I. Martinetz, Thomas. II. Shulten, K. (Klaus) III. Title. IV. Title: Neuronale Netze.
QA76.87.R58 1991 006.3—dc20 91-30541
ISBN 0-201-55443-7 (hbk.)
ISBN 0-201-55442-9 (pbk.)

This book was typeset by the authors using the TEX typesetting language.

1 2 3 4 5 6 7 8 9 10-MA-95949392

COMPUTATION AND NEURAL SYSTEMS SERIES

SERIES EDITOR

Christof Koch
California Institute of Technology

Recent advances in the mathematical theory of nonlinear feedback networks, combined with new methods in neurophysiology and the development of digital/analog VLSI and optical computing technologies, have led to the emergence of a new paradigm in information processing: 'Neural Networks'.

The Addison-Wesley Series in *Computation and Neural Systems* attempts to reflect the diversity of this new field by publishing textbooks, course materials and monographs, including the following topics:

- Biophysical Modelling of Synapses, Dendrites and Neurons
- Modelling Neurophysiological and Psychophysical Data at the Network and System Levels
- Computational Theories of Vision, Audition, Olfaction, Language Understanding, and Motor Control
- Cybernetics and System Theory
- Pattern Recognition
- Theory of Neural Networks (e.g. Learning)
- Theory of Dynamic Systems
- Hardware Implementation of Networks (e.g. VLSI, Optics)

The series editor, Dr Christof Koch, is Assistant Professor of Computation and Neural Systems at the California Institute of Technology. Dr Koch works at both the biophysical level, investigating information processing in single neurons and in networks such as the visual cortex, as well as studying and implementing simple resistive networks for computing motion, stereo and colour in biological and artificial systems.

Foreword

The wave of interest in artificial neural networks (ANNs) that started in the mid-1980s was inspired by new prospects not visible ten years earlier. First of all, it should be realized that ANNs have been intended for a new *component technology*. There are many computation-intensive tasks such as preprocessing of natural signals, pattern classification and recognition, coordination of movements in complex mechanisms, decision making on the basis of extensive but uncertain data, and high-definition animated graphics that can no longer be handled by digital computers. Even supercomputers are soon unable to cope with the growing dimensionality of such problems. It has become more and more obvious that one has to resort to special analog computing methods; with the aid of modern VLSI technology and optics it will be possible to produce analog picowatt circuits by the billions, and so the cost of massively parallel computation can be cut to a fraction. Breakthroughs in analog semiconductor and active optical component technology around 1980 were thus crucial for the acceptance of ANN computing principles.

Before digital technology can be replaced or at least augmented by "neuromorphic" technology in practice, one must fully understand *what* and *how* to compute. As even the most fundamental operations are different from those of digital computing, and the innumerable system parameters of ANNs are time variable, designers are faced with new phenomena, and have to learn how to deal with them. This revolution in paradigms and standards will not be easy; however, if ANNs prove cost-effective in practice, this change will be inevitable.

Therefore, we must welcome every teaching effort in this new field. Books, especially monographs, of which the present one is an excellent example, are invaluable aids for education in these new technologies.

Excitement about ANNs has been accompanied by a sense that we finally understand how the brain works. The collective computations performed by ANNs, and the automatic adaptive changes of the system parameters and structures, have often been identified with mental processes and learning ability. However, it should already have become clear even to the most enthusiastic supporter of these ideas that mere increase in parallel computing capacity is not sufficient for duplication or even imitation of brain function. Every biological cell makes use of many information processing principles, of which only two or three have been utilized in ANNs. The immensely complex structures of biological neural networks have been formed in innumerable cycles of evolution, under continuous bombardment of complex signals from the environment and other sources of natural information. There exists yet nothing similar in ANNs, which are usually dedicated only to restricted tasks.

While it is obvious that ANNs cannot accurately imitate even the simplest biological circuits, it is also necessary to realize that the *functions* and *processes* at work in the nervous system are not all that mysterious. Since they are based on physical and chemical phenomena, it is possible to approximate their behavior, at least on some level of abstraction. For their *understanding*, it will be sufficient to set up a model that takes into account a number of basic operations and relationships in the elementary functions of the spatial and temporal domain. If certain essential modeling assumptions are made, one cannot avoid starting to see phenomena that very much resemble those observed in biological systems. This is an irrefutable fact, and can certainly be interpreted as partial explanation of these phenomena.

When working with ANNs, it is therefore necessary to realize that while the principles and components thereby applied have been inspired by brain-theoretic considerations, the artificial implementations need not necessarily do exactly the same as their biological counterparts. It may not be possible to achieve the complexity, flexible learning ability, and high-level abstraction capability characteristic of biological organisms. On the other hand, the stability and accuracy of artificial components can be orders of magnitude higher than those of biological ones. In some tasks it can be a significant advantage that ANNs do not exhibit fatigue, and are not panicked in alarming situations. It is plausible that in the future the computing capacity of ANNs can be increased far beyond that of biological systems. All this gives us promises of development that we may not yet fully foresee.

Teuvo Kohonen

Professor, Helsinki University of Technology
Research Professor at the Academy of Finland

Preface

The understanding of biological brains—with their capacity for learning as well as for the processing of sensory impressions and the control of movements—is one of the most fascinating research challenges of our time. In the still-young discipline of *Neural Computation,* scientists from such distinct fields as biology, information theory, physics, mathematics, psychology, and medicine have joined forces to pursue this challenge. *Neural Computation* seeks to simulate "biological intelligence" in artificial *"neural networks"* the structure and dynamics of which attempt to imitate the function of biological neural systems.

In the past few years, a number of promising successes have been achieved in this endeavor, triggering lively research activities in diverse research groups. The present book took shape during this period. Its aim is to provide an introduction to the field of neural computation and it is equally intended for those working in the fields of computer science, physics, biology, mathematics, engineering, psychology, and medicine, as well as for all those readers with an interest in computer models of neural networks and of the brain.

The first part of the book gives a general overview of the most important current models of neural nets together with a short sketch of the relevant biological background. The second part of the book is devoted to the central question of how functional neural circuitry in the brain can arise by means of a *self-organizing process.* It is shown how, by means of a few simple mechanisms, neural layers can learn representations or "maps" of important stimulus features under the influence of nothing more than a random sequence of sensory stimuli. A series of examples demonstrates the simulation of observed organization processes in the brain. However, these examples also show how solutions of abstract tasks from traditional information science can be obtained by the same mechanisms. The third part of this book is concerned with the question of what extensions of these mechanisms are required in order to enable the learning of simple motor skills, such as the balancing of a pole or the control of eye movements. Building on this foundation, the fourth part of the book describes several studies concerning problems of robot control. It is shown how a neural network can implement the coordination of robot arm movements under visual feedback control. Finally, the last part of the book treats important theoretical questions connected with the learning process, in particular the question of convergence and the influence of the element of chance during the learning phase.

At several points, a basic mathematical knowledge of elementary analysis and linear algebra may be useful to the reader, but they are not required in large parts of the book. Only in the last part, which is concerned with a more thorough mathematical analysis, some familiarity with vector analysis will be helpful.

Here, we would like to thank all those who have contributed to the creation of this book. We are grateful to the friendship and advice we received from Hans-Ulrich Bauer, Joachim Buhmann, Anita Govindjee, Leo van Hemmen, Karl Hess, Teuvo Kohonen, Christoph von der Malsburg, Sabine Martinetz, Jeanette Rubner, Zan Schulten, Werner von Seelen, Larry Smarr, Paul Tavan, and Udo Weigelt. We want to mention particularly our colleague Klaus Obermayer, whose work on self-organizing maps enriched our own views in many important ways, and who provided two of the color pictures on the front cover. Daniel Barsky, Ron Kates, and Markus Tesch have helped us tremendously with the translation from the original German text. Allan Wylde and Pam Suwinsky of Addison Wesley have been patient supporters. The book would have been impossible without grants which we received over the years from the National Science Foundation, the National Institute of Health, the State of Illinois, as well as from the German Ministry of Research and Development. Thomas Martinetz received a fellowship from the Volkswagen Foundation. Computer time and much good advice had been available to us from the National Center for Supercomputing supported by the National Science Foundation.

We are especially grateful to the Beckman Institute of the University of Illinois where we had the privilege to work and in whose stimulating atmosphere the book could be completed.

This book was written with the TEX typesetting system and the program Textures. Typesetting and graphics were produced on a Macintosh II computer.

Thomas Martinetz, Helge Ritter, Klaus Schulten
Urbana, Illinois, and Bielefeld, Germany

Table of Contents

Introduction and Overview

The emergence of the electronic computer and its incredibly rapid development have revived humankind's age-old curiosity about the working of the brain and about the nature of the human mind. The availability of the computer as a research tool has raised hopes of at least partial answers to these questions. There are three reasons for regarding this hope as justified.

First, the accomplishments of computers have forced us to define, in a precise manner, our concepts of the phenomenon "mind" — in this context generally under the heading of "intelligence." The rapid evolution of computers also demands a redefinition of the previously clear and unproblematic concept of "machine." In particular, the high flexibility made possible through programming has led us to regard the capabilities of computers as being separate from their material substrate, the *hardware,* but rather as residing in their program, the *software.* This "hardware-software duality" has enriched our conceptual framework on the relationship between mind and matter.

Secondly, as a tool, the computer has tremendously accelerated scientific progress, including progress in areas that are important for a better understanding of the brain. For example, computers made it possible to carry out and evaluate many neurophysiological, psychophysical, and cognitive experiments. Other relevant branches of science, in particular computer science and its subfield "artificial intelligence" ("AI") came into being as computers became available.

Thirdly, with the ability to manufacture computer hardware of high enough performance, discoveries concerning the functioning of the brain, in addition to their former purely intellectual benefit, have also become valuable for their technical applicability. This circumstance has opened up important resources for theoretical studies of the brain, and will probably continue to do so.

However, the demand for practical applications of artificial intelligence made evident the limitations of previous concepts of hardware and software. Characteristically, today's computers solve problems that are difficult for humans, but fail miserably at everyday tasks that humans master without a great deal of effort. This circumstance, so far, has limited the use of computers to narrow problem areas and indicates a fundamental difference between AI methods and the operation of biological nervous systems.

Most computers, until recently, were based on the so-called *von Neumann architecture.* They derive their performance from one or only a few central processors which carry out long sequential programs at extremely high speed. Therefore, signal-propagation times within the computer have already begun to emerge as limiting factors to further gains in speed. At the same time, efforts to master multifaceted problem situations, *e.g.*, those encountered in driving a car, by means of conventional programming techniques lead to programs of a complexity that can no longer be managed reliably.

A way out of this dilemma requires an abandonment of the von Neumann architecture used up to now, and instead to apply a large number of computational processors *working in parallel*. For the programming of such computers, new kinds of algorithms are required that must allow a distribution of computational tasks over a great number of processors. In order to keep the necessary task of integrating such algorithms into complex software systems manageable, the algorithms must be error tolerant and capable of learning. These features seem to be realized in biological brains with nerve cells as processors, which, by technical standards, are slow computational elements and of only limited reliability, but which on the other hand are present in huge numbers, processing sensory data and motor tasks concurrently.

In order to make this "biological know-how" available, the

interdisciplinary research area of *Neural Computation* has developed in the last few years. While its main aim is an understanding of the principles of information processing employed by biological nervous systems, this discipline also seeks to apply the insights gained to the construction of new kinds of computers with more flexible capabilities. In the pursuit of this goal, Neural Computation combines the efforts of computer scientists, neurobiologists, physicists, engineers, mathematicians, psychologists, and physicians.

Although we are still far from a true understanding of how the brain works, a great deal of progress has been made, especially in the last few years. On the experimental side, modern techniques are opening new "windows into the brain". Today, optical dyes allow one to stain living brain tissue such that the optical properties of the dyes provide a measure of the electrical activation of the nerve cells. In this way, optical recording of neural activity patterns has become possible. Other staining methods allow precise reconstructions of the three-dimensional shape of single nerve cells. By means of modern computer tomographic methods (PET, NMR) the momentary metabolic activity level of brain tissue can be recorded up to spatial resolutions in the range of millimeters. Sensitive magnetic field detectors based on superconducting devices (SQUID's) can measure the spatial distribution of brain currents with a similar resolution from outside the head. This has made it possible to monitor patterns of brain activity with noninvasive methods — and, therefore, also in humans — and to investigate its dependence on experimentally preselected mental tasks.

Nevertheless, the task of integrating the multitude of experimental data collected up to now into predictive theories of information processing in the brain is anything but simple. The first efforts go back to 1943, when McCulloch and Pitts originally postulated that nerve cells play the role of "logical elements," *i.e.*, evaluate Boolean (logical) functions. With the advent of digital computers, a strong additional motivation for the further development of these ideas arose, since quantitatively formulated models were suddenly no longer dependent on mathematical analysis alone, often both very difficult and feasible only to a limited degree, but could now be investigated in computer simulations. At this time the "perceptron" was being developed by Rosenblatt (1958). Rosenblatt derived a network model capable of learning to classify patterns making use only of simple principles for the change of connection strengths between neurons. These resembled the principles previously suggested by the psychologist Hebb (1949) on theoretical grounds to explain memory performance. Thus, the "perceptron" represents one of the first "brain models" that could successfully demonstrate the ability to "learn."

At about the same time the availability of computers led to the advent of a competing research direction, which regarded orientation toward the structure of biological nerve systems as of little aid in the investigation and simulation of intelligence. Instead, this direction attempted a more direct approach: by introducing sufficiently elaborate programming based on "problem solution heuristics," it was hoped that ultimately the goal of intelligent machines would be reached. Due to rapid initial successes, this research direction, now forming most of traditional AI, managed to push the investigation of neural networks for a number of years into obscurity. Even so, a series of important insights were gained in the theory of neural networks during this period: examples are the discovery of models for associative memory (Taylor 1956; Steinbuch 1961), models for self-organization of feature detectors (von der Malsburg 1973) and of ordered neural connections (Willshaw and von der Malsburg 1976), as well as pioneering studies concerning mathematical properties of important classes of network models by Amari, Grossberg, Kohonen, and numerous other researchers.

A highly significant stimulus for the further development of the subject was contributed by Hopfield (1982). Exploiting the formal equivalance between network models with "Boolean" neural units and physical systems consisting of interacting "elementary magnets" or "spins" (Cragg and Temperley 1954, 1955; Caianiello 1961; Little 1974; Little and Shaw 1975), he showed that the dynamic of such networks can be described by an *energy function* and that patterns stored in these networks can be regarded as attractors in a high-dimensional phase space. As a consequence, a whole arsenal of mathematical methods of statistical physics became available for the analysis of such network models. Many questions previously approachable only by computer simulations found an elegant mathematical solution (see, *e.g.*, Amit et al. 1985ab, Derrida et al. 1987, Gardner 1988, Buhmann et al. 1989). At the same time, new kinds of network models were found, two of which deserve special mention because of their promise: The *backpropagation model* (rediscovered several times, most recently by Rumelhart et al. 1986) constituted a significant improvement of the earlier perceptron models. In spite of a few aspects that are implausible from a biological point of view, its extremely broad applicability triggered considerable new research activity. Kohonen's model of *self-organizing neural maps* (Kohonen 1982a) represented an important abstraction of earlier models of von der Malsburg and Willshaw; the model combines biological plausibility with proven applicability in a broad range of difficult data processing and optimization problems.

All of these models provide us with a much more refined picture of the function of the brain than could have been anticipated a few decades ago. Nevertheless, most of the work has yet to be done. Compared to the capabilities of biological systems, the performance of our present "neurocomputers" is quite rudimentary. We still are unable to relate more than a relatively small number of experimental observations to properties of our models. There are still enormous gaps between the complexity of the brain, our theoretical models, and the capacity of today's computers. However, the modest amount of "biological know-how" which has been accumulated in order to bridge these gaps is already promising and suggests that further research will be rewarding. In particular, a new generation of computers with thousands of processors has put us in a position to simulate at least small areas of the brain in much greater detail than previously possible, and to use for the first time realistic numbers of neurons and synapses for such simulations (Obermayer et al. 1990a-c, 1991).

The first part of the book furnishes an overview of the major concepts on which much of the current work in Neural Computation is based. In Chapter 1, our present view of the brain as a "neurocomputer" is briefly outlined. The second chapter contains a sketch of the biological background, emphasizing its significance in understanding the various brain models. The third chapter introduces the most prominent model approaches of neural networks, including the perceptron model, the Hopfield model, and the back-propagation algorithm. A particular type of network, Kohonen's model of self-organizing maps, is the focus of Chapter 4. This network model is capable both of reproducing important aspects of the structure of biological neural nets and of a wide range of practical applications. It will serve as a basis for much of the discussion in the later chapters.

The later parts of the book take the reader through a series of typical issues in neural computation. We devote each chapter to an information-processing task that is characteristic of those confronting a biological organism in its environment. It is not our intention in the later chapters to present a complete survey of the by now large field of neural computation. Rather than a broad overview of the many different approaches, we present a highly focused and detailed description of network models based on self-organizing maps.

As an introductory example, it is shown in Chapter 5 how an adaptive "neural frequency map" can be formed in the cortex of a bat, which enables the bat to perform an extremely precise analysis of sonar ultrasound signals. Chapter 6 is concerned with the relationship of this example to the solution of a task appearing completely different at first glance, namely the determination of a route that is as short as possible in the "traveling salesman problem." A further example (Chapter 7) considers the creation of an ordered connectivity between touch receptors of the hand surface and the cortical area responsible for the sense of touch in the brain. Here, as in the case of the bat, we are concerned with the processing of *sensory information*. However, in nature this is never an end in itself. The processing of sensory information always has as its eventual goal the triggering and control of *motor functions*, probably the oldest task of biological nerve systems. This points to the need for the investigation of strategies for *neural control* and for *learning to execute movements*; it also brings us to the theme of the third part of the book.

The task of balancing a pole already contains a number of important features of motor control problems, and it is therefore discussed thoroughly in Chapter 8. We show how a neural network can learn the task of balancing a pole, first in a version with the help of a "teacher," then in an improved version by "independent trial and error." The main point of this task is to learn how to maintain an unstable equilibrium. An equally important aspect of motor function is the support of our sensory perception. In vision, for example, this purpose is served by unconscious, sudden eye movements. The precise "calibration" of these movements is provided by a permanently operating adaptation process, and Chapter 9 describes a simple neural network model demonstrating such capability in a computer simulation.

It is clear that, for the control of their movements, biological organisms and intelligent robots are confronted with tasks that are in many respects similar. Hence, in Part IV of the book, we turn our attention to issues of robotics (Chapter 10). In Chapter 11, it is shown how a robot arm observed by two cameras can learn in the course of a training phase to position its "hand" within the field of view of the cameras by means of visual feedback. Here, by trial and error, the network gradually learns to take properly into account the geometry of the arm and the visual world "seen" by the cameras.

The capability of proper positioning forms the basis for the more complex motor behavior of object gripping. Chapter 12 demonstrates that this ability can also be acquired by a network through learning. However, in view of the higher complexity of the procedure, a network with a hierarchical construction is required. Chapter 12 offers an interesting example of the implementation and training of nets structured in this way.

For the control problems of Chapters 11 and 12, consideration of purely geometrical relationships, *i.e.,* the so-called *kinematics* of the robot, is sufficient. However, for sudden movements, *arm inertia* also plays a role. Chapter 13 shows how the network can take such *dynamic aspects* into account. Here, the network learns the control of "ballistic arm movements" in a training phase by triggering short torques about the joints of the robot arm.

The preceding examples attempt to illustrate the multitude of tasks that biological brains have learned to master in the course of evolution. At best, we can solve a few isolated tasks today, and in many cases we must develop new solution heuristics which are often ad hoc and without substantial theoretical foundation. This may be compared to the situation prevailing in chemistry during the middle ages, when many chemical reactions were indeed known empirically, but it was not yet appreciated that the huge number of distinct chemical substances could be attributed to barely one-hundred chemical elements. The number of different "neural modules" in the brain appears to be of the same order of magnitude as the number of chemical elements. This suggests that in the area of information processing, a reduction of the great variety of phenomena to a manageable number of "elements" might also exist.

Our present level of understanding provides us with little

more than a vague idea of which principles might be fundamental in this reduction. However, we have available some network models that are encouragingly versatile. The present book illustrates this by demonstrating that the solution of the tasks discussed above can succeed using only a few variants of a single network model, Kohonen's "self-organizing neural map" (Kohonen 1982a). The biological basis for this model is the organization encountered in many regions of the brain in the form of two-dimensional neuron layers. These layers receive their input signals from nerve fibers emerging either from other neural layers or from peripheral sensory receptors. As a rule, the activities in the individual nerve fibers encode different features of the input stimulus. The nerve fibers coming into contact with a neuron thus determine which input features are particularly effective in exciting this neuron. As experiments show, the connections between neurons and incoming nerve fibers are frequently structured in such a way that adjacent neurons respond to similar input features. This corresponds to a mapping of the (usually higher-dimensional) space of stimulus features, which are coded in the nerve fibre activities, to the two-dimensional neuron layer. Important similarity relationships of abstract stimulus features can be translated into spatial relations of excited neurons of a two-dimensional layer in the manner of a "topographic map." Kohonen's model explains the creation of appropriate connection patterns and the resulting "maps" of stimulus features as a consequence of a few simple assumptions. The connection pattern forms step by step during a learning process requiring as its only information a sufficiently long sequence of input stimuli. By means of appropriate variants of the basic model, this procedure can be exploited for a broad spectrum of interesting information-processing tasks.

Our book is not limited to the discussion of a series of examples. Rather, each example serves to introduce a mathematical analysis of some particular aspect of the model and, in the course of the discussion, serves as an illustration of the application of a number of important mathematical methods to concrete questions of Neural Computation. The mathematical aspect takes center stage in Part V of the book. First, in Chapter 14, the relationship of the model to procedures for data compression and to factor analysis for the determination of "hidden variables" is presented. This is followed by a discussion of those aspects of the model whose investigation requires a higher degree of mathematical sophistication. The learning process is treated as a stochastic process and described by means of a partial differential equation. Statements concerning convergence properties and statistical fluctuations of the learning process can then be made. The capacity for automatic selection of the most important feature dimensions is discussed mathematically in greater depth, and the relationship to the periodic structure of certain sensory maps in the brain is pointed out. Finally, Chapter 15 discusses the use of local linear transformations as output (needed to solve control tasks), and provides a mathematical analysis of the improvement of the learning process as a consequence of "neighborhood cooperation" between processing units.

I

The Brain as a Neural Computer

1. Contemporary View of Brain Function

The brain plays a most particular role among all of our organs: in contrast to other organs, it does not process metabolic products, but rather a "substance" that did not become the subject of systematic scientific investigation until this century, namely *information*. As late as in the eighteenth century, the brain was considered to be a gland whose secretions were distributed throughout the body along the nerve pathways. The structure of the brain as a complex intertwined fabric of multiply networked cells exchanging signals with one another was first recognized during the past century, principally through the research of Golgi and Ramón y Cajal.

With this modern point of view, the specialization of the brain into areas, so-called cortices, responsible for particular activities, such as vision, hearing, or the movement of muscles, was soon discovered. Countless experiments and studies have extended and refined this picture in many respects; the invention of the computer has augmented this refined view of the concrete "machinery" with an equally refined view of its abstract task, the processing of "data." According to our present understanding, these data are represented on at least two distinct functional levels, differing in their time scales. One level is characterized by rapid changes (on the scale of milliseconds to seconds), the other by much slower processes (taking seconds to years).

The "fast" level consists of the instantaneous activity state of single neurons. The corresponding patterns of activity encode data that can change continuously and are presumably responsible for the contents of our short-term memory as well as for our immediate sensations. Our sensory receptors determine a part of these activity patterns through incoming nerve bundles by imprinting their activity more or less completely onto some subset of the neurons. The remainder of these changes is determined by the interactions among the neurons themselves, which can be either "excitatory" or "inhibitory" in nature.

The connection pattern, which determines the rapid activity changes in a decisive way, is not static, but can gradually evolve. It thus constitutes the second, "slow" level and codes those data which change either gradually or not at all. In particular, our long-term memory belongs to this level. Changes on this level concern the effectivity of the connections between neurons and take place primarily at the *synapses*, the neural "contacts," whose capacity to change and adapt forms the basis for the brain's learning ability. According to a hypothesis going back to Hebb (1949), the efficacy of a synapse changes depending on the correlation between the activity of the *presynaptic* neuron, *i.e.*, the neuron that triggers the activity of the synapse, and the *postsynaptic* neuron, *i.e.*, the neuron that is affected by the synapse. This hypothesis has been experimentally verified at individual synapses (Kelso et al. 1986). Changes on the fast and the slow level are thus coupled in both directions: The rapidly varying activity states of neurons gradually mold and change the network of connections between neurons, and these gradual changes in turn exert a back-reaction on the activity states of the neurons themselves.

According to our current understanding, the coupled, nonlinear dynamical processes for neuron activities and synaptic strengths form the basis for the functioning of the brain. This concept departs completely from the way sequential computers work. Thus, although the reaction time of a neuron (typical timescale 1 ms) and the signal propagation velocity along a nerve fibre (typical value 10 m/s) are extremely slow by the standards of modern computers, nature more than compensates for this disadvantage by the massive parallelism of the neural network. The underlying strategies of information processing must be significantly different from those of present-day computers. For example, only a few dozen sequential processing stages can possibly be involved in the observed, rapid formation of complex percepts, such as the visual recognition of a scene in a fraction of a second. This represents an important constraint on what can be considered as possible brain algorithms.

Since an individual neuron plays a minor role in what is happening globally, a high level of error tolerance results. A further property is the nearly complete lifting of any distinction between data and algorithm: an algorithm is embodied in the unfolding of the system dynamics and, hence, is determined by the synaptic strengths as well as by the instantaneous neuron activities. At the same time, the synaptic strengths also determine which activity states can be attained and thus determine which memories can be recalled. Interestingly enough, in programming languages used for artificial intelligence such as LISP, the rigid distinction between data and program has also been relaxed.

The framework provided by the coupled dynamics of neurons and synaptic strengths is still enormously broad. Obtaining concrete insights into the capabilities and properties of such information-processing systems requires the identification of important paradigmatic classes of such systems and of the problems that they can solve. The following chapters give an overview of some important and typical models of neural networks. However, it is reasonable to begin with a brief (and hence by necessity very fragmentary) sketch of the biological background. The reader may obtain more thorough information on this subject in the books by, for example, Creutzfeld (1983), Kandel, Schwartz (1985), and Brooks (1981).

2. Biological Background

The site of the intelligent capabilities of the brain is the *neocortex*; from an evolutionary point of view the most recent and in people the most highly developed part of the brain. Viewed superficially, the human neocortex consists of a layer of nerve cell tissue of about 0.2m^2 in area and on the average 2–3 mm in thickness, strongly convoluted to save space, and forming the exterior of both brain hemispheres. Within this layer, various areas can be distinguished which are specialized for specific tasks such as visual perception *(visual cortex)*, motor control *(motor cortex)*, or touch *(somatosensory cortex)* (Fig. 2.1). Additional areas *(association areas)* link information affecting multiple sensations.

In the human neocortex, about 100,000 closely interconnected nerve cells, called *neurons*, lie under every square millimeter and constitute the "computational units" of the cortex. Fig. 2.2 shows a vertical cut through the neocortex of a cat and gives some impression of the complexity of the cortical circuitry. Of the neurons actually present in the slice, only a fraction is shown in Fig. 2.2, in order that single neurons be recognizable for the observer. The actual neuron density is a factor of about 100 larger and would correspond to a completely black picture of the slice.

Three main structures can be distinguished in a typical neuron: *dendritic tree*, *cell body*, and *axon*, roughly corresponding to the input, processing, and output functions, respectively. The dendritic tree, a branched structure of thin cell extensions, forms the main input pathway of a neuron. It is spread out within a region of up to 400 μm in radius around the neuron and sums the output signals of the surrounding neurons in the form of an electric potential, which it then sends to the cell body (*soma*) of

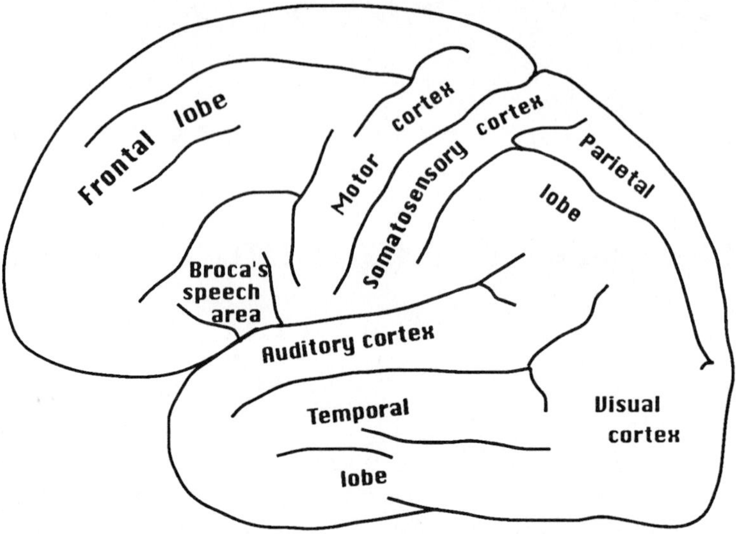

Figure 2.1 Lateral (schematic) view of the human left-brain hemisphere. Its convoluted surface is composed of a 2–3mm thick cortical area (neocortex). Various cortical areas specialized to specific tasks can be distinguished on this layer.

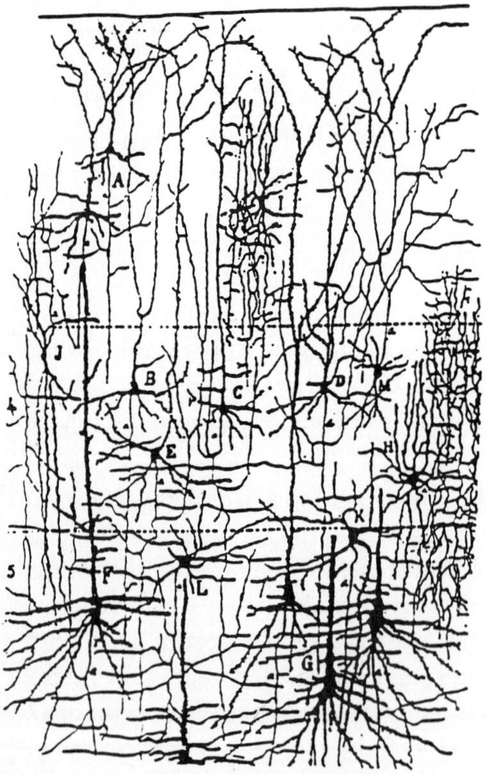

Figure 2.2 Vertical section through the neocortex of a cat (the thickness dimension of the cortex lies in the vertical direction of the figure). The pyramidal cells (A–G) are recognizable from their conical cell body, their root-like dendrites, and their long axon which extends to the surface of the cortex (in the upper part of the figure). In contrast, the extensions of the stellate cells (H–M) are spread out only in the immediate neighborhood. Only a fraction of the neurons in the figure section is reproduced. The true packing density is a factor of about 100 higher (Ramón y Cajal 1909).

the neuron. If this potential exceeds a certain threshold value, the cell body produces a short *electrical spike*, which is then conducted along the axon, a nerve fibre ranging from a fraction of a millimeter to several meters in length. The axon also branches out and, in this manner, conducts the pulse to several thousand target neurons. The contacts of an axon are either located on the dendritic tree or direcly on the cell body of the target neuron and are known as *synapses*. Most synapses are "chemical contacts," *i.e.*, at the synapse, the electrical pulse of the axon causes secretion of a transmitter substance (*neurotransmitter*), which in turn leads to a change in the potential at the dendritic tree or cell body of the target neuron. Depending on the type of synapse and its state, an incoming pulse causes a more or less strong potential rise (*excitatory* synapse) or potential drop (*inhibitory* synapse) at the target neuron. Hence, the synapses act like analog switches regulating the communication between neurons and, thus, represent sites where important information is stored.

Two main classes of cortical neurons are distinguished on the basis of their shape: *pyramidal cells* (*Golgi Type I neurons*, comprising about 60% of the total) and star-shaped *"stellate cells"* or *astrocytes* (*Golgi Type II neurons*, about 40%). The pyramidal cells usually have long-range axons with synapses acting excitatory, whereas in the stellate cells the axon, with its stellate branching, affects only its immediate environment, acting usually in an inhibitory fashion (see Fig. 2.3). It is commonly believed that the important information is coded in the activity state of the pyramidal cells, and the astrocytes serve as stabilizers of the system by inhibiting activity around excited regions (*lateral inhibition*).

In many regions of the cortex, groups of adjacent neurons give evidence for aggregation in higher functional units (Mountcastle 1978; Blasdel and Salama 1986). These units, known as *microcolumns*, usually include the neurons of a small vertical cylindrical volume in the cortex of typically tenths of a millimeter in diameter or smaller. Such a cylinder can serve to analyze some particular stimulus feature, such as the orientation of an edge of an image (as in the primary visual cortex), or the innervation of a common muscle (as in the *primary motor cortex*). Adjacent microcolumns cannot be precisely separated, but rather there is a gradual transition in the membership of individual neurons.

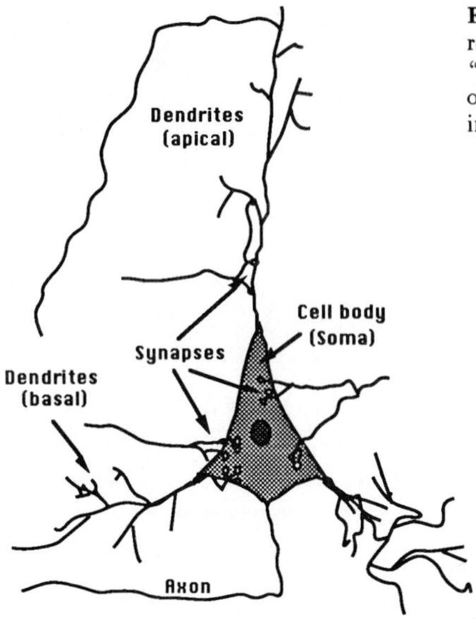

Figure 2.3 Structure of a neuron (schematic). Besides the "pyramidal cell" shown, numerous other kinds of neurons occur in the brain.

At the next higher level of organization, microcolumns of one type are arranged in specialized areas. Today, about 80 such "cortical areas" are known in the human cortex, each of which represents a highly parallel "special purpose" module for a specific task. For example, one can identify in the visual cortex areas for the analysis of edge orientation, of color shades, and of velocity fields, while other cortical areas host modules for various aspects of speech comprehension, recognition of faces, spatial orientation, and planning and execution of movements. To the extent that simple features can be identified relating to the properties of cortical neurons, one often finds a regular variation of these features along the two directions parallel to the surface of the layer, *i.e.*, there is a *continuous, two-dimensional feature map*. The formation — and the benefits — of such a representation of, *e.g.*, sensory data, constitutes one of the subjects of this book.

Most cortical areas can be assigned to one of three groups: (*i*) *primary* and *secondary* sensory areas, whose input stems directly (via noncortical "relay stations") from sensory receptors or primary cortices, (*ii*) *association fields*, in which the various sensory signals which have been preprocessed by primary and secondary cortical areas converge, and (*iii*) *primary* and *secondary motor areas*, which (again via noncortical intermediaries) are connected with the musculature or the primary motor areas. Each of these cortical areas is also connected to and interacts

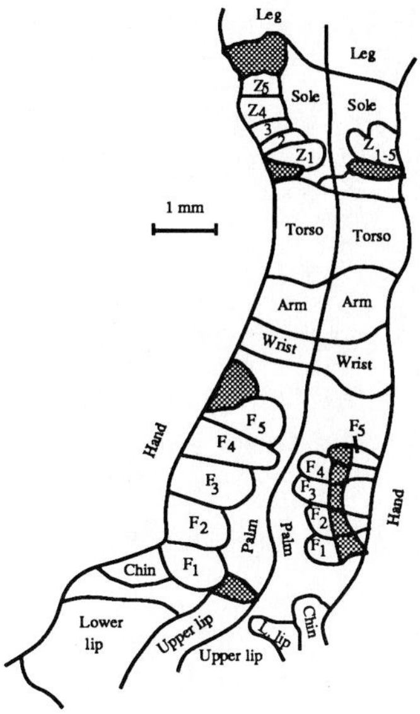

Figure 2.4 Map of a part of the body surface in the somatosensory cortex of a monkey. Most of the neighborhood relations of the body regions shown are preserved in the map. Richly innervated skin regions (*e.g.* finger F_1 — — F_5) are strongly enlarged in the map (after Kaas et al. 1979).

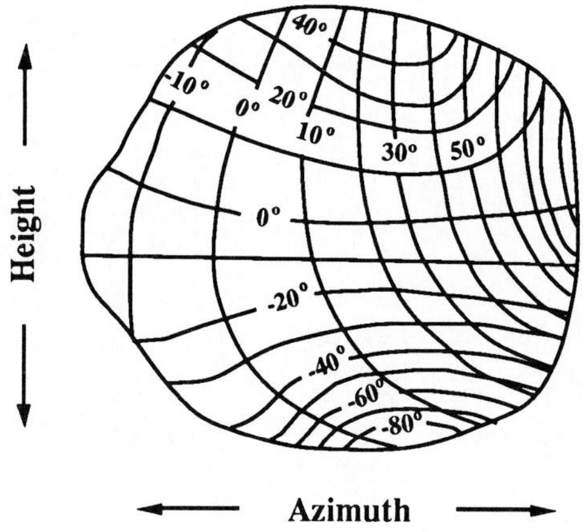

Figure 2.5 Direction map for sound signals in the so-called "optical tectum" of an owl. The horizontally directed lines connect neurons responding to sound signals from directions with the same longitude. The vertically directed lines connect neurons corresponding to sound directions with the same incident latitude (after Knudsen et al. 1987).

with numerous additional cortical areas as well as brain and nerve structures outside of the cortex. This leads to a highly coupled and parallel global system.

In spite of the differences between the tasks addressed by different cortical areas, the cortex possesses a surprisingly homogeneous structure. For example all cortical areas consist of six layers (I–VI), one above the other, which differ from one another in their relative thickness. At the risk of oversimplifying, one can say that layer IV generally serves as the input layer of a cortical area. Next to this, association fibers project out to other, distant cortical regions. The main source of output is layer V. Layer VI sends out "feedback" nerve fibers to the neurons, which are directed to the input layer IV. Layers II and III are the main output location for short-range association fibers to surrounding cortex points. These fibers themselves form the upper layer I.

The circuitry connecting individual modules with one another is generally subject to a common "topographic" organizational principle: adjacent neurons of an output field are almost always connected to adjacent neurons in the target field. This organizational structure is especially evident in the primary cortical areas, *i.e.*, those that, from the point of view of circuitry, are located "close to the outside world."

Most signals from the environment are received by the brain from "sensory surfaces" which are covered with receptors. Our largest sensory surface is the skin with its touch and thermal receptors; perhaps our most important sensory surface is the retina. The ear gives an example of a one-dimensional sensory "surface:" there, the receptors are arranged along the spiral-shaped *cochlea*.

Although the wiring connecting these sensory surfaces to their primary sensory areas in the cortex passes through several "relay stations," it also exhibits a "topographic ordering" and conducts signals from adjacent receptors to neurons which are adjacent in the cortex. In this way a mapping of the respective sensory surfaces to the relevant cortical area is established. Due to its preservation of adjacency and neighborhood relationships, this mapping can be regarded as a (frequently more or less distorted) *image* or *topographic map* of the sensory surface. For example, in the case of the sense of touch, one finds various such maps of the body surface in the *somatosensory cortex* (Kaas et al. 1979). An example is shown in Fig. 2.4. A similar situation holds for the primary visual cortex. However, there it is already evident that the brain also constructs *maps of abstract features* of the environment in which, *e.g.*, the association of neurons with local properties of visual images, such as edge orientation or velocity of movement, varies in a regular way with the location of the neurons. An especially illustrative example is the image in the *optical tectum* of owls. There, the direction of sound signals is mapped in a regular way within a layer (Fig. 2.5). A map coding pitch in one direction is found in the *auditory cortex* of many higher brains. In bats, the amplitude of the signal is coded in the direction orthogonal to the direction of pitch. In this way, a "sound spectrogram" is created on the cortex. In addition, bats also possess a map representing the time difference between two acoustic events. This map is important for the sonar orientation of the animal (Suga and O'Neill 1979).

However, maps are not limited to sensory regions. There

are also "motor" maps, on which the location of an activity peak specifies the execution of a movement. While sensory maps generate a spatially localized "activity peak" from the activity pattern of preceding receptor neurons whose location represents the signal features being analyzed, motor maps create — from a spatially localized activity peak — an activity pattern (in space and time) among subsequent motor neurons that triggers a particular movement (Lemon 1988). The best investigated example of such a map can be found in the *"superior colliculus"* in the midbrain (Sparks and Nelson 1987). In this map, the spatial location of an excitation peak encodes the direction and amplitude of an eye movement. A map organized in the form of a ring can be observed in the primary motor cortex (Murphy et al. 1977). Localized electrical stimulation within this map triggers flexion and extension movements of the arm joints, varying systematically with the location of the stimulus.

It is highly probable that a large portion of the organization of such maps is genetically determined. However, considering the estimated 10^{13} synapses of a brain, it would be impossible to specify this organization on the basis of a detailed connectivity scheme. A way out of this dilemma is the genetic coding of mechanisms of structure formation, as a result of whose operation the desired connectivity would then be created. The formation of structure could either take place before birth or as part of a later maturation phase, and in the latter case it could be driven by suitable sensory stimuli. For example, it has been established that the normal formation of an edge orientation map in the primary visual cortex of a newborn is suppressed in the absence of sufficient visual experience (Rauschecker and Singer 1981). Moreover, experimental investigations, *e.g.*, in the somatosensory cortex, show that even in a mature animal many maps are not at all rigidly determined, but can change slowly depending on sensory stimuli (Jenkins et al. 1984; Harris 1986).

This condensed description provides only an extremely limited impression of the "brain as a neural computer" and its structural variety. Nevertheless, in the last few years we have gained numerous theoretical insights in the functioning of the brain that can be tested by means of mathematically formulated models. In Chapter 3, we discuss some of their most important representatives.

3. Neural Network Models

3.1. Early Approaches

The first neural network models go back to the 1940s. Around this time, two mathematicians, McCulloch and Pitts (1943) suggested the description of a neuron as a *logical threshold element* with two possible states. Such a threshold element has L input channels (*afferent axons*) and one output channel (*efferent axon*). An input channel is either active (input 1) or silent (input 0). The activity states of all input channels thus encode the input information as a *binary sequence* of L bits. The state of the threshold element is then given by linear summation of all afferent input signals x_i and comparison of the sum with a threshold value s. If the sum exceeds the threshold value, then the neuron is *excited;* otherwise, it is in the quiescent state. The excited and quiet state should correspond to the firing or not firing of an action potential of biological neurons and are represented in the model by the binary values 1 and 0 for the activity of the output channel. Excitatory and inhibitory input signals are modulated by "synaptic strengths" $w_i = \pm 1$. The output signal y of a neuron is thus given by

$$y = \theta\left(\sum_i w_i x_i - s\right), \tag{1}$$

where $\theta(x) = 1$ for $x \geq 0$ and $\theta(x) = 0$ for $x < 0$. McCulloch and Pitts demonstrated that any arbitrary logical function can be constructed by an appropriate combination of such elements.

Their proof is based on the observation that, in particular, AND-gates and inverters can be realized as special cases of (1); therefore, any other logical function can be constructed from these. The model of McCulloch and Pitts for the first time suggested how neurons might be able to carry out logical operations. Their idea of the neuron as a logical threshold element was a fundamental contribution to the field and has found entrance into numerous later models, albeit often in modified form.

However, the theory of McCulloch and Pitts failed in two important respects. Firstly, it did not explain how the necessary interconnections between neurons could be formed, in particular, how this might occur through *learning*. Secondly, such networks depended on error-free functioning of all their components and did not display the (often quite impressive) error tolerance of biological neural networks.

The psychologist Hebb (1949) suggested an answer to the first question in his now famous book *Organization of Behaviour* (Hebb 1949). According to his suggestion, the connection between two neurons is *plastic* and changes in proportion to the activity correlation between the presynaptic and the postsynaptic cell.

This *Hebb hypothesis* has survived up until today in various mathematical formulations as the essential feature of many network models with learning ability, although its experimental verification remains in dispute. One of its simplest mathematical formulations is

$$\Delta w_i = \epsilon \cdot y(\mathbf{x}) \cdot x_i \tag{2}$$

for the change in the synaptic strengths w_i ($i = 1, 2, \ldots, n$) of a neuron receiving an input $\mathbf{x} = (x_1, x_2, \ldots, x_n)^T$ when x_i is the input at the ith synapse. $y(\mathbf{x})$ denotes the excitation of the neuron and $\epsilon > 0$ is a parameter measuring the size of a single learning step. The quantities $y(\mathbf{x})$ and w_i can also be considered as continuous.

With the advent of the computer, it became possible to simulate in more detail the learning capacity of networks made of neurons subject to rules of the above kind and to demonstrate practical applications of such systems.

3.2. The Perceptron

The *perceptron* proposed by Rosenblatt (1958) constituted an important step in this direction. It consists of a fixed number N of elements, each of which is supplied with an "input pattern" through L channels. Each of the input patterns is described by an L-component feature vector $\mathbf{x} = (x_1, x_2, \ldots, x_L)^T$ and belongs to one of N "pattern classes." The classification of the input patterns and the required number and the interpretation of the components x_i depends on the application; the x_i might, for example, describe gray levels of image pixels or quantities of a more complex feature extracted from the input pattern by some preprocessing stage. The perceptron shall learn the correct classification of the pattern vectors using known classification examples during a "training phase." For the classification of an input pattern $\mathbf{x}$, each element r computes a binary output value y_r according to

$$y_r = \theta(\sum_{i=1}^{L} w_{ri} x_i). \tag{3}$$

The coefficients w_{ri}, $i = 1, 2, \ldots, L$ determine the behavior of the element r. The absence of an "excitation threshold" in (3) does not imply a loss of generality. The action of such a threshold can be taken into account without changing the general form of (3) by agreeing on a constant input signal $x_1 = 1$. The threshold is then given by the value $-w_{r1}$.

During a training phase, each element adjusts its coefficient w_{ri} in such a way that it only reacts to the input patterns of "its" class C_r with an output value $y_r = 1$. For this to be possible, the *existence of a solution* must first be guaranteed, *i.e.*, there must exist weights w^*_{ri} for which (3) correctly solves the classification problem. The satisfaction of this condition depends both on how the problem is posed and on the coding chosen for the pattern vector $\mathbf{x}$. This can be illustrated as follows: Within a particular choice of coding, *i.e.*, an assignment of "features" x_1, $x_2, \ldots, x_L$ to each pattern, each pattern corresponds to a point $\mathbf{x}$ in a "feature space"(possibly of very high dimension). The individual classes C_r can be considered as subsets of points in this space. Each element must assign its output values y_r to

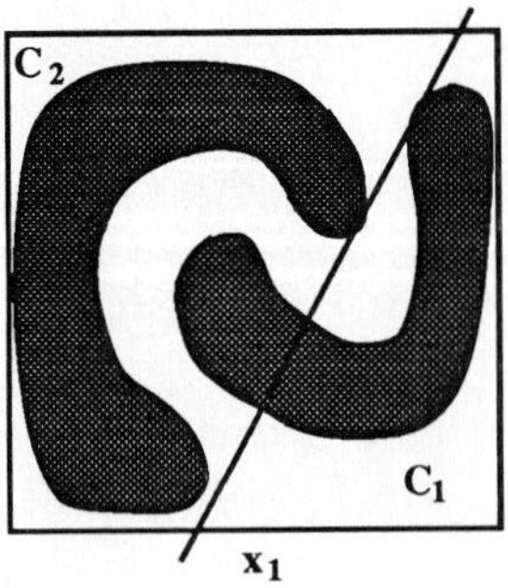

Figure 3.1 Example of two pattern classes C_1 and C_2 in a two-dimensional feature space of the variables x_1 and x_2 which are not linearly separable.

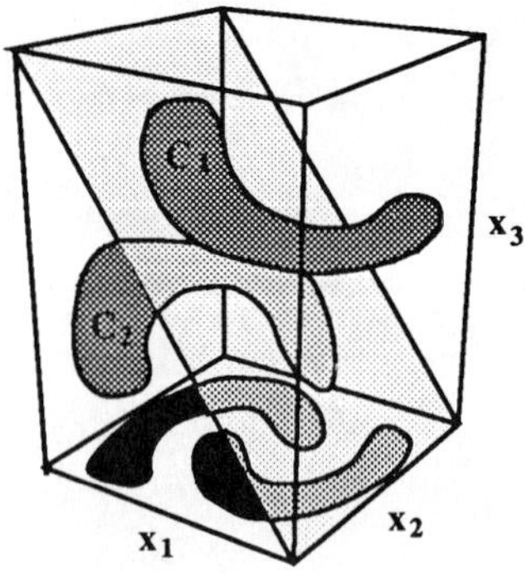

Figure 3.2 The addition of a further feature x_3 leads to a higher-dimensional feature space, in which the two classes may be linearly separable. Projection onto the $x_1 - x_2$-plane leads back to the nonseparable situation of Fig. 3.1.

points in such a way that the spatial region belonging to the output value $y_r = 1$ includes the points of the class C_r and excludes the points of all other classes C_s, $s \neq r$. However, the flexibility of the separation afforded by the threshold elements of the form (3) is limited: geometrically, every choice of weights w_{ri} corresponds to a separation of the feature space by an $L-1$-dimensional "hyperplane" into two regions, one with $y_r = 1$ and the other with $y_r = 0$. If the classes in the space of pattern vectors x are arranged in a manner which is too "convoluted," then the desired separation by hyperplanes cannot be achieved, and the perceptron algorithm is doomed to fail from the outset. Figure 3.1 offers a simple example. We assume $L = 2$, *i.e.*, each pattern is characterized by a two-dimensional "feature vector," and only two classes are considered. In this case, the available "hyperplanes" are lines ($L - 1 = 1$), by means of which a complete separation of the classes C_1 and C_2 is evidently impossible.

A way out of such a situation can often be found by appropriate extension of the feature vectors by additional feature variables. These can increase the distinguishability of the classes to the extent that a separation by hyperplanes becomes possible. If, for example, in addition to C_1 and C_2 a further feature variable x_3 can be found that differs sufficiently from C_1 and C_2, the situation shown in Fig. 3.2 may occur in the resulting $L = 3$-dimensional feature space. A separation of C_1 and C_2 by a plane is now possible. This geometric property of two classes is called *linear separability.*

Linear separability of each class from the union of all the other classes thus guarantees that the perceptron of Eq. (3) can correctly classify all pattern instances, provided its weights w_{ri} are chosen appropriately. The task of finding such a set of weights remains. An attractive approach makes use of a number of *classification examples, i.e.,* vectors x together with a specification of their respective classes. These constitute the input to the perceptron in a "training phase." Every time an element r provides an incorrect output value $y_r \neq y_r^{(corr)}$ in response to some input $\mathbf{x} \in C_s$, its coefficients w_{ri}, $i = 1, 2, \ldots, L$, are changed by an amount

$$\Delta w_{ri} = \epsilon \cdot \left(y_r^{(corr)} - y_r \right) \cdot x_i \tag{4}$$

This no longer exactly corresponds to Hebb's rule, but rather the postsynaptic activity y_r in (2) is replaced by the difference $d_r = y_r^{(corr)} - y_r$ between the correct output value and the perceptron's current output value y_r. The factor ϵ in front of the expression determines the "learning step size" and must be positive. Eq. (4) then acts as an *error correction rule*: In case of a correct answer from the element r, $d_r = 0$, and all of the weights w_{ri} remain unchanged. In case of an incorrect output value, $d_r = \pm 1$ and Eq. (4) implies a change in the sum $\sum_i w_{ri} x_i$ by $\pm\epsilon \sum_i x_i^2$. If the output value was too small, this causes an increase in the sum ($d_r = 1$) if the input pattern x is repeated, and a reduction ($d_r = -1$) if the output was too large. This procedure is known as the *perceptron algorithm*, for which the following *convergence theorem* holds:

Perceptron Convergence Theorem: (Rosenblatt 1961; Block 1962; Minsky and Papert 1969) Let the classification problem be solvable with appropriate weights w_{ri}^* by means of the perceptron *ansatz* (3), and suppose that the feature vectors x are all bounded, *i.e.,* there exists a constant M, such that $\|\mathbf{x}\| < M$ is always satisfied. Then, with the choice

$$\epsilon_r = 1/\|\mathbf{x}\| \tag{5}$$

the perceptron algorithm (5) will always find a solution after finitely many adaptation steps for the weights w_{ri} (only the "true" modification steps, *i.e.,* steps with $d_r \neq 0$, are counted).

In the following, we give a proof of this theorem for the mathematically interested reader. However, for an understanding of what follows, there is no harm in skipping the mathematical derivation.

Since all elements operate independently of one another, in the proof of the preceding theorem it suffices to consider a single element, and in the following we can thus suppress the index r. We denote by $\mathbf{w}^* = (w_1^*, w_2^*, \ldots, w_L^*)^T$ a weight vector for which the perceptron solves the classification problem correctly (the existence of a vector with this property is required by the theorem). Hence, there exists a constant $\delta > 0$, such that†

$$\begin{aligned} \mathbf{w}^* \cdot \mathbf{x} &> \delta, & \text{if } y^{(corr)}(\mathbf{x}) = 1, \\ \mathbf{w}^* \cdot \mathbf{x} &< -\delta, & \text{if } y^{(corr)}(\mathbf{x}) = 0. \end{aligned} \tag{6}$$

Here, $y^{(corr)}(\mathbf{x})$ designates that output value which corresponds to a correct classification of the input $\mathbf{x}$ by the element under consideration. Let $\mathbf{w}(t)$ denote the weight vector of the perceptron obtained after t modification steps from some (arbitrary) starting value. For $\mathbf{w}(t)$, the next modification step, *i.e.*, $d = y^{(corr)} - y = \pm 1$, yields

$$\mathbf{w}(t+1) = \mathbf{w}(t) + \epsilon \cdot d \cdot \mathbf{x}, \tag{7}$$

and thus

$$\begin{aligned} \mathbf{w}^2(t+1) &= \mathbf{w}^2(t) + 2\epsilon d \cdot (\mathbf{w}(t) \cdot \mathbf{x}) + \epsilon^2 d^2 \mathbf{x}^2 \\ &\leq \mathbf{w}^2(t) + \epsilon^2 d^2 \mathbf{x}^2 = \mathbf{w}^2(t) + 1. \end{aligned} \tag{8}$$

In (8), we have made use of the relations $d \cdot (\mathbf{w} \cdot \mathbf{x}) = (y^{(corr)} - y)(\mathbf{w} \cdot \mathbf{x}) \leq 0$ and $d^2 \epsilon^2 = 1/\|\mathbf{x}\|^2$. From Eq. (8), we obtain an upper bound for the increase in the length $\|\mathbf{w}(t)\|$ with the number of modification steps that have occurred

$$\|\mathbf{w}(t)\| \leq \sqrt{\|\mathbf{w}(0)\|^2 + t}. \tag{9}$$

On the other hand, at each modification step, the scalar product $\mathbf{w} \cdot \mathbf{w}^*$ satisfies

$$\begin{aligned} \mathbf{w}(t+1) \cdot \mathbf{w}^* &= \mathbf{w}(t) \cdot \mathbf{w}^* + \epsilon \cdot d \cdot (\mathbf{x} \cdot \mathbf{w}^*) \\ &\geq \mathbf{w}(t) \cdot \mathbf{w}^* + \epsilon \cdot \delta. \end{aligned} \tag{10}$$

†For classes with infinitely many elements, there could always be vectors demanding arbitrarily small δ. In this case, we consider Eq. (6) as a more precise statement of the requirement that a solution exist. Equation (6) implies that this solution is insensitive to sufficiently small perturbations of the weights $\mathbf{w}^*$.

The last step makes use of Eq. (6). Therefore, $\mathbf{w}(t)\cdot\mathbf{w}^*$ grows at least linearly with the number of modification steps

$$\mathbf{w}(t)\cdot\mathbf{w}^* \geq \mathbf{w}(0)\cdot\mathbf{w}^* + t\cdot\delta/M. \tag{11}$$

With the help of (10), (11) and the Cauchy-Schwarz inequality, we thus have

$$\begin{aligned}\mathbf{w}(0)\cdot\mathbf{w}^* + t\cdot\delta/M \leq \mathbf{w}(t)\cdot\mathbf{w}^* &\leq \|\mathbf{w}(t)\|\cdot\|\mathbf{w}^*\| \\ &\leq \|\mathbf{w}^*\|\sqrt{\|\mathbf{w}(0)\|^2 + t}.\end{aligned} \tag{12}$$

Since the left side of this inequality is linear and thus grows faster with t than the right side, t cannot become arbitrarily large, *i.e.*, only a finite number of modification steps can occur. This concludes the convergence proof for the perceptron. For a thorough discussion and other approaches to a proof, see for example (Minsky and Papert 1969).

A more flexible variant of the perceptron results if the individual elements do not work completely independently of one another, but rather compete with one another for the correct classification. Equation (3) is then replaced by

$$y_r = \begin{cases} 1 & \text{if } \mathbf{w}_r\cdot\mathbf{x} > \mathbf{w}_s\cdot\mathbf{x} \text{ for all } s \neq r, \\ 0 & \text{else.}\end{cases} \tag{13}$$

A learning step occurs every time the index r of the element with $y_r = 1$ deviates from the correct classification s of the input vector. In this case, the weight vectors of the two elements r and s are changed according to (4). The resulting learning rule is (note $y_r^{(corr)} = 0$ and $y_s^{(corr)} = 1$)

$$\begin{aligned}\Delta\mathbf{w}_s &= \epsilon\mathbf{x}, \\ \Delta\mathbf{w}_r &= -\epsilon\mathbf{x}.\end{aligned} \tag{14}$$

Here, the procedure also finds a solution after a finite number of modification steps, as long as a solution exists. The greater flexibility of this approach stems from the fact that now each element r can close off for its class not just a half-space, but a conical region bounded by those hyperplanes where $\mathbf{w}_r\cdot\mathbf{x} = \mathbf{w}_s\cdot\mathbf{x}$.

Aside from the convergence theorems, numerous other interesting and important statements can be derived with mathematical rigor for the perceptron (Minsky and Papert 1969). This is possible because the individual elements "interact" either not at all or at most in a very simple way. In spite of this relative simplicity, the insights gained from the perceptron illustrate many typical problems posed by parallel and adaptive systems. In particular, the perceptron permits a relatively far-reaching analysis of its performance and also of its limitations. The convergence theorem guarantees that whenever a perceptron solution exists, the learning algorithm will find it. Similarly far-reaching results are usually not known for learning rules in more complex, multilayered networks. On the other hand, it soon became evident that for a whole series of practical classification problems, the requirement of the existence of a perceptron solution, *i.e.*, of appropriate weights w_{ri}, is not satisfied, and that the perceptron thus cannot solve such problems. Moreover, other problems do admit a solution in principle but demand that the weights be maintained with a precision growing exponentially with the size of the problem, a requirement which in practice cannot be satisfied (Minsky and Papert 1969). Such limitations of the perceptron have been overcome recently by means of multilayer network models. We will return to this in Section 3.9.

3.3. Associative Memory

Hebb's learning rule in the form of Eq. (2) led to another class of models, those of *associative memory*. One of the remarkable properties of the human brain is its ability to draw inferences or *associations* between all types of mental images. For a long time the location of this mental capacity and the respective mode of information storage posed a great puzzle. Although Hebb proposed the synapse as a relevant storage element, it was not compatible with neurophysiological experiments to ascribe to individual synapses a role requiring a degree of reliability similar to that of storage locations in a conventional computer. On the contrary, information storage in neural networks turned out to be remarkably robust with respect to loss or malfunction of some limited portion of the neurons. One possible explanation was provided by storage concepts in which each newly arriving piece of information is stored in a way that is "distributed" over many storage elements. Thus, loss or malfunction of a portion of the memory causes merely a general degrading of the quality of the stored information but not the total loss of individual entries.

A proposal for a network model with such properties was made by Willshaw, Bunemann, and Longuet-Higgins (1969), whose network uses threshold value elements of the type (1). The information to be stored is presented in the form of *training pairs* $(\mathbf{x}, \mathbf{y})$. x plays the role of the *input pattern*, y that of the *output pattern*, and both are represented as binary vectors for which the components take values 0 or 1. x plays the role of the "key" for the associated pattern y. Proper operation of the network model of Willshaw et al. requires that x be a vector with a large number of components, whereas y may be of low dimension. The dimension N of y determines the number of threshold value elements required. Each threshold value element computes, as in the perceptron, a single component y_r of the output pattern. It is given by

$$y_r = \theta\left(\sum_{i=1}^{L} w_{ri}x_i - s_r\right). \tag{15}$$

Here, s_r is the threshold of element r and $\theta(.)$ is again the step function defined in connection with (1). The right side of (15) can be evaluated by N McCulloch-Pitts neurons, which receive the input pattern x through N common input channels. Information storage occurs in the matrix of the $L \times N$ "synaptic strengths" w_{ri}. These are to be chosen in such a way that (15) assigns the correct output pattern y to each input pattern x.

Willshaw et al. considered the case where p training pairs $(\mathbf{x}^{(1)}, \mathbf{y}^{(1)}), (\mathbf{x}^{(2)}, \mathbf{y}^{(2)}), \ldots, (\mathbf{x}^{(p)}, \mathbf{y}^{(p)})$ are to be stored, whose input patterns of 1s and 0s each contain the same number k of 1s, *e.g.*, $\mathbf{x} = 010100100$ for $k = 3$. Suppose that the positions of these 1s are not correlated with each other and that their number k is small compared to the total number L of components of a pattern. The input patterns thus consist almost completely of 0s. On the other hand, the number of 1s in the output patterns $\mathbf{y}^{(\nu)}$ need not be restricted in any way.

The storage of a training pair $(\mathbf{x}, \mathbf{y}) = (\mathbf{x}^{(\nu)}, \mathbf{y}^{(\nu)})$ consists of setting all weights w_{ri} satisfying both $x_i = 1$ and $y_r = 1$ to the value one (all the weights are zero before storage of the first pattern). The remaining weights remain unchanged. This is illustrated in Fig. 3.3a–c for the example of the storage of three training pairs. The horizontal input lines carry the input pattern, the vertical output lines the output pattern. A value $w_{ri} = 1$ is designated by a mark at the intersection of input line i and output line r. Those weights that have been changed for the storage of the most recently offered pattern pair are identified by open circles.

After all of the p training pairs have been stored, the resulting memory matrix becomes

$$w_{ri} = \max_{\nu=1,\ldots,p} \left(y_r^{(\nu)} x_i^{(\nu)} \right). \tag{16}$$

The threshold is set to the value $s_r = k - 1/2$.

This choice of a memory matrix and threshold guarantees that all output lines that were active during the storage of a training pair $\left(\mathbf{x}^{(\nu)}, \mathbf{y}^{(\nu)}\right)$ are reactivated if the input pattern $\mathbf{x}^{(\nu)}$ is presented alone. Formally, this results from the relation

$$\sum_i w_{ri} x_i^{(\nu)} = \sum_i w_{ri} \cdot y_r^{(\nu)} x_i^{(\nu)} = \sum_i y_r^{(\nu)} x_i^{(\nu)} = \sum_i x_i^{(\nu)} = k > s_r, \tag{17}$$

which holds provided $y_r^{(\nu)} = 1$.

Figure 3.3d offers an illustrative example. Here, the memory array formed after the steps shown in Fig. 3.3a–c is presented with the input pattern of the training pair stored in step (b). In this case, $k = 2$, and all thresholds take the value $s_r = 3/2$. Each output line r active in storage step (b) has left exactly k weights $w_{ri} = 1$ (r fixed) in the memory matrix; these are highlighted in Fig. 3.3d by open circles. These weights "belong" precisely to those k input lines which together were active in step (b), and, if the same input lines are again activated, they produce the sum $\sum_i w_{ri} x_i = k > s_r$ and thus the excitation of all those output lines r that were active during storage step (b).

Note that Fig. 3.3d also shows that the output pattern can contain, in addition to the correct 1s, a few erroneous 1s. Such an "erroneous 1" is present on the second output line of Fig. 3.3d and is designated by an $(*)$. As illustrated by the example, such errors occur whenever many training pairs activate the same output line r and the opposite output value $y_r = 0$ is to be assigned to an input pattern which agrees partly with many of these pairs. However, it can be shown that for pattern vectors with a sufficiently small proportion of 1s (this assumption is strongly violated in the example of Fig. 3.3), these errors occur with very low probability.

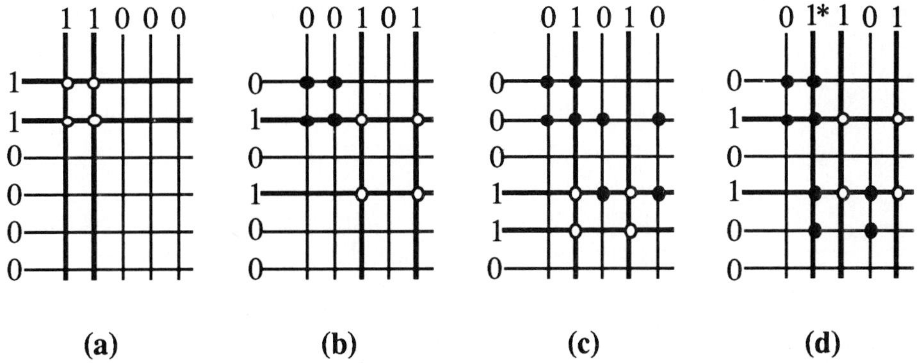

Figure 3.3 Pattern storage in an associative memory matrix. The input information is provided by the horizontal lines as a 0-1-pattern **x** of "activities." The output information **y** is the 0-1-pattern on the vertical lines. Each intersection of an output line r and an input line i is assigned a "weight" w_{ri} (marked by a symbol), which is set to the value one if both lines are active simultaneously. The associations between the input and output patterns are stored in the matrix determined in this manner. Fig. 3.3a–c show the implications of this rule for three consecutive training pairs. The output **y** corresponding to the input pattern **x** can be approximately reconstructed for each output line by summation and thresholding, $\mathbf{y}_r = \theta(\sum_r w_{ri}x_i - s_r)$ (Fig. 3.3d). In Fig. 3.3d, the output pattern reconstructed in this way deviates from the correct pattern in the component designated by an $(*)$.

For a statistical estimate of the error probability of 0s, we introduce the additional assumption that every output pattern contains a fixed fraction f' of 1s. However, we make this assumption for convenience of the mathematical discussion only; it is not important for the function of the memory. We denote the fixed fraction of 1s in each input pattern by $f = k/L$.

We consider a pattern ν and a component r of the output, to which the value $y_r^{(\nu)} = 0$ is assigned for pattern ν. What is the probability for equation (15) to provide the wrong output value $y_r = 1$ if altogether p patterns are stored?

An incorrect value $y_r = 1$ always occurs if

$$\sum_i w_{ri} x_i^{(\nu)} > s_r. \tag{18}$$

Because of the choice $s_r = k - 1/2$ for the threshold, the left side of (18) would have to assume its maximal value k. This can only occur if all of the k 1s of the input pattern $\mathbf{x}^{(\nu)}$, *i.e.*, $x_i^{(\nu)}$, coincide with elements $w_{ri} = 1$. Since $y_r^{(\nu)} = 0$, these elements can only come from training pairs $\mu \neq \nu$. Those k values of the index i for which $w_{ri} = 1$ or $x_i = 1$ are therefore uncorrelated with one another. The probability for all k input 1s to coincide with elements $w_{ri} = 1$, and thus the probability for the occurrence of an error in the output value y_r, is therefore

$$P \approx q^k. \tag{19}$$

Here, q is the fraction of all weights which have been set to the value 1 during the storage procedure. Since a weight w_{ri} keeps its initial value 0 if and only if it "avoids" the coincidence of $x_i = 1$ (probability f) and $y_r = 1$ (probability f') for all p training pairs (probability each time $1 - ff'$), q is thus given by

$$q = 1 - (1 - ff')^p \approx 1 - \exp(-pff'). \tag{20}$$

Equations (19) and (20) thus yield the estimate for the probability of a "false 1" ($f = k/L$)

$$P \approx \left(1 - \exp(-pf'k/L)\right)^k. \tag{21}$$

The average fraction γ of "false 1s" in the output pattern then becomes

$$\gamma = P(1 - f')/f'. \tag{22}$$

For fixed f', γ depends only on k, the ratio p/L of the number of stored patterns, and on the input dimension L. A convenient parameter for discussing the behavior of P is $\alpha = f'p/L$. Figure 3.4 shows the behavior of the error probability P with the number k of 1s per input pattern for several values of α. Below $\alpha \approx 0.1$, the error probability falls off rapidly with decreasing α. There is always an optimal value $k_{opt} = \ln 2/\alpha$ of k that minimizes the error probability for fixed α. The minimum is given by $P_{min} = 2^{-k_{opt}} \approx 0.618^{1/\alpha}$.

The choice $s_r = k - 1/2$ for the thresholds "just barely" enables the activation of an output line. If any 1s at all are lacking from the input pattern, the value zero results in all output lines. Similarly, even a single missing "synapse" ($w_{ri} = 0$ instead of $w_{ri} = 1$) prevents the output value $y_r = 1$. Thus, the system has practically no error tolerance with respect to failure of a few "synapses" or a few missing input bits. However, the choice of a lower threshold s_r gives rise to such an error tolerance. This raises the error probability P to

$$P = \sum_{\nu > s_r}^{k} q^\nu (1 - q)^{k-\nu} \binom{k}{\nu} \tag{23}$$

(for $s_r = k - 1/2$ this reduces to the simpler expression (21)), but this worsening can be compensated by choosing a correspondingly smaller value for the ratio p/L , *i.e.*, by a storage of

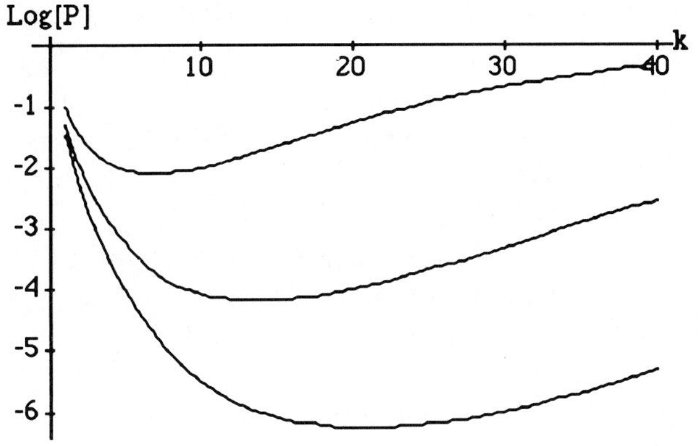

Figure 3.4 Dependence of error probability (logarithmic scale) P on the number k of 1s of the input pattern in the model of Willshaw et al. for parameter values $\alpha = 0.1$ (upper graph), $\alpha = 0.05$ (middle graph) and $\alpha = 0.025$ (lower graph). For every α, there is an optimal value of k minimizing the error probability. For $\alpha << 1$, errors rapidly become very rare.

a smaller number of patterns. This corresponds to utilization of a smaller fraction of the "storage capacity." The advantage compared to the choice of threshold $s_r = k - 1/2$, however, is that the error rate P is now robust with respect to a limited fraction of missing synapses or with respect to the absence of some percentage of the input 1s. The tolerable fraction of such errors can be estimated as follows: since $s_r < k$ correct input 1s of an input pattern already suffice for activation of all the correct output 1s, even if a relative fraction $\kappa \approx 1 - s_r/k$ of all input 1s were absent, an incorrect output pattern would not result. Here, it is of no consequence whether these errors occur in the input pattern itself or whether they arise due to the lack of a corresponding fraction of the "synapses" $w_{ri} = 1$. In this way, the model offers a way to realize a distributed pattern storage. A similar kind of storage is believed to be realized in the brain.

An especially interesting feature is that one can obtain the matrix w_{ri} using Hebb's Rule (2) by adding the condition that the value of a weight must be strictly increasing and be bounded from above by the maximal value one. Beginning with the initial values $w_{ri} = 0$, during a training phase one "forces" the input and output lines to take on successively the binary values of all training pairs $(\mathbf{x}^{(1)}, y^{(1)})$, $(\mathbf{x}^{(2)}, \mathbf{y}^{(2)})$, ..., $(\mathbf{x}^{(L)}, \mathbf{y}^{(L)})$ which are to be stored. For each pair (2) is applied with $\epsilon = 1$. Thus, one sets $w_{ri} = 1$ in the first training pair satisfying both $x_i^{(\nu)} = 1$ and

$y_r^{(\nu)} = 1$ simultaneously. All w_{ri} for which this never happens remain zero, which finally results in (16).

The nonlinear threshold operation by means of the function $\theta(.)$ defined in (15) does not allow a mathematical analysis. However, a matrix memory can also be realized by means of a *linear ansatz*. In this case, the threshold operation does not occur, and the binary values may be replaced by continuous variables. The resulting *linear associative memory* has been investigated by Kohonen (1972, 1984a) and forms the subject of the following section.

3.4. Linear Associative Memory

An important difference between nonlinear and linear systems is the validity of the *superposition principle* in the latter. The linear superposition of several input patterns yields the same superposition of the corresponding output pattern. Whether or not this is a desired property depends on the intended application. However, in general this circumstance does imply a limitation of linear models compared to nonlinear models: only in the latter case can a linear combination of input patterns be associated with an independent output pattern.
In the following, we consider the linear *ansatz*

$$y_r = \sum_{i=1}^{L} w_{ri} x_i. \tag{24}$$

Like Eq. (15), Eq. (24) can be interpreted as the transformation of an input signal $\mathbf{x}$ by a number of "neurons," now assumed linear, into an output signal $\mathbf{y}$.

We are again interested in the use of a system described by Eq.(24) as a *memory* for a number of given "training pairs" $(\mathbf{x}^{(\nu)}, \mathbf{y}^{(\nu)})$, $\nu = 1, 2, \ldots, p$. In contrast to the previous section, the components $x_i^{(\nu)}$ and $y_i^{(\nu)}$ can now take arbitrary continuous values. For example, $\mathbf{x}^{(\nu)}$ might be an array of pixel intensities of a gray-level image, and $\mathbf{y}^{(\nu)}$ might contain some information which is to be "associated" with this image. In particular, $\mathbf{y}^{(\nu)}$ may even coincide with $\mathbf{x}^{(\nu)}$. In this case, one has a so-called *autoassociative memory* . At first glance the association of a pattern with itself seems to promise little new information. However, a useful effect results if the association succeeds even in the case of an erroneous or incomplete input pattern. Autoassociation leads in this case to elimination of errors and/or to completion of incomplete input data.

The requirement that the p training pairs $(\mathbf{x}^{(\nu)}, \mathbf{y}^{(\nu)})$ be stored constitutes a condition on the $N \times L$-matrix $\mathbf{W}$ of weights w_{ri}. The simplest approach consists in minimizing the squared error $E[\mathbf{W}]$, averaged over all input patterns of the matrix, which is dependent on the matrix $\mathbf{W}$:

$$E[\mathbf{W}] = \sum_{\nu=1}^{p} \sum_{r=1}^{N} \left(y_r^{(\nu)} - \sum_{i=1}^{L} w_{ri} x_i^{(\nu)} \right)^2 = \text{Minimum}. \qquad (25)$$

Several solution strategies are possible for minimizing $E[\mathbf{W}]$. The three most important are: (i) exact algebraic minimization by means of the so-called *pseudoinverse*, (ii) application of an iterative *gradient-descent procedure* for stepwise minimization of $E[\mathbf{W}]$, and (iii) use of the *correlation matrix* of training pairs as an approximate solution for the weight array $\mathbf{W}$.

The approaches (i) and (ii) lead essentially to the same solution and maximize the achievable "storage capacity." However, as a solution technique, (i) has the disadvantage of requiring a completely new computation of all w_{ri} for each newly arriving pattern. Hence, this approach is unrealistic, at least as far as applications to neural models are concerned. On the other hand, method (ii) can be formulated as an iterative "learning rule" which, for sufficiently frequent sequential "presentation" of the training pairs to be stored, gradually produces the optimal weights w_{ri}. However, the change of a weight w_{ri} in a learning step also depends on all the other weights w_{rj}, $j \neq i$. In this sense, alternative (iii) is still simpler. Moreover, the required correlation matrix is easy to compute, and its formulation as an iterative "learning rule" takes the form of Hebb's rule. However, in general (iii) does not yield the minimum of $E[\mathbf{W}]$ and hence its utilization of storage capacity is worse than that of the optimal techniques (i) and (ii). This disadvantage is only avoided in the case of pairwise orthogonal pattern vectors, *i.e.*, $\mathbf{x}^{(\nu)} \cdot \mathbf{x}^{(\mu)} = 0$ for $\mu \neq \nu$. In this case, all three techniques are equally good, and (i) and (ii) reduce to (iii).

Following this survey, we now discuss approaches (i), (ii) and (iii) in more detail.

3.5. The Pseudoinverse as a Memory Array

The average error $E[\mathbf{W}]$ is a quadratic polynomial in the weight variables w_{ri}. Minimality of $E[\mathbf{W}]$ demands the vanishing of all first derivatives with respect to weight variables w_{ri}, *i.e.*, the existence of the $L \times p$ equations

$$\frac{\partial E}{\partial w_{ri}} = 2 \cdot \sum_{\nu=1}^{p} \left(\sum_j w_{rj} x_j^{(\nu)} - y_r^{(\nu)} \right) \cdot x_i^{(\nu)} = 0, \tag{26}$$

or, in matrix notation,

$$\mathbf{W}\mathbf{X}\mathbf{X}^{\mathbf{T}} = \mathbf{Y}\mathbf{X}^{\mathbf{T}}. \tag{27}$$

Here, $\mathbf{W}$ is the $N \times L$-matrix of weights w_{ri}, $\mathbf{X}$ is a $L \times p$-matrix, whose elements $X_{i\nu}$ are given by the components of the input vector $\mathbf{x}_i^{(\nu)}$, and $\mathbf{Y}$ is a $N \times p$-matrix with elements $Y_{r\nu} = y_r^{(\nu)}$.

Equation (26) is a *linear equation* for the weight array $\mathbf{W}$. Comparison with the original "storage condition" (24), which in matrix notation takes the form

$$\mathbf{W}\mathbf{X} = \mathbf{Y}, \tag{28}$$

shows that (27) results from (28) after "right-multiplication" of both sides by the matrix $\mathbf{X}^T$. If the square matrix $\mathbf{X}\mathbf{X}^T$ is invertible, one can solve (27) for $\mathbf{W}$, and one obtains

$$\mathbf{W} = \mathbf{Y}\mathbf{X}^T(\mathbf{X}\mathbf{X}^T)^{-1}. \tag{29}$$

However, the invertibility of $\mathbf{X}\mathbf{X}^T$ requires the presence of N linearly independent input pattern vectors $\mathbf{x}^{(\nu)}$, which is usually not satisfied. For example, the number p of input vectors might be smaller than N; or, although $p > N$, the dimension of the space spanned by the input vectors might be lower than N.

The noninvertibility of the matrix $\mathbf{X}\mathbf{X}^T$ indicates that (28) possesses a whole family of solution matrices $\mathbf{W}$ forming an affine space. However, the uniqueness of the minimal solution can be restored by imposing an additional requirement. An appropriate condition is the minimization of the squared sum $\sum_{ri} w_{ri}^2$ of all weights w_{ri}. This requirement can be incorporated easily into the original *ansatz* by minimizing the new functional $E[\mathbf{W}] + \alpha \sum_{ri} w_{ri}^2$ instead of $E[\mathbf{W}]$. This, besides measuring error, also measures the magnitude of an average weight. Here, α is a positive constant, and we take the limit of α approaching zero at the end in order to recover the original minimization problem.

This leads to the new minimization condition

$$\mathbf{W}(\mathbf{X}\mathbf{X}^T + \alpha\mathbf{1}) = \mathbf{Y}\mathbf{X}^T. \tag{30}$$

For every $\alpha > 0$, the matrix $\mathbf{X}\mathbf{X}^T + \alpha\mathbf{1}$ has a well-defined inverse (because $\mathbf{u}^T(\mathbf{X}\mathbf{X}^T + \alpha\mathbf{1})\mathbf{u} \geq \alpha\|\mathbf{u}\|^2$, all its eigenvalues are positive). Hence, combining this with the limit $\alpha \rightarrow 0$, we obtain the closed expression

$$\mathbf{W} = \lim_{\alpha\rightarrow 0} \mathbf{Y}\mathbf{X}^T(\mathbf{X}\mathbf{X}^T + \alpha\mathbf{1})^{-1} \equiv \mathbf{Y}\tilde{\mathbf{X}} \tag{31}$$

for a minimal solution of $E[\mathbf{W}]$. The matrix

$$\tilde{\mathbf{X}} = \lim_{\alpha\rightarrow 0} \mathbf{X}^T(\mathbf{X}\mathbf{X}^T + \alpha\mathbf{1})^{-1} \tag{32}$$

is known as the *pseudoinverse* or *Moore-Penrose inverse* of $\mathbf{X}$.

Whereas the inverse $\mathbf{X}^{-1}$ of a matrix $\mathbf{X}$ arises in solving the matrix equation $\mathbf{W}\mathbf{X} - \mathbf{Y} = 0$ for given $\mathbf{X}$ and $\mathbf{Y}$ in terms of the variables $\mathbf{W}$, (and exists if and only if there is a unique solution $\mathbf{W}$, which is then given by $\mathbf{W} = \mathbf{Y}\mathbf{X}^{-1}$), the pseudoinverse $\tilde{\mathbf{X}}$ arises in the present, more general problem of minimizing the squared sum $E[\mathbf{W}]$, Eq. (25), of the matrix elements of the difference matrix $\mathbf{W}\mathbf{X} - \mathbf{Y}$. In contrast to the stronger condition $\mathbf{W}\mathbf{X} - \mathbf{Y} = 0$, this problem always has at least one solution, which can be expressed in terms of the pseudoinverse $\tilde{\mathbf{X}}$ in the form $\mathbf{W} = \mathbf{Y}\tilde{\mathbf{X}}$. If more than one solution exists, the pseudoinverse chooses the one with the smallest possible sum of the squares of the matrix elements. Unlike the ordinary inverse, which is defined only for quadratic, nonsingular matrices $\mathbf{X}$, the pseudoinverse exists for any matrix (hence in particular for rectangular matrices), and it coincides with the inverse $\mathbf{X}^{-1}$ whenever the inverse is defined.

3.6. Gradient Descent for the Computation of the Memory Matrix

Frequently, it is desired to "memorize" new patterns and/or to change already stored patterns adaptively — while the memory is being used — without having to carry out a completely new computation of the weight array **W** every time. This seems to be an important property for a neural model as well.

Such requirements can be taken into account by an iterative procedure for minimization of $E[\mathbf{W}]$. Each iteration step consists of changing all the weights w_{ri} in the direction of the negative gradient of $E[\mathbf{W}]$, or, in matrix notation,

$$\Delta \mathbf{W} = \epsilon \sum_{\nu=1}^{p} \left(\mathbf{y}^{(\nu)} - \mathbf{W}\mathbf{x}^{(\nu)}\right) \left(\mathbf{x}^{(\nu)}\right)^T, \qquad 0 < \epsilon << 1. \tag{33}$$

Since $E[\mathbf{W}]$ is a quadratic function of the matrix elements w_{ri}, this procedure leads to a monotonic decrease and eventually to the global minimum of E. In the case of a family of minimal solutions, the asymptotic solution depends on the initial value of **W**, and, in contrast to the solution using the pseudoinverse, it is generally not characterized by having the smallest possible sum of the w_{ri}^2.

Equation (33) can be regarded as the result of the superposition of p "learning steps," where each learning step corresponds to a term in the ν-summation and can be interpreted as a change of the weights during a "presentation" of the training pair $(\mathbf{x}^{(\nu)}, \mathbf{y}^{(\nu)})$. If every training pair occurs with the same probability and the "learning step size" ϵ is sufficiently small, then on the average (33) corresponds to the simpler prescription

$$\Delta \mathbf{W} = \epsilon'(\mathbf{y}^{(\nu)} - \mathbf{W}\mathbf{x}^{(\nu)})(\mathbf{x}^{(\nu)})^T, \qquad \epsilon' = \epsilon/p. \tag{34}$$

Comparison of (34) and (4) shows that (34) is nothing more than a variant of the perceptron rule discussed above. The present derivation augments the previous discussion of the perceptron rule by showing us that this rule can be interpreted as a gradient descent procedure for the average squared response error.

3.7. The Correlation Matrix Memory

The perceptron rule (34) requires that a matrix multiplication $\mathbf{W}\mathbf{x}^{(\nu)}$ is carried out for each learning step. Hence, the change of any single weight w_{ri} involves the values of all the remaining weights w_{rj}, $j = 1, \ldots, L$. In order to carry out the procedure in practice, for example in very large scale integrated (VLSI) circuits, it would be desirable to have a simpler rule that would work without this dependence. In fact, in many cases one can do without the term $\mathbf{W}\mathbf{x}^{(\nu)}$ in (34). This leads to a rule of the form

$$\Delta\mathbf{W} = \epsilon\left(\mathbf{y}^{(\nu)}(\mathbf{x}^{(\nu)})^T - \mathbf{W}\right), \qquad \epsilon > 0. \tag{35}$$

Here, as opposed to (34), an additional decay term $-\mathbf{W}$ has been introduced for the sole purpose of automatically normalizing $\mathbf{W}$; it can be left out if the normalization is otherwise guaranteed.

In the limit of small step size ϵ the matrix $\mathbf{W}$ converges by means of (35) to the *correlation matrix* $\langle \mathbf{y}\mathbf{x}^T \rangle$, where $\langle . \rangle$ denotes averaging over the presented pattern pairs. A matrix memory based on this choice of $\mathbf{W}$ is therefore known as a *linear correlation matrix memory* . If the training pairs all occur with equal frequency, one has

$$\mathbf{W} = \frac{1}{p}\sum_{\nu=1}^{p} \mathbf{y}^{(\nu)}\left(\mathbf{x}^{(\nu)}\right)^T. \tag{36}$$

For pairwise orthogonal pattern vectors $\mathbf{x}^{(\nu)}$, one easily sees that (36) leads to a memory matrix with the desired property $\mathbf{W}\mathbf{x}^{(\nu)} = \|\mathbf{x}^{(\nu)}\|^2 \cdot \mathbf{y}^{(\nu)}$. In this case, the correlation matrix memory evidently works in an error-free manner, (the factor in front, $\|x^{(\nu)}\|^2$, can be regarded as an "intensity normalization" and disappears if normalized input vectors $\mathbf{x}^{\nu}$ are used). In particular, a maximum of $p = N$ such pattern vectors can be stored in this manner.

Deviations from pairwise orthogonality lead to "cross-talk" between different patterns and, thus, to a decreased storage capacity: for an input pattern $\mathbf{x}^{(\nu)}$, the resulting output signal is

$$\mathbf{y} = ||\mathbf{x}^{(\nu)}||^2 \left(\mathbf{y}^{(\nu)} + \sum_{\mu \neq \nu} \mathbf{y}^{(\mu)} \frac{\mathbf{x}^{(\mu)} \cdot \mathbf{x}^{(\nu)}}{||\mathbf{x}^{(\nu)}||^2} \right). \tag{37}$$

Equation (37) shows that, superimposed on the correct output pattern $\mathbf{y}^{(\nu)}$, there are contributions from all the remaining patterns μ, $\mu \neq \nu$ for which the scalar product $\mathbf{x}^{(\nu)} \cdot \mathbf{x}^{(\mu)}$ with the input pattern $\mathbf{x}^{(\nu)}$ does not vanish. A proper functioning of the linear correlation matrix memory thus requires that these scalar products be small and, hence, that the patterns be at least approximately orthogonal.

As a consequence, the operation of a linear correlation matrix memory can be significantly improved by a previous *orthogonalization* of the input patterns $\mathbf{x}^{(\nu)}$. A simple and often appropriate procedure (*e.g.*, for many kinds of image data) is a *high-pass filtering* of the input signal. The slowly varying parts of signals are then suppressed, and only the "high-frequency" (in space or time) part of the signal is kept. Subtracting from each component, its average value can be regarded as the simplest version of such *high-pass filtering*.

The models discussed so far have no *feedback*. Feedback is present if some of the input is provided by the output lines. This situation, which complicates a theoretical analysis considerably, is almost always found in real nerve systems. The smallest degree of complication occurs in the case of the linear matrix memory, considered here. A qualitative summary of its behavior when feedback is present can easily be given. If the dimensions of the input and output vectors agree, ($L = N$), the process of repeatedly feeding the output back into the input is equivalent to replacing the memory matrix $\mathbf{W}$ by the matrix taken to some higher power. After t loops, the initial vector $\mathbf{x}(0)$ becomes

$$\mathbf{x}(t) = \mathbf{W}^t \mathbf{x}(0). \tag{38}$$

For a diagonalizable memory matrix $\mathbf{W}$, $\mathbf{x}(t)$ converges (up to a normalization factor) for large t to its projection on the eigenspace corresponding to the eigenvalue of $\mathbf{W}$ with the largest absolute value. The components of $\mathbf{x}(0)$ along the eigenvectors with small eigenvalues of $\mathbf{W}$ fall off most rapidly. If, for example, $\mathbf{W}$ has been determined using (36), and if p stored patterns are approximately orthogonal to each other, then the eigenvalues of $\mathbf{W}$ may form two "clusters", one cluster consisting of p eigenvalues of nearly the same magnitude near

$1/p$, the other consisting of $N - p$ eigenvalues near zero. The eigenvectors corresponding to the latter eigenvalues are approximately orthogonal to the stored patterns. Hence, an input vector is generally "driven" in the direction of the "most similar pattern" among the p stored patterns. Competition between the stored patterns eventually occurs after many iterations, and $\mathbf{x}(t)$ converges to the eigenvector whose eigenvalue has the largest absolute value. Since $\mathbf{W}$ is nearly degenerate in the space spanned by the stored patterns, this eigenvector need not necessarily agree with any of the stored patterns.

Since the eigenvalue of greatest magnitude will usually differ from unity, the norm of $\mathbf{x}(t)$ gradually tends either to zero or infinity. Hence, for a realistic model, the introduction of nonlinearities is unavoidable, at least for stabilization. One of the earliest suggestions of this kind goes back to Anderson et al. (1977) and is known as the "Brain State in a Box" ("BSB" model), since an appropriate nonlinearity constrains $\mathbf{x}(t)$ within a multidimensional box.

The mathematical analysis of systems with feedback of this type turns out to be much more difficult than in the linear case. In particular, it seemed quite hopeless for a long time to go much beyond computer simulations for nonlinear threshold value models with McCulloch-Pitts neurons. This changed in 1982 due to an important idea of Hopfield (1982), which forms the subject of the following section. For other important contributions related to these questions see, for example, the papers by Grossberg (1976ab,1978), Kohonen (1984a), as well as Cohen and Grossberg (1983).

3.8. The Hopfield Model

If a portion of the output lines is fed back to the inputs, the corresponding portion of the output patterns $\mathbf{y}$ can contribute to the input pattern $\mathbf{x}$. An especially interesting case arises for $\mathbf{y} = \mathbf{x}$, *i.e.*, every input pattern is associated with itself as output (*autoassociation*). If one presents an incomplete input pattern to a recurrent system in which such training pairs are stored, then at first a correspondingly incomplete output pattern results. However, if output is fed back, the intact portion may be sufficient for reconstruction of part of the missing input data.

The system may react to the improved input pattern with an improved output, which in turn reconstructs even more of the input pattern, etc. until finally the system winds up in a state in which the input pattern is completely restored.

Such feedback mechanism can enable recall of the complete pattern on the basis of an *incomplete input fragment.* Such a capability of pattern restoration is an important requirement for high-performance data processing and a prominent feature of biological nervous systems, which are highly optimized in the processing of incomplete information from their natural environment.

Due to feedback, every neuron affects the inputs to all the other neurons. The behavior of such a system is generally quite difficult to analyze. However, by exploiting an analogy to interacting many-particle systems from statistical physics, Hopfield (1982) was able to characterize the behavior of an interesting class of such systems in an elegant model.

Hopfield's original model employs McCulloch-Pitts neurons. In the following, we give a version with "± 1-neurons". Because of the feedback, now the input pattern of each neuron i is constructed from the states y_j of all the other neurons. The state of neuron i at the latest time step is determined according to

$$y_i^{(new)} = \text{sgn}\left(\sum_{j,j\neq i} w_{ij} y_j^{(old)}\right). \tag{39}$$

Here, sgn(x) denotes the "sign function", *i.e.*, is equal to +1 for $x \geq 0$ and -1 otherwise. The "update-steps" (39) are carried out "asynchronously," *i.e.*, the state of a neuron is updated at discrete times chosen to be uncorrelated among the neurons.

The solvability of the models follows from the requirement of *symmetric matrix elements, i.e.*, $w_{ij} = w_{ji}$ for all index pairs (i, j). In this case, (39) describes the stochastic dynamic of a *physical spin system* with an "energy function"

$$H(\mathbf{y}) = -\frac{1}{2}\sum_{i,j} w_{ij} y_i y_j, \tag{40}$$

where $w_{ii} = 0$.

Whenever (39) leads to a change $\Delta y_i \neq 0$ of y_i, it can be written in the form

$$\Delta y_i = 2 \cdot \text{sgn}\left(\sum_{j,j\neq i} w_{ij} y_j\right) \tag{41}$$

By symmetry of the w_{ij}, the corresponding change ΔH of H is then

$$\begin{aligned} \Delta H &= -\Delta y_i \cdot \sum_j w_{ij} y_j \\ &= -2 \cdot \left\| \sum_j w_{ij} y_j \right\| \leq 0, \end{aligned} \tag{42}$$

i.e., H decreases until either the quantities $\sum_j w_{ij} y_j$ all vanish (an exceptional situation arising only for "pathological" choices of w_{ij}), or the adaptation rule (39) does not yield any further change in state. In this (common) case, the system reaches a stationary "fixed point."

This allows a rather clear interpretation of the time evolution of the neural activities described by (39). $H(\mathbf{y})$ defines a "potential surface" on the state space of all possible binary vectors $\mathbf{y}$. Starting from an initial state $\mathbf{y}(0)$, the system moves downhill along the gradient of $H(\mathbf{y})$ until it comes to rest at a local minimum (a "perpetual" descent is impossible, since only finitely many states are available to the system). If the input pattern defines the initial state $\mathbf{y}(0)$, the minimum attained by the network is the output associated with the input. Every minimum in the potential surface is the lowest point of a "basin" or "sink" surrounding it. All the input patterns within this basin are attracted to the basin minimum by the system dynamics and, thus, yield the same output pattern. Hence, one also refers to *basins of attraction* surrounding the local minima.

By an appropriate choice of w_{ij}, one can "mold" the potential surface and, in particular, place local minima at desired target patterns ξ^ν. The system dynamics will then be able to restore a fragmentary input pattern to that target pattern ξ^ν, whose basin of attraction encloses the input pattern. The completion of fragmentary information in the Hopfield model thus is obtained through gradient descent on a potential surface.

The choice of the w_{ij} is based on the specified target patterns to be stored. For uncorrelated binary patterns consisting of equally many positive and negative elements an appropriate choice is

$$w_{ij} = \frac{1}{N} \sum_{\nu=1}^{p} \xi_i^\nu \cdot \xi_j^\nu. \tag{43}$$

Here, N is the number of neurons, p is the number of patterns and ξ_i^ν the ith component of the νth pattern vector ξ^ν, $\nu = 1, 2, \ldots, p$.

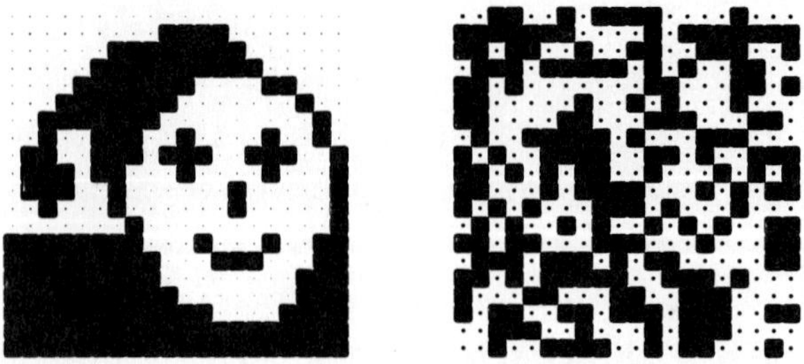

Figure 3.5 *(left)* This pattern is stored together with 19 others in a Hopfield model consisting of 400 neurons. *(right)* All of the other 19 patterns are "random patterns" of the type shown; 50% of randomly chosen pixels are black.

In the following, we present an example of a simulation for a network consisting of 400 neurons. In this case, 20 patterns are stored according to the prescription (43). The first two of these patterns are shown in Figure 3.5. Each -1 is represented by a white pixel, each +1 by a black pixel. Only the first pattern represents a recognizable motif (Fig. 3.5a); all of the remaining 19 patterns are "random patterns," each consisting of 50 percent randomly chosen white and black pixels; a representative example is shown in Figure 3.5b.

In Figure 3.6, we see the reaction of the network, if just the upper quarter of pattern 1 is presented as input. In the course of a few timesteps (each timestep includes update steps for all neurons) the pattern is correctly completed.

Figure 3.7 shows a similar simulation. This time, pattern 1 is corrupted by changing each pixel of the image with a probability P=0.3. This corresponds to the presence of intense "signal noise." Although the original motif is hardly recognizable, within a few time steps all of the "errors" have been corrected.

Figure 3.8 shows a repetition of this simulation, but this time with P=0.4. In this case, the network is no longer able to restore the original motif, and the output pattern converges to one of the other stored random patterns.

The weight choice (43) is sufficient for pattern recall, provided that the number p of stored patterns is not too large. If the number of patterns is increased beyond a critical threshold, the character of the potential surface changes, and the system no longer functions as a memory for the specified input patterns. This can be qualitatively understood as follows. If all of the

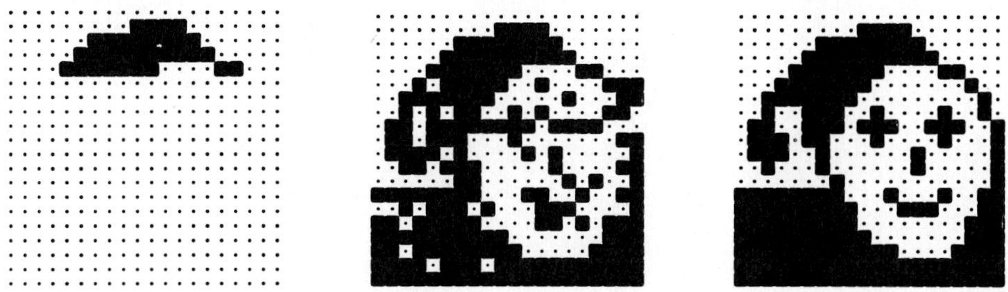

Figure 3.6 Completion of a fragmentary input pattern. Only the upper 25% of pattern 1 is presented to the network (*left*). After one timestep, the complete pattern can already be recognized (*middle*); two steps later, the pattern has been correctly completed (*right*).

Figure 3.7 Reconstruction of a noisy input pattern. This time, the input is the complete pattern 1, but, with a probability of P=0.3, every pixel of the image has been changed (*left*). After only one timestep, nearly all of the errors are eliminated (*middle*), and after an additional step the correct pattern 1 is restored (*right*).

Figure 3.8 Like the preceding sequence of images, but for P=0.4. In this case, the network is no longer able to restore the original pattern, and it converges to one of the 19 other random patterns.

neurons are in a pattern state, for example $y = \xi^1$, then

$$\begin{aligned}\sum_j w_{ij} y_j &= \frac{1}{N} \sum_j \left(\xi_i^1 \cdot (\xi_j^1)^2 + \sum_{\nu=2}^{p} \xi_i^\nu \xi_j^\nu \xi_j^1 \right) \\ &= \xi_i^1 + \frac{1}{N} \sum_{j,\nu>1} \xi_i^\nu \xi_j^\nu \xi_j^1 .\end{aligned} \tag{44}$$

After separation of the terms with $\nu = 1$, the remaining summation on the right side consists of $N \cdot (p-1)$ uncorrelated terms of value ± 1 and with average value zero. Hence, the sum is itself again a random variable with average value zero, but with variance $\sqrt{N(p-1)}$, and we can write (44) approximately as

$$\sum_j w_{ij} \xi_j^1 = \xi_i^1 + \eta \cdot \sqrt{\frac{p-1}{N}}, \tag{45}$$

where η is a normally distributed random variable with variance one. The second term in (45) shows that the stored patterns act like "Gaussian noise" superimposed on the currently active pattern. Nevertheless, provided $p << N$, the first term in (45) dominates, and the system is immune to the noise, since in this case (39) does not lead to a change in any neuron states. However, if p gets to be of order N, the influence of the noise becomes comparable to the effect of the currently active pattern itself. In that case, we can no longer expect to find stability for any stored pattern. A more precise computation shows that the critical transition occurs at $p \approx 0.146N$. In the analogous physical spin system, one encounters at this value a *phase transition* to a so-called *spin glass state* (Amit et al. 1985).

The choice (43) for the storage of given patterns is not the only possible one. By means of more general procedures, for example iterative methods, or by a more sophisticated coding of the patterns, on can store a larger number of patterns. However, for an estimate of the *storage capacity* of a network, the mere number of patterns that can be stored is not the only important variable. In addition, one has to consider the *information content* per pattern as well as the information contained in the synaptic strengths w_{ij}. For a thorough discussion of these interesting questions, the reader is referred to the literature (see Palm 1980, 1981; Amit et al. 1985, 1987; Gardner and Derrida 1988; Buhmann et al. 1989).

The Hopfield model of associative memory is less than optimal in many respects. For example, it is ill suited for the storage of correlated patterns. Another problem arises in connection with invariance: the model judges the similarity of patterns exclusively according to the number of pixels that coincide. Hence, it is unable to recognize the equivalence of patterns that differ only by a simple transformation, such as, by a translation.

Nonetheless, the model is of great conceptual significance, since it constitutes a fully connected neural network for which many questions can be given an analytical answer. In particular, the Hopfield model initiated the use of many highly developed mathematical methods of statistical physics and thus made important new tools available for the field of neural computation. Therefore, it formed the basis for numerous new developments and motivated important new questions, and it was thus a forceful stimulus for the major upsurge in "neural computing" at the beginning of the eighties.

3.9. The Back-Propagation Algorithm

In the Hopfield model, every neuron is connected to every other neuron. Hence, with respect to its connections, the model has no "internal structure" and is "homogeneous." However, neural networks are usually structured. A structure encountered frequently results from connecting several layers of neurons in series. The first layer is usually reserved for input patterns. Every neuron of this layer sends out connections to every neuron of the next layer. This continues until the last layer has been reached, whose activity pattern constitutes the output.

Each individual layer can perform a partial transformation of the activity pattern of the preceding layer. For the perceptron — corresponding essentially to a single layer — we saw that a serious limitation of the possible transformations between input and output occurs. Hence, an important question concerns how to overcome the limitations of the perceptron by connecting several layers in series and thus concatenating their transformations.

In contrast to the perceptron and to nets of the Hopfield type, a layered feed-forward network contains *hidden units* that are not directly connected to input or output lines. Therefore, the activity state of these neurons cannot be affected directly by the "outside world," but can only be influenced indirectly

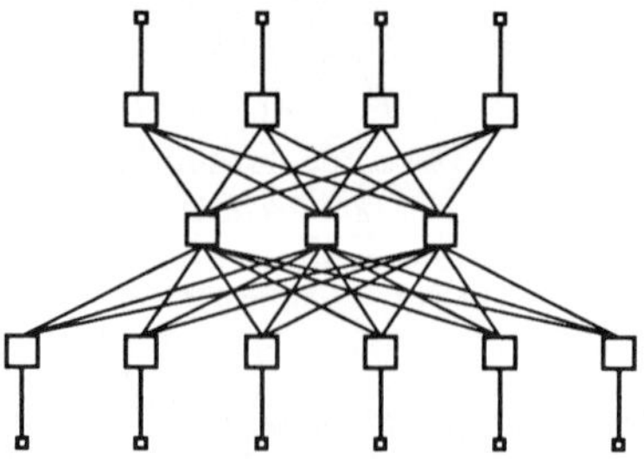

Figure 3.9 Three-layer neural net. Each layer sends connections to the layer just above it. The input pattern is applied to the neurons of the bottom layer, while the neuron activities of the top layer constitute the output pattern.

through the internal circuitry of the network. The perceptron convergence theorem described in Section 3.2 guarantees that the weights of a network with a single layer of units can be trained with a finite number of adaptation steps. However, this theorem cannot be generalized to feed-forward networks with hidden units. Because the hidden units are only indirectly affected by input signals, the following problem arises: if the given task has been performed badly, it is not clear which of the weights are responsible for the bad result and how they have to be changed. This problem is known as the *credit assignment problem* and was one of the reasons which led to the demise of the perceptron and its multilayer successors in the 1960s. The *back-propagation algorithm* (Werbos 1974; Rumelhart, Hinton and Williams 1986) is an interesting approach to solve this problem. We describe this procedure for a network which consists of three layers: an input layer, a "hidden layer," and an output layer, as shown schematically in Fig. 3.9.

We designate neurons of the output layer, the hidden layer, and the input layer by denoting indices i, j and k, respectively. In contrast to the earlier models, here each neuron has a continuous output activity between zero and one. The activity s_j of a neuron j of the hidden layer is given by

$$s_j = \sigma\left(\sum_k w_{jk} s_k\right). \tag{46}$$

Here, s_k are the activities of the neurons k in the input layer, *i.e.*, we identify s_k with the components x_k of the input vector. $\sigma(x)$ is a *sigmoid function*, *i.e.*, $\sigma(x)$ is nonnegative, everywhere monotonically increasing, and approaches the asymptotic saturation values zero or one, respectively for $x \to \pm\infty$. $\sigma(x)$ describes the response of a neuron to a total synaptic input x. A frequent

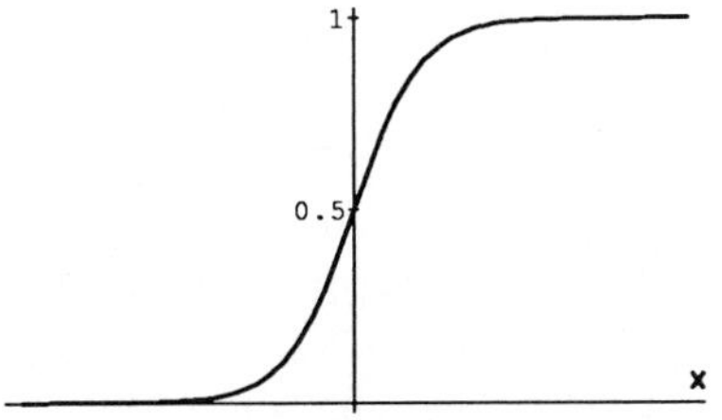

Figure 3.10 Graph of the Fermi function $\sigma(x) = (1 + \exp(x))^{-1}$, a typical choice for the response function σ of a neuron.

choice for $\sigma(x)$ is the "Fermi function"

$$\sigma(x) = \frac{1}{1 + \exp(-x)} \tag{47}$$

presented in Fig. 3.10.

The activities of the neurons of the output layer are

$$s_i = \sigma\left(\sum_j w_{ij} s_j\right), \tag{48}$$

and provide the output values $y_i \equiv s_i$. According to (46) and (48), for each input pattern x an output pattern y is assigned. This assignment depends on the values of the synaptic strengths w_{ij} from the hidden layer to the output layer and on the synaptic strengths w_{jk} from the input layer to the hidden layer.†

We now seek w_{ij} and w_{jk} such that the network maps some given number of input patterns $\mathbf{x}^\nu$ onto given output patterns $\mathbf{y}^\nu$, $\nu = 1, 2, \ldots, p$. A measure of how well the network performs this task is the sum of the squared errors over all training pairs $(\mathbf{x}^\nu, \mathbf{y}^\nu)$

$$E = \frac{1}{2} \sum_{\nu=1}^{p} \sum_i \left(y_i^\nu - s_i(\mathbf{x}^\nu)\right)^2. \tag{49}$$

For a set of given, fixed training pairs, E is a function of all the synaptic strengths w_{ij} and w_{jk}. Here, the w_{ij} and w_{jk} are optimally chosen if the error E is minimized. The determination of appropriate synaptic strengths is hence equivalent to the problem of minimizing the function E. The gradient descent procedure offers the simplest way of doing this. The back-propagation algorithm is a parallelized computational scheme for carrying out an approximate gradient descent for E.

†Equations (46) and (48) do not contain explicit "excitation thresholds". These can be taken into account in the form of synaptic strengths w_{i0} and w_{j0} by taking for each layer $s_0 = -1$.

To do this, all of the w_{ij} and w_{jk} are modified iteratively according to $w_{ab}^{new} = w_{ab}^{old} + \Delta w_{ab}$ where

$$\Delta w_{ab} = -\alpha \cdot \frac{\partial E}{\partial w_{ab}}. \tag{50}$$

For sufficiently small $\alpha > 0$, one will then move along the direction of steepest descent of E. The change of E during such an iteration step is approximately

$$\Delta E = \sum_{ab} \frac{\partial E}{\partial w_{ab}} \Delta w_{ab} = -\alpha \sum_{ab} \left(\frac{\partial E}{\partial w_{ab}} \right)^2 \leq 0. \tag{51}$$

The derivatives $\partial E / \partial w_{ab}$ are obtained using the chain rule. For the connections w_{ij} between the hidden layer and the output layer we have

$$\frac{\partial E}{\partial w_{ij}} = -\sum_{\nu} (y_i^{\nu} - s_i(\mathbf{x}^{\nu})) \cdot \sigma'(\sum_{j'} w_{ij'} s_{j'}) \cdot s_j; \tag{52}$$

and for the connections w_{jk} from the input layer to the hidden layer we have

$$\begin{aligned} \frac{\partial E}{\partial w_{jk}} &= -\sum_{\nu} \sum_{i} (y_i^{\nu} - s_i(\mathbf{x}^{\nu})) \cdot \sigma'(\sum_{j'} w_{ij'} s_{j'}) \cdot w_{ij} \cdot \frac{\partial s_j}{\partial w_{jk}} \\ &= -\sum_{\nu} \sum_{i} (y_i^{\nu} - s_i(\mathbf{x}^{\nu})) \cdot \sigma'(\sum_{j'} w_{ij'} s_{j'}) \cdot w_{ij} \\ &\quad \times \sigma'(\sum_{k'} w_{jk'} s_{k'}) \cdot s_k. \end{aligned} \tag{53}$$

Both expressions consist of sums over contributions from specified input training pairs $(\mathbf{x}^{\nu}, \mathbf{y}^{\nu})$. If α is sufficiently small, it makes little difference if just one ν-term of (52) or (53) is taken into account at each iteration (50), provided that every term is on the average included equally often. This leads to the update rules

$$\begin{aligned} \Delta w_{ij} &= \alpha \cdot \epsilon_i^{\nu} \cdot s_j s_i (1 - s_i), \\ \Delta w_{jk} &= \alpha \cdot \sum_i \epsilon_i^{\nu} \cdot s_k s_i (1 - s_i) \cdot w_{ij} \cdot s_j (1 - s_j) \end{aligned} \tag{54}$$

for the w_{ij} and w_{jk} connecting hidden and output layer, and connecting input and hidden layer, respectively. Here, we have defined $\epsilon_i^{\nu} = y_i^{\nu} - s_i(\mathbf{x}^{\nu})$ for the ith "output error" in the νth input pattern, and we have employed the expression $\sigma'(x) = \sigma(x)(1 - \sigma(x))$ which is valid for the Fermi function (47).

Expressions (54) can easily be generalized to the case of more than one hidden layer. In the following, let a and b designate arbitrary neurons of two consecutive layers, and let b lie in the layer preceding a. The change Δw_{ab} of the weight w_{ab} under an iteration with the specified input training pair ν is a summation over contributions D_{γ_i}. Each contribution belongs to one neuron i of the output layer and to a sequence γ_i of connections leading from neuron a to neuron i. The summation is to be performed both over all the different sequences of this kind, visiting each layer between a and the output layer only once and over all possible choices of the output neuron i, *i.e.*,

$$\Delta w_{ab} = \sum_i \sum_{\gamma_i} D_{\gamma_i}. \tag{55}$$

Each contribution D_{γ_i} consists of a product of factors along the "connecting path" γ_i. The individual factors are obtained according to the following rules:

1. For each "visited" neuron n along the path γ_i, one obtains a factor $s_n(1 - s_n)$, where s_n is the activity of neuron n.
2. For each connection between two consecutive neurons n, n' along the path γ_i, one obtains a factor $w_{nn'}$.
3. Additionally, one has a factor $\alpha \cdot \epsilon_i^\nu \cdot s_b$. Here, ϵ_i^ν is the output error of the neuron i at the end of the connecting path.

Equations (54) allows the following interpretation: for each iteration, a training pair $(\mathbf{x}^\nu, \mathbf{y}^\nu)$ is selected and the activities of the neurons in the input layer are set to values $\mathbf{x}^\nu$. On the basis of the resulting neuron activities in the remaining layers and the error ϵ_i^ν occurring at the output layer, the network carries out a "learning step" such that the output error for pattern ν is decreased.

The hope is to gradually reduce the error E to zero or at least to negligibly small values for all specified input patterns, provided sufficiently many learning steps are made. However, the problem of *local minima* can arise. As a rule, E is an extremely complicated function of all the synaptic strengths w_{ab} and, hence, it can have numerous local minima. Depending on the initial values specified for the w_{ab}, the gradient-descent method always leads to the nearest minimum, independently of how far it lies above the absolute minimum. Thus, the learning procedure can get "stuck" prematurely although the network has not yet solved the problem. Whether or not a good minimum is attained depends in a generally unpredictable way on the initial values for the synaptic strengths and on the (generally unknown) form of the "error surface" E. A further difficulty is caused by parameter regions, for which the height of the error surface hardly varies with w_{ab}. There, the gradient is very small and, thus, the adaptation steps (55) yield negligible changes. This difficulty is the price for a completely "general" learning algorithm, which is supposed to solve a given problem without any a priori information.

In spite of these problems, the back-propagation algorithm represents a significant step forward. In particular it allows the solution of problems that cannot be solved with a single-layer perceptron. One problem of this kind that is frequently considered is the logical "exclusive-or-gate," which assigns the output value 1 to an input if and only if one input is equal to 0 and the other is equal to 1.

In the back-propagation algorithm, the solution of such problems becomes possible because, in contrast to the perceptron, the system has access to additional, "hidden" neurons. The activity of these neurons provides an *internal representation* of the input patterns. By evolving appropriate connections w_{jk}, the system can develop internal representations that make the problem solvable for the following layer. We demonstrate this by means of a simulation example, the so-called "encoder problem" (Rumelhart et al. 1986).

We consider a network consisting of three layers. The input and output layers each contain N neurons, numbered from one to N. The middle layer contains $M < N$ neurons. The learning task of the network is to respond to the activation of a single neuron n in the input layer with the activation of a single neuron n in the output layer, *i.e.*, activation of that neuron whose index coincides with the index of the activated input neuron.

If the hidden layer also had N neurons, the solution would be simple and evident: each input neuron would be connected directly via one of the hidden neurons to "its" output neuron. However, since the layer in between possesses *less than* N neurons, it constitutes a "bottleneck" for the transfer of information, and the network must find some way of getting the information through this bottleneck. One possibility consists in discovering an appropriate data coding — hence the name "encoder problem" — which can make do with M elements for the representation of the information.

Figure 3.11 shows the result of a computer simulation for a network with $N = 8$ and $M = 3$ after 10,000 learning steps with a step size of $\alpha = 0.25$. The initial values of all connections were chosen to be pseudo-random numbers in the interval $[-2,\ 2]$. Each of the eight specified input patterns $\mathbf{x}^\nu$ was given by $x_k^\nu = 0.1 + 0.8\delta_{k\nu}$, *i.e.*, the νth neuron received the input 0.9, all others 0.1. The inputs 0.9 and 0.1 for "active" and "inactive" were used to avoid convergence difficulties, since the Fermi function $\sigma(x)$ produces binary outputs zero and one only for $x = \pm\infty$ (this would require infinitely large weights w_{ab}).

Figure 3.11 shows for each of the eight possible input patterns the resulting neuron activities. The bottom row of each picture shows the input layer, the middle row consists of the three "hidden" neurons, and the upper row shows the output layer. Each square symbol stands for one neuron, whose activity is indicated by the size of the square.

One sees that the network has solved the problem successfully. A look at the activity patterns of the middle layer reveals the solution strategy developed by the network. The neurons of this layer have organized their connections in such a way as to assign to each of the eight input patterns a 3-bit binary code, thus enabling the transfer of the required information through the "bottleneck."

This example shows how a network can "discover" interesting *internal data representations*, in this case the binary code. This is relevant to a key question of neural computing: What internal data representations are required in order to solve a given problem by means of a massively parallel network? With the back-propagation algorithm one has a method to construct networks performing some desired task. One then can analyze the structure of the networks thus obtained in order to gain new insights how parallel networks can solve various computational tasks. This approach, occasionally termed "neurophysiology in the computer," may also help to interprete neurophysiological findings about "real" neural networks and to guide new experiments. For instance, interesting parallels have been noted between the response of "neurons" in the computer and neurons in biological networks (Sejnowski and Rosenberg 1987; Zipser and Andersen 1988).

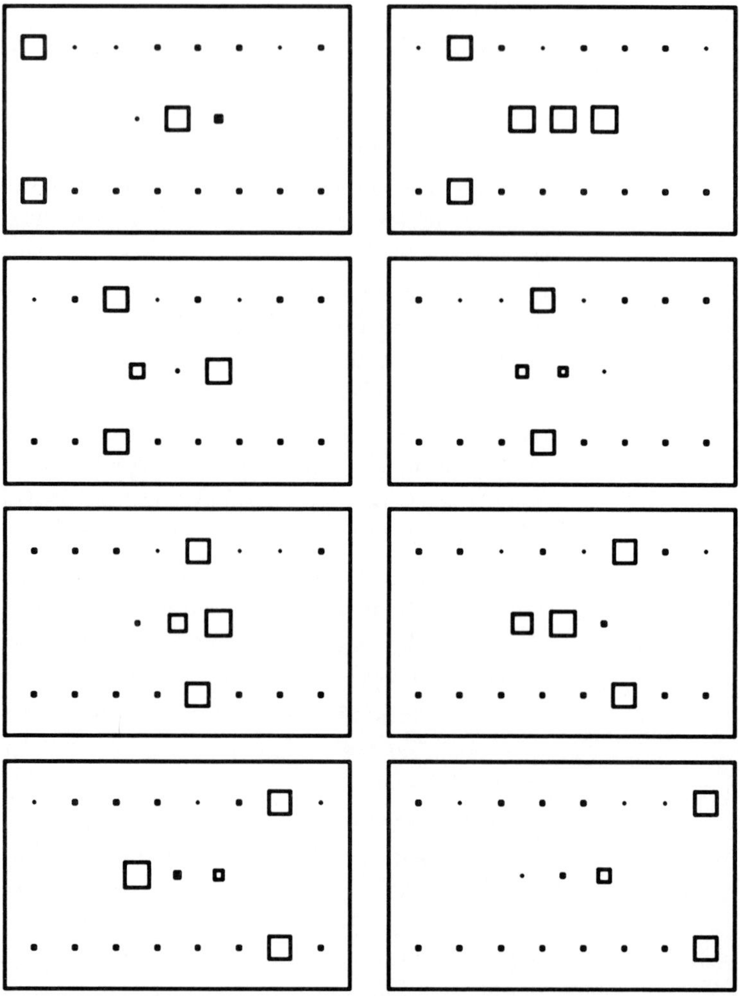

Figure 3.11 Internal data coding found by the back-propagation algorithm for the "encoder problem." In each picture, one of the eight lower input neurons is activated. The task of the network is the activation of the corresponding output neuron in the upper layer. The input neurons cannot reach the output neurons directly, but only by imposing an "intermediate coding pattern" on the three neurons of the middle layer. From their activities it is evident that the network has "discovered" in essence a binary coding of the eight input patterns.

3.10. Self-Organizing Maps

In all of the previous models, a key role was played by the connections between neurons. In the Hopfield model, every neuron was connected to every other one, and the only (but, from a biological point of view rather restrictive) constraint was the symmetry $w_{ij} = w_{ji}$. The feed-forward nets of the previous chapter were already organized into a number of layers connected in a fixed order. However, thus far the *location of each neuron within a layer* has played no role for the outgoing or incoming connections. This was a direct consequence of connecting every neuron of one layer to every neuron of the subsequent layer. With *self-organizing maps*, one deals with models in which the ordering of the neurons, *i.e.*, within a layer structure, plays an important role. One is concerned with the question of how the neurons should organize their connectivity in order to optimize the *spatial distribution of their responses within the layer*. Here, the purpose of the optimization is to convert the *similarity of signals* into *proximity* of excited neurons. Neurons with similar tasks can thus communicate over especially short connection paths. This is a very important property for a massively parallel system. A further consequence of such optimization is the formation of *topographic maps* of the input signals, in which the most important similarity relationships among the input signals are converted into *spatial relationships* among the responding neurons. This conversion can be viewed as a process of *abstraction*, suppressing trivial details and mapping the most important properties or features along the dimensions of the map; this is once again relevant to the important problem of the construction of internal data representations.

An important special case of such maps is the occurrence of topographically organized projections from a receptor layer to a layer of sensory neurons. This corresponds to the occurrence of simple maps, representing on the neuron layer a (distorted) image of the receptor layer. A theory of the formation of such projections on the basis of synaptic plasticity was suggested by von der Malsburg and Willshaw (Willshaw and von der Malsburg 1976; von der Malsburg and Willshaw 1977). These authors consider a neural layer A, from which output nerve fibers are supposed to grow into a second layer B such that the neighborhood relationships in A are preserved under this "projection." To this end they postulate in layer A the presence of at least two different "marker substances" $i = 1, 2, \ldots,$ with concentration gradients such that their local concentrations $c_i(\mathbf{r})$ uniquely determine the position $\mathbf{r}$ everywhere in A. The nerve fibers leaving $\mathbf{r}$ are assumed to transport these marker substances in a mixing ratio characteristic of their origin $\mathbf{r}$ and to give them off at all points in B with which they make synaptic contact. In this way, position-dependent concentrations $c_i'(\mathbf{r}')$ of the marker substances are formed in B as well. The evolution of the strength of each synapse in B is then determined by two competing contributions. One contribution is a decay term driving the strength of a synapse slowly to zero. The other is a growth term. The better the agreement between the mixing ratios of the marker substances present at the position of the synapse in B and the mixing ratio of the markers given off by the synapse itself, the larger is this growth term. This favors establishment of neighboring synaptic contacts in B for nerve fibers that originate from neighboring positions in A and, as demonstrated by von der Malsburg and Willshaw, leads to the formation of a topographically ordered projection between A and B. By means of computer simulations, von der Malsburg and Willshaw were able to demonstrate a good agreement between the properties of this model and experimentally known findings. In a series of papers, this model was elaborated further in various directions, and new variations were proposed that were capable of explaining additional details, such as the formation of cortical microcolumns (Takeuchi and Amari 1979).

These models often endeavored to be more or less faithful to biological details. A more abstract, and at the same time more general, approach was subsequently suggested by Kohonen (1982a) for the formation of self-organizing sensory maps. We will discuss his model for the formation of such maps in more detail in the subsequent chapters of this book. The Kohonen maps offer a very good point of departure for presenting how a multitude of data processing problems can be solved by means of a small number of powerful basic principles. At the same time, the simplifications and computational savings due to abstraction from biological details not only allow computer simulations of interesting applications, but also are suited for a far-reaching mathematical analysis.

II

Self-Organizing Sensory Maps

4. Kohonen's Network Model

This chapter describes Kohonen's network model. We will discuss how the cells of a neuron layer coordinate their sensitivity to sensory signals in such a way that their response properties to signal features vary in a regular fashion with their position in the layer, an organization observed in many parts of the brain. After some neurophysiological background information, a mathematical formulation of the model will be presented. Simulations will give a first impression of the main features of the model.

4.1. Neurophysiological Background

The model employs a neuron layer A, usually assumed to be a two-dimensional sheet. This layer is innervated by d input fibers (*axons*), which carry the input signal and excite or inhibit the neurons of the layer via synaptic connections, as illustrated schematically in Fig. 4.1. In the following, we consider conditions under which the excitation of the neurons is restricted to a spatially localized region in the layer. The location of this region is then determined by those neurons that respond most intensively to the given stimulus. The neuron layer acts as a *topographic feature map*, if the location of the most strongly excited neurons is correlated in a regular and continuous fashion with a restricted number of signal features of interest. Neighboring excited locations in the layer then correspond to stimuli with similar features. Of course, a single layer can only make a few important features visible in this way. In the simplest case, we may be dealing with the stimulus position on a sensory

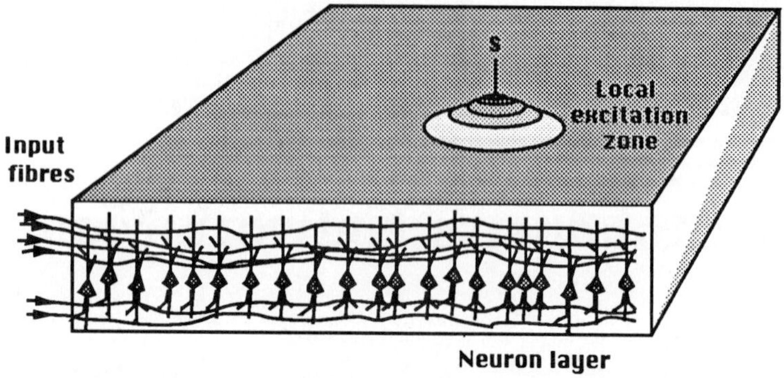

Figure 4.1 Schematic representation of the neuron layer in Kohonen's model. The nerve fibers running horizontally provide the input signal ("stimulus") and excite the layer neurons via synaptic connections. Lateral interactions between the neurons constrain the reaction to a spatially bounded "excitation zone." The layer acts as a "topographical feature map" if the position **s** of the excitation zone varies in a continuous way with the presence of stimulus features of interest.

surface, such as the retina or the body's outer surface; simple examples of more abstract features are pitch and intensity of sound signals.

We now describe the principles which enable the formation of such topographic feature maps in Kohonen's model by means of a self-organizing process. An incoming signal $\mathbf{v}$ is given by the average activities v_l of the individual incoming fibers $l = 1, 2, \ldots$. We identify the neurons of the layer by their two-dimensional position vectors $\mathbf{r} \in A$, with A being a two-dimensional grid. Every neuron $\mathbf{r}$ forms in its dendritic tree a weighted sum $\sum_l w_{\mathbf{r}l} v_l$ of the incoming activities v_l, where $w_{\mathbf{r}l}$ expresses the "strength" of the synapse between axon l and neuron $\mathbf{r}$. Here, $w_{\mathbf{r}l}$ is positive for an excitatory synapse and negative for an inhibitory synapse. The resulting excitation of an isolated neuron $\mathbf{r}$ is described by its average spike frequency $f_{\mathbf{r}}^0$. Usually, a relation

$$f_{\mathbf{r}}^0(\mathbf{v}) = \sigma\left(\sum_l w_{\mathbf{r}l} v_l - \theta\right) \tag{56}$$

is assumed for $f_{\mathbf{r}}^0$. Here, $\sigma(x)$ is a "sigmoid" function, increasing monotonically with x, with a qualitative behavior as shown in Fig. 3.10. In particular, $\sigma(x)$ tends asymptotically to the saturation values 0 or 1 for $x \to \pm\infty$. The quantity θ acts as an excitation threshold, below which the neuron responds weakly.

In addition to the coupling to the input fibers, the neurons are connected to each other via synapses. Thus, the layer has internal feedback. If one designates by $g_{\mathbf{rr}'}$ the coupling strength from neuron $\mathbf{r}'$ to neuron $\mathbf{r}$, any excitation $f_{\mathbf{r}'}$ of neuron $\mathbf{r}'$ provides a contribution $g_{\mathbf{rr}'} f_{\mathbf{r}'}$ to the total input signal of neuron $\mathbf{r}$. The contributions of all neurons $\mathbf{r}'$ in the layer are additively superimposed onto the external input signal $\sum_l w_{\mathbf{r}l} \mathrm{v}_l$. In the stationary case, the neuron activities $f_{\mathbf{r}}$ are thus the solution of the nonlinear system of equations

$$f_{\mathbf{r}} = \sigma \left(\sum_l w_{\mathbf{r}l} v_l + \sum_{\mathbf{r}'} g_{\mathbf{rr}'} f_{\mathbf{r}'} - \theta \right). \tag{57}$$

Frequently, the feedback accounted for by $g_{\mathbf{rr}'}$ is due to excitatory synapses ($g_{\mathbf{rr}'} > 0$) at small distances $\|\mathbf{r} - \mathbf{r}'\|$ and inhibitory synapses ($g_{\mathbf{rr}'} < 0$) at larger distances $\|\mathbf{r} - \mathbf{r}'\|$. It can be shown that the effect of such "center-surround" organisation of synaptic interactions on the solutions of (57) consists in the formation of excitatory responses that are confined to a neighborhood around the neuron receiving maximal external excitation. In the following, we will not prove this in general, but we would like to demonstrate it using a simplified version of (57).

To this end, we consider the limiting case when the "sigmoid function" $\sigma(x)$ approximates a step function $\theta(x)$ (as defined in Section 3.1). Further, we restrict ourselves to a one-dimensional system without an external input signal (*i.e.*, $v_l = 0$) and with thresholds $\theta = 0$. We assume for $g_{rr'}$ the function

$$g_{rr'} = \begin{cases} 1 & \text{if } |r - r'| \leq a, \\ -g & \text{else.} \end{cases} \tag{58}$$

Here, we assume $g > 2a + 1$, *i.e.*, neurons at distances exceeding a act inhibitory, while neurons closer than a act excitatory; the strength of the inhibition is given by the value of g. Defining the quantities

$$M = \sum_r f_r, \tag{59}$$

$$m_s = \sum_{r=s-a}^{s+a} f_r, \tag{60}$$

we see that (57) becomes

$$f_r = \theta\Big([1 + g] \sum_{r'=r-a}^{r+a} f_{r'} - g \sum_{r'} f_{r'}\Big), \tag{61}$$

or, by using the property $\theta(gx) = \theta(x)$ which holds for $g > 0$,

$$f_r = \theta\Big([1 + g^{-1}]m_r - M\Big). \tag{62}$$

Because of the θ-function, every neuron can be in only one of the two states $f_r = 0$ or $f_r = 1$. Equation (62), together with (59) and (60) represents a system of equations for the neuron activities f_r. We now show that, as a consequence of the "center-surround" organization of the lateral interactions, (62) only has solutions in which the total excitation is concentrated within a single, connected "cluster" of $a + 1$ consecutive neurons with $f_r = 1$. All of the neurons outside of this cluster are in the quiescent state ($f_r = 0$). To this end, we first prove the following lemma:

Lemma: If the quantities f_r constitute a solution of (62), and if $g > 2a + 1$, then $f_r = 1$ always implies $f_s = 0$ for all $s > r + a$ and all $s < r - a$.

Proof: From (62) it follows because of $f_r = 1$ that the inequality $m_r + g^{-1}m_r > M$ is satisfied. From the definitions (59) and (60) one also has $m_r \leq M$, and together

$$m_r \leq M < m_r + \frac{m_r}{g} \leq m_r + \frac{2a+1}{g} < m_r + 1.$$

Since M and all the m_r are integers, one has $M = m_r$ and, thus, the lemma is proven.

The lemma implies that two active neurons r, s can never be located more than a positions apart ($|r - s| \leq a$). From this, it follows that $M \leq a + 1$, *i.e.*, at most $a + 1$ neurons can be excited at the same time. If s is the leftmost of these neurons, then it follows for each of the a neurons $r \in [s, s + a]$ adjacent to s on the right

$$\begin{aligned}
[1 + g^{-1}]m_r - M =& [1 + g^{-1}] \sum_{r'=r-a}^{r+a} f_{r'} - M \\
=& [1 + g^{-1}] \sum_{r'=s-a}^{s+a} f_{r'} - M \\
=& [1 + g^{-1}]m_s - M > 0.
\end{aligned} \tag{63}$$

Here, the shift of the limits of summation in the next to last step is based on the vanishing of all the $f_{r'}$ for $r' < s$ and $r' > s + a$. For each of the $a+1$ neurons $r = s, s+1, \ldots, s+a$, (63) yields then $f_r = 1$, and since $M \leq a + 1$ all the remaining neurons satisfy

$f_r = 0$. Every solution of (62) therefore consists of a cluster of $a+1$ adjacent excited neurons.

Similarly, in higher dimension, a sufficiently strong lateral inhibition also leads to the production of a spatially localized excitatory response. In the case of a continuous sigmoid function $\sigma(.)$, the spatial behavior of the excitation is no longer that of a step function, but rather takes a maximum at a position $\mathbf{r}'$ and from there decreases to zero in all directions. The location $\mathbf{r}'$ of the excitatory center is dependent on the input signal v_l (not taken into account in the above derivation). We pay special attention to this position $\mathbf{r}'$, since by mapping every input signal to a position $\mathbf{r}'$, the layer provides the desired map of the space of input signals. One could obtain $\mathbf{r}'$ by solving the nonlinear system of equations (57). Instead of this tedious step, Kohonen suggests an approximation for $\mathbf{r}'$, replacing it with the position of maximum excitation *on the basis of the external signal v_l alone, i.e.*, $\mathbf{r}'$ is determined from

$$\sum_l w_{\mathbf{r}'l} v_l = \max_{\mathbf{r}} \sum_l w_{\mathbf{r}l} v_l. \tag{64}$$

Under the two assumptions that the "total synaptic strength" per neuron $\sqrt{\sum_l w_{\mathbf{r}l}^2}$, is constant and the same for every neuron, and that all of the input signals $\mathbf{v}$ have the same "intensity" $\|\mathbf{v}\| = 1$, the condition

$$\|\mathbf{w}_{\mathbf{r}'} - \mathbf{v}\| = \min_{\mathbf{r}} \|\mathbf{w}_{\mathbf{r}} - \mathbf{v}\|, \tag{65}$$

which often is more convenient from a mathematical point of view, yields the same result for $\mathbf{r}'$. Here, $\|\mathbf{x}\|$ indicates the Euclidean vector norm $\sqrt{\sum_l x_l^2}$, and vector $\mathbf{w}_{\mathbf{r}} \equiv (w_{\mathbf{r}1}, \ldots, w_{\mathbf{r}d})^T$ is a compact notation for the synaptic strengths of neuron $\mathbf{r}$.

Thus, we now see how the map is related to the synaptic strengths $w_{\mathbf{r}l}$. An input signal $\mathbf{v}$ is mapped to the position $\mathbf{r}'$ implicitly defined by (65). For fixed synaptic strengths, (65) defines a nonlinear projection of the space of input signals onto the two-dimensional layer. In the following, we will use the notation

$$\phi_{\mathbf{w}} : \mathbf{v} \mapsto \mathbf{r}' = \phi_{\mathbf{w}}(\mathbf{v}) \tag{66}$$

to refer to this mapping. The index $\mathbf{w}$ shall remind us of the mapping's dependence on the synaptic strengths of all neurons.

This leads to the second important issue, the determination of synaptic strengths $\mathbf{w}$ providing "useful" maps. In the nervous systems of higher animals, a detailed genetic specification of all synaptic strengths is not possible. This specification would require an exact knowledge of the way input signals are coded, a condition which even for technical applications, for example due to tolerances, is difficult to satisfy. Moreover, a system with fixed values $w_{\mathbf{r}l}$ could not respond to subsequent changes of the coding, *e.g.*, due to drift or aging processes; this obviously would contradict the high capacity for adaptation of biological systems. Apparently, such flexibility requires that the neurons be able to find suitable synaptic strengths, starting from arbitrary or only roughly correct initial settings.

In the present model, the only source of information for this process is assumed to be a sequence of input stimuli entering the layer, occurring randomly according to some statistical probability distribution. Each stimulus causes at synapse $w_{\mathbf{r}l}$ the coincidence of a presynaptic activity v_l and the resulting postsynaptic activity of neuron r. The postsynaptic activity of neuron r is just the value of the excitatory response of the layer at the position r. Its magnitude includes all interaction effects within the layer and should be computed from (57). Kohonen's model now makes the simplifying assumption that this response can be written as a function $h_{\mathbf{r}\mathbf{r}'}$ of two position variables r and r′, whose "shape" (with respect to variation of r) is fixed, but whose position (denoted by the second variable r′) depends on the stimulus. Specifically, the position r′ is taken to be the position of the excitation maximum, *i.e.*, r′ is defined by (64) or (65), and r is the location of the neurons whose response is to be described by $h_{\mathbf{r}\mathbf{r}'}$. The model then prescribes for the change of synaptic strengths $w_{\mathbf{r}l}$ the expression

$$\Delta w_{\mathbf{r}l} = \epsilon(h_{\mathbf{r}\mathbf{r}'}v_l - h_{\mathbf{r}\mathbf{r}'}w_{\mathbf{r}l}). \tag{67}$$

The first term corresponds to the "Hebbian learning rule" mentioned earlier, according to which a synapse is strengthened in the case of correlated pre- and postsynaptic activity. The second term is a decay term for the synaptic strengths, which is proportional to the postsynaptic activity. The relative scaling between the first term and the second (decay) term is normalized to unity by appropriate scaling of v. Here, ϵ determines the size of a single adaptation step ($0 < \epsilon < 1$). If ϵ is chosen to be a function $\epsilon(t)$, decreasing gradually with the number t of learning steps from large initial values to small final values, then at the beginning the system is rapidly able to learn coarsely the correct synaptic strengths. However, for large ϵ, the fluctuation of the map caused by each learning step is also large. Hence, if the map is to stabilize asymptotically in an equilibrium state, one must let ϵ decrease to zero. On the other hand, a permanent "residual plasticity" can be realized with low fluctuations of the map by means of a small, nonvanishing final value for ϵ.

Based on (67), every synaptic change is limited to a neighborhood zone about the excitation center. In this zone, the synaptic connections are changed such that a subsequent reoccurrence of the same or a similar stimulus will lead to an increased excitation. The shape of the function $h_{\mathbf{rr}'}$ controls the size of the neighborhood zone and, thus, of the number of neurons affected by a single adaptation step.

4.2. Simplification and Mathematical Definition

The precise form of the excitatory response $h_{\mathbf{rr}'}$ appears not to be critical for the qualitative behavior of the system under the learning rule (67) and could only be obtained by numerical solution of (57). Hence, in the present model, the exact solution is only approximated qualitatively by means of a given choice of $h_{\mathbf{rr}'}$. To this end, for $h_{\mathbf{rr}'} \geq 0$ a unimodal function depending only on the distance $\mathbf{r} - \mathbf{r}'$ with its maximum at $\mathbf{r} = \mathbf{r}'$ and approaching zero for large distances is assumed. An appropriate choice is given by the Gaussian

$$h_{\mathbf{rr}'} = \exp(-(\mathbf{r} - \mathbf{r}')^2 / 2\sigma_E^2). \tag{68}$$

The radius σ_E of this excitatory function determines the length scale on which the input stimuli cause corrections to the map. As a rule, it is better if the coarse structure of the map is allowed to form first, before the fine structure is incorporated into the map. This is made possible by choosing σ to be a function $\sigma(t)$ starting with a rather large initial value $\sigma(0)$ and decreasing slowly with the number of learning steps toward a small final value. This can be interpreted as gradually increasing the "selectivity" of the individual neurons in the course of the learning process.

Each learning step requires the arrival of an input stimulus $\mathbf{v}$. For the model, these input stimuli are treated as independent random variables from a vector space V, and their occurrence is determined by a probability density $P(\mathbf{v})$.

A final simplification is that the neuron positions $\mathbf{r}$ are taken to be the points of a discrete periodic lattice A.

Thus, Kohonen's model can be described by the following algorithm (Kohonen 1982a, 1984a):

0. *Initialization*: Start with appropriate initial values for the synaptic strengths $w_{\mathbf{r}l}$. In the absence of any a priori information, the $w_{\mathbf{r}l}$ can be chosen at random.
1. *Choice of Stimulus*: Choose, according to the probability density $P(\mathbf{v})$, a random vector $\mathbf{v}$ representing a "sensory signal."
2. *Response*: Determine the corresponding "excitation center" $\mathbf{r}'$ from the condition

$$\|\mathbf{v} - \mathbf{w}_{\mathbf{r}'}\| \leq \|\mathbf{v} - \mathbf{w}_{\mathbf{r}}\| \quad \text{for all } \mathbf{r} \in A. \tag{69}$$

3. *Adaptation Step*: Carry out a "learning step" by changing the synaptic strengths according to

$$\mathbf{w}_{\mathbf{r}}^{new} = \mathbf{w}_{\mathbf{r}}^{old} + \epsilon h_{\mathbf{r}\mathbf{r}'}(\mathbf{v} - \mathbf{w}_{\mathbf{r}}^{old}) \tag{70}$$

   and continue with step 1.

The mapping

$$\phi_{\mathbf{w}} : V \mapsto A, \quad \mathbf{v} \in V \mapsto \phi_{\mathbf{w}}(\mathbf{v}) \in A, \tag{71}$$

where $\phi_{\mathbf{w}}(\mathbf{v})$ is defined through the condition

$$\|\mathbf{w}_{\phi_{\mathbf{w}}(\mathbf{v})} - \mathbf{v}\| = \min_{\mathbf{r} \in A} \|\mathbf{w}_{\mathbf{r}} - \mathbf{v}\| \tag{72}$$

which constitutes the *neural map* of the input signal space V onto the lattice A which is formed as a consequence of iterating steps 1.–3.

To illustrate this algorithm, the relationships are schematically shown again in Fig. 4.2. The ensemble of all possible input values forms the shaded manifold V, from which a point $\mathbf{v}$ is chosen as "stimulus" for the network in step 1. This leads to a selection (step 2) of an excitation center $\mathbf{s}$ among the neurons (lattice A). All neurons in the neighborhood of this center (highlighted) participate in the subsequent adaptation (step 3). It consists in a "shift" of the vectors $\mathbf{w}_{\mathbf{r}}$ towards $\mathbf{v}$. The magnitude

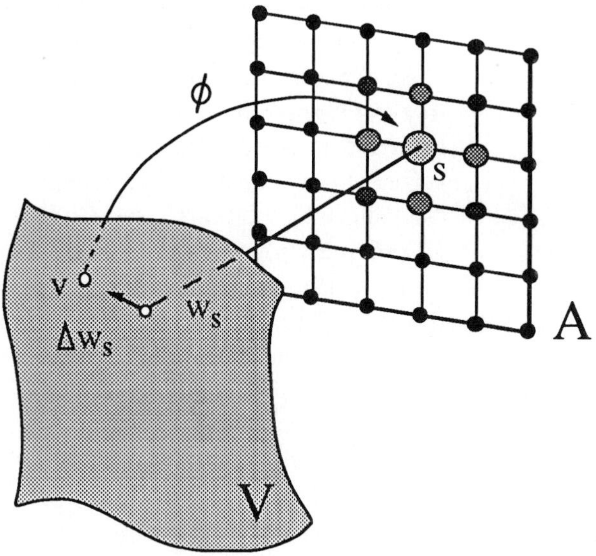

Figure 4.2 The adaptation step in Kohonen's model. The input value $\mathbf{v}$ selects a center $\mathbf{s}$ in whose neighborhood all neurons shift their weight vectors $\mathbf{w_s}$ towards the input $\mathbf{v}$. The magnitude of the shift decreases as the distance of a unit from the center $\mathbf{s}$ increases. In the figure, this magnitude is indicated by different sizes and gray values. The shift of weights is only depicted, though, for unit s.

of this shift is fixed by the learning step size ϵ and by the function $h_{\mathbf{rs}}$.

Mathematically, the algorithm represents a so-called *Markov process*. A Markov process is defined by a set of states and a set of transition probabilities between states. These transition probabilities determine a stochastic process that, given some initial state, produces a sequence of states. This sequence is obtained by using the transition probabilities from the current state to choose a successor, which then becomes the current state for the next step (for a thorough discussion of Markov processes see for example Gardiner 1985 or van Kampen 1981).

In the present model, each possible state is given by a set of values for all the synaptic strengths $w \equiv (\mathbf{w}_{\mathbf{r}_1}, \mathbf{w}_{\mathbf{r}_2}, \ldots, \mathbf{w}_{\mathbf{r}_N})$ in the system (N denotes the number of neurons). The function $\phi_\mathbf{w}$ associates with each such state a mapping that, as we have discussed, has the interpretation of a "neural map" of some feature space. The update of a state w is obtained as a result of applying (70), *i.e.*, the decision for the update is caused by the input stimulus $\mathbf{v} \in V$. Each update represents a "learning step" and can be thought of as a local "distortion" of the associated "neural map." Beginning with an initial state that corresponds to a completely disordered map, the goal of the algorithm is to arrive at a state (more precisely, the system shall enter a subset of its state space comprising states differing only by small "statistical fluctuations", see Chapter 14) that corresponds to an ordered, "topology-conserving map" of the stimulus space V, in which some relevant features of input stimuli are two-dimensionally (in the case of a neural sheet) represented. In order to reach such state and make it stationary asymptotically, the learning step length ϵ must slowly tend to zero.

The training process is qualitatively in good agreement with observed features of the formation of certain neural projections in the brain. The resulting maps predominantly represent those directions of the stimulus space V along which the input stimuli change most strongly. These directions, which often correspond to stimulus features of particular interest, may vary locally within V. Therefore, a good projection requires a nonlinear mapping. Usually, the map tries to maintain the neighborhood relationships between the input stimuli under this mapping process. Therefore, Kohonen named the resulting maps "topology-conserving feature maps." Furthermore, the map automatically takes into account the statistical weight $P(\mathbf{v})$ of the input stimuli. Regions of V from which many input stimuli occur become "magnified" and are thus projected with better resolution than regions of less frequently occurring signals. An appropriate choice for the rate of decrease of ϵ and σ with the number of learning steps is important for good results and rapid convergence. If the decrease is too rapid, the synaptic strengths "freeze" before the map has reached an equilibrium state. If the decrease is too slow, the process takes longer than necessary.

To illustrate the basic properties of this approach, we now consider a few simulation examples of the process.

4.3. Simulation Examples

In the first example, a neural network creates a map or image of an unknown region G with curved boundary. Only indirect sensory signals are available to the network. These come from

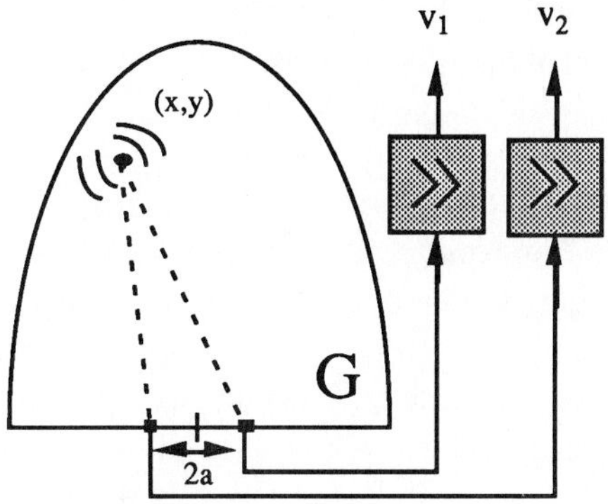

Figure 4.3 Region G containing the sound source. The two microphone positions are marked at the lower boundary of G. The microphone signals are fed into two logarithmic amplifiers, whose output signals v_1, v_2 serve as input for the network.

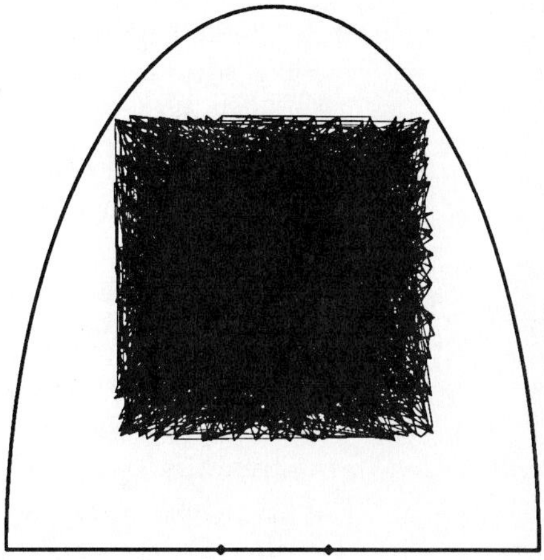

Figure 4.4 Initial relation between neurons and points in G. Initially, each neuron is assigned to a point of G chosen randomly from the filled quadrant. This assignment ignores any neighborhood relations. This is evident from the completely irregular "embedding" of the lattice in the quadrant.

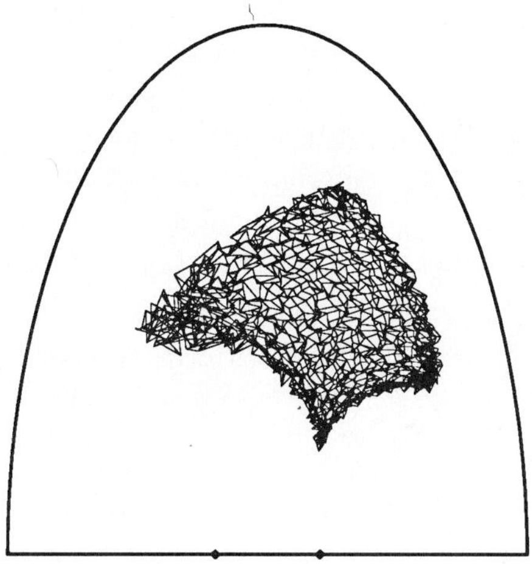

Figure 4.5 After 100 learning steps, an assignment has already formed which roughly reproduces the neighborhood relations of points of G in the lattice. However, the distribution of "responsibilities" of neurons for the region G is still very inhomogeneous.

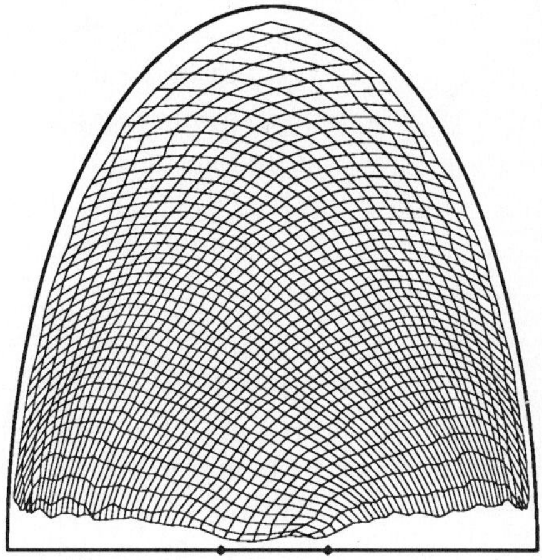

Figure 4.6 After 40,000 learning steps, a good correspondence between lattice neurons and points of G has formed. This corresponds to the choice of curvilinear coordinates, mapping the region G onto the square neuron lattice.

a source of sound moving around in G. From time to time, the sound source emits a sound signal (of constant intensity), and the position in G of each sound emission is random. The sound signal is received by two microphones, each connected to an amplifier with logarithmic characteristics (Fig. 4.3). The two amplifier output signals v_1, v_2 are the "sensory signals," and they are fed via two "axons" to the 1600 "neurons" of a model network.† The "neurons" are arranged in a planar 40×40 lattice. Every single model neuron $\mathbf{r}$ is characterized by a two-component vector $\mathbf{w_r} = (w_{\mathbf{r}1}, w_{\mathbf{r}2}) \in G$ of "synaptic strengths." Each neuron is to adjust its vector $\mathbf{w_r}$ gradually in such a way as to become sensitive for a small subset of input signals $\mathbf{v} = (v_1, v_2)^T$. This subset corresponds to a small subarea of G within which the moving source may be located. This subarea constitutes the "receptive field" of the particular neuron in the "environment" G. The neurons are to coordinate the formation of their receptive fields in such a way that — in the manner of a topographic map — the arrangement of neurons in the lattice reflects the arrangement of their respective receptive fields in the environment. This is achieved if each point of the region G corresponds to a point in the neural lattice such that the neighborhood relation between points is preserved under the correspondence, *i.e.*, the network becomes associated with a "continuous" image of G. This correspondence gives a simple example of a sensory map or sensory image of an environment, here the region in front of the two microphones. Similar "auditive maps" occur in the brain. However, this simulation example is only intended to serve as an illustration of the algorithm and makes no claim of corresponding to any brain map.

In Figs. 4.4–4.6, the evolution of the assignment of neurons to positions is shown in detail. For each neuron $\mathbf{r} \in A$, the location (x, y) of its receptive field in G has been marked, as assigned by the map. Marked locations are connected by a line if their corresponding neurons are adjacent on the lattice. (Thus, in place of the image itself, the embedding of the lattice A in G is shown,

† In the computer simulation, sound source, microphone, and amplifier are represented as follows: if the sound source is at the position (x, y), the output signals v_1 and v_2 of the two amplifiers are given by

$$\mathbf{v} = \begin{pmatrix} v_1 \\ v_2 \end{pmatrix} = \begin{pmatrix} -\log[(x-a)^2 + y^2] \\ -\log[(x+a)^2 + y^2] \end{pmatrix},$$

where $2a$ is the separation of the microphones.

from which the map can be obtained as its inverse.) Initially, the assignment is completely random, and there is no agreement between the arrangement of neurons and the corresponding locations (Fig. 4.4). After only a few signals, the coarse structure of the assignment has been found (Fig. 4.5), until finally after 40,000 sound signals a good assignment is achieved (Fig. 4.6). In this case, the algorithm has automatically found a nonlinear coordinate transformation mapping the region G with curved boundary onto a square lattice A. The resulting coordinate transformation takes the frequency distribution of the arriving signals into account, as illustrated in the simulation result shown in Fig. 4.7. Instead of a homogeneous distribution of source locations, the signals from the indicated circular region in G were now emitted with a three times higher probability than in the remaining part of G. Within both regions the probability density was constant. In all other respects the simulation was identical to that presented in Fig. 4.4–4.6. As a consequence of the inhomogeneous stimulus distribution, substantially more neurons are assigned to positions in the circular region. This corresponds to a higher resolution of the map for this part of G, which is a desirable result, since a concentration of assignments within regions where signals frequently occur leads to a more efficient use of the network.

However, the frequency with which a signal occurs is not always an indication of its importance. Varying importance of signals can also be taken into account by regulating the plasticity of the network. For example, one can adjust the size of a learning step according to an a priori importance attributed to the signals. This increases the "attentiveness" of the network for signals deemed more important and has the same effect as correspondingly more frequent occurrence. This is illustrated in Fig. 4.8, which shows the result of a simulation with sound emission probability again uniform throughout all of G. However, in contrast to Fig. 4.4–4.6, the network reacted to every sound event from within the circle with an adaptation step that was three times larger than for a sound event from the remaining part of G. The result thus obtained is practically identical to that of Fig. 4.7.

In the example presented, the space of stimuli G is mapped onto a lattice A of the same dimensionality. If the space of stimuli possesses a higher dimensionality, the map tries to project the higher-dimensional space as faithfully as possible by means

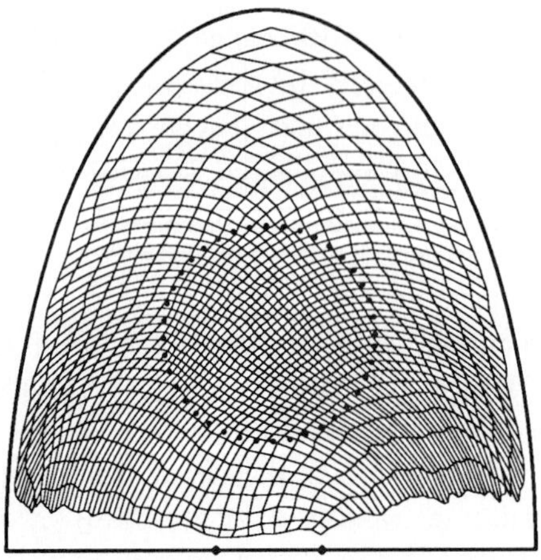

Figure 4.7 Result of the same simulation as in Fig. 4.6, except that within the circular region marked by dots signals were emitted with a three times higher probability than in the remaining region of G. In this case, more neurons code positions in the circular region. This corresponds to a higher resolution of the map created for this region.

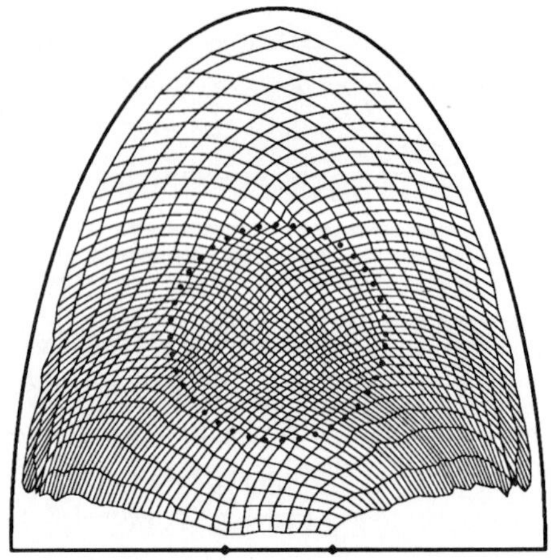

Figure 4.8 The same effect as in Fig. 4.7 can be achieved by a signal-dependent adjustment of the plasticity of the neurons. In this simulation, the sound signals were again emitted as in Fig. 4.4–4.6 with a homogeneous probability everywhere in G, but the learning step size ϵ was increased by a factor of three if the sound source was located in the circular region.

of an appropriate "convolution." To illustrate this behavior, we consider a one-dimensional neural "net," *i.e.*, a neuron chain. For the input signal, we take a random sequence of two-dimensional vectors **v**, whose values are homogeneously distributed in the unit square. For $h_{\mathbf{rr}'}$, we choose the Gaussian (68) with $\sigma(t) = 100 \cdot (0.01)^{10^{-5}t}$. The correspondence between neurons and points of the square is again represented as an embedding of the neuron chain into the square, as in the previous example. This assignment is initially made at random as shown in Fig. 4.9a. After 200 iterations, the curve has attained a U-shaped configuration (Fig. 4.9b). At this time, the range σ of the function $h_{\mathbf{rr}'}$ is still large and, hence, structure has formed only at this length scale. As σ decreases further, structures gradually form at shorter length scales as well (Fig. 4.9c, 50,000 iterations). Eventually, after 100,000 iteration steps, the hierarchically convoluted graph of Fig. 4.9d has emerged. The network thus tries to fill the two-dimensional region while reproducing the neighborhood relations as well as possible. The degree of success is evident from the similarity of the curve created in this way to the finite approximation of a so-called "Peano curve." This is an

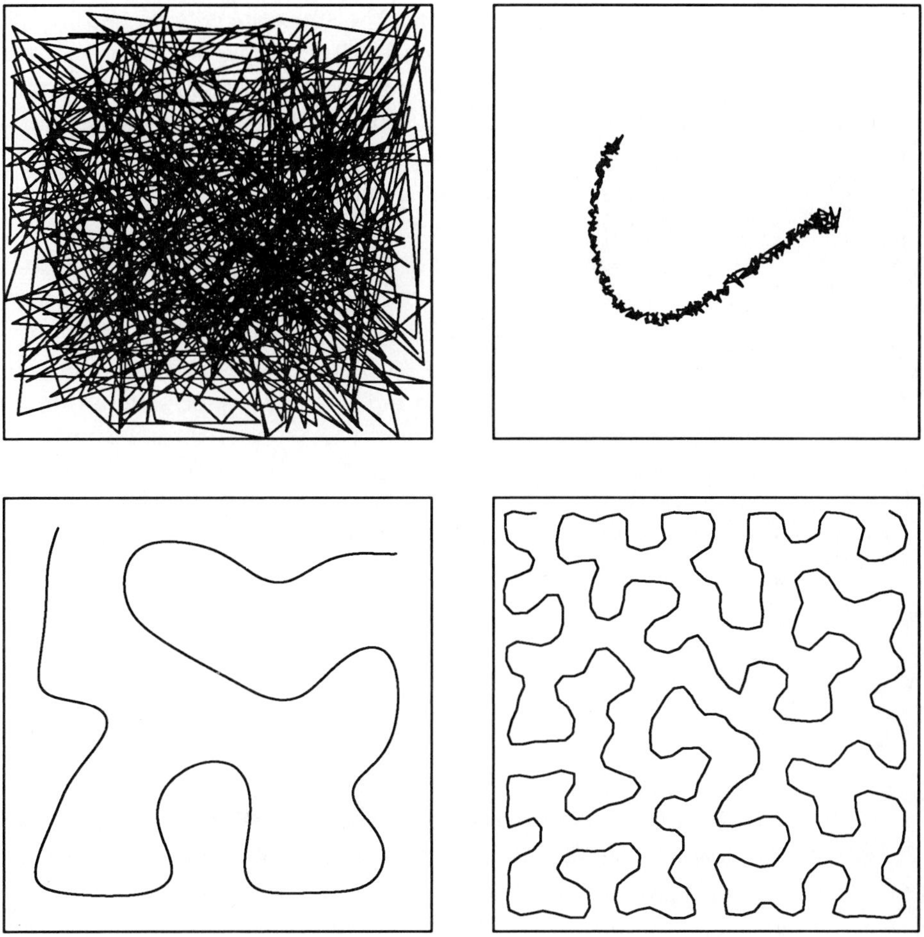

Figure 4.9 Mapping between a "neural" chain and a squared stimulus space. From top left to bottom right: a) randomly chosen initial assignment; b) coarse assignment after 200 Markov steps; c) after 50,000 Markov steps; d) assignment obtained after 100,000 Markov steps resembling a "Peano curve."

infinitely, recursively convoluted fractal curve representing the solution of the problem of mapping a one-dimensional interval continuously onto a two-dimensional surface.

However, as a rule one is interested in mapping of higher-dimensional regions onto a two-dimensional image. Indeed, Kohonen used the procedure successfully to map spectra of different speech sounds (phonemes) to separate map positions. Here, the tonal similarity relations between the individual phonemes are translated into locational relations in the image. This constitutes a very important preprocessing step for the problem of artificial speech recognition. The subsequent steps require the analysis of transitions between individual phonemes, *i.e.*, of time sequences. The possibility of employing the procedure also for such purposes shall be indicated in the following concluding example. At the same time, this example will clarify how in the course of the formation of a map hierarchic relations can also be represented.

The source of the signal is a Markov process (here used as a simple model of a temporal signal and to be distinguished from the learning algorithm itself) with 10 states. The aim is to create a map of the possible transitions between states of the process. Transitions to the same successor state are to be adjacent in the map. A state i, $i = 0, \ldots, 9$, is assumed to have one of the five states $i-3$, $i-2$, $i-1$, $i+1$ or $i+2$ (modulo 10) as a possible successor. A transition from state i to state j is coded by a 20-component vector v with components $v_k = \delta_{k,i} + \delta_{k,j+10}$. A transition occurs at each time step, and all transition probabilities have the same value 0.2. A lattice consisting of 20×20 neurons is used, and the Gaussian (68) is chosen for $h_{\mathbf{rr}'}$. The remaining parameter values of the simulation are $\sigma(t) = 5 \cdot 0.2^{t/t_{max}}$, $\epsilon(t) = 0.9 \cdot (0.05/0.9)^{t/t_{max}}$ and $t_{max} = 5,000$ learning steps. Additionally, for the computation of the distances $\|\mathbf{v} - \mathbf{w}(\mathbf{r})\|$, a "metric" was used which weights the differences in the last 10 components of v twice as strongly as those of the first 10 components. In Fig. 4.10, the 20×20-lattice of neurons is represented. For each lattice site, two numbers $i, j \in \{0, \ldots, 9\}$ indicate the initial and final state of the transition assigned to the respective neuron. The initial distribution was again chosen randomly. Figure 4.10 shows the map obtained after 5,000 learning steps. For each of the 50 allowed transitions, an "island" of neurons responding to this transition has formed, and the islands are in turn arranged in such a way that islands corresponding to transitions to the same successor state form a larger cluster. This corresponds to a hierarchical arrangement and is a consequence of the described choice of weight, the successor state obtaining a higher weight than the predecessor state in the choice of the excitation center. This choice dominates the formation of the "large-scale" structure of the map, *i.e.*, the structure on the level of "clusters of islands." This illustrates that, by an appropriate choice of metric (the choice of weight corresponds to a choice of metric), it is possible to arrange for certain features (here successors) to be grouped together hierar-

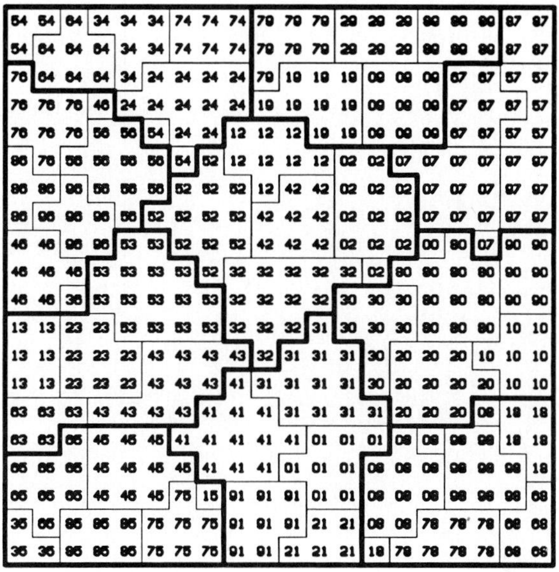

Figure 4.10 Mapping of the transitions $i \longrightarrow j$ of a Markov process with states $i, j = 0, ..., 9$ onto a lattice consisting of 20×20 neurons. For each lattice location, the transition to which the corresponding neuron best responds is indicated as jk. Neurons with the same transition are adjacent to one another within islands. Islands with the same successor in turn form "clusters." This corresponds to a hierarchical distribution of the neuron specificities over the lattice.

chically in the map. By the inclusion of *contextual information,* such a hierarchical grouping can emerge from the data itself. For example one can create "semantic maps" which arrange words in hierarchies of meaning. This ordering is gradually found by the system itself in the course of a learning phase, where simple English sentences can serve as "training data" (Ritter and Kohonen 1989).

After this initial overview, we consider in the following chapters a series of information processing tasks, for which the choice is motivated by their significance for biological systems. At the same time, we investigate how self-organizing maps can be useful in solving such problems. While viewing biological examples as a guide, we will occasionally consider technical applications when appropriate. This applies particularly to Chapter 6, which gives a solution to the "traveling salesman problem" and Chapters 10–13, which are concerned with applications to robotics.

5. Kohonen's Network for Modeling the Auditory Cortex of a Bat

In this chapter we employ Kohonen's model to simulate the projection of the space of the ultrasound frequencies onto the auditory cortex of a bat (Martinetz, Ritter, and Schulten 1988). The auditory cortex is the area of the cerebrum responsible for sound analysis (Kandel and Schwartz, 1985). We will compare the results of the simulation with available measurements from the cortex of the bat *Pteronotus parnelli rubiginosus,* as well as with an analytic calculation.

For each animal species, the size of an area of neural units responsible for the analysis of a particular sense strongly depends on the importance of that sense for the species. Within each of those areas the extent of the cortical representation of each input stimulus depends on the required resolution. For example, the fine analysis of the visual information of higher mammals is accomplished in the *fovea*. The fovea is a very small area of the retina in the vicinity of the optical axis with a very high density of *rods* and *cones*, the light sensitive receptors in the eye. The especially high density gives rise to a significantly higher resolution in this area than in the regions of the retina responsible for the peripheral part of the visual field. Although the fovea is only a small part of the total retina, the larger part of the visual cortex is dedicated to the processing of signals from the fovea. Similarly nonproportional representations have also been found in the somatosensory system and in the motor cortex. For example, particularly large areas in the somatosensory and the motor cortex are assigned to the hand when compared to the area devoted to the representation of other body surfaces or limbs (Woolsey 1958).

In contrast no nonproportional projections have been found so far in the auditory cortex of higher mammals. The reason for this is perhaps that the acoustic signals perceived by most mammals contain a wide spectrum of frequencies; the signal energy is usually not concentrated in a narrow range of frequencies. The meow of a cat, for example, is made up of many harmonics of the base tone, and no region of the frequency spectrum plays any particular function in the cat's survival. The auditory cortex of cats was thoroughly examined, and the result was that frequencies, as expected, are mapped onto the cortex in a linearly increasing arrangement without any regard for particular frequencies. The high-frequency units lie in the *anterior* and the low-frequency units lie in the *posterior* region of the cortex. According to available experimental evidence, the auditory cortex of dogs and monkeys is structured very similarly (Merzenich et al. 1975).

5.1. The Auditory Cortex of a Bat

In bats, nonproportional projections have been detected in the auditory cortex. Due to the use of sonar by these animals, the acoustic frequency spectrum contains certain intervals which are more important. Bats utilize a whole range of frequencies for orientation purposes. They can measure the distances to objects in their surroundings by the time delay of the echo of their sonar signals, and they obtain information about the size of the detected objects by the amplitude of the echo.

In addition, bats are able to determine their flight velocity relative to other objects by the Doppler shift of the sonar signal that they transmit. This ability to determine the Doppler shift has been intensively studied in *Pteronotus parnelli rubiginosus*, a bat species which is native to Panama (Suga and Jen 1976). This species has developed this ability to the extent that it is able to resolve relative velocities up to 3 cm/s, enabling it to detect even the beating of the wings of insects, its major source of nutrition. The transmitted sonar signal consists of a pulse that lasts about 30 ms at a frequency of 61 kHz. For the analysis of the Doppler-shifted echoes, this bat employs a special part of its auditory cortex (Suga and Jen 1976).

The Doppler shift Δf of the sonar frequency by an object moving in the same line with the bat is determined by

$$\frac{\Delta f}{f_e} = \frac{2v_{bat}}{c} - \frac{2v_{obj}}{c}. \tag{73}$$

Here f_e is the bat's sonar frequency, *i.e.*, 61 kHz, v_{bat} is the bat's velocity, v_{obj} is the object's flight velocity, and c is the velocity of sound. The factor of two is due to the fact that both the transmitted signal and the echo are Doppler shifted. If the bat knows its own velocity, it can determine v_{obj} from the Doppler shift Δf.

Excellent sonar capabilities are certainly indispensable for the bat's survival. To be able to detect a frequency shift of 0.02% which corresponds to the stated relative velocity of 3 cm/s, assuming a sound velocity of 300 m/s, a particularly high resolution of frequencies around the sonar frequency is necessary. Therefore, it would not be surprising if the interval around 61 kHz of the frequency spectrum were disproportionately represented in the part of the auditory cortex responsible for the Doppler analysis. Investigations on *Pteronotus parnelli rubiginosus* indeed support this expectation (Suga and Jen 1976).

Figure 5.1 shows the results of observations by Suga and Jen (1976). In part B of Fig. 5.1 one can clearly see that the one-dimensional frequency spectrum essentially extends continuously and monotonically from the posterior to the anterior region of the auditory cortex. In addition, one recognizes a region around the sonar frequency of 61 kHz with a very high resolution. To emphasize this anomaly, the region shaded in part A of Fig 5.1 has been displayed separately in part C. This region corresponds to the frequency interval which is especially important for the bat and extends monotonically from a minimum frequency of about 20 kHz up to a maximum frequency of about 100 kHz. The position and *best frequency* for each measurement in the shaded region of A is also shown in part C of Fig. 5.1. As "best frequency" for a neuron, one picks the frequency that causes the highest excitation of that neuron. One clearly sees that the majority of the measured values are clustered around the sonar frequency, as is expected. Almost half of the anterior-posterior region is used for the analysis of the Doppler-shifted signals. This provides the particularly high resolution of 0.02% which gives the bat its fine navigational and insect hunting abilities.

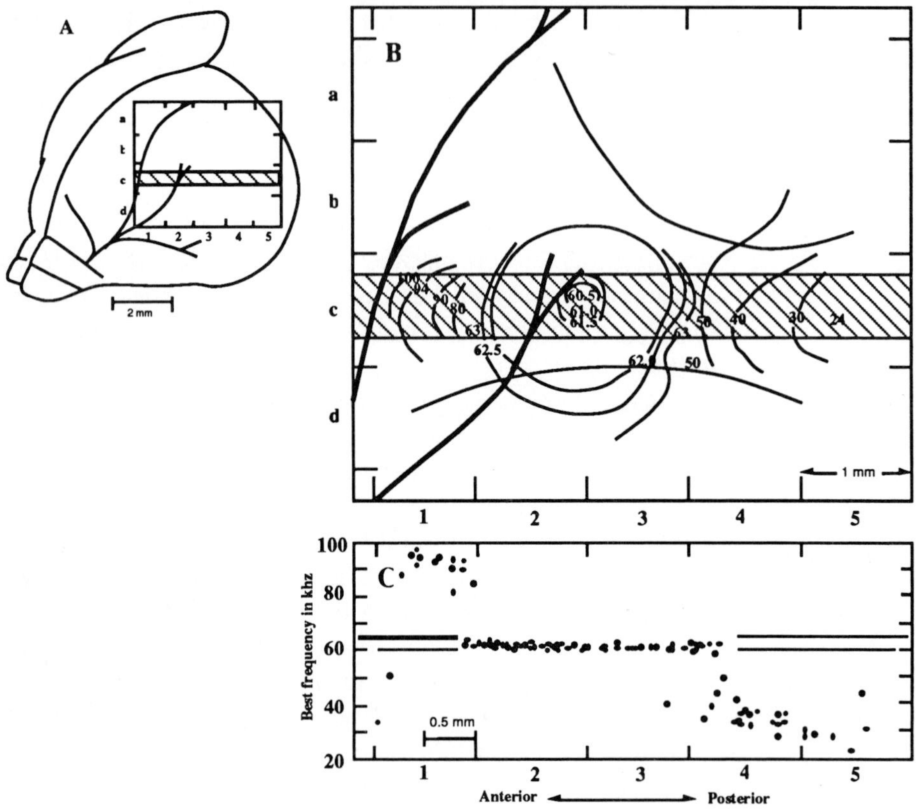

Figure 5.1 (A) Dorsolateral view of the bat's cerebrum. The auditory cortex lies within the inserted rectangle. (B) Distribution of "best frequencies" on the auditory cortex, the rectangle in (A). (C) Distribution of "best frequencies" along the region shaded in (A) and (B). The distribution of measured values around 61 kHz has been enlarged (after Suga and Jen 1976).

5.2. A Model of the Bat's Auditory Cortex

The development of the projection of the one-dimensional frequency space onto the auditory cortex, with special weighting of the frequencies around 61 kHz, will now be simulated by Kohonen's model of self-organizing maps. For this purpose we will model the auditory cortex by an array of 5×25 neural units.

The space of input stimuli is the one-dimensional ultrasound spectrum of the bat's hearing. In our model this spectrum will be simulated by a Gaussian distribution of Doppler-shifted

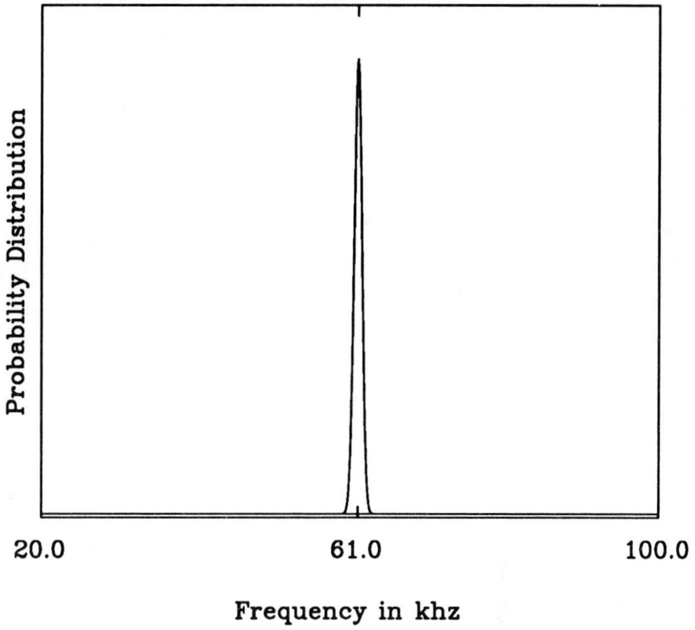

Figure 5.2 The relative probability density of the input signals versus frequency. Doppler-shifted echoes occur exactly three times as often as signals from the white background noise.

sonar echoes on top of a white background noise. The background noise in the range from 20 to 100 kHz depicts signals from external ultrasound sources. In addition, there is a peak near 61 kHz which consists of the echoes from objects moving relative to the bat. We describe this peak of Doppler-shifted sonar signals by a Gaussian distribution centered at 61 kHz with a width of σ_r=0.5 kHz. This corresponds to a root mean square speed difference of the sonar-detected objects of about 2 m/s. Doppler-shifted sonar signals occur in our model three times as often as signals from the white background noise. Figure 5.2 shows the weighted probability distribution.

Initially, a random frequency is assigned to each model neuron of our model cortex. This corresponds to Step 0 of Kohonen's model as described in the last chapter. Due to the one-dimensionality of the space of input stimuli, the synaptic strengths $\mathbf{w_r}$ of the model neurons r have only a single component.† An input signal according to a probability distribution

† This is only an idealization that is caused by the explicit use of frequency values. In a more

$P(\mathrm{v})$ causes that model neuron whose momentarily assigned frequency (the so-called "best frequency" of that neuron) lies closest to the input frequency to determine the center of the "activity peak" within which the neurons become significantly excited (Step 2). Next, the "best frequencies" of all neurons of the cortex are modified according to Step 3 of Kohonen's algorithm. After a sufficient number of steps this modification should result in an arrangement of "best frequencies" on the model cortex that is continuous and is adapted to the particular probability distribution of the input signals.

5.3. Simulation Results

In Fig. 5.1B it can be seen that the region of the auditory cortex of *Pteronotus parnelli rubiginosus* responsible for the resolution of the echo is greatly elongated, it being much more extended along the anterior-posterior axis than it is along the perpendicular direction. A similar length-width ratio for the model cortex was chosen in the simulation we will describe. There, the anterior-posterior length contains 25 model neurons and is five times longer than the width of the array.

Figure 5.3 shows the model cortex at different stages of the learning process. Each model neuron is represented by a box containing (the integer part of) the assigned frequency. Figure 5.3a presents the initial state. Each neuron was assigned randomly a frequency value in the range 20 to 100 kHz. As we see in Fig. 5.3.b, after 500 learning steps a continuous mapping between the space of input frequencies and the model cortex has already emerged. The final state, achieved after 5000 learning steps, is depicted in Fig. 5.3.c. One can see the special feature of Kohonen's model that represents the input stimuli on the net of neural units according to the probability with which stimuli occur. The strong maximum of the probability density in our model causes a wide-ranging occupation of the "cortex" with frequencies in the narrow interval around the sonar frequency of 61 kHz.

In this simulation the time dependence of the excitation zone

realistic model one could, for example, code the frequency by different output amplitudes of a set of overlapping filters as they are actually realized in the inner ear. The ordering process demonstrated in the simulation would, however, not be affected by this.

78	45	63	43	75
51	77	28	86	91
52	80	24	34	45
52	85	91	85	84
23	97	26	27	37
96	28	98	86	82
44	99	50	81	42
52	86	74	92	75
66	39	56	41	34
99	23	77	69	61
42	47	81	38	100
93	86	56	45	23
36	70	46	59	22
62	59	80	97	25
64	92	94	23	84
83	59	31	89	47
76	71	41	41	89
72	27	85	27	67
51	23	93	100	27
89	52	32	42	65
48	44	30	65	45
21	34	83	77	31
25	38	82	38	79
47	75	43	86	64
20	73	43	51	64

28	28	30	32	35
28	29	31	33	36
30	31	32	35	37
33	33	35	37	39
36	37	38	39	41
40	41	41	43	44
44	44	45	46	47
48	48	49	49	50
51	52	52	52	53
54	54	55	55	55
57	57	57	57	57
58	58	58	58	58
59	59	59	59	59
60	60	60	60	60
60	60	60	60	60
60	60	60	60	60
60	60	60	60	60
60	60	60	60	60
61	61	61	61	61
62	61	61	61	61
62	62	62	62	62
63	63	63	63	62
64	64	63	63	63
64	64	64	64	63
65	64	64	64	64

36	33	29	26	25
38	35	32	30	27
40	39	37	35	33
44	42	41	39	39
47	46	44	44	44
50	49	48	48	49
54	53	53	54	54
58	58	58	58	58
59	59	59	59	59
60	60	60	60	60
60	60	60	60	60
61	61	61	61	61
61	61	61	61	61
61	61	61	61	61
61	61	61	61	61
62	62	62	62	62
62	62	62	62	63
62	62	63	63	63
64	64	64	64	65
68	68	68	69	68
72	73	73	74	73
75	77	79	81	81
78	80	84	87	88
81	83	87	91	93
82	85	90	94	96

Figure 5.3 (a)*(left)* The initial state with random frequencies assigned to the neural units. The length-to-width ratio of the array of model neurons is five (anterior-posterior) to one (dorsolateral). Each box represents a neuron and contains the integer part of the current "best frequency" assigned to that neuron. **(b)***(middle)* The state of the "auditory cortex" after 500 learning steps. The field has evolved into a state where neighboring neurons have similar "best frequencies;" *i.e.*, the space of input stimuli is represented continuously on the array. **(c)***(right)* The "auditory cortex" in the final state, after 5000 learning steps. The region of "best frequencies" around the sonar frequency, which represents the Doppler-shifted input signals, occupies almost half of the model cortex.

σ and of the adaptation step widths ϵ were chosen as follows: $\sigma(t) = \sigma_i[1 + \exp(-5\,(t/t_{max})^2)]$ and $\epsilon(t) = \epsilon_i \exp(-5\,(t/t_{max})^2)$ with $\sigma_i = 5$ and $\epsilon_i = 1$, where t denotes the number of performed learning steps. The final number of learning steps at the end of the simulation was $t_{max} = 5000$.

In accordance with the experimental results from the auditory cortex of *Pteronotus parnelli rubiginosus,* the representation of the input frequencies on our model cortex increases monotonically along the "anterior-posterior" axis. In order to compare the results of our simulation with the measurements, we have presented the distribution of "best frequencies" as in

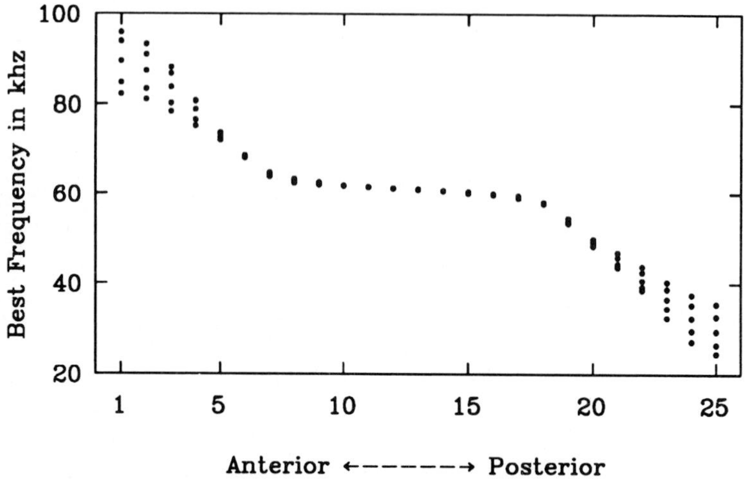

Figure 5.4 The simulation results presented as in Fig. 5.1C. Along the abscissa are the positions 1 through 25 of the model neurons along the "anterior-posterior" axis. The ordinate shows the corresponding "best frequencies." For every value between 1 and 25 five frequency values are represented, one for each of the five neural units along the "dorso-lateral" direction.

Fig. 5.1C. Figure 5.4 depicts the simulation results of Fig. 5.3 in the same way as Fig. 5.1C represents the data of Fig. 5.1A-B. Each model neuron has been described by its position 1 to 25 on the "anterior-posterior" axis as well as by its "best frequency." This representation of the results of the simulation produces a picture very similar to that of the experimental measurements (Fig. 5.1). In both cases a plateau arises that occupies almost half of the cortex and contains the neural units specialized in the analysis of the Doppler-shifted echoes. The size of this plateau is determined by the shape of the probability distribution of the input stimuli. In Section 5.4 we will look more closely at the relation between the shape of the probability distribution and the final cortical representation in Kohonen's model.

5.4. Mathematical Description of the "Cortical Representation"

We want to investigate what mappings between a neural lattice and an input signal space result asymptotically for Kohonen's model. For "maximally ordered" states we will demonstrate a quantitative relation between the "neural-occupation density" in the space of input stimuli which corresponds to the local enlargement factor of the map, and the functional form of the probability density $P(\mathbf{v})$ of the input signals (Ritter and Schulten 1986a). The result will enable us to derive an analytical expression for the shape of the curve shown in Fig. 5.4, including the size of the plateau. Unfortunately, such analytical expressions will be limited to the special case of one-dimensional networks and one-dimensional input spaces. The following derivation is mainly directed at the mathematically inclined reader; it can be skipped without loss of continuity.

To begin, we consider a lattice A of N formal neurons $\mathbf{r}_1, \mathbf{r}_2, \ldots, \mathbf{r}_N$. A map $\phi_{\mathbf{w}} : V \mapsto A$ of the space V onto A, which assigns to each element $\mathbf{v} \in V$ an element $\phi_{\mathbf{w}}(\mathbf{v}) \in A$, is defined by the synaptic strengths $\mathbf{w} = (\mathbf{w}_{\mathbf{r}_1}, \mathbf{w}_{\mathbf{r}_2}, \ldots, \mathbf{w}_{\mathbf{r}_N})$, $\mathbf{w}_{\mathbf{r}_j} \in V$. The image $\phi_{\mathbf{w}}(\mathbf{v}) \in A$ that belongs to $\mathbf{v} \in V$ is specified by the condition

$$\|\mathbf{w}_{\phi_{\mathbf{w}}(\mathbf{v})} - \mathbf{v}\| = \min_{\mathbf{r} \in A} \|\mathbf{w}_{\mathbf{r}} - \mathbf{v}\|, \tag{74}$$

i.e., an element $\mathbf{v} \in V$ is mapped onto that neuron $\mathbf{r} \in A$ for which $\|\mathbf{w}_{\mathbf{r}} - \mathbf{v}\|$ becomes minimal.

As described in Chapter 4, $\phi_{\mathbf{w}}$ emerges in a learning process that consists of iterated changes of the synaptic strengths $\mathbf{w} = (\mathbf{w}_{\mathbf{r}_1}, \mathbf{w}_{\mathbf{r}_2}, \ldots, \mathbf{w}_{\mathbf{r}_N})$. A learning step that causes a change from $\mathbf{w}'$ to $\mathbf{w}$ can formally be described by the transformation

$$\mathbf{w} = \mathbf{T}(\mathbf{w}', \mathbf{v}, \epsilon). \tag{75}$$

Here $\mathbf{v} \in V$ represents the input vector invoked at a particular instance, and ϵ is a measure of the plasticity of the synaptic strengths (see Eq. (70)).

The learning process is driven by a sequence of randomly and independently chosen vectors $\mathbf{v}$ whose distribution obeys a probability density $P(\mathbf{v})$. The transformation (75) then defines a Markov process in the space of synaptic strengths $\mathbf{w} \in V \otimes V \otimes \ldots \otimes V$ that describes the evolution of the map $\phi_{\mathbf{w}}(\mathbf{v})$. We will now show that the stationary state of the map which evolves asymptotically by this process can be described by a partial differential equation for the stationary distribution of the synaptic strengths.

Since the elements $\mathbf{v}$ occur with the probability $P(\mathbf{v})$, the probability $Q(\mathbf{w}, \mathbf{w}')$ for the transition of a state $\mathbf{w}'$ to a state $\mathbf{w}$, via adaptation step (75), is given by

$$Q(\mathbf{w}, \mathbf{w}') = \int \delta(\mathbf{w} - \mathbf{T}(\mathbf{w}', \mathbf{v}, \epsilon)) P(\mathbf{v})\, d\mathbf{v}. \tag{76}$$

$\delta(\mathbf{x})$ denotes the so-called delta-function which is zero for all $\mathbf{x} \neq 0$ and for which $\int \delta(\mathbf{x}) d\mathbf{x} = 1$. More explicitly, Eq. (75) can be written

$$\mathbf{w_r} = \mathbf{w'_r} + \epsilon\, h_{\mathbf{rs}}(\mathbf{v} - \mathbf{w'_r}) \quad \text{for all } \mathbf{r} \in A. \tag{77}$$

Here $\mathbf{s} = \phi_{\mathbf{w}'}(\mathbf{v})$ is the formal neuron to which $\mathbf{v}$ is assigned in the old map $\phi_{\mathbf{w}'}$.

In the following we take exclusive interest in those states $\phi_{\mathbf{w}}$ that correspond to "maximally ordered maps," and we want to investigate their dependence on the probability density $P(\mathbf{v})$. We assume that the space V and the lattice A have the same dimensionality d. A "maximally ordered map" can then be characterized by the condition that lines in V which connect the $\mathbf{w_r}$ of $\mathbf{r}$ adjacent in the network are not allowed to cross. Figure 5.5 demonstrates this fact with an example of a two-dimensional Kohonen lattice on a two-dimensional space V of input stimuli with a homogeneous probability distribution $P(\mathbf{v})$. The square frame represents the space V. The synaptic strengths $\mathbf{w_r} \in V$ determine the locations on the square which are assigned to the formal neurons $\mathbf{r} \in A$. Each mesh point of the lattice A corresponds to a formal neuron and, in our representation, is drawn at the location that has been assigned to that neuron through $\mathbf{w_r}$. Two locations $\mathbf{w_r}$ are connected by a line if the two corresponding formal neurons $\mathbf{r}$ are neighbors in the lattice A. Figure 5.5a shows a map that has reached a state of "maximal order" as seen by the lack of line crossings between lattice points. In contrast Fig. 5.5b presents a map for which even in the final stage some connections still cross. Such a map is not "maximally ordered."

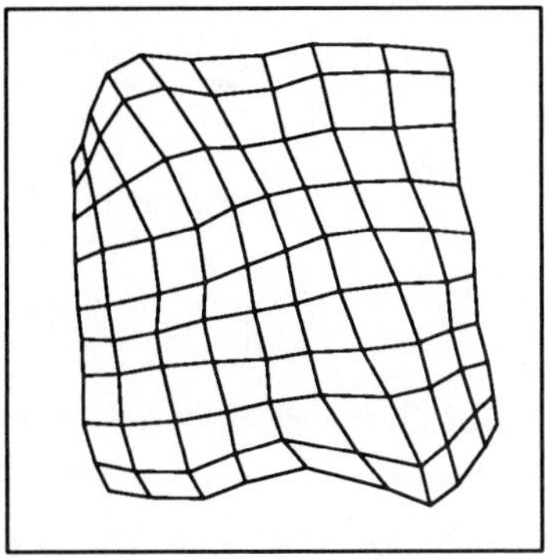

Figure 5.5a An example for a "maximally ordered" state of the network. Network and input signals are both two-dimensional. All input signals originate from the limiting square. In the continuum limit the network nodes are infinitely dense and specify a one-to-one mapping between the network and the square.

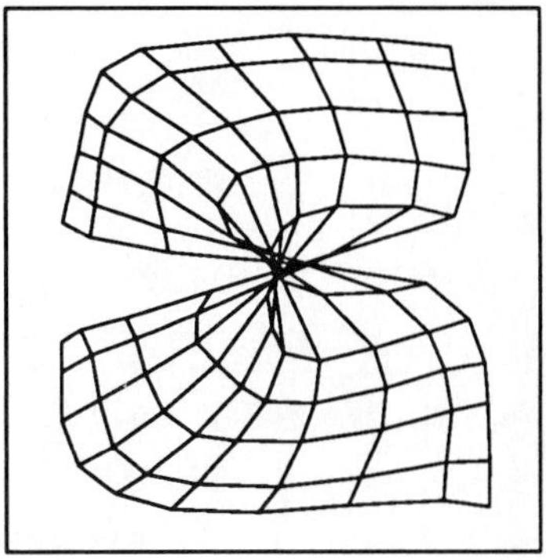

Figure 5.5b An example of an incompletely ordered state of the network, evolved as a consequence of the range $\sigma(t)$ of $h_{\mathbf{rs}}$ to be too short initially (see Eq. (68)). In this case a topological defect develops and the connections between neighboring lattice points cross. In the continuum limit a one-to-one mapping cannot be obtained.

In the following calculation we will make a transition from discrete values of $\mathbf{r}$ to continuous ones. This is possible because in the following we restrict ourselves to "maximally ordered" states where in the transition to a continuum $\mathbf{w_r}$ becomes a smooth function of the spatial coordinate $\mathbf{r}$ in the network.

We consider an ensemble of maps that, after t learning steps, are all in the vicinity of the same asymptotic state and whose distribution is given by a distribution function $S(\mathbf{w}, t)$. In the limit $t \to \infty$, $S(\mathbf{w}, t)$ converges towards a stationary distribution $S(\mathbf{w})$ with a mean value $\bar{\mathbf{w}}$. In Chapter 14 we will show that the variance of $S(\mathbf{w})$ under the given conditions will be of the order of ϵ. Therefore, for an ϵ that is sufficiently slowly approaching zero, all members of the ensemble will result in the same map characterized by its value $\bar{\mathbf{w}}$.

We want to calculate $\bar{\mathbf{w}}$ in the limit $\epsilon \to 0$. In the stationary state, the condition $S(\mathbf{w}) = \int Q(\mathbf{w}, \mathbf{w}')S(\mathbf{w}')\, d\mathbf{w}'$ holds, and, therefore, it also holds that

$$\bar{\mathbf{w}} = \int \mathbf{w} S(\mathbf{w})\, d\mathbf{w} = \int\int \mathbf{w} Q(\mathbf{w}, \mathbf{w}')S(\mathbf{w}')\, d\mathbf{w} d\mathbf{w}'. \tag{78}$$

In the limit $\epsilon \to 0$ it follows $S(\mathbf{w}) \to \delta(\mathbf{w} - \bar{\mathbf{w}})$ and, therefore,

$$\bar{\mathbf{w}} = \int \mathbf{w} Q(\mathbf{w}, \bar{\mathbf{w}})\, d\mathbf{w}$$

$$= \int \mathbf{T}(\bar{\mathbf{w}}, \mathbf{v}, \epsilon) P(\mathbf{v}) \, d\mathbf{v}. \tag{79}$$

Applying Eq. (77) we obtain

$$0 = \epsilon \int h_{\mathbf{rs}}(\mathbf{v} - \bar{\mathbf{w}}_{\mathbf{r}}) P(\mathbf{v}) \, d\mathbf{v} \quad \text{for all } \mathbf{r} \in A. \tag{80}$$

We formulate the restriction of maximally ordered maps by two approximating assumptions:

(i) We assume that for sufficiently large systems $\bar{\mathbf{w}}_{\mathbf{r}}$ is a function that varies slowly from lattice point to lattice point so that its replacement by a function $\bar{\mathbf{w}}(\mathbf{r})$ on a continuum of r-values is justified.

(ii) We assume that $\bar{\mathbf{w}}(\mathbf{r})$ is one-to-one.

We demand also that $h_{\mathbf{rs}}$ at $\mathbf{r} = \mathbf{s}$ has a steep maximum and satisfies

$$\begin{aligned} \int h_{\mathbf{rs}}(\mathbf{r} - \mathbf{s}) \, d\mathbf{r} &= 0, \\ \int h(\mathbf{r} - \mathbf{s})(r_i - s_i)(r_j - s_j) \, d\mathbf{r} &= \delta_{ij}\sigma^2, \quad i, j = 1, \ldots, d \end{aligned} \tag{81}$$

where d is the dimension of V and r_j, s_j describe the d Cartesian components of r, s. The constant σ is the range of $h_{\mathbf{rs}}$ which coincides with σ in (68) in case of a Gaussian $h_{\mathbf{rs}}$.

From the above we will derive a differential equation for $\bar{\mathbf{w}}$. Due to the continuum approximation (i), the quantity $\min_{\mathbf{r} \in A} \|\mathbf{w}_{\mathbf{r}} - \mathbf{v}\|$ in Eq. (74) vanishes because now for each v there exists exactly one r for which $\mathbf{w}_{\mathbf{r}} = \mathbf{v}$ holds. Therefore, we can replace v in Eq. (80) by $\bar{\mathbf{w}}(\mathbf{s})$. Here $\mathbf{s} := \phi_{\bar{\mathbf{w}}}(\mathbf{v})$ is the image of v under the map that belongs to $\bar{\mathbf{w}}$. This provides the condition

$$\int h_{\mathbf{rs}} \big(\bar{\mathbf{w}}(\mathbf{s}) - \bar{\mathbf{w}}(\mathbf{r}) \big) P(\bar{\mathbf{w}}(\mathbf{s})) J(\mathbf{s}) \, d\mathbf{s} = 0. \tag{82}$$

Here

$$J(\mathbf{s}) := \left| \frac{d\mathbf{v}}{d\mathbf{s}} \right| \tag{83}$$

is the absolute value of the Jacobian of the map $\phi_{\bar{\mathbf{w}}}$. With $\mathbf{q} := \mathbf{s} - \mathbf{r}$ as a new integration variable and $\bar{P}(\mathbf{r}) := P(\bar{\mathbf{w}}(\mathbf{r}))$ the expansion of Eq. (82) in powers of q yields (with implicit summation over repeated indices; *e.g.*, $q_i\partial_i$ is to be summed over all values of i)

$$\begin{aligned}0 &= \int h_{\mathbf{q}0}(q_i\partial_i\bar{\mathbf{w}} + \frac{1}{2}q_iq_j\partial_i\partial_j\bar{\mathbf{w}} + \ldots)\cdot \\ &\quad \cdot(\bar{P} + q_k\partial_k\bar{P} + \ldots)\cdot(J + q_l\partial_l J + \ldots)\, d\mathbf{q} \\ &= \int h_{\mathbf{q}0}q_iq_j\, d\mathbf{q}\cdot\Big((\partial_i\bar{\mathbf{w}})\partial_j(\bar{P}J) + \frac{1}{2}\bar{P}J\cdot\partial_i\partial_j\bar{\mathbf{w}}\Big)(\mathbf{r}) + O(\sigma^4) \\ &= \sigma^2\cdot\Big[(\partial_i\bar{\mathbf{w}})(\partial_i(\bar{P}J) + \frac{1}{2}\bar{P}J\cdot\partial_i^2\bar{\mathbf{w}}\Big](\mathbf{r}) + O(\sigma^4),\end{aligned} \tag{84}$$

where we made use of (81). In order for the expansion (84) to hold it is necessary and sufficient for small σ that condition

$$\sum_i \partial_i\bar{\mathbf{w}}\left(\frac{\partial_i\bar{P}}{\bar{P}} + \frac{\partial_i J}{J}\right) = -\frac{1}{2}\sum_i \partial_i^2\bar{\mathbf{w}} \tag{85}$$

or, with the Jacobi matrix $J_{ij} = \partial_j\bar{w}_i(\mathbf{r})$ and $\Delta = \sum_i \partial_i^2$, condition

$$\mathbf{J}\cdot\nabla\ln(\bar{P}\cdot J) = -\frac{1}{2}\Delta\bar{\mathbf{w}} \tag{86}$$

is satisfied. For the one-dimensional case we obtain $\mathbf{J} = J = d\bar{w}/dr$ and $\Delta\bar{\mathbf{w}} = d^2\bar{w}/dr^2$ with $\bar{w}$ and r as scalars. In this case the differential equation (86) can be solved. For this purpose we rewrite (86) and obtain

$$\frac{d\bar{w}}{dr}\left(\frac{1}{\bar{P}}\frac{d\bar{P}}{dr} + \left(\frac{d\bar{w}}{dr}\right)^{-1}\frac{d^2\bar{w}}{dr^2}\right) = -\frac{1}{2}\frac{d^2\bar{w}}{dr^2} \tag{87}$$

from which we can conclude

$$\frac{d}{dr}\ln\bar{P} = -\frac{3}{2}\frac{d}{dr}\ln\left(\frac{d\bar{w}}{dr}\right). \tag{88}$$

This result allows us to determine the local enlargement factor of the map in terms of the generating probability distribution $P(\mathbf{v})$.

Since $\phi_{\bar{\mathbf{w}}}(\bar{\mathbf{w}}(\mathbf{r})) = \mathbf{r}$ holds, the local enlargement factor M of $\phi_{\bar{\mathbf{w}}}$ can be defined by $M = 1/J$ (compare Eq. (83)). For the one-dimensional case $M = (d\bar{w}/dr)^{-1}$ and we obtain as a relation between input stimulus distribution and cortical representation

$$M(v) = J^{-1} = \frac{dr}{d\bar{w}} \propto P(v)^{2/3}. \tag{89}$$

The local enlargement factor $M(v)$ depends on the probability density $P(v)$ according to a power law. It can be shown that the exponent 2/3 that we found in the continuum approximation undergoes a correction for a discrete one-dimensional system and is then given by $\frac{2}{3} - [3(1+n^2)(1+[n+1]^2)]^{-1}$, where n is the number of neighbors that are taken into account on each side of the excitation center, (*i.e.*, $h_{\mathbf{rs}} = 1$ for $\|\mathbf{r}-\mathbf{s}\| \leq n$ and zero elsewhere) (Ritter 1989). The continuum corresponds to the limit of infinite density of neighbors. Then $n = \infty$ for each finite σ and we obtain the previous result of 2/3.

5.5. "Cortical Representation" in the Model of the Bat's Auditory Cortex

We now apply the mathematical derivation of Section 5.4 to the particular input stimulus distribution that we assumed for our model of the bat's auditory cortex and compare the result with a simulation.

The input stimulus distribution that we assume can be written in the range $v_1 \leq v \leq v_2$ as

$$P(v) = \frac{P_0}{v_2 - v_1} + (1 - P_0)\frac{1}{\sqrt{2\pi}\sigma_r}\exp\left(-\frac{(v - v_e)^2}{2\sigma_r^2}\right) \tag{90}$$

with the parameters σ_r=0.5 kHz, v_e=61.0 kHz, v_1=20 kHz, v_2=100 kHz and P_0=1/4. The width of the distribution of the Doppler-shifted echoes is given by σ_r, and P_0 is the probability for the occurrence of an input stimulus from the white background noise. v_1 and v_2 are the limits of the ultrasound spectrum that we assume the bat can hear.

The integral $I = \int_{v_1}^{v_2} P(v)dv$ is not exactly unity because of the finite integration limits. Since, due to the small σ_r of 0.5 kHz, nearly all the Doppler-shifted echo signals lie within the interval $[20, 100]$ and the deviation of I from unity is negligible. With the choice $P_0 = 1/4$, the Doppler-shifted signals occur three times as often as signals due to the background noise (see also Fig. 5.2). From Eqs. (89) and (90) we find

$$\frac{dr}{d\bar{w}} = C \cdot \left(\frac{P_0}{v_2 - v_1} + (1 - P_0)\frac{1}{\sqrt{2\pi}\sigma_r}\exp\left(-\frac{(v - v_e)^2}{2\sigma_r^2}\right)\right)^{2/3} \tag{91}$$

where C is a proportionality constant. In integral form one has

$$r(\bar{w}) - r_1 = C \cdot \int_{\bar{w}_1}^{\bar{w}} \left(\frac{P_0}{v_2 - v_1} + \frac{1 - P_0}{\sqrt{2\pi}\sigma_r} \times \exp\left(-\frac{(v - v_e)^2}{2\sigma_r^2} \right) \right)^{2/3} dv. \tag{92}$$

We will solve this integral numerically and then compare the resulting $\bar{w}(r)$ with the corresponding values from a simulation.

Since these considerations apply only to the case where the dimensionality of the net and the dimensionality of the space of input stimuli is identical, we stretch the "auditory cortex" and, instead of a 5×25 net as in Figs. 5.3 and 5.4, assume a one-dimensional chain with 50 elements for the present simulation. Starting from a linear, second-order differential equation, we need two boundary conditions, *e.g.*, $\bar{w}_1(r_1)$ and $\bar{w}_2(r_2)$, from our simulation data to be able to adjust the function $r(\bar{w})$ of Eq. (92) uniquely. Since boundary effects at the beginning and the end of the chain were not taken into account in our analytic calculation, the end points can in some cases deviate slightly from our calculated curve. To adjust the curve to the simulation data, we take values for w_1 and w_2 that do not lie too close to the end points; in this case we have chosen $\bar{w}$ at the third and forty-eighth link of the chain, *i.e.*, at $r_1 = 3$ and $r_2 = 48$. The solid curve in Fig. 5.6 depicts the function $\bar{w}(r)$ calculated numerically from Eq. (92) and adjusted to the simulation data. The dots show the values $\bar{w}_r$ that were obtained by simulating the Markov process (75). The representation corresponds to the one in Fig. 5.4. The time dependence of the excitation zone σ and of the adaptation step width ϵ for the simulation were chosen as follows: $\sigma(t) = \sigma_i[1 + \exp(-(5t/t_{max})^2)]$ with $\sigma_i = 10$, $\epsilon(t) = \epsilon_i \exp(-(5t/t_{max})^2)$ with $\epsilon_i = 1$. For the maximal number of learning steps $t_{max} = 20000$ was chosen.

Clearly, the function $\bar{w}(r)$ resulting from Eq. (92) is in close agreement with the simulation results, and even the deviations at the end points are small. One may have expected intuitively that for the magnification holds $M(v) \propto P(v)$, *i.e.*, a magnification proportional to the stimulus density. The corresponding result is presented in Fig. 5.6 as well to demonstrate that this expectation is, in fact, incorrect.

For the present input stimulus distribution, it is possible to estimate the size of the region relevant for the analysis of

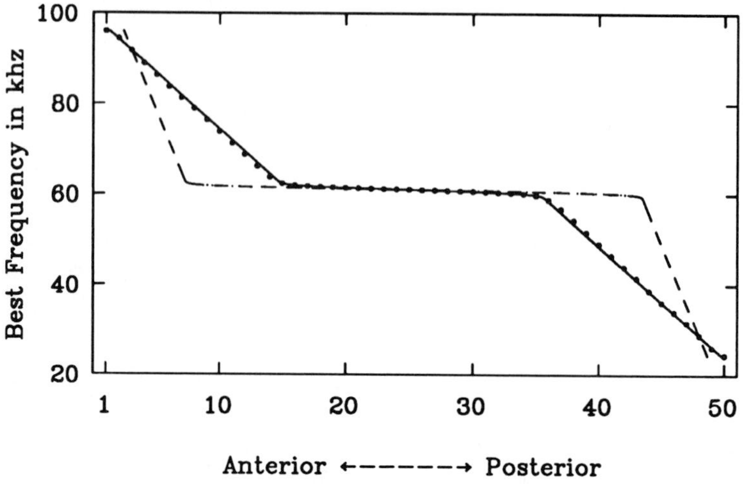

Figure 5.6 A bat's sensitivity to accoustic and sonar signals (cf. Fig. 5.4). The solid curve represents the function $\bar{w}(r)$ calculated from Eq. (92). The dots show the values obtained from simulating the Markov process (75). For comparison we show the result for $M(v) \propto P(v)$ with a dashed line. This result strongly deviates from the simulation data.

the Doppler-shifted signal, *i.e.*, the extension of the 61 kHz plateau in Fig. 5.6. In Eq. (92) we integrate over $P(v)^{2/3}$ and, therefore, the function $r(\bar{w})$ increases sharply for large values of $P(v)$. Hence, the plateau starts where the Gaussian distribution of the Doppler-shifted echoes increases strongly relative to the background. This is approximately the case for $v = v_e - 2\sigma_r$. Accordingly, the plateau ends where the Gaussian peak recedes back into the homogeneous background, *i.e.*, at $v = v_e + 2\sigma_r$. Therefore, the relation

$$\begin{aligned}\Delta r_{plateau} = &C \cdot \int_{v_e-2\sigma_r}^{v_e+2\sigma_r} \left(\frac{P_0}{v_2 - v_1} + (1 - P_0) \frac{1}{\sqrt{2\pi}\sigma_r} \right. \\ &\left. \times \exp\left(-\frac{(v - v_e)^2}{2\sigma_r^2} \right) \right)^{2/3} dv. \end{aligned} \tag{93}$$

for the size of the plateau holds. Within these integration limits the background portion in the integrand is negligible compared to the values of the Gaussian. Furthermore, we can extend the integration of the integrand that results without the background towards infinity without significant error. The integral can then be evaluated, yielding the approximation

$$\Delta r_{plateau} \approx C \cdot (1-P_0)^{2/3} \int_{-\infty}^{\infty} \frac{1}{(\sqrt{2\pi}\sigma_r)^{2/3}} \exp\left(-\frac{2}{3}\frac{v^2}{2\sigma_r^2}\right) dv$$
$$\approx C \cdot \sqrt{\frac{3}{2}} \left(\sqrt{2\pi}\sigma_r(1-P_0)^2\right)^{1/3}. \tag{94}$$

In order to determine the part of the plateau relative to the overall "auditory cortex," we also need an estimate of the integral in Eq. (92), where we have to integrate over the full band width of input frequencies. To obtain this we split the integration range from v_1=20 kHz to v_2=100 kHz into three regions as follows

$$\Delta r_{total} \propto \int_{v_1}^{v_e-2\sigma_r} (P(v))^{2/3}\, dv + \int_{v_e-2\sigma_r}^{v_e+2\sigma_r} (P(v))^{2/3}\, dv + \int_{v_e-2\sigma_r}^{v_2} (P(v))^{2/3}\, dv. \tag{95}$$

We have already estimated the second integral in the sum by Eq. (94). Within the integration limits of the other two integrals the contribution of the Gaussian distribution is so small that it can be neglected relative to the background. In addition, $\sigma_r \ll (v_2 - v_1)$, enabling us to write

$$\Delta r_{total} \approx \Delta r_{plateau} + C \cdot (v_2 - v_1) \left(\frac{P_0}{v_2 - v_1}\right)^{2/3}$$
$$\approx \Delta r_{plateau} + C \cdot {P_0}^{2/3} (v_2 - v_1)^{1/3}. \tag{96}$$

If we insert the parameters of our above model of the input stimulus distribution of the bat into the two estimates (94) and (96), we obtain for the size of the 61 kHz region, relative to the size of the total "cortex," the value

$$\frac{\Delta r_{plateau}}{\Delta r_{total}} \approx 39\%.$$

This implies that for our case of a 50-unit chain, the plateau should consist of 19 to 20 neurons. This value agrees very well with the simulation results presented in Fig. 5.6.

By now we have extensively described the basics of Kohonen's model—the self-organization of a topology-conserving map between an input stimulus space and a network of neural units. We have compared the simulation results of Kohonen's model to experimental data as well as to a mathematical description valid for certain limiting cases. The simulation data have agreed at least qualitatively with the experimental findings. More than a qualitative agreement should not have been expected, considering the many simplifications of Kohonen's model. In contrast to that, the mathematical result for the representation of the input signals relative to their probability corresponds, even quantitatively, very well to the results obtained from simulations.

In Chapter 6 we will become acquainted with a completely different application of Kohonen's model. Instead of a mapping onto a continuum, we will generate a mapping that projects a linear chain onto a discrete set of points. Such a mapping can be interpreted as a choice of a connection path between the points. The feature of the algorithm to preserve topology as much as possible manifests itself in a tendency to minimize the path-length. In this way, very good approximate solutions for the well-known travelling salesman problem can be achieved.

6. Application to the "Traveling Salesman Problem"

The properties that have the most significant influence on the maps constructed by Kohonen's algorithm are the dimensionality of the neural network and the dimensionality and distribution of the input signals. The simplest case arises for a one-dimensional net, *i.e.*, a chain of neurons, and one-dimensional input signals. As shown in Chapter 5, one encounters this apparently quite unbiological case in the auditory cortex of mammals, where approximately linearly arranged neurons are assigned to a frequency interval. This situation is especially interesting also from a theoretical point of view, because it admits a closed solution, yielding the dependence of the resultant mapping on the probability density of the input signals. In this chapter, we extend our discussion to the case of multidimensional input signals, but we continue to assume a one-dimensional chain for the arrangement of the neurons. An analytical solution for the stationary maps which are possible under these circumstances can no longer be given. Instead, we will see that under appropriate conditions the resulting maps can be interpreted as approximate solutions of an interesting but analytically not tractable optimization problem, the "traveling salesman problem."

6.1. Paths as One-Dimensional Maps

In the case of a chain of neurons there exists a fixed order among the neurons given by their arrangement along the chain. Each neuron r carries a vector $\mathbf{w}_r$ marking a point in the space V of input signals. Hence, the corresponding "map" of V is one-dimensional. Whenever V is of higher dimension than the space of the lattice A, a substantial loss of information is inevitable, and the topology of V can only be reproduced to a very limited degree by a map $V \mapsto A$. Nevertheless, such maps may contain important and highly nontrivial information. We demonstrate this for the example of one-dimensional maps.

If one runs through the neurons of the chain A, the points $\mathbf{w}_r$ run through a corresponding sequence of stations in the space V, which can be thought of as a *path*. This path is the image of the neuron chain under the mapping $r \mapsto \mathbf{w}_r$. From this point of view, Kohonen's algorithm for the formation of a one-dimensional map appears as a procedure for the stepwise optimization of a path in the space V (Angeniol et al. 1988). Initially, the path visits N randomly distributed stations. Each input signal $\mathbf{v} \in V$ chooses that station $\mathbf{w}_s$ of the path which is closest to $\mathbf{v}$ and deforms the path a bit toward $\mathbf{v}$ by shifting all stations corresponding to neurons in the neighborhood of s towards $\mathbf{v}$ as well. Thus, a path gradually develops, whose course favors regions from which input signals $\mathbf{v}$ are frequently chosen. Hence, by specification of an appropriate probability density $P(\mathbf{v})$, one can influence how important the presence of the path is in the individual regions of V. Since neurons neighboring on the chain become assigned to points $\mathbf{w}_r$ adjacent in the space V, the resulting path tends to be as short as possible. Hence, one-dimensional topology-conserving maps (approximately) solve an interesting optimization problem, that is, to find the shortest possible path, where $P(\mathbf{v})$ plays the role of a position-dependent "utility function" (cf. Angeniol et al. 1988).

6.2. The Model for a Discrete Stimulus Distribution

In this section we supplement the very qualitative remarks of the preceding section by a more precise, mathematical formulation. This is simplified if we assume a discrete probability distribution $P(\mathbf{v})$ instead of a continuous one. In this case, the input signal $\mathbf{v}$ can only take values from a discrete set $\{\mathbf{q}_1, \mathbf{q}_2, \ldots, \mathbf{q}_L\}$. Denoting by p_i the probability that $\mathbf{v}$ takes the value $\mathbf{q}_i$ ($\sum_i p_i = 1$), we see that $P(\mathbf{v})$ is of the form

$$P(\mathbf{v}) = \sum_{i=1}^{L} p_i \delta(\mathbf{v} - \mathbf{q}_i), \quad \mathbf{q}_i \in V, \tag{97}$$

where $\delta(.)$ denotes the "Dirac delta function" or "unit point measure" and represents a probability density concentrated entirely at the origin. In the context of the path optimization problem described above, the $\mathbf{q}_i$, $i = 1, 2, \ldots, L$, designate the location L of specified positions where the probability function is entirely concentrated, and through which the path is supposed to pass. The p_i enable one to vary the relative importance of the positions.

Taking the discrete probability density (97), we can drop the assumption of a one-dimensional neuron chain for the following derivation and temporarily admit an arbitrary topology of the neural network, without introducing additional complications. We now ask for the expectation value $E(\Delta\mathbf{w}_\mathbf{r}|\mathbf{w}')$ for the change $\Delta\mathbf{w}_\mathbf{r} := \mathbf{w}_\mathbf{r} - \mathbf{w}'_\mathbf{r}$ of the synaptic strengths of neuron $\mathbf{r}$ under a single learning step. The notation $E(\Delta\mathbf{w}_\mathbf{r}|\mathbf{w}')$ indicates that the expectation value is conditional, *i.e.*, it depends on the state $\mathbf{w}'$ of the neural network before the learning step. In analogy to Eq. (70), $E(\Delta\mathbf{w}_\mathbf{r}|\mathbf{w}')$ is given by

$$\begin{aligned} E(\Delta\mathbf{w}_\mathbf{r}|\mathbf{w}') =& \epsilon \int h_{\mathbf{r}\phi_{\mathbf{w}'}(\mathbf{v})}(\mathbf{v} - \mathbf{w}'_\mathbf{r}) P(\mathbf{v})\, d\mathbf{v} \\ =& \epsilon \sum_\mathbf{s} h_{\mathbf{rs}} \int_{F_\mathbf{s}(\mathbf{w}')} (\mathbf{v} - \mathbf{w}'_\mathbf{r}) P(\mathbf{v})\, d\mathbf{v}. \end{aligned} \tag{98}$$

Here, $F_\mathbf{s}(\mathbf{w})$ is the set of all $\mathbf{v} \in V$ leading to the selection of "neuron" $\mathbf{s}$, *i.e.*,

$$F_\mathbf{s}(\mathbf{w}) = \left\{ \mathbf{v} \in V \,\middle|\, \|\mathbf{v} - \mathbf{w}_\mathbf{s}\| \le \|\mathbf{v} - \mathbf{w}_\mathbf{r}\| \; \forall \mathbf{r} \in A \right\}. \tag{99}$$

Since we will encounter the set $F_{\mathbf{s}}(\mathbf{w})$ (called "indicator function" in probability theory) very often throughout the rest of this book, let us give a further explanation of (99): $F_{\mathbf{s}}(\mathbf{w})$ entails the sub-volume of the space V, whose center of gravity is given by $\mathbf{w_s}$, enclosing all points of V lying closer to $\mathbf{w_s}$ than to any other $\mathbf{w_r}$, $\mathbf{r} \neq \mathbf{s}$. With regard to the biological interpretation of Kohonen's model, $F_{\mathbf{s}}(\mathbf{w})$ thus plays the role of the set of all input patterns exciting the "neuron" s most strongly and, hence, can be interpreted as the "receptive field" of this neuron.

For the discrete probability distribution (97), expression (98) simplifies to

$$E(\Delta \mathbf{w_r}|\mathbf{w}) = \epsilon \sum_{\mathbf{s}} h_{\mathbf{rs}} \sum_{\mathbf{q}_i \in F_{\mathbf{s}}(\mathbf{w})} p_i(\mathbf{q}_i - \mathbf{w_r}). \tag{100}$$

The right-hand side (RHS) can be expressed as the gradient of a "potential function"

$$E(\Delta \mathbf{w_r}|\mathbf{w}) = -\epsilon \nabla_{\mathbf{w_r}} V(\mathbf{w})$$

where $V(\mathbf{w})$ is given by†

$$V(\mathbf{w}) = \frac{1}{2} \sum_{\mathbf{rs}} h_{\mathbf{rs}} \sum_{\mathbf{q}_i \in F_{\mathbf{s}}(\mathbf{w})} p_i(\mathbf{q}_i - \mathbf{w_r})^2. \tag{101}$$

According to (100), a single learning step *on the average* leads to a decrease

$$E(\Delta V|\mathbf{w}) = -\epsilon \sum_{\mathbf{r}} \|\nabla_{\mathbf{w_r}} V\|^2 \tag{102}$$

of $V(\mathbf{w})$. However, an *individual* learning step can also lead to an increase in $V(\mathbf{w})$. Hence, as in Monte-Carlo annealing (Kirkpatrick et al. 1983, Kirkpatrick 1984), for $\epsilon > 0$ there is some possibility of escaping from local minima. However, for this to happen, the RHS of (102) must be comparable to the depth of the minimum. Otherwise, escaping the minimum requires the joint action of several steps. But the change in the potential for k steps tends approximately to $k \cdot E(\Delta V|\mathbf{w})$, *i.e.*, to a strongly negative value. Therefore, the chance of leaving the minimum by the joint action of several steps is small. This indicates that the learning step size ϵ is qualitatively analogous to the temperature in Monte-Carlo annealing. In particular, in the limit $\epsilon \to 0$, a deterministic trajectory in the potential $V(\mathbf{w})$ results.

†For a continuous probability density, a potential cannot be derived in this manner because of the dependence of (98) on the regions of integration, $F_{\mathbf{r}}(\mathbf{w})$.

For small ϵ, the stationary states correspond to the stationary points of $V(\mathbf{w})$. If $N \geq L$, then $V(\mathbf{w})$ assumes particulary small values if one sets $\mathbf{w_r} \approx \mathbf{q}_{i(\mathbf{r})}$, where $i(\mathbf{r})$ is an assignment of lattice sites $\mathbf{r}$ to positions $\mathbf{q}_i$ with the property that lattice sites $\mathbf{r}$, $\mathbf{s}$ for which $h_{\mathbf{rs}}$ has large values, are assigned to positions $\mathbf{q}_{i(\mathbf{r})}$, $\mathbf{q}_{i(\mathbf{s})}$ that are as close as possible in V. The minimization of $V(\mathbf{w})$ can thus be viewed as the mathematical formalization of seeking a mapping from the positions $\mathbf{q}_i$ to the lattice A such that the neighborhood relations in the image on A (being defined by the function $h_{\mathbf{rs}}$: the larger $h_{\mathbf{rs}}$, the closer $\mathbf{r}, \mathbf{s}$) reproduce the corresponding neighborhood relations of the $\mathbf{q}_i \in V$ as faithfully as possible. The success of this minimization, and hence the "quality" of the obtained mapping, depends to a considerable degree on the form of the potential surface $V(\mathbf{w})$ and on the possible presence of local minima corresponding to "more poorly arranged" maps.

Now, $V(\mathbf{w})$ is differentiable for all configurations $\mathbf{w}$ in which none of the $\mathbf{q}_i$ happens to be on the boundary $\partial F_{\mathbf{s}}$ of one of the regions $F_{\mathbf{s}}(\mathbf{w})$, and in this case one has

$$\frac{\partial^2 V}{\partial w_{\mathbf{r}m} \partial w_{\mathbf{s}n}} = \delta_{\mathbf{rs}} \delta_{mn} h_{\mathbf{rs}} \sum_{\mathbf{q}_i \in F_{\mathbf{s}}(\mathbf{w})} p_i \geq 0. \tag{103}$$

At those values $\mathbf{w}$ for which one of the $\mathbf{q}_i$ lies on the border between two regions $F_{\mathbf{r}}$ and $F_{\mathbf{s}}$, one has $\|\mathbf{q}_i - \mathbf{w_r}\| = \|\mathbf{q}_i - \mathbf{w_s}\|$ and hence V is still continuous. However, the first derivative has a discontinuity at these positions, and the potential surface above the state space has a "cusp." Thus, in spite of (103), V as a rule possesses numerous local minima of finite width. This situation is shown in Fig. 6.1, where the state space is represented schematically as a one-dimensional abscissa. For sufficiently small ϵ, the system can become trapped in any one of the "valleys" and converges in the limit $\epsilon \to 0$ to that state $\bar{\mathbf{w}}$ which corresponds to the local minimum of the "valley" that the system has chosen.

The number of minima depends on the range of $h_{\mathbf{rs}}$. For an infinite range, *i.e.*, $h_{\mathbf{rs}} = h$ =const., V becomes

$$V(\mathbf{w}) = \frac{h}{2} \sum_{i,\mathbf{r}} p_i (\mathbf{q}_i - \mathbf{w_r})^2 \tag{104}$$

with a single minimum at $\mathbf{w_r} = \sum_i p_i \mathbf{q}_i$. Decreasing the range, the cusps in V emerge, and with decreasing range of $h_{\mathbf{rs}}$ they

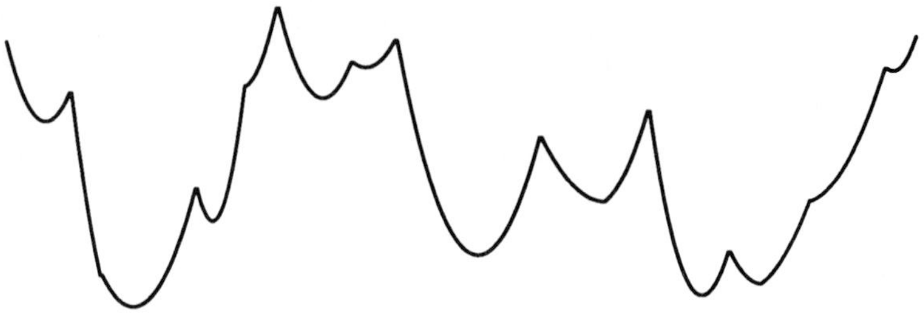

Figure 6.1 Behavior of the potential $V(\mathbf{w})$ above the state space. This space is actually $N \cdot d$-dimensional, and its representation in the figure as a one-dimensional abscissa is only schematic.

become more prominent. In this way, additional local minima enter the picture. Finally, in the limit $h_{\mathbf{rs}} = \delta_{\mathbf{rs}}$, one has

$$V(\mathbf{w}) = \frac{1}{2} \sum_{\mathbf{q}_i \in F_{\mathbf{r}}(\mathbf{w})} p_i (\mathbf{q}_i - \mathbf{w}_{\mathbf{r}})^2. \tag{105}$$

For $N \geq L$, every configuration $\mathbf{w}_{\mathbf{r}} = \mathbf{q}_{i(\mathbf{r})}$ for which $i(\mathbf{r})$ is surjective is a local minimum of V. For instance, for $N = L$ this leads to $N!$ minima. For $N >> L$, one has about L^N such minima (aside from these, there are further minima in which some of the $\mathbf{w}_{\mathbf{r}}$ are averages of several of the $\mathbf{q}_i$). Hence, for short-range $h_{\mathbf{rs}}$, V possesses very many local minima, and the minimization of V generally represents an extremely difficult problem.

Nevertheless, one can obtain a close to minimal path in this case by beginning with a very long-range $h_{\mathbf{rs}}$, for which V has only a single minimum. If the $h_{\mathbf{rs}}$ are slowly adjusted toward their desired final values, additional local minima successively emerge. For a sufficiently slow change, the system will fall into those new minima which are created in the current valley. But these are just the most promising candidates for an especially low final value. We can thus appreciate the importance of a slow decrease of the range of $h_{\mathbf{rs}}$ for the construction of a good map.

6.3. Application to the "Traveling Salesman Problem"

The occurrence of numerous local minima is a frequent characteristic of difficult optimization problems that belong to the class of so-called NP-complete problems and is one of the causes for the difficulty of finding their solution (although there are also NP-complete problems without local minima; see for example Baum 1986). For a problem to be efficiently tractable, there must exist a deterministic algorithm that generates a solution with a computational effort that rises no faster asymptotically than polynomially with the size of the problem. The set of all problems with this property forms the class P of so-called deterministic Polynomial problems. The class NP of Non-deterministic Polynomial problems arises if one weakens this requirement and just demands that the *correctness* of a solution is verifiable with a computational effort growing at most as some polynomial with the size of the problem. Evidently $P \subset NP$, but it is to be expected that NP contains in addition problems that are considerably more "difficult" than those in P, since every problem in NP not contained in P must require a computational effort for finding a solution which by definition grows faster asymptotically than any power of the problem size (Garey and Johnson 1979). A subclass of NP which is not contained in P is the class of so-called *NP-complete* problems. NP-complete problems can be characterized as being at least as hard as any other NP problem and not being solvable deterministically in polynomial time. Today, many NP-complete problems are known, however, it is not possible in any case to decide whether a deterministic solution procedure may be discovered someday that would reduce the computational effort to within polynomial bounds. (It has not been proven that $NP \neq P$, i.e., *every* NP-complete problem might be reducible to a "merely" P problem, although at present hardly anyone believes this).

The best-known example of an NP-complete problem, for which the computational effort rises exponentially with the problem size for every algorithm known up to now, is the "Traveling Salesman Problem" (TSP). In this problem, one seeks the short-

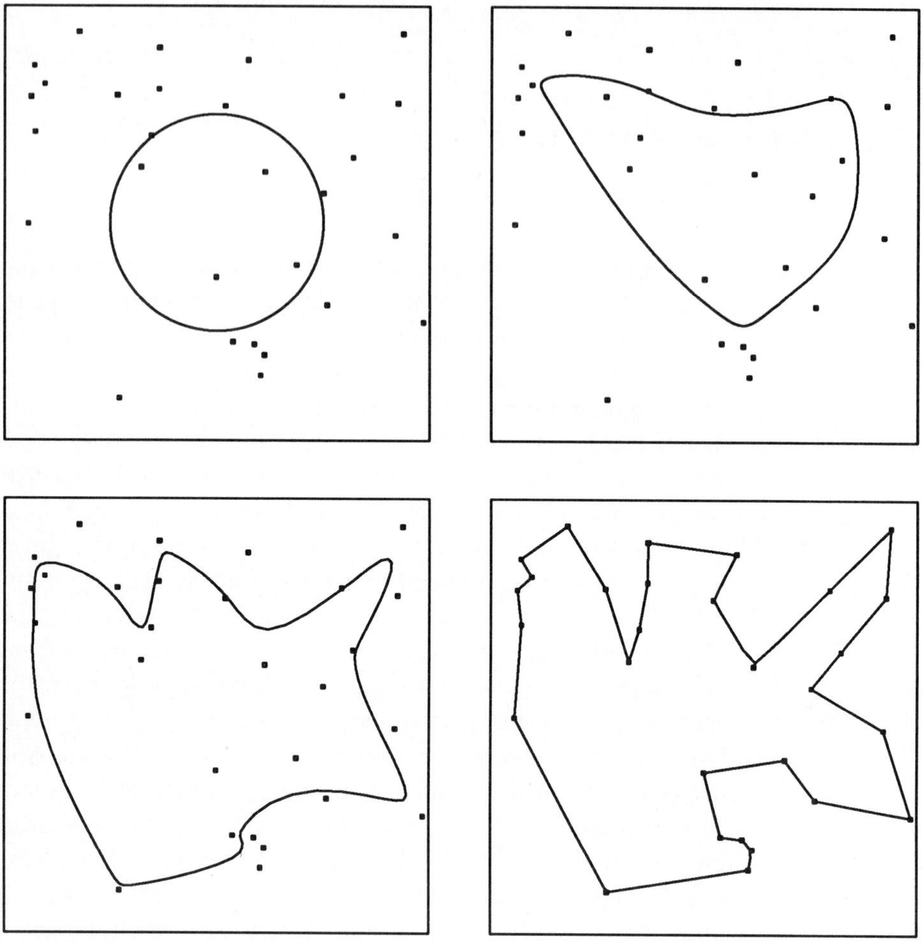

Figure 6.2 Simulation of the Markov-Process (70) for the TSP problem with $L = 30$ cities chosen at random in the unit square. Top left to bottom right: Initially chosen polygon tour, polygon tour obtained after 5,000, 7,000 and 10,000 learning steps, respectively. Simulation parameters: $N = 100$, $\epsilon = 0.8$, $\sigma(0) = 50$, $\sigma(10,000) = 1$.

est possible tour passing through N given cities. By testing all $\frac{1}{2}(N-1)!$ possible tours, one can always find the shortest tour, but the computational effort for this "direct" strategy, called "exhaustive search," rises exponentially with N and rapidly becomes unmanageable (for $N = 30$ the required processing time, even using a Cray–XMP supercomputer, would exceed the age of the universe.) The exponential character of this growth behavior persists for all improved algorithms discovered so far, although one has been successful at postponing the increase to considerably large values N. The root of this difficulty lies in the extremely irregular structure of the function "path length" over the state space of the problem. In particular, this function possesses numerous local minima, very many of which lie only very little above the global minimum. In order to find at least good approximations to the global minimum for such functions, several methods have been developed (Lin and Kerninghan 1973; Kirkpatrick et al. 1983). They are mostly based on a stochastic sampling of the state space in the direction of decreasing path lengths, together with some provision to escape from unfavorable local minima.

The usefulness of models of the formation of neural projections for treating the traveling salesman problem was first recognized by Durbin and Willshaw (1987). In the following, we demonstrate in a computer simulation how an approximate solution can be obtained by means of Kohonen's model (see also Angeniol et al. 1988). To this end, we choose a closed chain of "neurons" in the form of a ring. The vectors $\mathbf{w}_r$ of the neurons are changed iteratively according to equation (70), where in each step an element of the set $\{\mathbf{q}_1, \mathbf{q}_2, \ldots, \mathbf{q}_L\}$ of position vectors $\mathbf{q}_i$ of the L cities is selected as the input vector $\mathbf{v}$. For each $\mathbf{q}_i$, the same selection probability $p_i = 1/L$ is chosen. The Gaussian (68) was chosen for $h_{\mathbf{rs}}$, and the remaining simulation data were $N = 800$, $\epsilon = 0.8$, $\sigma(t) = 50 \cdot 0.02^{t/t_{max}}$ and $t_{max} = 10,000$ Markov steps. For the simulation example, $L = 30$ cities, randomly located in a unit square, were given. The initial values of the N vectors $\mathbf{w}_r$ were assigned to the corners of a regular 30-sided polygon. This results in the initial configuration shown in the upper left part of Fig. 6.2. Each iteration causes a local deformation of this path. Initially, as long as $h_{\mathbf{rs}}$ is still long-range, each deformation affects rather large path segments. In this way, first the rough outline of the eventual path is formed (Fig. 6.2, upper right, 5000 iterations). As the range of $h_{\mathbf{rs}}$ gradually decreases, the deformations along the chain become more localized and finer details of the path emerge (Fig. 6.2, lower left, 7000 iterations). Towards the end of the simulation $h_{\mathbf{rs}}$ differs significantly from zero only for immediate chain neighbors r, s. In this phase, the path takes on its final shape, passing through all of the given cities (Fig. 6.2, lower right, 10000 iterations). The path found after 10,000 steps has length 4.5888 and, in this example, happened to be the optimal solution.[†] However, this is not guaranteed for every case. Depending on the initial conditions, a slightly longer path may result, especially if the number of cities becomes larger.

We have seen in the previous chapters how even one-dimensional maps make possible interesting applications. In the following chapters, we will extend the discussion to two-dimensional maps. In Chapter 7, we will use them to model the formation of a "somatotopic map" of the palm of the hand. An extension of the algorithm to the task of *learning of output values* will then open up applications to *control problems* and thus introduce the subject of the Part III of this book.

[†]Only a "naive" comparison of all possible paths would require a computational time which exceeds the age of the universe. In fact, there are clever search techiques which reduce the computational effort significantly. With those sophisticated search techniques it has even been possible to find the shortest path through a nontrivial distribution of 2430 points, the current "world record" (1990).

7. Modeling the Somatotopic Map

7.1. The Somatotopic Map of the Body Surface

In this chapter we demonstrate the formation of a "somatotopic map" by means of a computer simulation of Kohonen's algorithm (Ritter and Schulten 1986). The *somatotopic map* is the projection of the body surface onto a brain area that is responsible for our sense of touch and that is called the *somatosensory cortex*. This projection connects neurons of the cortex with touch receptors in the skin surface such that neighborhood relations are preserved. Adjacent touch receptors in the skin surface are thus connected to adjacent neurons (Kaas et al. 1979). However, the projection is strongly distorted, since the density of touch receptors is very different in various skin regions. For example, hand and face regions are considerably more densely innervated with touch receptors than the skin on the arms and on the trunk. Correspondingly, the former have a much larger image area in the somatosensory cortex. Interestingly, the neural projections giving rise to these images are not rigid. Instead, they can change under the influence of sensory experience or as the result of a loss of sensory input, *e.g.*, after nerve damage. The necessary modifications of the connections between receptors and sensory neurons are thought to be, at least in part, activity driven. For example, experiments have revealed that frequent stimulation of confined skin regions leads to an expansion of their representation in the somatotopic map (Jenkins et al. 1984). Conversely, neurons whose receptors no longer receive any stimuli become sensitive to other receptors which are still active (Kaas et al. 1983). Such findings imply that a significant part of cortical organization may be shaped by a principle of competition between neurons, most likely operating at the synaptic level.

In the following we show that from a completely disordered initial connectivity, the structure of an ordered, neighborhood-preserving connection pattern between touch receptors and neurons of a "model somatosensory cortex" as well as a series of experimentally observed adaptation phenomena, can come about as a result of Kohonen's strongly idealized algorithm alone. According to current thought, this represents an idealization of the actual phenomena in which chemical control processes are also significantly involved (Campenot 1977). However, the value of such a demonstration is not primarily the description of biological detail, but the isolation of significant and simple functional principles and their capacity for contributing to important organizational processes in the nervous system.

A considerably more ambitious simulation model for the formation of somatotopic connectivity, as far as reproduction of biological details is concerned, was investigated by Pearson et al. (1987). Pearson's model assumes an initial connectivity which is diffuse, but already topographically ordered. The simulation investigates how, by aggregation into competing groups, individual neurons can focus their initially diffuse receptive fields into smaller regions while maintaining the initial topographic ordering. The main intention is a test of the group selection theory of Edelman (1978). According to this theory, aggregation of adjacent neurons into localized "functional groups" occurs. The "formal neurons" in Kohonen's model may possibly be viewed as an abstraction of such larger, functional units.

7.2. Simplification of the Dynamics

For the simulation, we consider a "model hand surface" with touch receptors distributed at locations $\mathbf{v}_\alpha \in \mathbb{R}^2$, $\alpha = 1, 2, \ldots K$. Figure 7.1 shows the hand surface used, together with $K = 1200$ randomly distributed touch receptor points. The touch receptors are connected through synapses to the 30×30 neurons

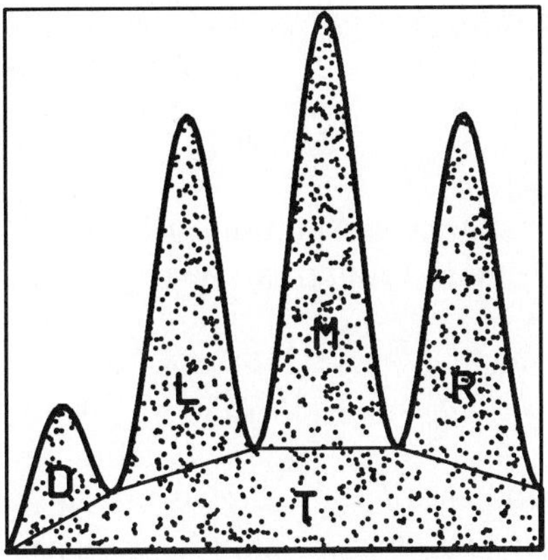

Figure 7.1 Model hand surface with touch receptors. Letters **D**, **L**, **M**, **R**, and **T** denote five subregions: thumb, left, middle, and right fingers as well as the palm. The dots mark the locations of 1,200 touch receptors distributed at random over the hand surface.

of a square "model cortex" A. Let $w_{\mathbf{r}\alpha}$ denote the strength of the synapse through which receptor α excites the neuron at the position r. Every localized touch stimulus on the hand surface leads to excitations ν_α of the receptors α. Receptors close to the stimulus location are strongly excited, and excitation decreases to zero with increasing distance. The excitations of the receptors are assumed to lead to an adaptation step

$$\Delta w_{\mathbf{r}\alpha} = \epsilon h_{\mathbf{rs}}(\nu_\alpha - w_{\mathbf{r}\alpha}), \tag{106}$$

for the synaptic strengths. Here, s again identifies the most strongly excited neuron and $h_{\mathbf{rs}}$ is the assumed excitation profile about s. We now show how (106) can give rise to the formation of an ordered connectivity between neurons and touch receptors such that each neuron has synaptic connections only to receptors from a localized region of the hand surface, and adjacent neurons are connected to adjacent regions. For a useful simulation, however, several hundred touch receptors would be required, and an equal number of synaptic strengths would have to be stored and updated at each learning step and for each of the 900 model neurons.

However, one can approximate the system behavior by mapping the original dynamic variables, the synaptic strengths $w_{\mathbf{r}\alpha}$, onto a much smaller set of new variables, whose evolution then is governed by a correspondingly simpler, "effective dynamics." In this way, the resulting simulation effort is reduced considerably. For this simplification, we must make the following two additional assumptions:

1. The sum $S = \sum_\alpha \nu_\alpha$ of the excitatory strengths of the touch receptors should be the same for each touch stimulus.

2. The synaptic strength of each neuron should satisfy initially

$$\sum_\alpha w_{\mathbf{r}\alpha} = S. \tag{107}$$

The first assumption corresponds to a preliminary normalization of the activity of the input signal. By (106), one has for a learning step

$$\Delta \sum_\alpha w_{\mathbf{r}\alpha} = \epsilon h_{\mathbf{rs}} \left(S - \sum_\alpha w_{\mathbf{r}\alpha} \right). \tag{108}$$

Thus, the second assumption implies that the sum of the synaptic strengths of each neuron takes its stationary value from the beginning, which by (108) would otherwise only hold after some relaxation time.

With these assumptions, we can describe the development of the correspondence between the hand surface and the neurons directly using two-dimensional surface coordinates. We describe the touch stimulus by the location $\mathbf{v}$ of the center of gravity of the excitatory pattern of the touch receptors, *i.e.*,

$$\mathbf{v} := \frac{1}{S} \sum_\alpha \nu_\alpha \mathbf{v}_\alpha, \tag{109}$$

and replace the K synaptic strengths $w_{\mathbf{r}\alpha}$ per neuron by the two "formal synaptic strengths"

$$\tilde{w}_{\mathbf{r}i} := \frac{1}{S} \sum_\alpha v_{\alpha i} w_{\mathbf{r}\alpha}, \quad (i = 1,\ 2). \tag{110}$$

Here, $v_{\alpha 1}$, $v_{\alpha 2}$ denote the cartesian coordinates at receptor location $\mathbf{v}_\alpha$, and we use arabic numerals as indices in order to distinguish the two formal synaptic locations $\tilde{w}_{\mathbf{r}i}$ from the K synaptic strengths $w_{\mathbf{r}\alpha}$. One can interpret $\tilde{\mathbf{w}}_\mathbf{r} := (\tilde{w}_{\mathbf{r}1}, \tilde{w}_{\mathbf{r}2})^T$ as the center-of-mass of the group of touch receptors attached to neuron $\mathbf{r}$. Here, each touch receptor is weighted in proportion to the strength of its connection with neuron $\mathbf{r}$. Thus, from (106) we obtain

$$\Delta \tilde{w}_{\mathbf{r}i} = \epsilon h_{\mathbf{rs}} (v_i - \tilde{w}_{\mathbf{r}i}), \qquad (i = 1,\ 2). \tag{111}$$

This equation establishes the desired "effective dynamics" for the new variables $\tilde{\mathbf{w}}_{\mathbf{r}i}$. Interestingly, it is of the same form as (106); however, now a simulation only requires taking into account the two-dimensional vectors $\mathbf{v}$ and $\tilde{\mathbf{w}}_\mathbf{r}$.

7.3. Results of the Simulation

The initial state of the simulation consisted of a random assignment of neurons to touch receptors. This assignment was arranged by setting the formal synaptic strengths $\tilde{\mathbf{w}}_{\mathbf{r}}$ to random values taken from a uniform distribution on the unit square circumscribing the hand surface in Fig. 7.1.† The resulting map is shown in Fig. 7.2. For each neuron **r**, a letter indicates which of the five regions **D**, **L**, **M**, **R**, and **T** contains the center of mass $\tilde{\mathbf{w}}_{\mathbf{r}}$ of the subset of receptors exciting that neuron. Neurons for which $\tilde{\mathbf{w}}_{\mathbf{r}}$ happens to lie outside of the hand surface are marked by a dot. This case occurs, for example, if a neuron has equally strong connections to the receptors of two adjacent fingers.

The initial connection pattern evidently leads to a map that does not reproduce the topological arrangement of the touch receptors in any way. For the subsequent learning steps, stimulus locations **v** were randomly selected from the hand region according to the the probability density $P(\mathbf{v}) = 1.5/\sqrt{4-3v_2}$. In this way, the increasing receptor density towards the finger tips, the locations of which correspond to $v_2 \approx 1$, was simulated (the touch receptor points illustrated in Fig. 7.1 are also distributed according to this density). During the first 5,000 learning steps, the Gaussian (68) with $\sigma(t) = 5 \cdot 0.4^{t/5000}$ and $\epsilon(t) = 0.5 \cdot 0.2^{t/5000}$ was assumed for $h_{\mathbf{rs}}$, while during the subsequent learning steps a Gaussian with $\sigma(t) = 2$ and $\epsilon(t) = 0.1$ was chosen. After 500 touch stimuli, a map has formed in which one can already recognize connected regions of neurons assigned to the same hand region (Fig. 7.3). Even the neighborhood relations between individual hand regions are already beginning to be reproduced correctly. Eventually, after 20,000 iterations, a map has been created (Fig. 7.4) which represents a topologically correct image of the individual hand regions, resembling maps obtained with electrode penetration

---

† Precisely speaking, the initial distribution of formal synaptic strengths could be obtained from the receptor distribution together with an assignment of the $w_{\mathbf{r}\alpha}$ to random values (preserving the sum condition 2.). The values thus obtained would all lie within the convex hull of the hand surface. However, this difference is not important for the qualitative course of the organization process from a disordered initial state.

```
M L . . L . . T T T L L . . L . . L R . L M T . . . . . . M
. T . L R R . . R . R . M M D . T . M . R . . R . R M L . .
. . . . R T T . . M . M . . T R R . . L . . . M M T . . R .
. . . . R L L . . . . . R . . L M . T . L D . T . T . R T M
. R T . T M . . . . . T . R D L . L . . M . L . R . . . D L
T . L L R . . T . M . . . L . . . . . T . T R . . . L T . M
. . . . . T . . R M . . . T . T . T . . M M . T . R R . . .
. . . . . . . . . . M . R M . T T . . . R . . . . L R . R .
. M . . T R . . . L T . R L . R R . . T R . T . M . . M R .
. M T T R . . T M . T . . . . T . . . T T . . D D M . R L R
R T R T T D . . . . . . R . D T L . T . . T . . . . . T . M
L T T M . . . . . . . . . . . T . . . M . . . L . M . M . R
M T . T . . . T . . . L . . . M . . . . . . . R T T . . . .
. T . . . M . . M . . . . T . . . . T . . . . M T T . . . T
. R . D . . L R M M . . R . . . . . . . M . T . T M L . . .
M L . . R . R . R . . . . . M . . M . . . . . M . M . T . R
M T . L . . L R L . R T . . . . L . T L . T T T R . T . L .
. . . . . T . T . T . . . M R . . T . . . . T L D . . T . T
. . L . . L . . D T . . . L M . . . L . T L . . . T M . R D
M M T M L . . L . . . . M L T M M . . . . . . . . . . T . .
. . . M . . L T . M . . . T . . . T M T T . . L . . . T L T
M M L L . . T . R R R . M . M . R . L . . R . T . . M R T .
. . . T . . R . . . T M . M R R R . L . . R . L L . . . L M
. . . . . . . . R . T . . . . L L . . M L M . . . . T . . .
. L M T . L . . . L . . . R . . T T . . . . . M M T . T T .
. . M . . . T . R . . T R . R L . . . . L . T . R . . L . .
. . . . . M R T . . . R M T R L T . M L . . . M T L M L L .
M . . M M D R . . M T M . . R . . L . T . . . . L . . T . .
. . . . R T M M M . . . . T M R T M M . . . . . . . M T . .
. . M . R M . . . . . . . . . R . . M . R M . . . . M . R T
```

Figure 7.2 Initial assignment of the 900 neurons of a model cortex of 30 × 30 lattice sites to the hand surface of Fig. 7.1. Each lattice site **r** corresponds to one neuron, which is connected through synapses to touch receptors on the hand surface. The location $\tilde{\mathbf{w}}_{\mathbf{r}}$ of the center of gravity of these receptors is indicated by labeling the lattice site with one of the letters **D,L,M,R** and **T**, according to the region in Fig. 7.1 containing $\tilde{\mathbf{w}}_{\mathbf{r}}$. A dot indicates that $\tilde{\mathbf{w}}_{\mathbf{r}}$ happens to lie in the space between the fingers. As can be seen, the initial correspondence between neurons and locations in the hand surface is completely random and in particular not neighborhood preserving.

```
M M M M M . . L L L L L T T T T T T T T T T T T T T T T T M
M M M M M M . L L L L L L T T T T T T T T T T T T T T T T T
M M M M M . . L L L L L L T T T T T T T T T T T T T T T T T
M M M M . . L L L L L L L T T T T T T T T T T T T T T T T T
M M M M . . L L L L L L L . T T T T T T T T T T T T T T T T
M M M . . L L L L L L L . . T T T T T T T T T T T T T T T T
M M . . . L L L L L L . . . D T T T T T T T T T T T T T T T
M M . . L L L L L L L . . . . . T T T T T T T T T T T T T T
M . . . L L L L L L L L . . . . . T T T T T T T T T T T T T
M . . . L L L L L L L L . . . . L L L L T T T T T T T T T T
M . . L L L L L L L L L L L L L L L L L L T T T T T T T T T
M . . L L L L L L L L L L L L L L L L L L T T T T T T T T T
M . . . L L L L L L L L L L L L L L L L . M T T T T T T T T
M . . . L L L L L L L L L L L L L L . M M M T T T T T T T T
M M . . L L L L L L L L L L L L L . . M M M M T T T T T T T
M M . . . L L L L L L L L L L L L . M M M M M T T T T T T T
M M M . . . L L L L L L L L L L . . M M M M M T T T T T T T
M M M . . . . L L L L L L L L . . . M M M M M T T T T T T T
M M M M . . . . . L L L L . . . . M M M M M M T T T T T T T
M M M M M . . . . . . . . . . M M M M M M M M T T T T T T T
M M M M M M M . . . M M M M M M M M M M M M M T T T T T T T
M M M M M M M M M M M M M M M M . . . . . . . T T T T T T T
M M M M M M M M M M M M . . . . . . R R R R R R T T T T T T
M M M . . . M M M M M M . . . R R R R R R R R R R T T T T T
. . . . . . . . M M M . . . R R R R R R R R R R T T T T T T
. . . . . . . . . M M . . . R R R R R R R R R R R T T T T T
. . . . . . . . . M M . . R R R R R R R R R R R R R T T T T
. . L L L L . . . . M M . . R R R R R R R R R R R R T T T T
L L L L L L L . . . M M . . R R R R R R R R R R R R T T T T
L L L L L L L L . . . M . . R R R R R R R R R R R R R T T T
```

Figure 7.3 After only 500 "touch stimuli," a coarsely ordered assignment has replaced the completely disordered initial state of Fig. 7.2. Adjacent neurons have begun to specialize to adjacent regions of the hand surface.

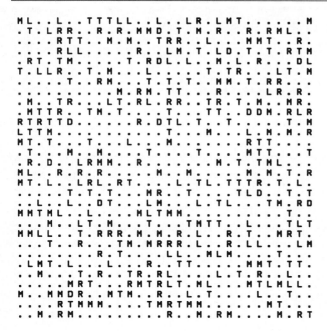

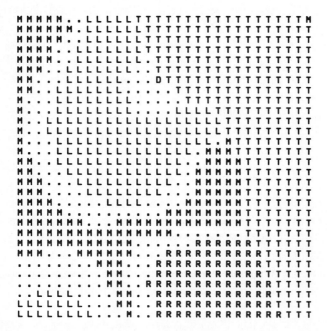

```
D D D D D D D D D T T T T T T T T T T T T T T T T T T T T T
D D D D D D D D D T T T T T T T T T T T T T T T T T T T T T
. D D D D D D D D D D T T T T T T T T T T T T T T T T T T T
. . . D D D D D D D D D T T T T T T T T T T T T T T T T T T
L L . . . . . . . . . . L L L T T T T T T T T T T T T T T T
L L L L L L L L L L L L L L L L L T T T T T T T T T T T T T
L L L L L L L L L L L L L L L L L L T T T T T T T T T T T T
L L L L L L L L L L L L L L L L L L L T T T T T T T T T T T
L L L L L L L L L L L L L L L L L L L T T T T T T T T T T T
L L L L L L L L L L L L L L L L L L L T T T T T T T T T T T
L L L L L L L L L L L L L L L L L . M M T T T T T T T T T T
L L L L L L L L L L L L L L L . M M M M M T T T T T T T T T
L L L L L L L L L L L L . . . M M M M M M T T T T T T T T T
L L L L L L L L L . . . M M M M M M M M M M T T T T T T T T
L L L L L L L L . . M M M M M M M M M M M M T T T T T T T T
L L L L L L . . M M M M M M M M M M M M M M T T T T T T T T
L L L L L . . M M M M M M M M M M M M M M M M T T T T T T T
L L L L . . M M M M M M M M M M M M M M M M M T T T T T T T
L L L . . M M M M M M M M M M M M M M M M M M T T T T T T T
L L . . M M M M M M M M M M M M M M M M M M M T T T T T T T
L . . M M M M M M M M M M M M M M M M M . . R T T T T T T T
. . M M M M M M M M M M M M M M M . . . R R R R T T T T T T
M M M M M M M M M M M M M M . . . R R R R R R R T T T T T T
M M M M M M M M M M . . . . R R R R R R R R R R R T T T T T
M M M M M M M M . . . R R R R R R R R R R R R R R T T T T T
M M M M M M . . . R R R R R R R R R R R R R R R R T T T T T
M M M M M . . R R R R R R R R R R R R R R R R R R R T T T T
M M M M . . R R R R R R R R R R R R R R R R R R R R T T T T
M M M . . R R R R R R R R R R R R R R R R R R R R R T T T T
M M M . R R R R R R R R R R R R R R R R R R R R R R R T T T
```

Figure 7.4 After a total of 20,000 touch stimuli, the connections between the neurons and the hand regions have become completely ordered. This assignment is now neighborhood preserving, and it reproduces the correct topological arrangement of the regions **D,L,M,R** and **T**. The map created here is also in good qualitative agreement with maps experimentally found in the cortex.

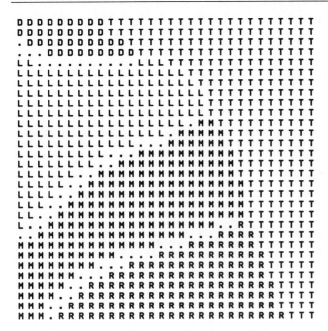

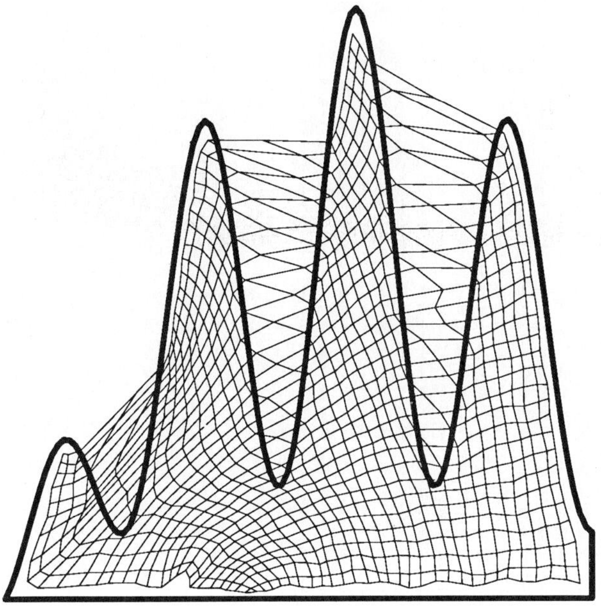

Figure 7.5 Here, the assignment of Fig. 7.4 is represented as the familiar "imbedding" of the neuron lattice in the space V, *i.e.*, on the hand surface. To this end, each neuron is marked at the position of the center of gravity $\tilde{\mathbf{w}}_{\mathbf{r}}$ of the touch receptors from which it receives input, and the resulting locations are connected by lines if the neurons are adjacent in the lattice.

```
D D D D D D D D D T T T T T T T T T T T T T T T T T T T T T
D D D D D D D D D T T T T T T T T T T T T T T T T T T T T T
. D D D D D D D D D D T T T T T T T T T T T T T T T T T T T
. . . D D D D D D D D D T T T T T T T T T T T T T T T T T T
L L . . . . . . . . . . L L L T T T T T T T T T T T T T T T
L L L L L L L L L L L L L L L L L T T T T T T T T T T T T T
L L L L L L L L L L L L L L L L L L T T T T T T T T T T T T
L L L L L L L L L L L L L L L L L L L T T T T T T T T T T T
L L L L L L L L L L L L L L L L L L L T T T T T T T T T T T
L L L L L L L L L L L L L L L L L L L T T T T T T T T T T T
L L L L L L L L L L L L L L L L L . . . T T T T T T T T T T
L L L L L L L L L L L L L L L . . . . . . T T T T T T T T T
L L L L L L L L L L L L . . . . . . . . . T T T T T T T T T
L L L L L L L L L . . . . . . . . . . . . . T T T T T T T T
L L L L L L L L . . . . . . . . . . . . . . T T T T T T T T
L L L L L L . . . . . . . . . . . . . . . . T T T T T T T T
L L L L L . . . . . . . . . . . . . . . . . . T T T T T T T
L L L L . . . . . . . . . . . . . . . . . . . T T T T T T T
L L L . . . . . . . . . . . . . . . . . . . . T T T T T T T
L L . . . . . . . . . . . . . . . . . . . . . T T T T T T T
L . . . . . . . . . . . . . . . . . . . . . R T T T T T T T
. . . . . . . . . . . . . . . . . . . . R R R R T T T T T T
. . . . . . . . . . . . . . . . . R R R R R R R T T T T T T
. . . . . . . . . . . . . . R R R R R R R R R R R T T T T T
. . . . . . . . . . . R R R R R R R R R R R R R R T T T T T
. . . . . . . . . R R R R R R R R R R R R R R R R T T T T T
. . . . . . . R R R R R R R R R R R R R R R R R R R T T T T
. . . . . . R R R R R R R R R R R R R R R R R R R R T T T T
. . . . . R R R R R R R R R R R R R R R R R R R R R T T T T
. . . . R R R R R R R R R R R R R R R R R R R R R R R T T T
```

Figure 7.6 After the map of Fig. 7.4 has been obtained, the middle finger **M** is "amputated", *i.e.*, for the rest of the simulation touch stimuli are no longer selected from this region; consequently the neurons designated by dots, which were previously connected to **M**, are now deprived of their former sensory inputs.

```
D D D T T T T T T T T T T T T T T T T T T T T T T T T T T T
D D D T T T T T T T T T T T T T T T T T T T T T T T T T T T
D D D D D T T T T T T T T T T T T T T T T T T T T T T T T T
D D D D D D T T T T T T T T T T T T T T T T T T T T T T T T
D D D D D D D D . L L T T T T T T T T T T T T T T T T T T T
D D D D D D . . L L L L L T T T T T T T T T T T T T T T T T
D D D D D . . L L L L L L L T T T T T T T T T T T T T T T T
D D D . . . L L L L L L L L L T T T T T T T T T T T T T T T
D D . . . L L L L L L L L L L L T T T T T T T T T T T T T T
. . . . L L L L L L L L L L L L L T T T T T T T T T T T T T
. . . L L L L L L L L L L L L L L T T T T T T T T T T T T T
. L L L L L L L L L L L L L L L L T T T T T T T T T T T T T
L L L L L L L L L L L L L L L L L T T T T T T T T T T T T T
L L L L L L L L L L L L L L L L . . T T T T T T T T T T T T
L L L L L L L L L L L L L L L L . . T T T T T T T T T T T T
L L L L L L L L L L L L L L L . . . T T T T T T T T T T T T
L L L L L L L L L L L L L L . . . . . T T T T T T T T T T T
L L L L L L L L L L L L . . . . . . . . T T T T T T T T T T
L L L L L L L L L . . . . . . . R R R . T T T T T T T T T T
L L L L L L L L . . . . . . R R R R R R R T T T T T T T T T
L L L L L L L . . . . . R R R R R R R R R R T T T T T T T T
L L L L L . . . . . R R R R R R R R R R R R T T T T T T T T
L L L L . . . . . R R R R R R R R R R R R R R T T T T T T T
L L L . . . . R R R R R R R R R R R R R R R R T T T T T T T
L . . . . . R R R R R R R R R R R R R R R R R R T T T T T T
. . . . . R R R R R R R R R R R R R R R R R R R T T T T T T
. . . R R R R R R R R R R R R R R R R R R R R R T T T T T T
. R R R R R R R R R R R R R R R R R R R R R R R R T T T T T
R R R R R R R R R R R R R R R R R R R R R R R R R T T T T T
R R R R R R R R R R R R R R R R R R R R R R R R R R T T T T
```

Figure 7.7 After another 50,000 touch stimuli, the map has reorganized itself in such a way that only a few neurons are still silent. The representation of the remaining hand regions **D, L, R** and **T** is now distributed over a larger number of neurons and, therefore, possesses a higher spatial resolution than before the "amputation."

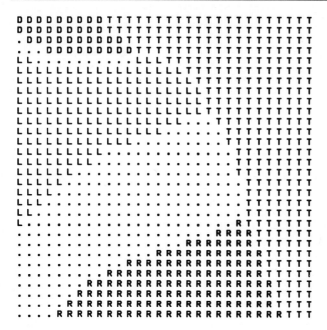

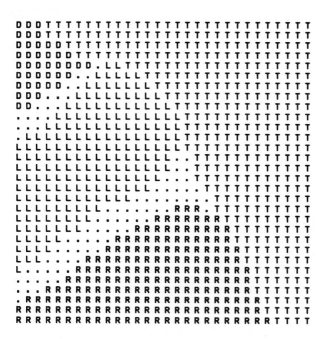

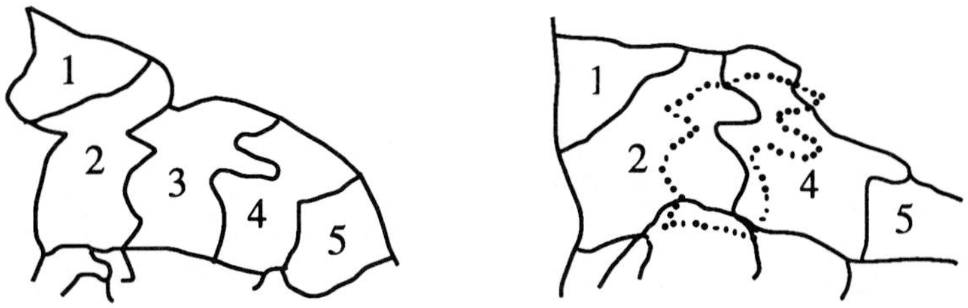

Figure 7.8 Readaptation of the somatosensory map of the hand region of an adult nocturnal ape due to the amputation of one finger. (a) (left) Before the operation, each finger in the map is represented as one of the regions 1-5. (b) (right) Several weeks after amputation of the middle finger, the assigned region 3 has disappeared, and the adjacent regions have correspondingly spread out (after Fox, 1984).

experiments in animals. Figure 7.5 again shows this assignment of neurons to hand locations, using the familiar imbedding of the neuron lattice in the space V. Following an experiment of Kaas et al. (1983), at this stage of development of the map we "remove" the middle finger by not selecting any further stimuli from the region **M** for the remainder of the simulation (Fig. 7.6). Because of the remaining plasticity in the mapping, the net readapts during the subsequent 50,000 learning steps, leading to the map in Fig. 7.7. The cortical region deprived of its former sensory inputs has established connections to receptors formerly driving neurons in the adjacent regions (labelled **L** and **R**). In the map, these regions "invade" the former territory of the amputated hand region **M**. Additionally, as a result of the readaptation, the local magnification factor of the mapping from the hand surface to the cortex has increased. This corresponds to an enhanced capacity for spatial discrimination in these regions. Qualitatively similar behavior has been observed experimentally (Kaas et al. 1983). To this end, the somatosensory map of the hand region of an adult monkey was determined using microelectrodes (Fig. 7.8a). The observed map resembles that in Fig. 7.4. To each finger corresponds one of the regions 1–5. Several weeks after amputation of the middle finger, the corresponding region 3 has "disappeared," and the adjacent regions have become correspondingly larger (Fig. 7.8b).

We have thus demonstrated that under Kohonen's algorithm a connection pattern forms between neurons and touch receptors; it arranges the centers of gravity $\tilde{\mathbf{w}}_{\mathbf{r}}$ of the neurons

$\mathbf{r}$ connected to the touch receptors in the hand surface topologically, just as the corresponding neurons $\mathbf{r}$ are arranged in the somatosensory cortex. However, because of the use of the centers of gravity $\mathbf{w_r}$ as simulation variables, the simulation makes no statement about the spatial scatter of the touch receptors in the hand surface to which a single neuron has finally formed synaptic contact. Therefore, we must still show that, under the algorithm, each neuron $\mathbf{r}$ concentrates its synaptic contacts to receptors from a small region about the center of gravity $\tilde{\mathbf{w}}_\mathbf{r}$.

7.4. Development of Receptive Fields

The skin region within which touch stimuli lead to excitation of a neuron $\mathbf{r}$ forms the *"receptive field"* of this neuron. A measure of the size of this field is the average surface area $G_\mathbf{r} = \pi\langle \mathbf{r}^2\rangle$ of the "scattering circle" of the touch receptors connected to the neuron. Here, $\langle \mathbf{r}^2\rangle$ is the average value of the squared distance of the receptors from the center of the circle (their center of gravity $\tilde{\mathbf{w}}_\mathbf{r}$), weighted by the synaptic strengths $w_{\mathbf{r}\alpha}$ of their connections with neuron $\mathbf{r}$. Thus

$$G_\mathbf{r} = \frac{\pi}{S}\sum_\alpha (\mathbf{v}_\alpha - \tilde{\mathbf{w}}_\mathbf{r})^2 w_{\mathbf{r}\alpha}. \tag{112}$$

A touch stimulus at location $\mathbf{v}$ leads to the following change of $G_\mathbf{r}$ (we neglect contributions of quadratic order in ϵ)

$$\begin{aligned} \Delta G_\mathbf{r} &= \frac{2\pi\epsilon}{S} h_{\mathbf{rs}} \sum_\alpha (\tilde{\mathbf{w}}_\mathbf{r} - \mathbf{v}_\alpha)\cdot(\mathbf{v} - \tilde{\mathbf{w}}_\mathbf{r}) w_{\mathbf{r}\alpha} \\ &\quad + \frac{\pi\epsilon}{S} h_{\mathbf{rs}} \sum_\alpha (\tilde{\mathbf{w}}_\mathbf{r} - \mathbf{v}_\alpha)^2 (\nu_\alpha - w_{\mathbf{r}\alpha}) \\ &= -\epsilon h_{\mathbf{rs}} \left[G_\mathbf{r} - \Gamma(\mathbf{v}) - \pi(\tilde{\mathbf{w}}_\mathbf{r} - \mathbf{v})^2\right]. \end{aligned} \tag{113}$$

In this equation, we have made the definition

$$\Gamma(\mathbf{v}) := \frac{\pi}{S}\sum_\alpha (\mathbf{v} - \mathbf{v}_\alpha)^2 \nu_\alpha. \tag{114}$$

One can interpret $\Gamma(\mathbf{v})$ as the surface area of the distribution of touch receptor excitations triggered by the touch stimulus. The expectation value $E(\Delta G_\mathbf{r}|G_\mathbf{r})$ for the change of $G_\mathbf{r}$ is therefore

$$E(\Delta G_\mathbf{r}|G_\mathbf{r}) = -\epsilon \int h_{\mathbf{r}\phi(\mathbf{v})} \left[G_\mathbf{r} - \langle\Gamma(\mathbf{v})\rangle - \pi(\tilde{\mathbf{w}}_\mathbf{r} - \mathbf{v})^2\right] P(\mathbf{v})\, d\mathbf{v}. \tag{115}$$

Here, ϕ is the mapping from the hand surface to the neuron lattice, and $\langle\Gamma(\mathbf{v})\rangle$ is the average excited surface area of the receptor layer due to the touch stimulus at position v. For sufficiently small learning step size ϵ, the resulting asymptotic value $G_{\mathbf{r}}^{\infty}$ of $G_{\mathbf{r}}$ becomes

$$G_{\mathbf{r}}^{\infty} \approx \frac{\int h_{\mathbf{r}\phi(\mathbf{v})}\left[\langle\Gamma(\mathbf{v})\rangle + \pi(\tilde{\mathbf{w}}_{\mathbf{r}} - \mathbf{v})^2\right]P(\mathbf{v})\, d\mathbf{v}}{\int h_{\mathbf{r}\phi(\mathbf{v})}P(\mathbf{v})\, d\mathbf{v}}. \tag{116}$$

This permits us to rewrite (115) in the more suggestive form

$$E(\Delta G_{\mathbf{r}}|G_{\mathbf{r}}) = -\epsilon\left[\int h_{\mathbf{r}\phi(\mathbf{v})}P(\mathbf{v})\, d\mathbf{v}\right]\cdot(G_{\mathbf{r}} - G_{\mathbf{r}}^{\infty}). \tag{117}$$

We see from (117) that on the average the surface area of a receptive field tends exponentially to its asymptotic equilibrium value $G_{\mathbf{r}}^{\infty}$. If any variation of $P(\mathbf{v})$ and $\langle\Gamma(\mathbf{v})\rangle$ occurs only on a much longer spatial scale than $h_{\mathbf{r}\phi(\mathbf{v})}$ and the mapping ϕ conserves angles (*i.e.*, is conformal) at the position $\mathbf{w}_{\mathbf{r}}$, then (116) can be simplified further to yield

$$G_{\mathbf{r}}^{\infty} \approx \langle\Gamma(\mathbf{v})\rangle + M^{-1}\pi\sigma^2, \tag{118}$$

where the quantity M is the local magnification factor of the mapping ϕ, and $\sigma^2 = \int h_{\mathbf{rs}}(\mathbf{r}-\mathbf{s})^2\, d^2\mathbf{s}/\int h_{\mathbf{rs}}\, d^2\mathbf{s}$. This equation shows that in the present model each neuron restricts its inputs to receptors within an area given by the the sum of two contributions. The first contribution is the average surface area $\langle\Gamma(\mathbf{v})\rangle$ of the excitation distribution in the receptor layer caused by each touch stimulus. The second contribution is the surface area $\pi\sigma^2/M$ of that region in the receptor layer which corresponds, under the mapping ϕ, to a cortical region of radius σ, *i.e.*, a cortical area the size of which is determined by the spread of the excitation profile $h_{\mathbf{rs}}$. Assuming localized touch stimuli, *i.e.*, small $\langle\Gamma(\mathbf{v})\rangle$, and a short-range excitation response $h_{\mathbf{rs}}$ towards the end of the simulation, the resulting synaptic connections for each neuron become concentrated to receptors of a narrowly focused region.

In this chapter we have shown that the rather abstract organizational principles in Kohonen's algorithm are sufficient to construct a neighborhood preserving connectivity between a receptor layer and a neuron layer from disordered initial connections. The only information driving this process is the stochastic stimulation of the receptors. At the end of the process, every neuron possesses synaptic connections to receptors of a narrowly limited region in the receptor layer. The assignment of neurons to regions preserves mutual neighborhood relations and represents a two-dimensional map of the hand surface. For the formation of this map, it turned out to be immaterial whether the algorithm obtains the information about touch stimuli explicitly in the form of two-dimensional coordinates or instead is directly supplied with high-dimensional receptor activity patterns. This illustrates the ability of the algorithm to automatically extract hidden lower-dimensional information, in this case the stimulus location, from a sequence of high-dimensional signals (the excitation at all the receptors on the hand), and to represent it in a two-dimensional map. In the present case, the dimensions of the implicit information and of the map agree and a continuous mapping results.

7.5. Simulating the High-Dimensional Model on a Parallel Computer

While the main purpose of the preceding sections was the investigation of a model for the self-organized formation of a topographically ordered somatosensory map, they also illustrate a typical methodological difficulty in the investigation of neural models: even if highly abstract approaches are used, such as Kohonen's model of self-organizing maps, the simulation of biological neural nets still requires in many cases an enormous computational effort. The previous sections demonstrate by means of an example how in such a situation a partial mathematical analysis can reduce the simulation effort to a more manageable level. However, such a simplification usually involves additional approximations and thus can no longer describe some properties of the original model. In the case of the somatosensory map, the introduction of the low-dimensional "effective dynamics" by means of (111) does offer the possibility of describing the average size of the receptive fields, but detailed questions concerning the form of receptive fields, such as the possibility of the formation of multiple centers (defined as a cortical neuron receiving input from two or more distinct areas of the hand surface), are excluded through this simplification, although these questions could have been addressed in the framework of the original model.

Therefore, even if there is some possibility of mathematical simplification, the capacity to carry out detailed simulations of the model in its original formulation is desirable. This capacity is offered by a new generation of high-performance computers, whose architecture, interestingly enough, is strongly influenced by the structure of neural systems. One of the most well-known computers of this kind, the "Connection Machine," can use 65,768 one-bit processors in parallel (Hillis 1985). Each of these processors is equipped with its own memory, and the data communication paths between the processors can be configured by software in such a way as to realize various lattice topologies. This offers the possibility of a very natural and direct "mapping" of neural algorithms and models onto the processors of this computer. In the following section, we report on some results of a simulation of Kohonen's model that were carried out on such a machine (Obermayer, Ritter, and Schulten 1989, 1990a,b).

The simulation again concerns the formation of a somatosensory map. This time, our point of departure is a "model cortex" consisting of 16,384 neurons arranged in a 128×128 square-lattice. Each neuron possesses synaptic connections to 800 touch receptors which are distributed stochastically over the hand surface (see Fig. 7.9a). Each neuron is assigned, along with the 800 values of its synaptic connections, to one processor of the Connection Machine. For each neuron, its 800 connection strengths to the receptors are initialized to independently chosen random values. Figure 7.9b illustrates this for a randomly selected neuron r: each receptor location is marked by a small spot, the brightness of which is proportional to the strength of the connection from the receptor to the selected neuron. The receptor excitation pattern caused by a touch stimulus is assumed to follow in its intensity a Gaussian centered at some location $\mathbf{v}_{stim}$, *i.e.*,

$$\nu_\alpha \propto \exp\Big(-(\mathbf{v}_\alpha - \mathbf{v}_{stim})^2/2a^2\Big).$$

The centers $\mathbf{v}_{stim}$ of the successive touch stimuli are scattered randomly over the complete hand surface. However, in contrast to the model using the "effective dynamics" simplification, every touch stimulus is now described by a 800-dimensional vector $(\nu_1, \nu_2, \ldots, \nu_{800})^T$, and the adaptation process takes place in the space of the 16,384 weight vectors $w_\mathbf{r} = (w_{\mathbf{r}1}, w_{\mathbf{r}2}, \ldots, w_{\mathbf{r}800})^T$,

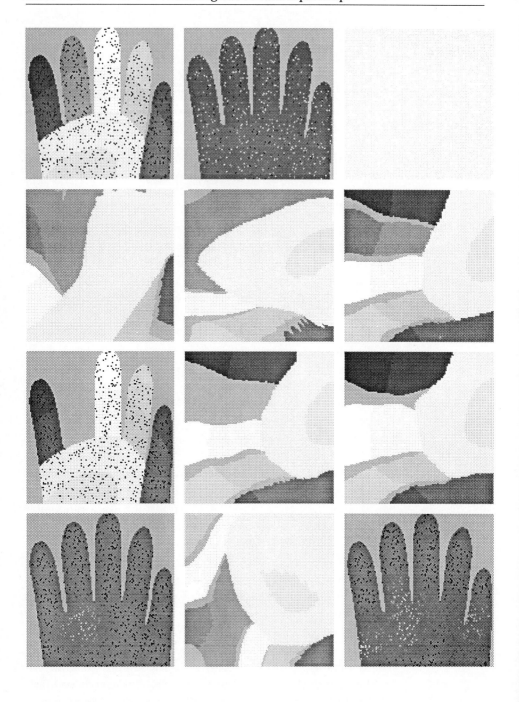

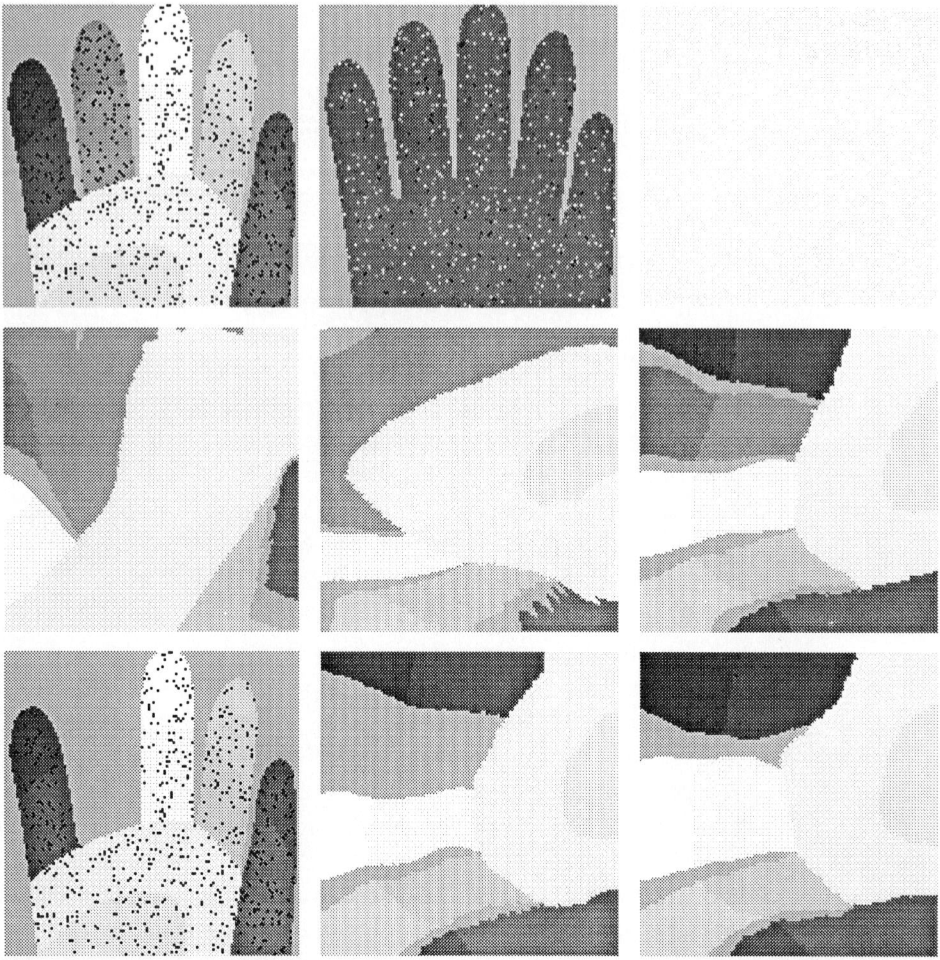

Figure 7.9 Formation of a somatosensory map. From upper left to lower right: Fig. 7.9a–l. For explanation see Section 7.5.

each of dimension 800 (for additional details of the simulation, see Obermayer, Ritter, and Schulten 1990a,b).

The figures 7.9c–f show the development of the somatotopic map. Each picture shows a view of the 128×128 model cortex, where each pixel corresponds to one neuron. To identify for each neuron the source of its receptor input, the same gray values as in Fig. 7.9a are used, *i.e.*, the gray value at a location $\mathbf{r}$ indicates which hand region of Fig. 7.9a contains the center of gravity $\tilde{\mathbf{w}}_{\mathbf{r}}$ of the receptors exciting neuron $\mathbf{r}$. The nearly uniform gray in Fig. 7.9c is a consequence of the initially random connectivity: each cell is "diffusely" connected to nearly the complete hand surface and all centers of gravity lie approximately in the central part of the hand surface. After about 200 touch stimuli, a specialization of the neurons begins to emerge (7.9d). After 1200 touch stimuli, this specialization has progressed further, and the correct topographic arrangement is already evident for four of the finger regions. After 10,000 touch stimuli, a complete and well-resolved topographic map of the hand surface has emerged (7.9f). Figs. 7.9g and 7.9h show a repeat of the "amputation experiment" depicted in Figs. 7.6 and 7.7. Figure 7.9g shows the region of the map which is deprived of its former input signals after the "amputation" of a finger. After a further 10,000 adaptive steps, the map has readjusted itself (7.9h) so that the representation of the fingers adjacent to the amputated digit has expanded to partially fill the "silent" region.

Figure 7.9j shows a typical "receptive field" of a cell from the map of Fig. 7.5f. A good spatial localization is discernible, and the extension of the field corresponds approximately to the diameter of the receptor excitation pattern caused by a touch stimulus. Figure 7.9k shows an only partially ordered map from another simulation run. Here, a "doubling" map of the sensory surface has formed. Such maps frequently contain cells the receptive fields of which have multiple centers as shown in Fig. 7.9l. Such cells are also encountered in the somatosensory cortex, but they are apparently rare. The investigation of the formation and the role of such receptive fields is an important motivation for carrying out simulations of this kind.

This aspect is even more evident in more complex maps such as those which occur in the visual cortex. There, signals from two sensory surfaces, the two retinas, are combined into one map. Aside from the information on the spatial location of a light stimulus, "ocularity information," *i.e.*, information about the origin of stimuli from the right or the left eye, as well as information about the orientation of, for example, brightness edges, is represented topographically in the map. This high-dimensional simulation model offers an extremely valuable tool for a theoretical understanding of the formation of such maps. The simulations, again performed on a Connection Machine, yield very close agreement to the visual maps observed in the striate cortex of monkeys, reproducing well the retinotopic characteristics as well as the organization of orientation columns and occularity stripes (see Obermayer, Ritter, and Schulten 1990c; Obermayer, Blasdel, and Schulten 1991).

In the brain such topographically ordered maps serve as the initial processing stages of sensory information. Subsequent cortical areas have the task of re-coding the received information step by step and transforming it into an appropriate form for the eventual control of muscles, which constitute the main output targets of the nervous system. However, in practically all cases, we are still far from understanding most of the phenomena that participate in that process. This is partly due to the fact that we often cannot precisely characterize the processing stages that are involved in the behavior of even simple organisms. For certain stages, however, the situation is a bit less unfavorable, particularly for such aspects of motor coordination that can be described mathematically as control problems or coordinate transformations. In Part III we therefore extend Kohonen's model in a suitable way to enable the solution of such problems. However, it would be improper to seek close biological correspondences. Instead, our intention will be to investigate biologically motivated model assumptions with respect to their performance in solving more complex problems, in particular those that biological nervous systems have to face.

III

Self-Organizing Motor Maps

8. Extension of Kohonen's Model

In the preceding chapters, motivated by the important role of topology-conserving maps in the brain, we considered a stochastic learning algorithm which, based only on a random sequence of sensory signals, generates such maps on a lattice of formal neurons. The aim of these maps was to represent the neighborhood relationships between the input signals in a two-dimensional, nonlinear projection as faithfully as possible.

8.1. Motor Maps

The brain cannot limit itself, however, to the representation of sensory input signals alone, but must also solve the complementary task of sending appropriate signals to the muscle system to react to the sensory input. The brain regions that are responsible for these tasks, such as the *motor cortex* and the *superior colliculus*, appear in many cases to be organized in a way similar to the sensory areas, *i.e.*, as maps that react to localized excitation by triggering a movement. This movement varies in a regular way with the focus of the excitation in the layer. Therefore, the layer can be considered as a *motor map* in which movement commands are mapped to two-dimensional locations of excitation (Lemon 1988).

By way of an abstraction that can also serve as a model for such motor maps, we consider in this chapter topology-conserving maps in which we additionally allow, as an extension of Kohonen's original learning algorithm, the storage of an *output* specific for each lattice point (Ritter and Schulten, 1986b, 1987, 1988). As we will see, the formation of a map then corresponds to the *learning of a control task.* The type of the output value can be, for example, a scalar, a vector, or a linear operator, *i.e.*, a tensor.

Several neural mechanisms for the storage of such outputs can be imagined. The information could be stored by a suitable selection of connections to subsequent motor neurons. Linear mappings could be realized by "de-inhibition" of local neuron groups. Furthermore, local "assemblies" of neurons also could act as local associative memories for the storage of more complex information. Such a neural network would form an active storage medium that reacts to a local activation caused by an input signal with the response stored at the site of excitation. Stored data are arranged in such a way that similar data are stored in spatial proximity to each other. A thoroughly investigated example of such organization, involving the case of a vectorial output quantity, is the *motor map* in the so-called *superior colliculus,* a mounded, multi-layered neuron sheet in the upper region of the brain stem (Sparks and Nelson 1987). In this sheet there are neurons which, when excited, trigger the execution of rapid eye movements (*saccades*). Usually, such excitation is caused by neurons located in the more superficial layers that process sensory signals. Through electrical stimulations by inserted electrodes, this excitation can also be induced artificially. Such experiments demonstrate that the resulting change of the vector of view direction varies in a regular fashion with the location of excitation in the layer. In Chapter 9 we will discuss more closely this example of a motor map and the control of saccades.

In much the same way as maps are learned or are adaptively modifiable, the assignment of output values to lattice sites must be plastic. Consequently, a learning algorithm is also required for the output values. In the following chapter we will show that with an appropriate algorithm the learning of the output values can benefit substantially from the neighborhood-, and hence, continuity-preserving spatial arrangement of the values within a map.

In the following we again onsider a space V of input signals and a lattice A of formal neurons. As in Chapter 4, $\phi_{\mathbf{w}}$ denotes the mapping of V onto A that is specified by the synaptic strengths. In addition, for maps intended to be used for motor control tasks, an output value $w_{\mathbf{r}}^{(out)}$ is assigned to each neuron

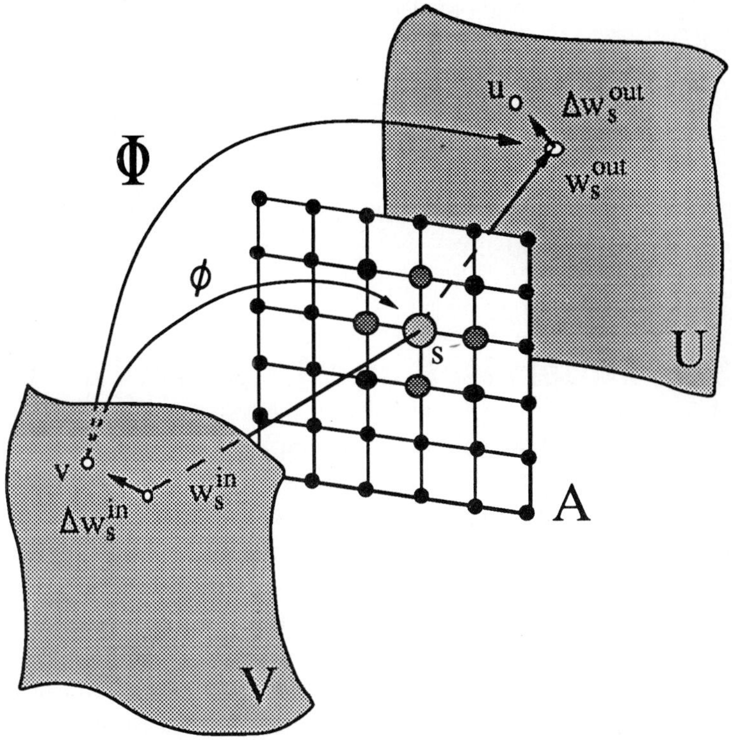

Figure 8.1 The extended model with the inclusion of output values. Each formal neuron s of the neuron layer (lattice A) has, in addition to its pre-existing weight vector $\mathbf{w}_\mathbf{s}^{in}$, a vector $\mathbf{w}_\mathbf{s}^{out}$ of output values assigned to it. A learning step now requires, with each presentation of an input vector $\mathbf{v}$, the specification of a corresponding output value u. The adaptation of the output values $\mathbf{w}_\mathbf{s}^{out}$ is completely analogous to the scheme used for the "input side:" all neurons in the vicinity of the particular neuron selected by the input value shift their output vectors towards the specified output value u.

r. (Here, as before, $w_\mathbf{r}^{(out)}$ can be a vectorial or tensorial value). Since the synaptic strengths, so far denoted by $\mathbf{w}$, determine the correspondence between *input signals* and neurons, we will denote them in this chapter by $\mathbf{w}^{(in)}$ so that they will not be confused with the recently introduced output values $\mathbf{w}^{(out)}$.

Together, all $\mathbf{w}_\mathbf{r}^{(out)}$ form a covering of the lattice with values in a second space U and extend the mapping $\phi_\mathbf{w}$ from V onto the lattice to a mapping Φ of V into the space U, given by

$$\Phi : V \mapsto U, \quad \mathbf{v} \mapsto \Phi(\mathbf{v}) := w_{\phi_{\mathbf{w}(\mathbf{v})}}^{(out)}. \tag{119}$$

Fig. 8.1 offers an illustration of this situation. In accordance with the motor maps formerly mentioned, we want to investigate mappings defined in this way, especially with regards to motor control tasks. In this case $\mathbf{v}$ represents the present state of the system which is to be controlled, and $\mathbf{w}_\mathbf{r}^{out}$ determines the required control action. This control action can specify a value for a *displacement*, a *force*, or a *torque* (Chapters 8, 9, and 13), or it can specify a *linear mapping* that determines these values in terms of the intended target state of the motion (Chapters 11 and 12).

8.2. Supervised and Unsupervised Learning

We begin with the simplest case, namely, that of a control task for which a sequence of correct *input-output pairs* $(\mathbf{v}, u)$ are available. Here, $\mathbf{v}$ denotes the system state and u the correct control action associated with that state (Ritter and Schulten 1987). This situation corresponds to *supervised learning* and requires the opportunity for observing the correct control, provided by a "teacher" for a sufficiently extended period of time. The synaptic strengths $\mathbf{w}_\mathbf{r}$ and the output values $w_\mathbf{r}^{(out)}$ are initialized with values chosen without any a priori information. They can be initialized, for example, with random values. The purpose of the learning process is a gradual improvement of the initial mapping Φ with the goal of an increasingly better imitation of the teacher's actions by Φ. This can be realized by the following algorithm:

1. Record the next control action $(\mathbf{v}, u)$.
2. Determine the lattice site $\mathbf{s} := \phi_\mathbf{w}(\mathbf{v})$ whose input weight vector $\mathbf{w}_\mathbf{s}^{(in)}$ best matches the present system state $\mathbf{v}$.
3. Perform a learning step

$$\Delta \mathbf{w}_\mathbf{r}^{(in)} = \mathbf{w}_\mathbf{r}^{(in)} + \epsilon h_{\mathbf{rs}}(\mathbf{v} - \mathbf{w}_\mathbf{r}^{(in)})$$

   for the input weight vectors $\mathbf{w}_\mathbf{r}^{(in)}$.
4. Perform a learning step

$$\Delta w_\mathbf{r}^{(out)} = w_\mathbf{r}^{(out)} + \epsilon' h'_{\mathbf{rs}}(u - w_\mathbf{r}^{(out)})$$

   for the set of output values $w_\mathbf{r}^{(out)}$ and return to step 1.

Steps 1–3 describe Kohonen's original algorithm for the formation of a topology conserving map on A. They are depicted in the front part of Fig. 8.1 where the different sizes and shades of the neurons in the vicinity of s indicate the shape and extent of the excitation zone as determined by the function $h_{\mathbf{rs}}$. The new step, step 4, changes the output values $w_{\mathbf{r}}^{(out)}$ assigned across A. This change is indicated in the rear part of Fig. 8.1. It occurs in an analogous manner to that of the learning step for the synaptic strengths $w_{\mathbf{r}}^{(in)}$, possibly with different learning step widths ϵ' and a different interaction function $h'_{\mathbf{rs}}$ as demanded by each situation. (This symmetric treatment of input values v and output values u can be mathematically interpreted in such a way that now the algorithm creates a topology-conserving mapping of a subset Γ of the product space $V \otimes U$ onto A. Here the subset Γ is just the set of the input-output values $(\mathbf{v}, u)$ provided by the teacher; *i.e.*, it is the graph of the input-output relation that correctly describes the control law.)

The proposed process creates, in the course of the learning phase, a look-up table for the function Φ (see (119)). The particular advantage of this process lies in the high adaptability of the table structure. The correspondence between table entries and input values is not rigidly specified from the outset, but instead develops in the course of the learning phase. This occurs in such a way that the table entries become distributed $(\mathbf{w}_{\mathbf{r}}^{(in)}, w_{\mathbf{r}}^{(out)})$ according to the required density of the control actions in the space $V \otimes U$. Regions in $V \otimes U$, from which control actions are frequently needed, are assigned a correspondingly higher number of table entries, resulting in a higher resolution of the input-output relation in these areas. Rarely or never used table entries are "redevoted." This facilitates a very economic use of the available storage space.

Due to the topology-conserving character of the assignment between value pairs and storage space, neighboring memory locations in the lattice A are usually assigned similar value pairs. In the case of a continuous relationship between input and output values, adjacent memory locations must, therefore, learn similar output values $w_{\mathbf{r}}^{(out)}$. Spreading the effect of learning steps for the output values $w_{\mathbf{r}}^{(out)}$ by virtue of the interaction function $h'_{\mathbf{rs}}$ into the vicinity of each selected storage location r represents a rudimentary form of generalization which accelerates the course of learning. If the function $h_{\mathbf{rs}}$ is given a long range at the beginning of the learning phase, then a large subset of all storage locations participates in each learning step, even if the learning steps for most of them are only approximately "correct." By this, a complete table, representing a good approximation to the correct input-output relation, can already develop after significantly fewer learning steps than there are storage locations. By gradually reducing the range of the function h_{rs} in the course of the learning phase the participation of storage locations at each learning step becomes increasingly more selective, so that eventually even fine details of the input-output relation can be learned.

In many cases, however, there is no teacher available, and the correct control actions must be found by the learning algorithm itself (*unsupervised learning*). The only source of information available in this case is a "reward function," which specifies at a given moment how well the control has mastered the given task. To execute the above algorithm the system must now create, at each learning step, the component u that in the previous case was delivered by the teacher. In the absence of any further information this requires a stochastic search in the space U of the available values, with the aim to maximize the "reward" received at each step.

8.3. The "Pole-Balancing Problem"

To demonstrate the learning algorithm, defined in the previous section by steps 1–4, we consider as a prototypical problem the task of balancing a vertical pole in a gravitational field by appropriate movements of the base of the pole. This is a favorite problem for the investigation of learning algorithms, and it has already been studied in connection with previous neural network approaches (Barto and Sutton 1983). As in the present case, these studies were directed at learning the connection between movement states of the pole and the required control forces in the form of a look-up table. In contrast to the approach presented here, the goal of the former studies was not to obtain an optimal organization of this table by an adaptive distribution of its entries over the state space. Instead, the connection between the table entries and states was initially given in a rigid way, and the focus of interest was the investigation of learning rules which gradually set the table entries using as the only criterion of success the absence of a signal indicating that the pole has fallen over.

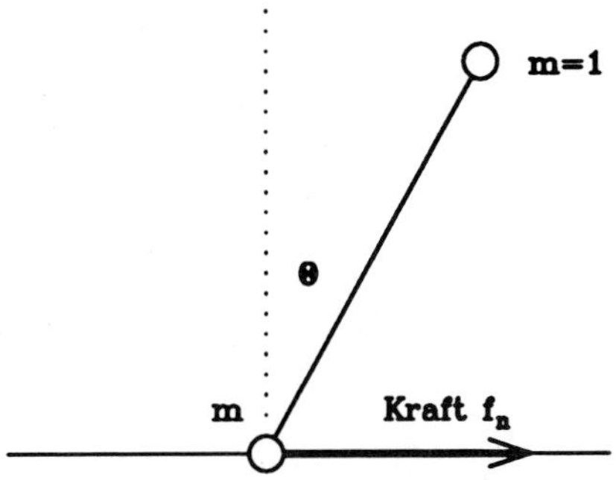

Figure 8.2 Model of the pole in the simulation. The bottom end of the pole can slide without friction along a horizontal line. By an appropriate force f the pole is to be balanced in the position $\theta = 0^0$. Units are shown such that the mass at the top end of the pole, the pole length, and the acceleration due to gravity all have values of unity. The mass at the bottom end is m. The shaft is assumed to be massless.

The motion of the pole is imitated by a computer simulation. A massless rod of unit length serves as the pole, with point masses of values m and unity at its bottom and top end, respectively. The motion of the pole is restricted to a vertical plane, and the bottom of the pole is confined to slide along the x-axis. The pole and its two degrees of freedom are presented in Fig. 8.2. For a gravitational field directed downward with unit strength, the equation of motion of the pole is

$$(m + \sin^2\theta)\ddot{\theta} + \frac{1}{2}\dot{\theta}^2 \sin(2\theta) - (m+1)\sin\theta = -f\cos\theta. \qquad (120)$$

Here, θ is the pole angle measured clockwise against the vertical, f is the horizontal force acting at the bottom end. The motion of the pole is simulated by the Runge-Kutta method using a time step of 0.1 in the units of Eq. (120).

8.4. Supervised Pole-Balancing

The first simulation demonstrates supervised learning. The Adoptation of a new movement often requires an adaptation period composed of partial, goal-oriented movements which must come together before the total course can be executed fluently and automatically. This indicates that in this phase a higher brain region might play the role of a teacher for a subor-

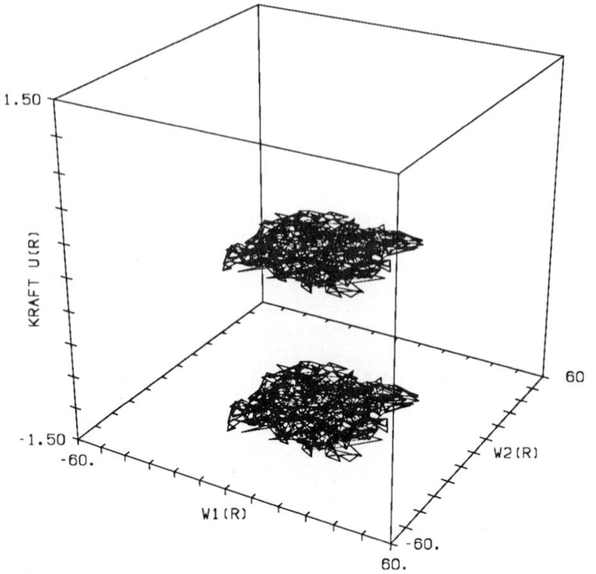

Figure 8.3 Initial state of the simulation. For each lattice point $\mathbf{r}$ the stored output force $w_{\mathbf{r}}^{(out)}$ is recorded along the vertical axis above the point $(w_{\mathbf{r}1}^{(in)}, w_{\mathbf{r}2}^{(in)})$ of the two-dimensional space V of input signals. $(w_{\mathbf{r}1}^{(in)}, w_{\mathbf{r}2}^{(in)})$ represents a pair of successive inclinations of the pole, at the occurrence of which the lattice delivers $w_{\mathbf{r}}^{(out)}$ as a control force. In the beginning all forces are chosen to be zero, and to each lattice site $\mathbf{r}$ a point, randomly selected from the square $[-30°, 30°] \times [-30°, 30°] \subset V$, is assigned.

dinate neural structure until the latter can execute the movement independently and without requiring conscious attention.

In the present simulation the neural network was chosen to be a lattice A of 25×25 formal neurons. Each formal neuron r is characterized by a two-dimensional vector $\mathbf{w}_{\mathbf{r}}^{(in)}$ and an output value $w_{\mathbf{r}}^{(out)}$. The vectors $\mathbf{w}_{\mathbf{r}}^{(in)}$ determine the correspondence between neurons and motion states of the pole, and the output values $w_{\mathbf{r}}^{(out)}$ are the forces to be applied. In this example the teacher has to deliver, for each motion state $(\theta, \dot{\theta})$, a force $f^L(\theta, \dot{\theta})$ that ensures the intended pole balance. In the simulation this force was chosen as

$$f^L(\theta, \dot{\theta}) = 5 \sin\theta + \dot{\theta}. \qquad (121)$$

The pole was controlled by choosing a force f_n at equidistant time instants $t_n = n\Delta t$, $\Delta t = 0.3$ and applying this force at the bottom of the pole until time t_{n+1}. At each time instant t_n the

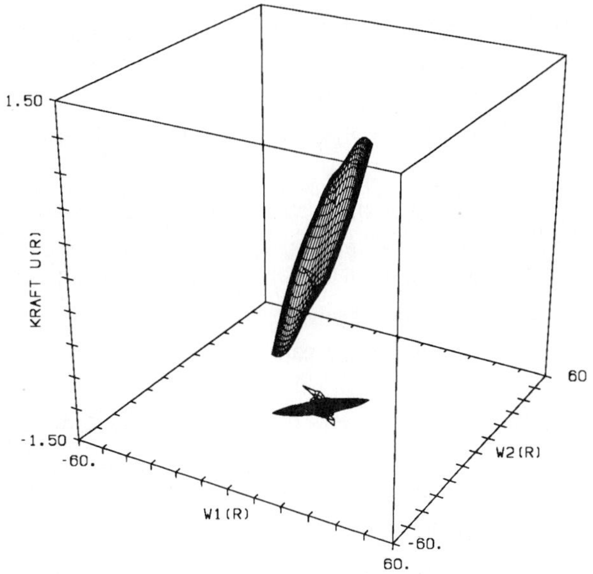

Figure 8.4 After 200 learning steps, most neurons have become asssociated with input values that are concentrated in a narrow region along the diagonal $w_1^{(in)} = w_2^{(in)}$. In the vicinity of $(0^0, 0^0)$ the learned output values already correspond quite well to the actions of the teacher.

learning steps 1-4 were executed for

$$(\mathbf{v}, u) = (v_1, v_2, u) := \Big(\theta(t_n), \theta(t_{n-1}), f^L(\theta(t_n), \dot{\theta}(t_n))\Big). \quad (122)$$

The force f_n for the next time step was determined according to

$$f_n = \alpha(t_n) w^{(out)}_{\phi_{\mathbf{w}}(\mathbf{v})} + (1 - \alpha(t_n)) f^L(\theta(t_n), \dot{\theta}(t_n)). \quad (123)$$

Here $w^{(out)}_{\phi_{\mathbf{w}}(\mathbf{v})}$ is the force proposed by A at the time t_n, and $\alpha(t)$ is a function that increases gradually from $\alpha = 0$ to $\alpha = 1$. Consequently, the control is initially done exclusively by the teacher, but it is gradually taken over by A until eventually at $\alpha = 1$, the neural net has completely replaced the teacher.

At the end of the learning phase, the map has learned to imitate the behavior of the teacher. One may object that by this procedure no new information has been gained because the solution of the balancing problem was already provided by the teacher. Nonetheless, this objection denies that an essential result of the learning process lies in the coding of the information in a new way, namely, as an optimized look-up table. The latter obviates recalculation of the correct control actions previously required at each time step; now, only a simple table look-up is required. In all cases where a recalculation is more wasteful or slower than a simple table look-up, a gain in efficiency will result.

The other data used in our simulations were $\sigma(n) = 6 \cdot (0.5)^{n/n_f}$, $h_{\mathbf{rs}} = h'_{\mathbf{rs}} = \exp[-\|\mathbf{r}-\mathbf{s}\|^2/\sigma(n)^2]$, $\epsilon(n) = \epsilon'(n) = 0.5 \cdot (0.04)^{n/n_f}$, $n_f = 1000$ and $m = 1$.

The learning phase consisted of a sequence of trials. At the beginning of each trial the pole was released from rest at an initial, randomly chosen angle $\theta \in [-30°, 30°]$. The pole was then balanced by the forces f_n either until the pole fell over, (Criterion: $|\theta(t_n)| > 60°$), or until 100 time steps had passed. Subsequently, the simulation was continued with a new trial until a total of $n_f = 1000$ time steps were completed.

Figures 8.3–8.5 show the development of the mapping Φ in the course of the simulation. Φ is displayed as a mesh surface in the $w_1^{(in)}$-$w_2^{(in)}$-$w^{(out)}$-space. At the beginning random pair values $w_1^{(in)}$-$w_2^{(in)}$ from the subset $[-30^0, 30^0] \times [-30^0, 30^0]$, together with a force $w_{\mathbf{r}}^{(out)} = 0$, were assigned to each neuron $\mathbf{r}$ (Fig. 8.3).

After 100 time steps most of the neurons have become associated with angle pairs in the vicinity of the diagonal $w_1^{(in)} = w_2^{(in)}$ and have roughly learned the corresponding forces (Fig. 8.4). Finally, after 1000 time steps, the result depicted in Fig. 8.5 is obtained. Now all neurons are associated with a narrow region near the diagonal $w_1^{(in)} = w_2^{(in)}$. This region represents, under the chosen coding of each state by two sequential angles, those states of the pole that are particularly important for the balancing problem (Fig. 8.6). The representation by neurons is especially dense in the vicinity of $(0°, 0°)$, because for these values forces are most frequently requested during the balancing. Figure 8.7 displays the learned balancing behavior after 200 steps (light curves) and after 1000 steps (heavy curves). The top diagram depicts the time course of the pole angle $\theta(t)$, which is monitored after release of the pole from rest and using the control furnished by A in the absence of a teacher, *i.e.*, for $\alpha = 1$. After 200 learning steps an initial angle of 20° away from vertical is handled well; at the end of the simulation even a trial starting with $\theta(0) = 30°$ succeeds. The bottom diagram shows the response of A for both cases.

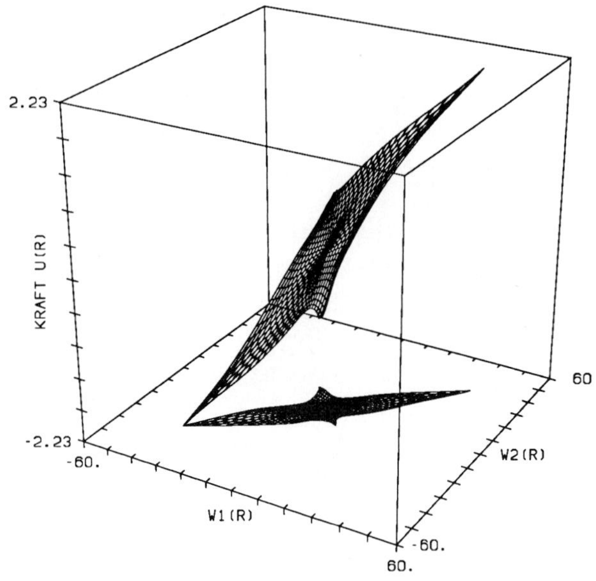

Figure 8.5 The stage reached after 1000 learning steps at the end of the simulation. All neurons have attached themselves to the part of the graph which is most important for the pole balancing, in accordance with the input-output relation delivered by the teacher. Since $w_1^{(in)}$, $w_2^{(in)}$ stands for sequential pole orientations, points with a small difference $w_1^{(in)} - w_2^{(in)}$ correspond to most of the pole states. The region of the represented differences is broader in the vicinity of the point $(0^0, 0^0)$ since near this point higher velocities occur on average than at the turning points. Also, the resolution is particularly high near $(0^0, 0^0)$ because forces are requested most frequently for these pole states.

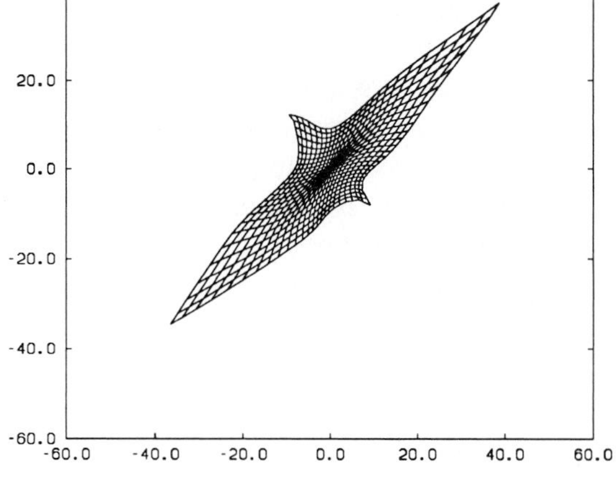

Figure 8.6 This graph depicts, in the $w_1^{(in)} - w_2^{(in)}$-plane, the mapping between lattice locations and those angle pairs $w_1^{(in)}, w_2^{(in)}$ which are important for the balancing process.

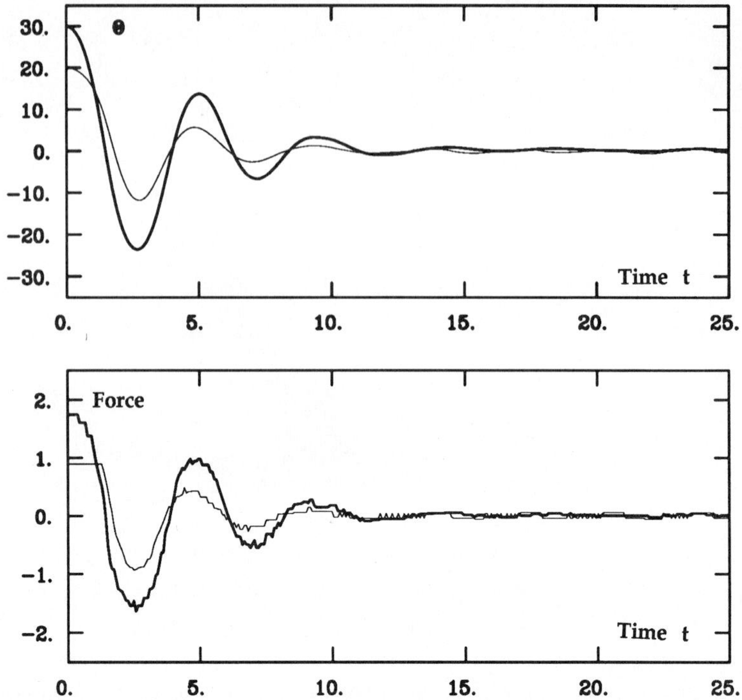

Figure 8.7 Balancing performance after 200 (light curves) and after 1000 learning steps (heavy curves). The curves in the top diagram show the time course of the pole angle θ after 200 learning steps. The pole was released from angles of 20^0 and 30^0, after 200 and 1000 learning steps, respectively. The bottom diagram displays the time course of the force that was applied by A.

8.5. Unsupervised Pole-Balancing

In the following, second simulation, the balancing of the pole is learned without a teacher by means of a "reward function" *(unsupervised learning).* In contrast to the teacher the reward function no longer directly specifies a suitable force, but only indicates "how well" the resulting state complies with the given task. An appropriate reward function for the balancing task is, *e.g.,*

$$R(\theta) = -\theta^2. \tag{124}$$

This function "rewards" vertical ($\theta \approx 0°$) orientations of the pole. As before, the lattice site s is selected by the pole motion at each time step. Since the teacher is no longer present, a force

f_n for a particular step is now determined by the selected lattice site s only. The learning goal is to find a force which yields a maximal increase of the reward function R towards the end of each time step. In the absence of any further information this can be accomplished in the most general way by a stochastic search process.†

Every time that s is chosen (step 2), instead of the most recently found output value $w_{\mathbf{s}}^{(out)}$ for f_n, the modified value

$$f_n := w_{\mathbf{s}}^{(out)} + a_{\mathbf{s}} \cdot \eta \tag{125}$$

is used. Here η is a Gaussian random variable with zero mean and unit variance, and $a_{\mathbf{s}} > 0$ is a new parameter that determines the mean value of the search step for lattice location s. The adaptation steps 3 and 4 are executed with $u = f_n$ only when, at the end of a time step, the increase ΔR of the reward function that has been caused by f_n exceeds the averaged increase $b_{\mathbf{s}}$ gained so far at lattice site s. The consequence of this is that A learns only from "actions" which lead to an improved performance, and thus A continually improves itself.

The mean increase of the reward function $b_{\mathbf{s}}$, necessary in addition to $a_{\mathbf{s}}$, has to be updated after each selection of s by using the actual increase ΔR that has been reached. This can be most simply accomplished by the instruction

$$b_{\mathbf{s}}^{new} = b_{\mathbf{s}}^{old} + \gamma(\Delta R - b_{\mathbf{s}}^{old}). \tag{126}$$

The effect of the latter procedure is a low-pass filtering and a corresponding "smoothing" of the most recent updates of the reward function with a time constant given by γ^{-1}.

At the beginning the average search step width $a_{\mathbf{s}}$ should be sufficiently large for each lattice location in order to rapidly find an approximately correct force. Each time an s is selected that has the opportunity to act, $a_{\mathbf{s}}$ is diminished. Therefore, the number of search steps for each lattice site is reduced as more experience is gained, and the stored output value can gradually converge. Because the neighboring lattice sites $\mathbf{r} \neq \mathbf{s}$

---

†More efficient searching methods can be applied when certain types of additional information are available. For example, one could use the differentiability of R and could replace the stochastic search method by the gradient descent method, which avoids searching steps in the "wrong" direction. Because we are less interested in variations of the detailed design for each application and would rather focus on a representation of the method's general structure, we will stay with the generally applicable stochastic search method.

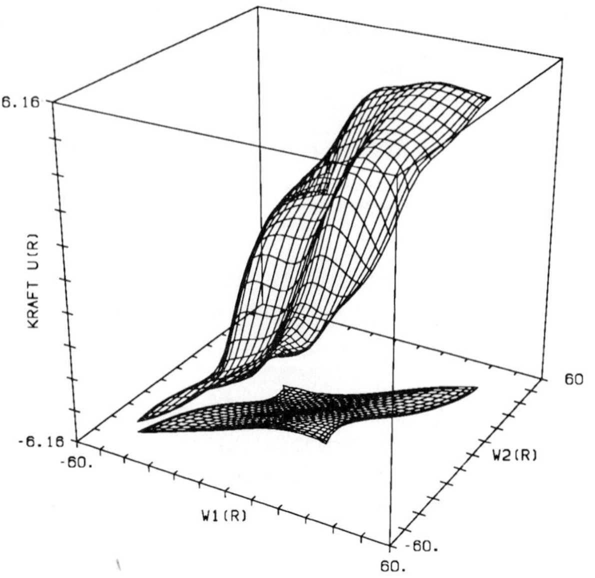

Figure 8.8 The association between pole motion states and control forces as it has been learned after 3000 learning steps without a teacher by using the reward function R (displayed as in Fig. 8.3-8.5). Again the states along the diagonal of the $w_1^{(in)}$, $w_2^{(in)}$ plane, *i.e.*, with a small difference $w_1^{(in)} - w_2^{(in)}$, are represented particularly well. For deviations from the vertical position the learned forces increase more strongly than in the simulation presented in Fig. 8.5 and lead to very rapid corrective adjustments of deviations from vertical.

are also involved in every adaption step of s (steps 3 and 4), the corresponding $a_{\mathbf{r}}$ are reduced in the same way as the $a_{\mathbf{s}}$. In analogy with steps 3 and 4, this can be achieved by including the following additional step.

5. Adaptation rule for the search step widths:

$$a_{\mathbf{r}}^{new} = a_{\mathbf{r}}^{old} + \epsilon'' h''_{\mathbf{rs}}(a - a_{\mathbf{r}}^{old}).$$

Here a is equal for all steps and defines the threshold towards which the search step widths should converge over long periods of time. If one intends for $w_{\mathbf{r}}^{(out)}$ to converge, one chooses $a = 0$. If one wishes a residual plasticity to remain for the capability of later readaptation under slow changes, one assigns a small corresponding positive value to a. The additional parameters ϵ'' and $h''_{\mathbf{rs}}$ (step 5) are varied analogously to ϵ and $h_{\mathbf{rs}}$, and ϵ' and $h'_{\mathbf{rs}}$, respectively.

For the simulation we chose $h''_{\mathbf{rs}} = h'_{\mathbf{rs}} = h_{\mathbf{rs}}$ where $h_{\mathbf{rs}}$ has the values of the simulation in Section 8.4. $\sigma(n)$ and $\epsilon(n)$ were

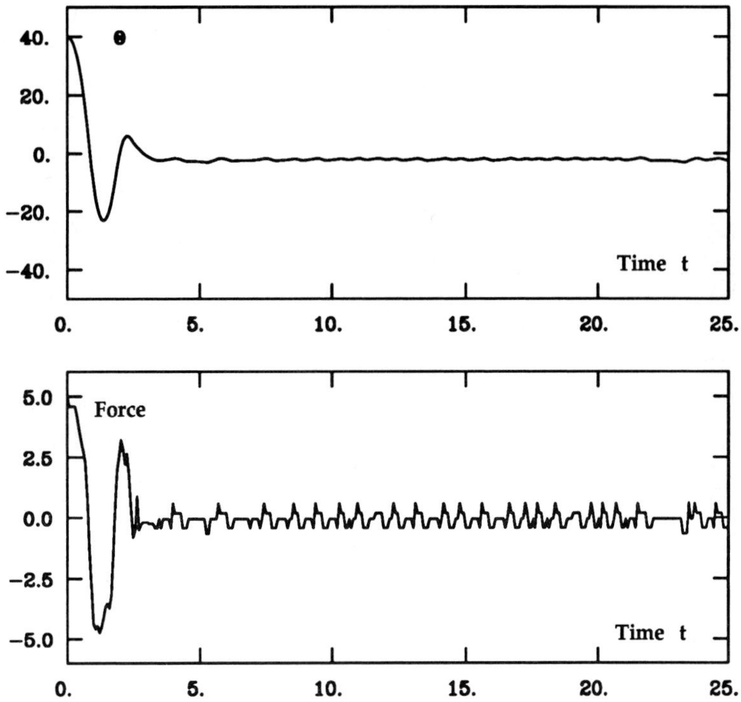

Figure 8.9 Pole-balance after 3000 learning steps using the reward function R. The top diagram shows how the pole angle θ changes in time after the pole has been released from a rest position $\theta = 40°$. The bottom diagram shows the corresponding control force that was applied.

chosen as in Section 8.4 but with $n_f = 3000$. Other quantities in the simulation were $\epsilon' = 0.2$, $\epsilon'' = 0.005$, $a = 0$, $\gamma = 0.05$. At the beginning of the simulation all averaged search step widths were set to $a_{\mathbf{r}} = 1$. The initial estimators $b_{\mathbf{r}}$ for the changes of the reward function were set to zero.

Starting with the same initial state as for supervised learning (Fig. 8.3) and with the parameters just given, the connection between pole motion states and control forces $w^{(out)}$ evolved as depicted in Fig. 8.8 in the course of 3000 learning steps. Again the preponderance of values along the $w_1^{(in)} - w_2^{(in)}$ main diagonal can be seen, particularly in the vicinity of $(0°, 0°)$. The resulting dependence of the control force on the pole positions evolves qualitatively as before, but has a steeper slope at deviations from $(0°, 0°)$, indicating a very rapid correction of any deviations from vertical. This is demonstrated in Fig. 8.9 where one can observe the time variation of the pole angle θ (top diagram) and the learned forces f (bottom diagram) that occur after the pole has been released from an initial angle of 40° from vertical.

Problems similar to the pole-balancing problem also arise in connection with upright walking, rendering the pole-balancing solution interesting for biological organisms as well as in robotics. Of presumably even higher interest, as far as applications are concerned, is the control of arm motions, especially under visual supervision. Chapters 10 and 11 are devoted to these issues. In the next chapter, however, we will first consider an issue with a biological background, namely the control of rapid eye movements that serve to center a visual object on the retina and, thus, solve the task of "visual grasping." This latter task is taken up in Chapter 9 which then leads naturally into issues in robotics.

9. The Oculomotor System: a Biological Example

9.1. Oculomotor Control and Superior Colliculus

When reading, looking at a painting, or steering a car the eyes make numerous movements, most of which consist of short, jerky jumps called *saccades*. Saccades function to direct a small, slightly deepened region (the *fovea*) in the center of the retina towards particular locations in the visual field. An extraordinarily high number of light sensitive cells reside in the fovea, providing particularly high resolution of any object whose image resides there. As soon as the attention of an observer is caught by an object the image of which is outside of the fovea, a saccade moves the eyeball such that the image leaps into the fovea. When reading, for example, only a few letters can be simultaneously in focus, and even single words longer than two or three letters must be viewed piecewise by successive saccades. Most of the time, the saccade traverses an angle between four minutes and forty degrees (Korn 1982). Larger changes in direction usually occur only when the eyes and head move simultaneously.

The control of eye movements, the oculomotor control, has often been the subject of neurophysiological investigations. The advantage one has in investigating the oculomotor system stems from the particularly close relation between eye motions and motor nerve signals. Due to the relatively small and constant mass of the eyeball and the capability of the muscle apparatus of the eye to react with a comparatively large and extremely rapid deployment of force, inertial effects play only a minor role, and the motions of the eyeball provide an accurate mapping of the nerve signals that control the muscle.

It is not precisely known where the decision is made concerning which object of the visual field should be in the primary focus. Clinical findings lead to the inference that parts of the *parietal lobe* play a vital role in this decision process (Wurtz et al. 1986). Experiments have shown that the saccades are triggered in the *superior colliculus*, a mounded, multilayered neuron sheet that is located in the upper region of the brain stem (Sparks and Nelson 1987). The relation between the location of receptors on the retina which are, *e.g.*, excited by a small light point, and the place of neurons in the upper layer of the *superior colliculus* that are simultaneously excited, is continuous and topology conserving. This implies that a topographic *sensory map* from the retina to the upper layer of the *superior colliculus*, a so-called *retinotopic map*, is realized. In contrast to that, and essential for the saccadic control of eye movements, the lower layer provides an example of a *motor map* similar to the one described in Chapter 8. Locations in this layer correspond in an ordered way to saccadic changes in view direction that can be triggered by excitation of neurons at the corresponding locations. Such excitations can be artificially created by stimulation via inserted electrodes. With excitations thus invoked, the direction of the saccades turns out to be quite independent from the intensity of the stimulus; rather, their direction is mainly determined by the *location of the stimulus* in the layer.

There is an interesting relationship between the retinotopic map in the upper layer and the motor map in the lower layer. The layers lie against one another such that local excitations of the neurons in the lower layer trigger a saccade which moves the fovea to a location which was previously kept by the receptive fields of the corresponding top-lying neurons of the upper layer. In other words, if one transfers an excitation in the upper layer that was caused by a localized light stimulus on the retina to the directly underlying neurons of the motor map, then the result is an eye motion that leads the fovea to the light stimulus. This correspondence led to the formulation of the *fovealization hypothesis:* According to this hypothesis, the alignment of the sensory and the motor map in the *superior colliculus* serves to create saccades for the centering of images in the fovea (Robinson 1972).

The correct functioning of such a system demands that both maps correspond precisely to one another. This requires an exact, topographically ordered wiring from the retina to the sensory layer and also an exact, topographically organized assignment of saccadic motion vectors to the neurons of the motor layer. As experiments have also shown, the oculomotor system can adaptively follow changes in the interrelation between visual input and the saccades needed for centering. For example, test subjects were equipped with both contact lenses and eye glasses such that the corrections of the glasses and the contact lenses exactly cancelled each other. Because of the distance between glasses and contact lenses, such a combination acts like a (weak) "Galileic telescope," and previously correct saccades now miss their target by some degrees because of the combined devices. In the beginning the eye reacts with additional corrective motions after each saccade to compensate for the errors artificially created. This state of affairs does not remain, however; it has been experimentally determined that already after 9–14 minutes the oculomotor system has adapted the saccades so well that subsequent eye motions can no longer be distinguished from eye motions of subjects without the contact lenses/glasses combination. Larger corrective motions were no longer required (Henson 1977). This shows that beyond the formation of appropriate, topographically ordered connections, the oculomotor system can use the appearance of errors to adaptively change its saccades.

In the following we present a simple model which, on the basis of a few simple learning principles, can adaptively form a sensory map and corresponding motor map in order to control saccades. As before, we consider only a minimum of biological detail in order to motivate the following mathematical model. The starting point of our model is a lattice A of formal neurons, as they were described in Chapter 8. Each formal neuron $\mathbf{r}$ corresponds to a receptive field centered on the retina at the location $\mathbf{w_r}$, and the excitation of this neuron leads to a saccade which causes a translation of a visual object on the retina by a vector $\mathbf{w}_\mathbf{r}^{(out)}$. The two layers of sensory and motor neurons are replaced by a single layer. The vectors $\mathbf{w_r}$ and $\mathbf{w}_\mathbf{r}^{(out)}$, respectively, bring together the location of the receptive field of a sensory neuron $\mathbf{r}$ and the corresponding saccade which is triggered when the underlying motor neuron $\mathbf{r}$ is stimulated. Furthermore, we describe the correspondence between the visual stimulus and the resultant saccade simply by a pair of values $(\mathbf{w_r}, \mathbf{w_r}^{(out)})$ of the centrally localized neuron. In reality, the resultant saccade is determined by a *group* of excited neurons localized at $\mathbf{r}$. (In particular, in our model we do not imitate the continuous interpolation which is caused by the simultaneous activity of many neurons.) As long as saccades $\mathbf{w_r}^{(out)}$ do not lead to a centering of the visual stimulus at the retina location $\mathbf{w_r}$, corrective saccades are necessary. The following section will show how these corrective saccades can be gradually reduced by a simple learning method and how, simultaneous to that, the arrangement of the receptive fields, whose center points are determined by the vectors $\mathbf{w_r}$, can organize itself topographically.

9.2. A Stepwise Method for Learning Saccades

The learning algorithm of our model is suggested by the corrective saccades of the oculomotor system. If an object within the visual field draws one's attention, a corresponding saccade is triggered. This saccade might not lead the object's image precisely into the fovea in which case a second, corrective saccade would occur to reduce this error. If this correction step really brings an improvement, *i.e.*, the image moves closer to the fovea, the corrective saccade will be accepted for later eye movements. This means that a model neuron that has triggered a wrong saccade will next time trigger a saccade that is the sum of the wrong saccade plus the correction step. Only a single correction step is allowed in our model. After that, a new stimulus is presented, *i.e.*, the attention is shifted to a new, randomly chosen object in the visual field.

The model assumes that the new object of attention is randomly chosen each time, yet the choice is governed by a fixed probability density which qualitatively follows the natural distribution of receptors on the retina. The region in the fovea is unused because, there, no saccades become triggered. Figure 9.1 shows the chosen probability distribution of input stimuli as a function of the distance from the center of the retina. It

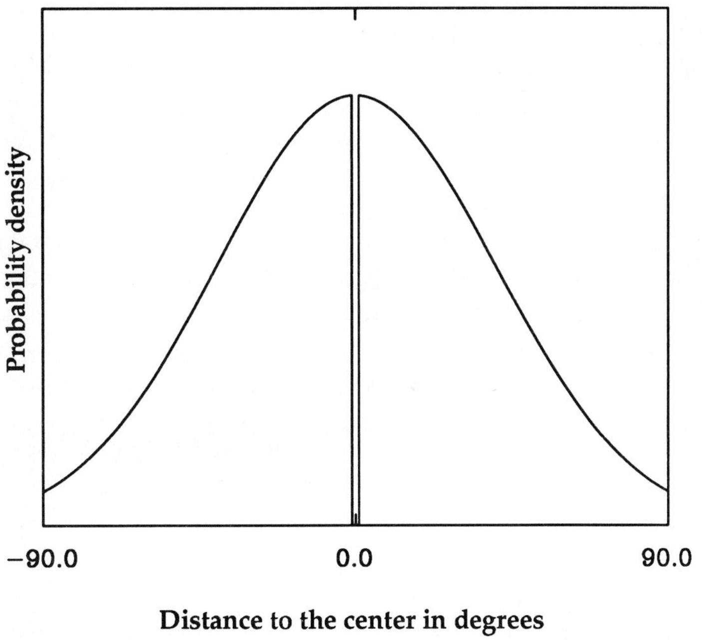

Figure 9.1 The probability density of the input stimuli in our model as a function of the distance to the center of the retina. This probability density roughly corresponds to the receptor density on the retina excluding the region of the fovea.

corresponds to a Gaussian distribution with a width of $\sigma_r = 40°$ notched out at the center. The region of the fovea has a radius of $1.0°$ (Korn 1982).

The formation of the wiring between neurons and light receptors in the retina, *i.e.*, the sensory map, occurs in analogy to the formation of the somatotopic map of the hand (Chapter 7). For the simulation we use the substitute dynamics described in Chapter 7 as well as two-dimensional coordinate vectors $\mathbf{w_r}$. Again, an image point at the location $\mathbf{v}$ on the retina selects that neuron $\mathbf{s}$ for which the distance $\|\mathbf{w_s} - \mathbf{v}\|$ is smallest and causes an adaptation step (70) for the vectors $\mathbf{w_r}$ which are the determining quantities of the "input wiring."

As a new feature, we add the learning of the output values, the saccade vectors $\mathbf{w}_\mathbf{r}^{(out)}$. The two-component vector $\mathbf{w}_\mathbf{r}^{(out)}$ depicts the displacement of an image point on the retina that results from this saccade. In the ideal case this displacement leads into the center, *i.e.*, if one considers each vector $\mathbf{w}_\mathbf{r}^{(out)}$ as "attached" to the receptor at $\mathbf{w_r}$, then all vectors must precisely end in the fovea.

These learning rules can now be mathematically formulated as follows. If $\mathbf{v}$ is the distance vector on the retina from the fovea to an image point and $\mathbf{w}_\mathbf{s}^{(out)}$ the saccade of the neuron $\mathbf{s}$ which is most strongly excited by the image at $\mathbf{v}$, then the new retinal location of the image after executing the saccade $\mathbf{w}_\mathbf{s}^{(out)}$ is given by $\mathbf{v}' = \mathbf{v} + \mathbf{w}_\mathbf{s}^{(out)}$. If $\mathbf{v}'$ does not fall into the fovea, *i.e.*, $\|\mathbf{v}'\| > R_{fovea}$, where R_{fovea} corresponds to a diameter of 1°, $\mathbf{v}'$ selects, as $\mathbf{v}$ did previously, a neuron $\mathbf{s}'$ which triggers another saccade $\mathbf{w}_{\mathbf{s}'}^{(out)}$, the *corrective saccade*. Every time this yields an improvement, *i.e.*, every time when $\|\mathbf{v} + \mathbf{w}_\mathbf{s}^{(out)} + \mathbf{w}_{\mathbf{s}'}^{(out)}\| < \|\mathbf{v} + \mathbf{w}_\mathbf{s}^{(out)}\|$, the original saccade $\mathbf{w}_\mathbf{s}^{(out)}$ becomes improved by the corrective saccade $\mathbf{w}_{\mathbf{s}'}^{(out)}$:

$$\mathbf{u} = \mathbf{w}_\mathbf{s}^{(out,old)} + \mathbf{w}_{\mathbf{s}'}^{(out,correction)}. \tag{127}$$

Here again, we take advantage of the continuity of the mapping between retinal locations and saccade vectors by allowing the model neurons in the neighborhood to participate in the learning process of the output value $\mathbf{w}_\mathbf{s}^{(out)}$, in analogy with the learning step for $\mathbf{w}_\mathbf{r}$. Just as in Chapter 8 we employ the formula

$$\mathbf{w}_\mathbf{r}^{(out,new)} = \mathbf{w}_\mathbf{r}^{(out,old)} + \epsilon' h'_{\mathbf{rs}}(\mathbf{u} - \mathbf{w}_\mathbf{r}^{(out,old)}). \tag{128}$$

Here $\mathbf{u}$ is the improved estimation for $\mathbf{w}_\mathbf{s}^{(out)}$ defined in Eq. (127), and just as $h_{\mathbf{rs}}$ did previously, $h'_{\mathbf{rs}}$ depends only on the lattice distance $d_{\mathbf{rs}} = \|\mathbf{r} - \mathbf{s}\|$ between the neurons $\mathbf{r}$ and $\mathbf{s}$. The parameter ϵ' measures the learning step width.

Thus, our model for the oculomotor system can be summarized by the following steps:

0. Begin with a random assignment of the elements $\mathbf{r}$ of the lattice A with receptive fields determined by the synaptic strengths $\mathbf{w}_\mathbf{r}$, and with a random assignment of the saccades $\mathbf{w}_\mathbf{r}^{(out)}$ to be triggered.
1. In accordance with the probability distribution $P(\mathbf{v})$ shown in Fig. 9.1, choose a vector $\mathbf{v}$ which represents a new "visual input." $\mathbf{v}$ points from the fovea to the retinal location of the new input.
2. Determine the center of excitation $\mathbf{s}$ in the layer A of formal neurons by the condition

$$\|\mathbf{v} - \mathbf{w}_\mathbf{s}\| \leq \|\mathbf{v} - \mathbf{w}_\mathbf{r}\|, \quad \text{for all } \mathbf{r} \in A. \tag{129}$$

3. Perform a learning step

$$\mathbf{w}_{\mathbf{r}}^{(new)} = \mathbf{w}_{\mathbf{r}}^{(old)} + \epsilon h_{\mathbf{rs}}(\mathbf{v} - \mathbf{w}_{\mathbf{r}}^{(old)}), \quad \text{for all } \mathbf{r} \in A \tag{130}$$

for the positions of the receptive fields.

4. Execute the saccade $\mathbf{w}_{\mathbf{s}}^{(out)}$, so that the position v of the image is changed according to

$$\mathbf{v}' = \mathbf{v} + \mathbf{w}_{\mathbf{s}}^{(out)}.$$

5.a) If the visual object lies in the fovea, *i.e.*, $\|\mathbf{v}'\| < R_{fovea}$, then go back to step 1.

5.b) If the image does not lie in the fovea, *i.e.*, $\|\mathbf{v}'\| \geq R_{fovea}$, then determine the new center of excitation $\mathbf{s}'$, belonging to the retinal location $\mathbf{v}'$ of the image, according to

$$\|\mathbf{v}' - \mathbf{w}_{\mathbf{s}'}\| \leq \|\mathbf{v}' - \mathbf{w}_{\mathbf{r}}\| \quad \text{for all } \mathbf{r} \in A. \tag{131}$$

Execute a corrective saccade $\mathbf{w}_{\mathbf{s}'}^{(out)}$. If the correction is an improvement , *i.e.*, $\|\mathbf{v}' + \mathbf{w}_{\mathbf{s}'}^{(out)}\| < \|\mathbf{v}'\|$, perform a learning step for the saccades according to

$$\mathbf{u} = \mathbf{w}_{\mathbf{s}}^{(out)} + \mathbf{w}_{\mathbf{s}'}^{(out)} \tag{132}$$

$$\mathbf{w}_{\mathbf{r}}^{(out,new)} = \mathbf{w}_{\mathbf{r}}^{(out,old)} + \epsilon' h'_{\mathbf{rs}}(\mathbf{u} - \mathbf{w}_{\mathbf{r}}^{(out,old)}) \quad \forall \mathbf{r} \in A \tag{133}$$

and go back to step 1. If the correction does not yield an improvement, *i.e.*, $\|\mathbf{v}' + \mathbf{w}_{\mathbf{s}'}^{(out)}\| \geq \|\mathbf{v}'\|$, then omit the learning step and return to step 1.

Steps 1–3 constitute the algorithm for the formation of the topology-conserving map onto A as explained in Chap. 7. The newly added steps 4 and 5 change the assignment of A with output values $\mathbf{w}_{\mathbf{r}}^{(out)}$. The change occurs according to the principle of *unsupervised learning* as mentioned in the previous chapter. The correct control actions must be discovered by the learning algorithm itself. This requires a search process in the space of possible values. In our algorithm this occurs by introducing corrective saccades. Again, a reward function is available only to tell how well the control has mastered the given task. In our case we employ the binary criterion "came closer to the fovea" versus "moved away from the fovea," which decides between the alternatives "learn" versus "ignore." By using the function $h'_{\mathbf{rs}}$, step 5 causes the neighboring neural units r to participate in the learning process when the search of the neural unit s is successful. This not only accelerates significantly the learning process but also contributes strongly to the convergence of the system to the desired state. Without the participation of neighboring neurons in the learning process, some of the neurons remain in a state in which saccades grossly deviate from the target value. This will be elucidated by the following presentation of simulation results.

9.3. A Computer Simulation

In a computer simulation of the above learning algorithm, we have chosen a ring-shaped lattice A with 20×30 neurons. The simulation parameters were chosen as follows: $\epsilon(t) = 1/(1 + 125t/t_{max})$, $\sigma(t) = 10 \cdot \exp(-5t/t_{max})$, $\epsilon'(t) = \exp(-5(t/t_{max})^2)$, and $\sigma'(t) = \exp(-5(t/t_{max})^2)$ with $t_{max} = 200,000$. Recorded at three different stages of the simulation, Figs. 9.2-9.4 show the assignment of A with receptive fields and the saccades to be executed.

The parameters for the learning of the receptive fields are chosen in such a way that they loose a large part of their plasticity at an early stage of the learning. This early freezing of the receptive fields is necessary because, when a receptive field is shifted, the target value of the saccade that is required at that location also changes. Without freezing, saccades that have already been correctly learned would become invalid under further changes of the receptive fields. For this reason the learning of the saccades requires the stabilization of the receptive fields.

Because of the rotational symmetry of the input stimulus distribution, the Kohonen net we employ is also rotationally symmetric. In the simulation the net consists of twenty concentric rings with thirty neural units each. Every neural unit has two radial and two circumferential neighbors. The depiction of the net is done in an imaginary "projection onto the retina," *i.e.*, each figure shows the retina, and for each neuron $\mathbf{r}$ the center $\mathbf{w_r}$ of its receptive field is marked on the retina. To indicate the adjacency of neural units, we have connected the marks of lattice neighbors by lines.

The outer ring represents the whole visual field from $-90°$ to $+90°$. The innermost ring encircles the fovea with a radius R_{fovea} which corresponds to an area of the visual field of $1°$.

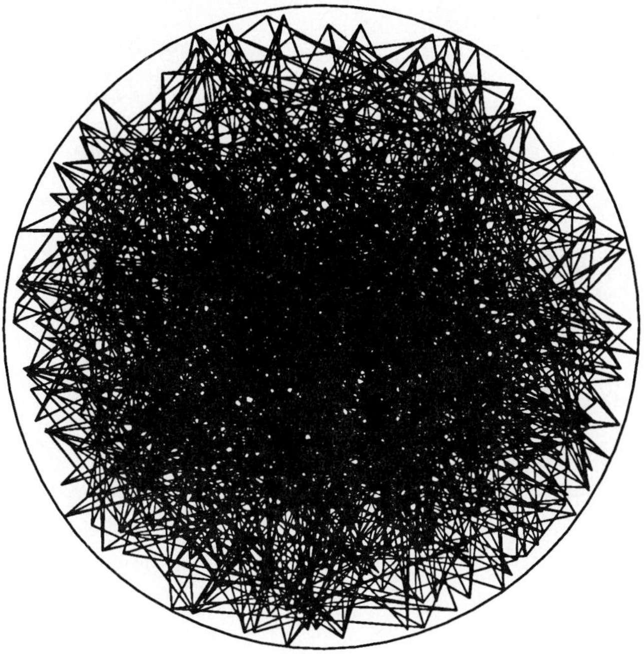

Figure 9.2a Learning saccadic eye movements according to Eqs. (129) – (133). The figure shows the lattice in its initial configuration on the retina. The wiring between the receptors and the neural net is chosen completely at random.

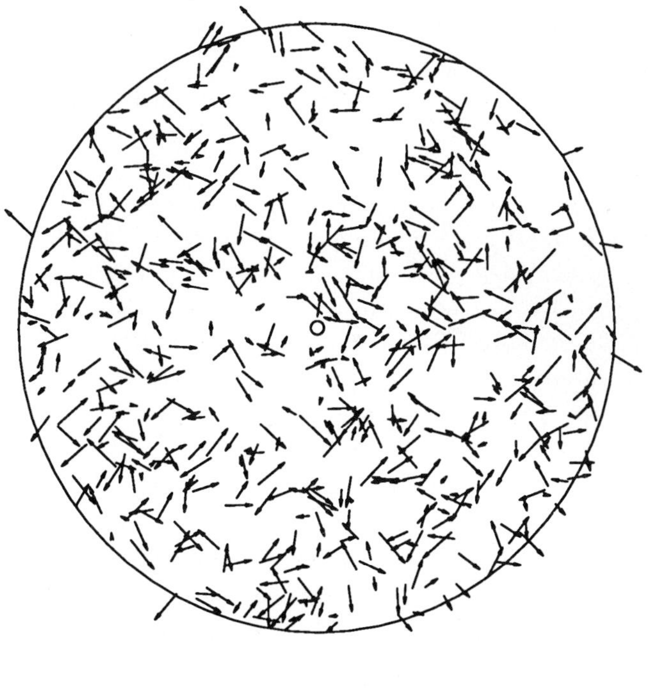

Figure 9.2b The saccades associated with the lattice points at the start of the simulation. The direction and length of each vector are chosen at random. The variation in length corresponds to eye rotation angles between 0° through 9°.

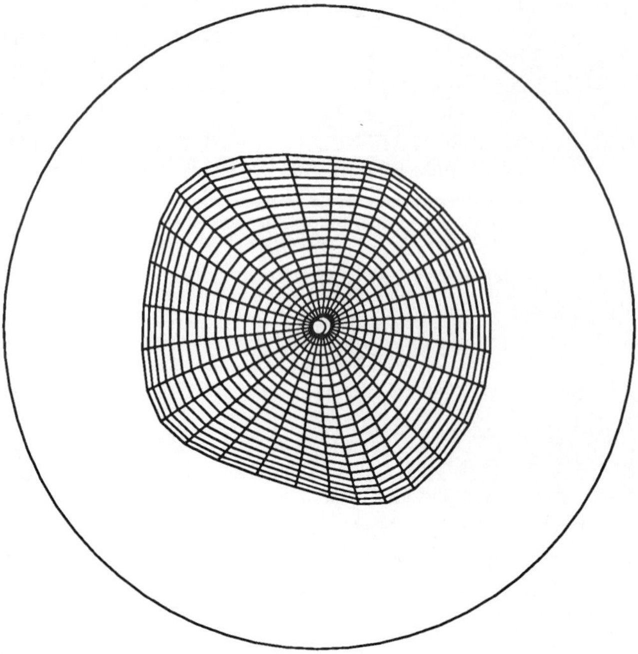

Figure 9.3a Learning saccadic eye movements according to Eqs. (129) – (133). The figure shows the lattice after 20,000 learning steps. At this time a recognizable ordering of the receptive fields has already taken place.

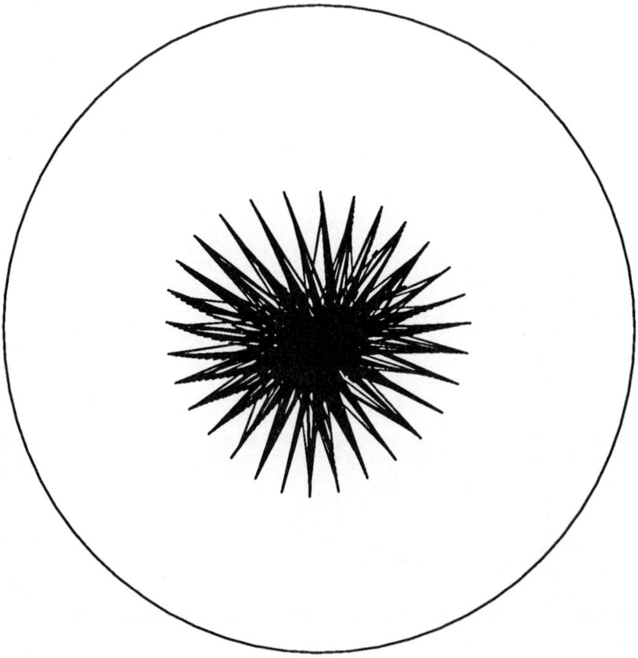

Figure 9.3b After 20,000 learning steps the saccades have already become crudely ordered. All vectors point towards the center.

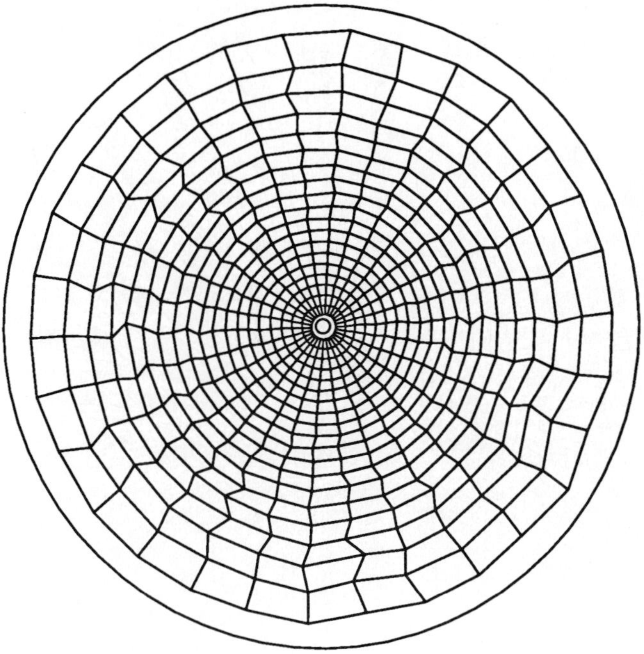

Figure 9.4a Learning saccadic eye movements according to Eqs. (129) – (133). The figure shows the state after 200,000 learning steps with an assignment between receptors and lattice points which is neighborhood-conserving and which follows the density $P(\mathbf{v})$.

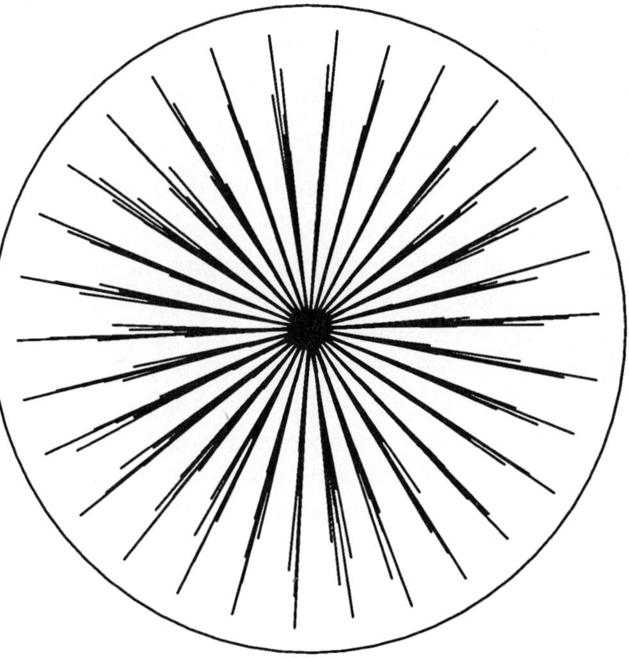

Figure 9.4b After 200,000 learning steps the saccades point towards the center of the retina. A blowup of the foveal region (Fig. 9.5) makes visible the precise positions of the endpoints of the vectors $\mathbf{w}_\mathbf{r}^{(out)}$.

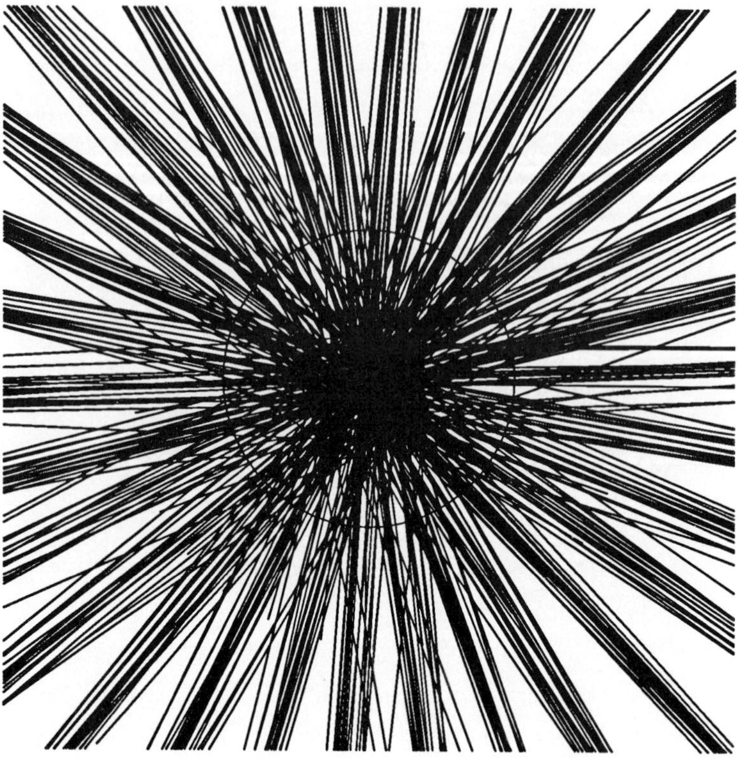

Figure 9.5 A blowup of Fig. 9.4b in the 1° foveal region which is indicated by the circle. One can see that all saccades actually lead into the foveal region and that the learning process has been successful.

The saccades $\mathbf{w}_\mathbf{r}^{(out)}$ at each lattice point are drawn as arrows; they specify the shifting of an image on the retina when the saccade is executed.

Figure 9.2 displays the initial-state assignment with random synaptic strengths $\mathbf{w}_\mathbf{r}$ and random saccades $\mathbf{w}_\mathbf{r}^{(out)}$. The magnitude of the saccades varies between 0° and 9°. Figure 9.3 shows the situation after 20,000 learning steps. At this stage a regular assignment between the retina and lattice points has already emerged and all the saccades are directed towards the center. In Fig. 9.4, after 200,000 learning steps, a well-ordered connectivity with the retina that is in accordance with the input stimulus distribution $P(\mathbf{v})$ has become established. The receptive fields lie more densely in the region around the fovea than farther out, where the decrease of the Gaussian input distribution gives rise to a lower resolution. All the corresponding saccades now actually point towards the center of the retina. Because, in Fig. 9.4b, the positions of the endpoints of the vectors $\mathbf{w}_\mathbf{r}^{(out)}$ cannot be clearly observed, Fig. 9.5 shows a blowup of the foveal region: one can notice that all saccades actually lead the targeted image into the fovea; the learning method has been successful.

The precise form of the distance measure between two neural units in the lattice is inconsequential for the organizational process to converge; however, sometimes a certain metric may fit a problem better than other distance measures. For example, in the above simulation we used the "Manhattan" rather than the Euclidean metric. (The "Manhattan-distance" between two lattice points $\mathbf{r}$ and $\mathbf{s}$ is the minimal number of lattice steps required to go from $\mathbf{r}$ to $\mathbf{s}$.) Equal distances in the lattice, *i.e.*, in the neuron layer, can correspond to completely different distances between the corresponding receptive fields in the space of input signals. It is the distances between the centers of receptive fields which become visible in pictures such as Figs. 9.2–9.4. In contrast, it is the distances in the lattice which determine the spatial interaction between the neurons themselves and, thereby, determine the distance-dependent adaptation steps in the model. This feature can be quite advantageous, as is particularly manifest in the vicinity of the fovea. There, receptors that are directly opposite to each other lie close together but have to learn saccades that differ as much as saccades that belong to receptive fields directly opposite and at the periphery of the retina. At both receptor pairs the required saccade directions of the partners differ by the same angle, namely $180°$. Therefore, it makes sense to use the "Manhattan" metric which yields, for the foveal and peripheral pair, the same lattice distance between the diametrically opposite neural units, namely 15 lattice sites.

9.4. The Convergence of the Learning Process

In this section we demonstrate that under certain conditions the algorithm which was employed to learn the saccadic eye movements must converge. For this purpose we make two assumptions. First, we consider a stage at which a corrective saccade always gives rise to an improvement. This is valid when all vectors have oriented themselves towards the center which is, as one can see in Fig. 9.3, already the case after comparatively few learning steps (in most cases 10% of the total number is sufficient). In addition, we assume that the receptive fields on the retina lie dense enough that we may make the transition from discrete lattice points to a continuum of r-values, as we did in Chapter 5 when we considered the representation of the ultrasonic spectrum on the bat's auditory cortex. By this assumption the sets of values $\mathbf{w_r}$ and $\mathbf{w_r}^{(out)}$ meld into continuous vector fields $\mathbf{w}(\mathbf{r})$ and $\mathbf{w}^{(out)}(\mathbf{r})$. Since we assume the lattice to be maximally ordered, the inverse $\mathbf{r}(\mathbf{w})$ exists, and we can define

$$\mathbf{w}^{(out)}(\mathbf{u}) = \mathbf{w}^{(out)}(\mathbf{r}(\mathbf{u})). \tag{134}$$

$\mathbf{w}^{(out)}(\mathbf{u})$ is the saccade which is triggered if the visual stimulus is at the retina location u. In addition, a glance at the simulation data shows that σ', the range of the interactions between neighbors, has a very small value from the start and decreases monotonically. We will see that from the time when all vectors are beginning to point towards the inner region, cooperation between neighbors is no longer necessary for convergence. If we set $h'_{\mathbf{rs}} = \delta_{\mathbf{rs}}$, then only the saccade at the lattice point s, in whose receptive field the stimulus v was located, experiences an adaptation step.

Under these conditions our learning algorithm can be mathematically formulated as follows: with an input stimulus v the saccade $\mathbf{w}^{(out)}(\mathbf{v})$ is triggered and leads to the retinal location $\mathbf{v} + \mathbf{w}^{(out)}(\mathbf{v})$. The corrective saccade is then given by $\mathbf{w}^{(out)}(\mathbf{v} + \mathbf{w}^{(out)}(\mathbf{v}))$. Thus, the saccade at v changes according to step 5 of our algorithm by

$$\Delta\mathbf{w}^{(out)}(\mathbf{v}) = \epsilon'\mathbf{w}^{(out)}(\mathbf{v} + \mathbf{w}^{(out)}(\mathbf{v})). \tag{135}$$

It is beneficial to introduce the new variable

$$\mathbf{x}(\mathbf{u}) = \mathbf{u} + \mathbf{w}^{(out)}(\mathbf{u}). \tag{136}$$

Here, $\mathbf{x}(\mathbf{u})$ is the shift which the saccade $\mathbf{w}^{(out)}(\mathbf{u})$ still lacks to lead an image into the fovea. In our algorithm $\mathbf{x}(\mathbf{u})$ should converge to zero since at the end it should be true that $\mathbf{w}^{(out)}(\mathbf{u}) = -\mathbf{u}$. Equation (135) then can be written

$$\begin{aligned} \mathbf{x}^{new}(\mathbf{v}) &= \mathbf{x}^{old}(\mathbf{v}) + \epsilon'\, \mathbf{w}^{(out)}_{old}(\mathbf{x}^{old}(\mathbf{v})) \\ &= (1-\epsilon')\mathbf{x}^{old}(\mathbf{v}) + \epsilon'\left[\mathbf{x}^{old}(\mathbf{v}) + \mathbf{w}^{(out)}_{old}(\mathbf{x}^{old}(\mathbf{v}))\right] \\ &= (1-\epsilon')\mathbf{x}^{old}(\mathbf{v}) + \epsilon'\mathbf{x}^{old}(\mathbf{x}^{old}(\mathbf{v})). \end{aligned} \tag{137}$$

For estimation purposes we now want to make mathematically precise the condition that at some point in time all vectors have become oriented towards the center. "All vectors are oriented towards the center" shall mean

$$\frac{\|\mathbf{u}\| - \|\mathbf{u} + \mathbf{w}(\mathbf{u})\|}{\|\mathbf{u}\|} > \delta, \quad \text{for all } \mathbf{u} \in V, \quad \text{with } \delta > 0. \tag{138}$$

There should exist a fixed $\delta > 0$ which satisfies Eq. (138) for all $\mathbf{u} \in V$ simultaneously. Rearranging (138) yields

$$\|\mathbf{x}(\mathbf{u})\| < \|\mathbf{u}\|(1 - \delta), \quad \text{for all } \mathbf{u} \in V. \tag{139}$$

If we replace u by x(u) in Eq. (139), then

$$\|\mathbf{x}(\mathbf{x}(\mathbf{u}))\| < \|\mathbf{x}(\mathbf{u})\|(1 - \delta) \quad \text{for all } \mathbf{u} \in V \tag{140}$$

is also true. Through the triangle inequality (137) becomes

$$\begin{aligned} \|\mathbf{x}^{new}(\mathbf{v})\| &\leq (1 - \epsilon')\|\mathbf{x}^{old}(\mathbf{v})\| + \epsilon'\|\mathbf{x}^{old}(\mathbf{x}^{old}(\mathbf{v}))\| \\ &< (1 - \epsilon'\delta)\|\mathbf{x}^{old}(\mathbf{v})\|, \end{aligned} \tag{141}$$

since $0 < \epsilon' < 1$ and, because of (138), $0 < \delta \leq 1$. Due to the nonexistent lateral interaction, the saccade of a lattice point is changed only if the stimulus falls into the lattice point's receptive field. But then, according to the above inequality, the residual error is diminished by at least a factor $(1 - \epsilon'\delta)$. On average, after N learning steps the neural unit s has been excited $H_\mathbf{s}N$ times by a stimulus, where

$$H_\mathbf{s} = \int_{F_\mathbf{s}} P(\mathbf{v})\, d\mathbf{v}. \tag{142}$$

$F_\mathbf{s}$ is the size of the receptive field of neural unit s on the retina. Therefore, as the number of learning steps N increases, the error of the saccade at s approaches zero on average faster than $(1 - \epsilon'\delta)^{H_\mathbf{s}N}$, resulting in the convergence of our algorithm under the above conditions.

If after only about 10% of the total number of simulation steps a state is reached where the learning algorithm for the saccades, even without interacting neighbors, safely converges towards the targeted values, then the question arises whether we need the cooperation between neighbors at all, especially since the range was very small from the start as we can see from the simulation parameters. An answer is apparent in

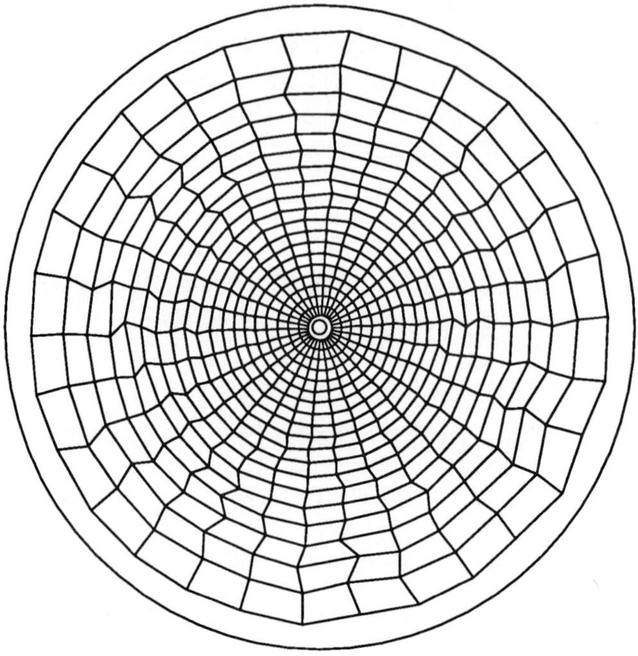

Figure 9.6a Learning saccadic eye movements according to Eqs. (129) – (133), but without cooperative learning as described through (133), *i.e.*, with $h_{\mathbf{rs}} = \delta_{\mathbf{rs}}$. After 200,000 learning steps the rotationally symmetric Kohonen net again displays the same assignment between receptors and lattice points.

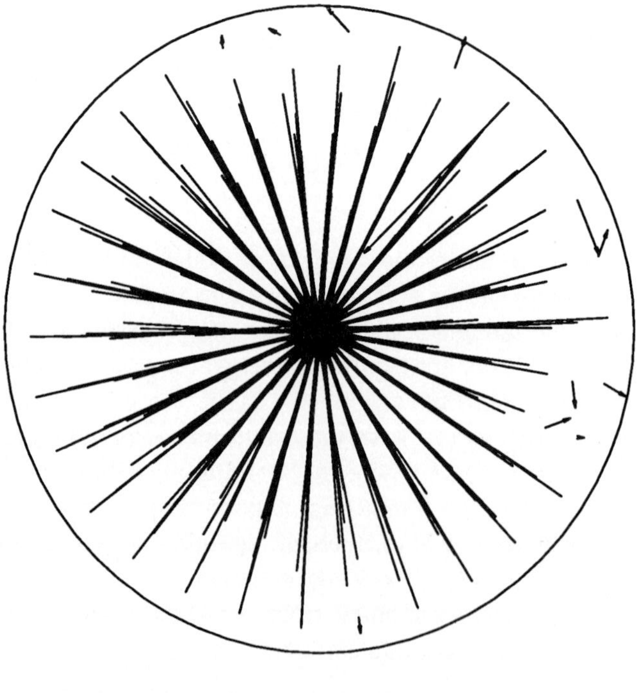

Figure 9.6b Without cooperation between neighbors, not all of the saccades learn the targeted value. In particular a few saccades in the outer region of the retina give rise to totally wrong directions.

Fig 9.6 where a simulation result is shown with the same simulation parameters as before, except with the cooperation between neighbors "turned off." There we recognize that a few saccades in the outer region of the retina deviate completely from their targeted output values and even point away from the center. This is due to those vectors, which after being acted upon by a stimulus, do not find an appropriate corrective saccade leading the stimulus closer to the center and, thereby, yielding a learning step (133). By an initial random assignment there are always a few saccades which evolve by the learning algorithm in a way that, at some point in time, they point into the receptive field of a neuron whose corrective saccade does not give rise to an improvement. These badly learned saccades appear mainly in the retina's outer region because there they often find only themselves for corrective saccades. In the learning algorithm without cooperation between neighbors these saccades have no longer the opportunity to rotate into the correct direction. Furthermore, we realize that the overall convergence of the system is slightly worse than in the case of cooperative learning. In particular, the end points of all vectors do not yet lead into the fovea even after the simulation has been terminated after 200,000 steps. This arises simply from the reduced rate of convergence. A reduced convergence rate is to be expected since without cooperation a saccade only changes if the center of a stimulation lies precisely in the saccade's receptive field, and neurons no longer profit from their neighbors. In principle, however, there is no reason why with further learning steps, except for some "runaways" in the outer region, the same desired state should not be reached.

At the beginning of the learning process, the cooperation between neighbors is essential. At this stage, it has the task of rotating all vectors towards the inner region. This cooperation is indispensable for a successful, overall convergence. The isolated saccades which continuously point towards the outside and which at the end of the simulation without cooperative learning would not have changed their direction are now shifted towards the center by their neighbors with more favorable starting values. Indeed, with cooperation between neighbors, all saccades point towards the center after only 10% of the learning steps (Fig. 9.3), creating a basis for the desired convergence of the total system.

9.5. Measurements on Human Subjects

In the model for the learning of oculomotor control presented above, we employed, with the introduction of corrective saccades, a very simple learning principle. Perhaps too simple, since measurements by Becker and Fuchs (1969) show that the simulation results of the algorithm do not quite agree with experimental observations. The experiments of Becker and Fuchs with human subjects show that the saccades almost never lead directly into the fovea. One can infer, however, that the "mistakes" occur by design since the errors of the first saccades are not randomly distributed around the fovea. The first saccades are, with few exceptions, too short (*undershoot*). In fact, it is believed that the intentional use of a first saccade which is too short gives rise to advantages, possibly in a better planning and easier execution of subsequent eye movements. Compared to those observations, our model learns its saccadic eye motions much too "well" because at the end of the learning process all of our saccades precisely lead in the fovea. In our simple example we have omitted the complicated aspect of planning and restricted ourselves to the images of immobile objects. An extension of the learning model must deal with the tracking of objects, where planning ahead will play an important role. Perhaps the intentional use of *undershoots* could provide advantages for a learning method extended in such a way.

Through the pole-balancing and saccadic-control problems, we have seen how self-organizing, topology-conserving maps can be used in a natural way for the learning of input/output relations in the form of adaptively organized "look-up" tables. The topology-conserving feature of the map makes possible the cooperation between neighboring neural units, which strongly contributes to the method's rapid convergence. This will be developed further in the following chapters. The adaptive capabilities of the map make possible an automatic optimization of the choice of value pairs represented in the table. Nonetheless, for mappings between higher dimensional spaces, a very high number of value pairs must be stored. This difficulty can be somewhat eased by the use of locally valid linear mappings instead of value pairs. With linear mappings, more complex control tasks can be handled, such as those that arise in the motion control of robots. In Chapters 10, 11 and 12 this will be demonstrated with a neural network which learns the control of a triple-jointed robot arm and one which learns to control a robot arm with redundant degrees of freedom.

IV
Applications in Robotics

10. Problems of Robot Control

At any given moment our brain manages to control 244 different mechanical degrees of freedom that involve more than 600 different body muscles (Nourse 1964, Saziorski 1984). In fact, dozens of different muscles routinely act simultaneously. For example, the muscles in each arm or leg control 30 mechanical degrees of freedom, utilizing rather complicated muscle combinations (Saziorski 1984). This control is accomplished through feedback control based on a variety of different sensors: stress and strain sensors in the muscle, tactile sensors in the skin, joint sensors, and—often essential—the visual system. Underlying these faculties lies the brain's vast, unconscious power of coordination of which we are fortunately unaware. The complexity of this control becomes obvious as soon as one attempts to equip a robot arm with only a small fraction of human dexterity.

Let us consider the simple example of grasping and inserting a screw. First the robot must sense the screw. To do so, the robot must determine the screw's position, and then choose a suitable gripper position. The choice depends on the shape of the screw, its location on the table, and the presence of other objects which might hinder the robot. The screw might, for example, lie in a box with other parts. The gripper position is also affected by the screw's purpose: it makes a big difference if the screw only needs to be moved, or if it should actually be inserted. As soon as such questions are answered, a trajectory to the screw's target location can be determined. The screw's orientation and any possible obstacles must be factored into the trajectory planning. The joint angles and torques required to move the arm as planned are then calculated. The joint angles and torques depend on the geometry and the moments of inertia of the robot arm and, while the movement should be as fast as possible, the corresponding joint angles and torques must not exceed, at any place in the trajectory, the mechanical limits of the robot. If such violations occur, the trajectory planning must be repeated. After the trajectory planning and after the screw has been brought to the appropiate location, the threads must be aligned with a precision in the hundredths of millimeters. This task seems, of course, much easier for people; after a rough placement of the screw, one can make use of counter forces from the threads in guiding the screw into the thread hole. In fact, our robot will need to use a similar strategy of compliant motion since the very precise location information is not achievable by cameras alone.

Presently, there are essentially two approaches for the solution of the problems mentioned. The first, *artificial intelligence*, is based on the development of a number of sophisticated programs, ideally designed to foresee all potential situations. This method has yielded a remarkable number of successes. Its weakness lies in the difficulty of finding the problem solving heuristics that work for all important practical situations.

The second approach attempts to understand the strategy of movement control by biological organisms for the purpose of abstracting *neural algorithms*. Our present state of knowledge of biological motion control, however, is still too fragmented to make possible the construction of robot control on a biological basis which could compete successfully with conventional algorithms. Nonetheless, there are a number of promising approaches based on conceptions of neural networks. Arbib (1981), and Arbib and Amari (1985), give a good overview of the problems to be solved and provide some conceptual presentations of their solutions.

Particularly important is the connection of motor action with sensory perception (*sensory-motor coordination*). It is the perfection of this feature that is so outstanding in higher biological organisms and that makes these organisms so superior to our present technical solutions. This sensory-motor coordination is not rigidly preprogramed, but rather, at least in higher animals, adapts and develops in a maturing phase by concerted actions of sensory and motor experience. If one artificially interrupts these concerted actions, then the development of a sensory controlled dexterity does not take place (Held and Hein 1963).

In Chapters 11 and 12 we show how such sensory motor coordination can emerge during the formation of neural maps. This will be demonstrated by a representative example, the problem of coordinating movements of a robot arm with pictures from a pair of stereo cameras. We will examine two computer simulations in order to focus on two different aspects of the problem.

In Chapters 11 and 12 we explore the *kinematics* of a robot arm. There a neural network will learn the relation between arm configurations as they appear in the camera and corresponding joint angles. That relation must take into account the geometrical features of the arm, the features of the optical projection through the cameras, and the position of the cameras relative to the arm. We will also see how the network model can gradually learn visuomotor control from a sequence of trial movements without any prior information. In Chapter 11 we will consider the task of positioning the end effector of a robot arm. In Chapter 12 we will be concerned with the problem of how an arm and its gripper can be properly oriented relative to an object that the robot is supposed to grasp.

Through kinematics one takes into consideration only the geometry. From this point of view all segments of the arm are massless and, therefore, without inertia. In all cases where effects of inertia do not play a significant role, a purely kinematic description is sufficient. For example, this is the case for joint motors that are sufficiently strong to comply with the movement commands. For fast movements or weaker motors, one must take into account the effects of inertia, *i.e.*, the *dynamics* of the arm. A network algorithm which allows to learn the corresponding control will be the subject of Chapter 13.

11. Visuomotor Coordination of a Robot Arm

In this chapter we again use the extension of Kohonen's model that includes the learning of output values. By employing this extended model we will enable a robot system to learn to automatically position its end effector at a target that has been presented in the robot's work space (Ritter, Martinetz, and Schulten 1989; Martinetz, Ritter, and Schulten 1989, 1990a, 1990b). "End effector" is the name given in robotics to a tool at the end of the robot arm, *e.g.*, a gripper, a welding electrode, etc. End effector positioning is an integral part of almost any task with which a robot system might be confronted. Examples of tasks include grasping of objects, application of welding points, insertion of devices, or, to mention a task from robotics that has not yet been satisfactorily accomplished, the planning of trajectories to circumvent obstacles. Obviously, end effector positioning is fundamental for all robot tasks and, therefore, we turn to this problem first.

Figure 11.1 shows a robot system as it has been simulated in the computer. The robot consists of a triple-jointed arm, positioned in front of the work space. The arm can pivot around its base (θ_1), and the other two joints (θ_2, θ_3) allow the arm to move in a vertical plane. For successful operation the robot requires information about the location of the targets. Humans obtain this information through their eyes. Correspondingly, we equip our robot with two cameras which can observe the work space. It is important to use *two* cameras in order to perceive the three-dimensionality of the space.

Since the work space of the robot is three-dimensional, we will now use, in contrast to examples in previous chapters, a

Figure 11.1 Model of the simulated robot system. The arm has three degrees of freedom: rotation around the vertical axis (θ_1), a middle joint (θ_2), and an outer joint (θ_3). The axes of the middle joint and the outer joint are parallel to each other, and are both horizontal and perpendicular to all three arm segments. Camera 1 is in front of the work space, and camera 2 is located on the left side of the robot.

three-dimensional Kohonen net, *i.e.*, a Kohonen lattice. With this step we seem to deviate from the networks actually realized in the brain, which appear to have a two-dimensional topology, because, as we know, the cortex consists of a two-dimensional arrangement of neural functional units, the so-called micro-columns. (see, *e.g.*, Kandel and Schwartz 1985). But this discrepancy is only an apparent one; the actual relevant topology, given by the connecting structure of the neurons or functional units, can very well deviate from the morphological arrangement on the cortex. Suppose we take a three-dimensional wire lattice and press it into a two-dimensional layer. The connecting structure between the lattice nodes has of course not been changed by this modification; it is still three-dimensional in spite of the fact that all lattice nodes now lie in a plane. Accordingly, the connecting structure between neural units in the brain might be multi-dimensional even if the neurons are arranged in a two-dimensional layer. The three-dimensional topology does not change any essential features of Kohonen's algorithm. Only the lattice vectors r are three-dimensional, and the distance $\|r - s\|$ to the excitation center is now measured in a three-dimensional lattice.

During the training phase, the position of the targets in the work space are chosen randomly. Before each movement the target is viewed by the cameras, the signals of which are fed into the neural net. Each neural unit is responsible for a particular region observed by the cameras. For each incoming signal that neuron which is momentarily responsible for the location of the target becomes activated and transmits its output values to the motor control. The three-dimensional coordinates of the location of the target, however, are not directly available; each camera only delivers the location at which the target appears in its two-dimensional visual field. The network must then derive proper output values for the joint motors to position the end effectors properly.

The neural network does not receive any prior information about, for example, the location of the cameras or the lengths of the robot arm segments. Rather it has to learn these geometrical relationships in order to correctly convert the camera information into motor signals. For this reason the untrained arm will initially not reach most targets. In each trial the deviation is observed by the cameras and then used to improve the output values. At each successive step a new target point is presented to the robot, providing the opportunity for further learning. The robot represents an autonomous system that works in a closed-loop mode and performs completely without a teacher. The robot system receives all the information needed for adaptation from its own stereo cameras and, thus, learns without an external teacher (See also Ginsburg and Opper 1969; Barto and Sutton 1981; Kuperstein 1987, 1988; Miller 1989).

11.1. The Positioning Action

As displayed schematically in Fig. 11.2, each target point generates an image point on the image plane of each camera. The two-dimensional position vectors $\vec{u}_1$, $\vec{u}_2$ of the image points in the image planes of cameras 1 and 2 implicitly transmit to the system the spatial position of the target point which is uniquely defined by $(\vec{u}_1, \vec{u}_2)$. We combine both vectors to one four-dimensional input signal $\mathrm{u} = (\vec{u}_1, \vec{u}_2)$. In order to be able to correctly position its end effector, the robot system must be able to perform the transformation $\vec{\theta}(\mathrm{u})$ from image point coordinates u of the target to the required set of joint angles $\vec{\theta} = (\theta_1, \theta_2, \theta_3)$ of the arm. This transformation depends on the geometry of the robot arm as well as on the location and imaging characteristics of the cameras, and should be adapted automatically through the learning method.

For each target u the neural unit whose receptive field entails the target location responds. As before, the receptive fields are defined by synaptic strengths $\mathbf{w_r}$ that now consist of four components as does u. A neural unit s is responsible for all targets u for which the condition $\|\mathbf{w_s} - \mathrm{u}\| \leq \|\mathbf{w_r} - \mathrm{u}\|$ holds, where r denotes all neurons on the lattice that are different from s. The responding neural unit provides as output values a suitable set of joint angles $\vec{\theta} = (\theta_1, \theta_2, \theta_3)$ that is transmitted to the three joint motors and that should lead the end effector to the target. To generate $\vec{\theta}$, two output elements that must be learned are assigned to each neuron: a three-dimensional vector $\vec{\theta}_\mathbf{r}$ and a 3×4-matrix $\mathbf{A_r}$. At the end of the learning phase, when $\vec{\theta}_\mathbf{r}$ and $\mathbf{A_r}$ have taken on the desired values, the angle positions $\vec{\theta}_\mathbf{r}$ will lead the end effector to the center of the receptive field of neuron r; *i.e.*, $\vec{\theta}_\mathbf{r}$ defines the move of the end effector into the target position $\mathrm{u} = \mathbf{w_r}$. The Jacobian matrix $\mathbf{A_r} = \delta\vec{\theta}/\delta\mathrm{u}$ serves to linearly correct the joint angles if the input vector u does not coincide with $\mathbf{w_r}$. This correction is accomplished by a linear expansion around $\mathbf{w_r}$ which is restricted to the region of responsibility of the particular neural unit r. The angular configuration $\vec{\theta}$ that is transmitted to the joints by unit s is then given by

$$\vec{\theta} = \vec{\theta}_\mathbf{s} + \mathbf{A_s}(\mathrm{u} - \mathbf{w_s}). \qquad (143)$$

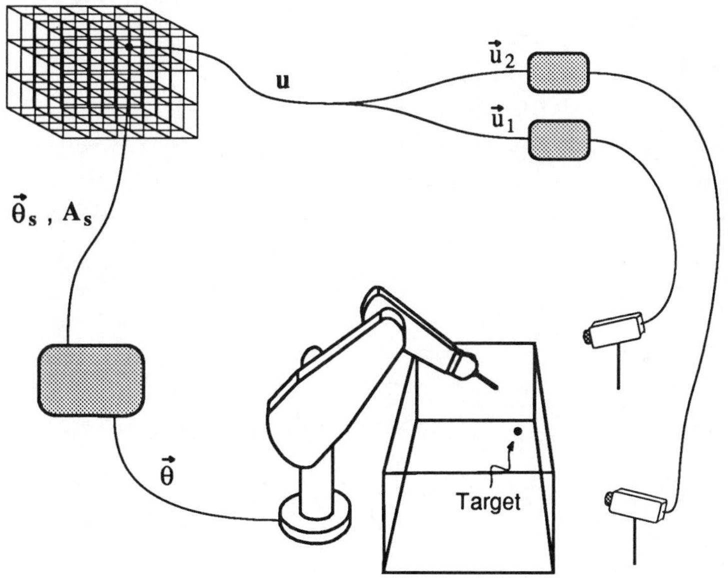

Figure 11.2 Schematic diagram of the positioning action. The two-dimensional coordinates $\vec{u}_1$ and $\vec{u}_2$ of the target in the image planes of cameras 1 and 2 are combined to a four-dimensional vector $\mathbf{u} = (\vec{u}_1, \vec{u}_2)$ and then transmitted to the three-dimensional Kohonen net. The neural unit s which is responsible for the region in which the target is momentarily located is activated and makes available its two output elements, the expansion terms of 0-th and first order, $\vec{\theta}_s$ and $\mathbf{A}_s$. These terms determine the joint angles needed for the movement towards the target.

At the end of the learning process this expression corresponds to a linear expansion around $\mathbf{w}_s$ of the exact transformation $\vec{\theta}(\mathrm{u})$. The vector $\vec{\theta}_s$ is given by the expansion term of zeroth order, and $\mathbf{A}_s$ is given by the Jacobian matrix for $\vec{\theta}(\mathbf{u})$ at $\mathbf{w}_s$.

The values $\vec{\theta}_r$ and $\mathbf{A}_r$ should assume values $\vec{\theta}_r^{\,0}$, $\mathbf{A}_r^0$ in the course of the learning which minimize the average output error. By the use of Eq. (143) the exact transformation of $\vec{\theta}(\mathrm{u})$ is approximated by an adaptive covering of the domain of $\vec{\theta}(\mathrm{u})$ with locally valid linear mappings. When compared with the sole use of discrete output values, the introduction of $\mathbf{A}_r$ implies that maps with less discretization points (neural units) are sufficient to reach a given precision.

The two vectors $(\vec{u}_1, \vec{u}_2)$, combined into the single vector u, span a four-dimensional space. All the target positions lie within the three-dimensional work space as indicated in Figs. 11.1 and 11.2. Hence, the input signals u of the cameras are all located in a three-dimensional submanifold of the four-dimen-

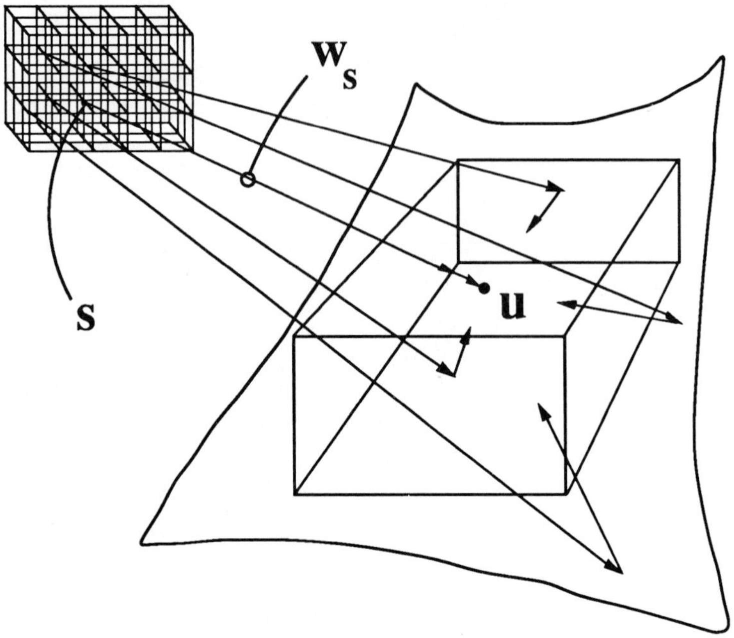

Figure 11.3 Occupation of the three-dimensional subspace with discretization points. The four-dimensional input signal space, U, schematically displayed, is initially homogeneously filled with the elements of the three-dimensional Kohonen net. The input signals $\mathbf{u}$ lie exclusively within the three-dimensional submanifold W. Therefore, all elements move rapidly into the relevant subspace of U, and a "waste" of unused discretization points W is avoided.

sional input signal space, making it unnecessary to use a four-dimensional Kohonen net to represent the input signal space—a Kohonen net with a three-dimensional lattice topology is sufficient. If we knew the relevant submanifold, *i.e.*, if we had precise knowledge about the position of the image planes relative to the work space, then we could, with the initialization, "plant" the nodes of the neural net into the submanifold, and the learning algorithm, as before, would in principle only have to "unfold" the net onto this submanifold.

However, supplying any a priori knowledge about the system to the learning algorithm, *e.g.*, precise information about the location of the cameras, should be avoided. Our goal is for the robot system to find out such information by itself while it is learning. Only then are the desired adaptive capabilities of an algorithm available to enable the robot to adapt to possible changes in the precise system data, *e.g.*, caused by corrosion, wear of its parts, or camera shifts. In our model this means that the robot system must find for itself the relevant three-dimensional submanifold in the space $U = U_1 \otimes U_2$ of the two connected image planes U_1, U_2 in order to distribute as homogeneously as possible the lattice points that are necessary for the discretization.

Lacking a priori knowledge about the location of the relevant subspace, we distribute the nodes of the neural lattice randomly within the four-dimensional input signal space at the beginning of the learning phase. The positions of the lattice nodes in the space U are described as before by four-dimensional vectors $\mathbf{w}_\mathbf{r}$. Because the incoming input stimuli $\mathbf{u} = (\vec{u}_1, \vec{u}_2)$ all lie within the yet unknown submanifold, just a few learning steps cause a "contraction" of all net nodes onto this relevant subspace. This contraction is schematically displayed in Fig. 11.3

The representation of only the submanifold by the network is a direct consequence of the feature of Kohonen's algorithm that has been discused extensively in Chapter 5, *i.e.*, adaptation of the density of the net nodes according to the probability density of the input signals. Since the input probability distribution in the present case differs from zero only on the submanifold, it follows that in equilibrium the density of the net nodes will be zero outside the submanifold. In this way the robot system can discover by itself the subspace relevant for its functioning. In the ensuing course of learning, the three-dimensional net will unfold within this three-dimensional subspace and will homogeneously distribute its nodes as discretization points.

This again demonstrates the effectiveness of the model in using a finite number of neural units, or more generally, memory units. We could have initialized the total, four-dimensional space with rigid discretization points. With this naive approach, the number of memory elements required to achieve a suitable representation would be much higher because the number of required memory elements increases exponentially with the dimensionality of the space. If we used a 20×20×20 lattice in our model, then the memory requirement to fill the total four-dimensional space with the same density of discretization points would be greater by at least a factor of twenty. In most cases the additional memory requirement would be even higher since the actual work space spans only part of the visual field of each camera.

The output values are learned by analysing the positioning error. The positioning of the arm occurs in two steps. If s is the node which responds to the target u, then in a first step the positioning of the end effector is achieved by means of the linear approximation (143) of the exact transformation $\vec{\theta}(\mathbf{u})$. The resulting position of the angle is denoted by $\vec{\theta}_i$. This first step causes the joint angles to assume a position given by

$$\vec{\theta}_i = \vec{\theta}_\mathbf{s} + \mathbf{A}_\mathbf{s}(\mathbf{u} - \mathbf{w}_\mathbf{s}). \tag{144}$$

The image point coordinates $\mathbf{v}_i$ of the end effector corresponding to $\vec{\theta}_i$ are recognized by the cameras and are then used for a second step, a corrective movement.

This correction is achieved in the following way: if the end effector is in the vicinity of the target after the first step of the positioning process, then the expression $\|\mathbf{u} - \mathbf{v}_i\|$ is already sufficiently small and, to a good approximation, $\vec{\theta}_{goal} - \vec{\theta}_i = \mathbf{A}^0_\mathbf{s}(\mathbf{u} - \mathbf{v}_i)$, where $\vec{\theta}_{goal}$ is the angle configuration needed to reach the target. Thus the corrective movement is simply given by the change in joint angles

$$\Delta\vec{\theta} = \mathbf{A}_\mathbf{s}(\mathbf{u} - \mathbf{v}_i). \tag{145}$$

The resulting image point coordinates $\mathbf{v}_f$ of the final position of the end effector are again recognized by the cameras and, along with $\mathbf{v}_i$, are put into a subsequent adaptation step. The corrective movement can be iterated several times, thereby reducing the positioning error as much as desired as far as imperfections of the equipment permit this. Satisfying results can often be obtained with just a single or very few corrective steps. In the following description we assume, therefore, two positioning steps, a gross movement described by (144) and a corrective movement described by (145).

11.2. The Learning Method

The learning algorithm for obtaining suitable elements $\vec{\theta}_\mathbf{r}$ and $\mathbf{A}_\mathbf{r}$ for each unit r uses a gradient descent on a quadratic error function. In each learning step the gradients of the error functions are calculated from the positioning error in order to obtain the direction to the minimum. If neural unit s was responsible for generating the arm movements, the improved values of $\vec{\theta}_{\mathbf{s}}$ and $\mathbf{A}_{\mathbf{s}}$ are then given by

$$\begin{aligned} \vec{\theta}^{\,*} &= \vec{\theta}_{\mathbf{s}}^{\,old} + \delta_1 \cdot \mathbf{A}_{\mathbf{s}}^{old}(\mathbf{u} - \mathbf{v}_i) \\ \mathbf{A}^* &= \mathbf{A}_{\mathbf{s}}^{old} + \delta_2 \cdot \mathbf{A}_{\mathbf{s}}^{old}(\mathbf{u} - \mathbf{v}_f)\Delta\mathbf{v}^T, \end{aligned} \tag{146}$$

where $\Delta\mathbf{v} = \mathbf{v}_f - \mathbf{v}_i$, $\mathbf{v}_f$ and $\mathbf{v}_i$ as defined in Section 11.1. A derivation of these learning rules will be given in Section 11.3. The factors δ_1 and δ_2 denote the step size of the gradient descent. On the one hand the step sizes should not be too small, for otherwise the number of iterations would be unnecessarily high. On the other hand, they should not be too large, for then a learning step could overshoot the minimum. As we will see later in a mathematical analysis of the learning method, the values $\delta_1 = 1$ and $\delta_2 = 1/\|\Delta\mathbf{v}\|^2$ are optimal.

The new estimates $\vec{\theta}^{\,*}$ and $\mathbf{A}^*$ that were obtained by the gradient descent (146) are used to improve the output elements of neural unit s as well as those of its neighbors. Here, as in previous chapters, we employ a learning procedure for the output elements that is analogous to Kohonen's original algorithm and is given by

$$\begin{aligned} \vec{\theta}_{\mathbf{r}}^{\,new} &= \vec{\theta}_{\mathbf{r}}^{\,old} + \epsilon' h'_{\mathbf{rs}}(\vec{\theta}^{\,*} - \vec{\theta}_{\mathbf{r}}^{\,old}) \\ \mathbf{A}_{\mathbf{r}}^{new} &= \mathbf{A}_{\mathbf{r}}^{old} + \epsilon' h'_{\mathbf{rs}}(\mathbf{A}^* - \mathbf{A}_{\mathbf{r}}^{old}). \end{aligned} \tag{147}$$

This learning step modifies a whole population of neural units in the vicinity of unit s. As a following display of simulation results will show, the cooperation between neighboring neural units resulting from Eq. (147) is crucial for rapid learning and for convergence to a satisfactory final state. Without cooperation between neighbors, some output elements $\vec{\theta}_{\mathbf{r}}$ and $\mathbf{A}_{\mathbf{r}}$ might not converge towards their desired values, and could become "stuck" in local minima during the gradient descent in a way similar to what occurred in the example of oculomotor control. A more detailed mathematical analysis of this behavior will be given in Chapter 15.

Our learning algorithm for the Kohonen net and the output elements $\vec{\theta}_{\mathbf{r}}$ and $\mathbf{A}_{\mathbf{r}}$ can be summarized into eight steps as follows:

1. Present a randomly chosen target point in the work space.
2. Let the cameras observe the corresponding input signal u.

3. Determine the lattice point (neural unit) $\mathbf{s} := \phi_{\mathbf{w}}(\mathbf{u})$ to which $\mathbf{u}$ is assigned in the lattice.
4. Move the end effector to an intermediate position by setting the joint angles to

$$\vec{\theta}_i = \vec{\theta}_{\mathbf{s}} + \mathbf{A}_{\mathbf{s}}(\mathbf{u} - \mathbf{w}_{\mathbf{s}}),$$

and register the corresponding coordinates $\mathbf{v}_i$ of the end effector in the image planes of the cameras.

5. Execute a correction of the end effector position from step 5 according to

$$\vec{\theta}_f = \vec{\theta}_i + \mathbf{A}_{\mathbf{s}}(\mathbf{u} - \mathbf{v}_i),$$

and observe the corresponding camera coordinates $\mathbf{v}_f$.

6. Execute the learning step for the receptive field of $\mathbf{r}$ according to

$$\mathbf{w}_{\mathbf{r}}^{new} = \mathbf{w}_{\mathbf{r}}^{old} + \epsilon h_{\mathbf{rs}}(\mathbf{u} - \mathbf{w}_{\mathbf{r}}^{old}).$$

7. Determine improved values $\vec{\theta}^{\,*}$ and $\mathbf{A}^*$ using

$$\begin{aligned}\vec{\theta}^{\,*} &= \vec{\theta}_{\mathbf{s}}^{\,old} + \delta_1 \cdot \mathbf{A}_{\mathbf{s}}^{old}(\mathbf{u} - \mathbf{v}_i)\\ \mathbf{A}^* &= \mathbf{A}_{\mathbf{s}}^{old} + \delta_2 \cdot \mathbf{A}_{\mathbf{s}}^{old}(\mathbf{u} - \mathbf{v}_f)(\mathbf{v}_f - \mathbf{v}_i)^T.\end{aligned}$$

8. Execute a learning step for the output values of the neural unit $\mathbf{s}$ as well as of its neighbors $\mathbf{r}$

$$\begin{aligned}\vec{\theta}_{\mathbf{r}}^{\,new} &= \vec{\theta}_{\mathbf{r}}^{\,old} + \epsilon' h'_{\mathbf{rs}}(\vec{\theta}^{\,*} - \vec{\theta}_{\mathbf{r}}^{\,old})\\ \mathbf{A}_{\mathbf{r}}^{new} &= \mathbf{A}_{\mathbf{r}}^{old} + \epsilon' h'_{\mathbf{rs}}(\mathbf{A}^* - \mathbf{A}_{\mathbf{r}}^{old})'\end{aligned}$$

and continue on with step 1.

The second phase of the positioning process (steps 5–8), aside from the correction of the end effector position that resulted from the first motion phase, generates pairs of camera coordinates $\mathbf{v}_i$ and $\mathbf{v}_f$ for the learning of $\mathbf{A}_{\mathbf{r}}$ and $\vec{\theta}_{\mathbf{r}}$. The Jacobian matrices $\mathbf{A}_{\mathbf{r}}$ describe the relation between a small change of the joint angles and the corresponding change in position of the end effector in the camera coordinates. The generally small corrective movements therefore deliver value pairs that must be connected by the Jacobian matrices that are to be learned, and thus, the corrective movements are used in Eq. (146) to iteratively improve the Jacobian matrices $\mathbf{A}_{\mathbf{r}}$.

As soon as the Jacobian matrices have been learned, they can be used to improve the expansion terms of zeroth order $\vec{\theta}_{\mathbf{r}}$. Each term should lead the end effector in camera coordinates towards the corresponding discretization point $\mathbf{w}_{\mathbf{r}}$. The corresponding error, as seen through the cameras, can be evaluated by the Jacobian matrices to obtain a suitable correction of $\vec{\theta}_{\mathbf{r}}$ which then results in an improved value $\vec{\theta}^{\,*}$ in learning step (146).

Thus, the Jacobian matrices $\mathbf{A}_{\mathbf{r}}$ contribute significantly to three important aspects of the learning algorithm:

1. Calculation of the joint angle changes for the corrective step in order to
   i) reduce the positioning error, and
   ii) generate a pair $(\mathbf{v}_i, \mathbf{v}_f)$ for an adaptation step of $\mathbf{A}_{\mathbf{r}}$ itself.
2. Improvement of the expansion terms of zeroth order by evaluating the error seen through the cameras to obtain a correction for $\vec{\theta}_{\mathbf{r}}$.

The Jacobian matrix $\mathbf{A}_{\mathbf{r}}$ is a most essential element of the presented algorithm for learning and controlling the kinematics of the robot arm. In the next section we present a mathematical derivation of the learning algorithm to further illuminate the crucial role of the Jacobian $\mathbf{A}_{\mathbf{r}}$ during the learning process.

11.3. A Derivation of the Learning Method

We now want to substantiate mathematically the method for determining the estimates $\vec{\theta}^{\,*}$ and $\mathbf{A}^*$. For this purpose we consider the neural lattice to be unfolded and stabilized to the extend that the space of input vectors is well represented by the network nodes and that larger shifts of the discretization points $\mathbf{w}_{\mathbf{r}}$ no longer occur. We can then assume the location of the discretization points to be sufficiently constant and can neglect their change by the Kohonen algorithm, so that in the following we only need to consider the behavior of the output elements $\vec{\theta}_{\mathbf{r}}$ and $\mathbf{A}_{\mathbf{r}}$.

If the end effector positions $\mathbf{v}_f$, $\mathbf{v}_i$, as provided by the cameras, lie sufficiently close to the currently implicated discretization point $\mathbf{w}_{\mathbf{s}}$, then the linear relation

$$\vec{\theta}_f - \vec{\theta}_i = \mathbf{A}^0_{\mathbf{s}}(\mathbf{v}_f - \mathbf{v}_i). \tag{148}$$

is approximately satisfied. The matrix $\mathbf{A}^0_{\mathbf{s}}$ in this equation is to be obtained by the learning algorithm using the pairs $(\vec{\theta}_i, \vec{\theta}_f)$ and $(\mathbf{v}_i, \mathbf{v}_f)$.

Knowing $\mathbf{A}_\mathbf{s}^0$, we can calculate the 0-th order expansion term $\vec{\theta}_\mathbf{s}{}^0 = \vec{\theta}(\mathbf{w}_\mathbf{s})$ since the linear relation

$$\vec{\theta}(\mathbf{w}_\mathbf{s}) - \vec{\theta}(\mathbf{v}_i) = \mathbf{A}_\mathbf{s}^0(\mathbf{w}_\mathbf{s} - \mathbf{v}_i) \tag{149}$$

holds in a sufficiently small vicinity around $\mathbf{w}_\mathbf{s}$. Since $\vec{\theta}(\mathbf{v}_i) = \vec{\theta}_i$ is given by Eq. (144) from the positioning process of the joint angles, we obtain for $\vec{\theta}_\mathbf{s}{}^0$ the expression

$$\vec{\theta}_\mathbf{s}{}^0 = \vec{\theta}_\mathbf{s} + \mathbf{A}_\mathbf{s}(\mathbf{u} - \mathbf{w}_\mathbf{s}) + \mathbf{A}_\mathbf{s}^0(\mathbf{w}_\mathbf{s} - \mathbf{v}_i). \tag{150}$$

Taking

$$\vec{\theta}^{\,*} = \vec{\theta}_\mathbf{s} + \mathbf{A}_\mathbf{s}(\mathbf{u} - \mathbf{v}_i) \tag{151}$$

as an improved estimate for $\vec{\theta}_\mathbf{s}$ (see Eq. (146)) leads to $\vec{\theta}^{\,*} \to \vec{\theta}_\mathbf{s}{}^0$ with $\mathbf{A}_\mathbf{s} \to \mathbf{A}_\mathbf{s}^0$. Therefore, it is sufficient to develop an algorithm which provides the correct Jacobian matrix $\mathbf{A}_\mathbf{s}^0$ for every network node s, since then learning step (151) is able to provide us with the correct zeroth order expansion terms $\vec{\theta}_\mathbf{s}{}^0$.

In the learning phase the points $(\vec{\theta}_i, \mathbf{v}_i)$, $(\vec{\theta}_f, \mathbf{v}_f)$, and every target point u are elements of a whole sequence $(\vec{\theta}_i^\nu, \mathbf{v}_i^\nu)$, $(\vec{\theta}_f^\nu, \mathbf{v}_f^\nu)$ and $\mathbf{u}^\nu$ of training data where $\nu = 1, 2, 3, \ldots$.[†] In the following we will consider a single lattice point s, and ν will index only that part of the sequence of training data that leads to an improvement of the output values of s.

In principle it is possible to calculate $\mathbf{A}_\mathbf{s}^0$ from $\mathbf{v}_i$, $\mathbf{v}_f$ and $\vec{\theta}_i$, $\vec{\theta}_f$ in Eq. (148) by using the method of least mean square error. The advantage of this method is that, in terms of the only approximate linear relation (148), the mean square error given by

$$E(\mathbf{A}_\mathbf{s}) = \frac{1}{2}\sum_\nu \left[(\vec{\theta}_f^\nu - \vec{\theta}_i^\nu) - \mathbf{A}_\mathbf{s}(\mathbf{v}_f^\nu - \mathbf{v}_i^\nu)\right]^2 \tag{152}$$

can be minimized for all training data simultanously. Concerning the adaptivity of the system, however, such a procedure has the disadvantage that first the quantities $(\vec{\theta}_i^\nu, \mathbf{v}_i^\nu)$, $(\vec{\theta}_f^\nu, \mathbf{v}_f^\nu)$ need to be accumulated before a result becomes available. After that

[†]It is not necessary that the values $\vec{\theta}_i$ and $\vec{\theta}_f$ are explicitly available to the learning algorithm. Here they are only listed as intermediate values for the derivation of the learning method and will later be replaced by expressions that will make it possible to use exclusively $\mathbf{v}_i$ and $\mathbf{v}_f$ provided by the cameras.

$\mathbf{A_s}$ is fixed, and the system can adapt to later slow variations of the relation $\vec{\theta}(\mathbf{u})$ only by a complete re-evaluation of $\mathbf{A_s}$. Moreover, a criterion would be needed to decide if a re-evaluation of $\mathbf{A_s}$ is necessary. To avoid these disadvantages we opt for an iterative method that improves an existing approximation $\mathbf{A_s}(t)$ of $\mathbf{A_s^0}$ for every new value pair $(\vec{\theta}_i^\nu, \mathbf{v}_i^\nu)$, $(\vec{\theta}_f^\nu, \mathbf{v}_f^\nu)$. A suitable iterative algorithm employes the technique of linear regression and was suggested for application in adaptive systems by Widrow and Hoff (1960).

By this method one obtains an improved value $\mathbf{A}^* = \mathbf{A_s} + \Delta\mathbf{A_s}$ for $\mathbf{A_s}$ by setting

$$\Delta\mathbf{A_s} = \delta \cdot \left(\Delta\vec{\theta}^\nu - \mathbf{A_s}\Delta\mathbf{v}^\nu\right)(\Delta\mathbf{v}^\nu)^T. \tag{153}$$

Here $\Delta\vec{\theta}^\nu = \vec{\theta}_f^\nu - \vec{\theta}_i^\nu$, $\Delta\mathbf{v}^\nu = \mathbf{v}_f^\nu - \mathbf{v}_i^\nu$, and δ is the learning step width. As long as $\delta \ll 1/\|\Delta\mathbf{v}\|^2$ and a stationary probability distribution of the quantities $(\vec{\theta}_i^\nu, \mathbf{v}_i^\nu)$, $(\vec{\theta}_f^\nu, \mathbf{v}_f^\nu)$ exists, then a sufficient number of steps (153) approximates a descent along the direction

$$\sum_\nu \left(\Delta\vec{\theta}^\nu - \mathbf{A_s}\Delta\mathbf{v}^\nu\right)(\Delta\mathbf{v}^\nu)^T = -\frac{dE(\mathbf{A_s})}{d\mathbf{A_s}} \tag{154}$$

where $E(\mathbf{A_s})$ is the error function (152) to be minimized. Obviously, the Widrow-Hoff method leads to a minimization of $E(\mathbf{A_s})$ by realising a gradient descent of the mean square error $E(\mathbf{A_s})$ "on average." Although an individual step (153) may even increase $E(\mathbf{A_s})$, many adaptation steps (153) lead to an decrease of the error $E(\mathbf{A_s})$.

In applying (145), the equation determining the corrective movement, one can eliminate the explicit input of angle positions in learning step (153) and, thereby, employ only values provided by the cameras, namely the image coordinates $\mathbf{u}$, $\mathbf{v}_i$, and $\mathbf{v}_f$ of the target and the actual end effector positions. With $\Delta\vec{\theta}^\nu = \mathbf{A_s}(\mathbf{u}^\nu - \mathbf{v}_i)$ from (145) the adaptation step (153) can be written

$$\mathbf{A}^* = \mathbf{A_s}^{old} + \delta \cdot \mathbf{A_s}^{old}\left(\mathbf{u}^\nu - \mathbf{v}_f^\nu\right)(\Delta\mathbf{v}^\nu)^T. \tag{155}$$

Since, in the course of learning, we approximate the Jacobian matrices with increasing accuracy, the learning step (151) for the expansion terms of 0-th order will deliver better and better values $\vec{\theta}^*$. Learning step (151) can also be interpreted as a gradient descent on a quadratic error function. In this case the quadratic error function is given by

$$E(\vec{\theta}_{\mathbf{s}}) = \frac{1}{2}\sum_{\nu}\left(\vec{\theta}_i^{\nu} - \vec{\theta}_{\mathbf{s}} - \mathbf{A}_{\mathbf{s}}^0\left(\mathbf{v}_i^{\nu} - \mathbf{w}_{\mathbf{s}}\right)\right)^2. \tag{156}$$

Taking the derivative with respect to $\vec{\theta}_{\mathbf{s}}$ and employing Eq.(144) yields

$$-\frac{dE(\vec{\theta}_{\mathbf{s}})}{d\vec{\theta}_{\mathbf{s}}} = \sum_{\nu}\left(\mathbf{A}_{\mathbf{s}}\left(\mathbf{u}^{\nu} - \mathbf{w}_{\mathbf{s}}\right) - \mathbf{A}_{\mathbf{s}}^0\left(\mathbf{v}_i^{\nu} - \mathbf{w}_{\mathbf{s}}\right)\right). \tag{157}$$

Since $\mathbf{A}_{\mathbf{s}}^0$ is initially unknown, we replace $\mathbf{A}_{\mathbf{s}}^0$ by the best available estimate, namely $\mathbf{A}_{\mathbf{s}}$. The error caused by this substitution is reduced by the improvement of $\mathbf{A}_{\mathbf{s}}$ with every trial movement and vanishes at the end of the learning process.† As for the Jacobian matrices, the adaptation step

$$\vec{\theta}^{\,*} = \vec{\theta}_{\mathbf{s}}^{\,old} + \delta\cdot\mathbf{A}_{\mathbf{s}}^{old}\left(\mathbf{u}^{\nu} - \mathbf{v}_i^{\nu}\right) \tag{158}$$

leads to a gradient descent "on average" on the function (156).

When this learning step is compared to Eq. (150) (where the index ν is again omitted), we recognize that both expressions become equivalent when $\mathbf{A}_{\mathbf{s}}^{old} = \mathbf{A}_{\mathbf{s}}^0$ and the step size is $\delta = 1$. Therefore, if the Jacobian matrices are learned correctly, we obtain through Eq. (158) also a correct new estimate $\vec{\theta}^{\,*}$ for the adjustment of the expansion terms of 0-th order, as long as we choose for the step size its optimal value $\delta = 1$.

11.4. Simulation Results

Having described the neural network algorithm for training the robot, we now present the results of a simulation involving this algorithm. The lattice which represents the work space consists of 7×12×4 neural units. As in previous simulations, the values of the parameters ϵ, ϵ', σ, and σ' decrease with the number of performed learning steps. For all four parameters we chose a time dependence of $x_i(x_f/x_i)^{t/t_{max}}$ with $t_{max} = 10,000$. For the initial and final values, x_i and x_f, we chose $\epsilon_i = 1$, $\epsilon_f = 0.005$,

†Due to this error, the learning step does not point exactly in the direction of the negative gradient.

$\epsilon'_i = 0.9$, $\epsilon'_f = 0.5$, $\sigma_i = 3$, $\sigma_f = 0.1$, $\sigma'_i = 2$ and $\sigma'_f = 0.05$. The learning step widths δ_1 and δ_2 were set to their optimal values $\delta_1 = 1$ and $\delta_2 = 1/\|\Delta \mathbf{v}\|^2$.

The three arm segments of the robot arm simulated have a length of 0.13, 0.31 and 0.33 units, respectively, starting with the segment at the base of the robot. In the same units, the work space is a rectangular cube with $0.1 < x < 0.5, -0.35 < y < 0.35, 0 < z < 0.23$, where the x- and y-axes lie in the horizontal plane with the x-axis along the short edge. The aperture of camera 1 is located at $(x, y, z) = (0.7,\ 0,\ 0.12)$ and points towards the coordinate $(0.15,\ 0,\ 0)$; the aperture of camera 2 is located at $(0.3,\ 1,\ 0.25)$ and points towards $(0.3\ ,0\ ,0.2)$. Both of the two cameras have a focal length of 0.05 units.

The Kohonen net in the four-dimensional space cannot, of course, be directly displayed. In lieu of a direct display we show a projection of the network nodes from the four-dimensional input space onto the image planes of cameras 1 and 2. Each lattice point appears in the center of its receptive field on the image plane of cameras 1 and 2. If $\mathbf{w_r} = (\vec{w}_{\mathbf{r}1}, \vec{w}_{\mathbf{r}2})$ is the four-dimensional spatial vector of the lattice point **r**, then we depict **r** at $\vec{w}_{\mathbf{r}1}$ on the image plane of camera 1 and at $\vec{w}_{\mathbf{r}2}$ on the image plane of camera 2. In this way the initial state of the net is shown in the two top frames of Fig. 11.4. The distribution of the network nodes was generated by assigning, on the image plane of camera 1, random values to the coordinate pairs $\vec{w}_{\mathbf{r}1}$ from a homogeneous probability distribution. The coordinate pairs $\vec{w}_{\mathbf{r}2}$ on the image plane of camera 2 were initialized accordingly. Therefore, we see in the top two frames of Fig. 11.4 a homogeneous distribution of the 336 lattice points. This implies that the initial distribution of the discretization points $\mathbf{w_r}$ in the four-dimensional space U is homogeneous, as well.

The two middle frames of Fig. 11.4 show the Kohonen net after 2000 learning steps. The work space and the robot arm have been displayed from the view of the corresponding camera. In Fig. 11.1 camera 1 is opposite to the robot arm, and camera 2 is to the right of the robot arm. Accordingly, we see the scene on the image planes of the cameras. In the top two frames of Fig. 11.4 no details can be seen yet because the connections between the elements of the Kohonen net completely cover the image planes. That the lattice, after 2000 learning steps, seems to "float" within the three-dimensional confines of the work space

Figure 11.4 Configuration of the neural lattice initially (top), after 2000 (middle), and after 6000 learning steps (bottom). The left column presents the image plane of camera 1, showing $\mathbf{w}_{\mathbf{r}1}$ for all lattice nodes; the right column shows the image plane of camera 2, showing $\mathbf{w}_{\mathbf{r}2}$

demonstrates that the Kohonen net represents already only the relevant subspace, however, only the central part of it.

The bottom frames of Fig. 11.4 show the Kohonen net after 6000 learning steps, a stage of the learning process where the positioning error has already reached its minimum value. The receptive fields of the network nodes have developed in a way that all possible target positions in the work space are equally represented. This gives rise to a "distortion" of the net to an extent that is determined by the affine projection of the work space onto the corresponding camera image plane and which in turn depends on the location of the camera. This can be seen particularly well in the image plane of camera 2 as shown in the right column of Fig. 11.4. For an homogeneous representation of the input signals, the network nodes on the image plane of camera 2 that are responsible for the back region of the work space must lie significantly more densely than the network nodes that represent target positions in the front part of the work space. By a proper distribution of its receptive fields according to the input stimulus density, the Kohonen algorithm yields this required "distortion" automatically.

To depict the learning of the output values, we again display frames from cameras 1 and 2 at different phases of the training. The two top frames of Fig. 11.5 show the initial state of the terms $\vec{\theta}_{\mathbf{r}}$ which provide the zero order contribution to the linear Taylor expansion (144) to be learned by each neural unit. The corresponding position of the end effector, after setting the joint angles $\vec{\theta}_{\mathbf{r}}$, is marked by a cross in each camera's visual field. These end effector positions are obtained by aiming at the target points $\mathbf{u} = (\vec{w}_{\mathbf{r}1}, \vec{w}_{\mathbf{r}2})$, for which the first order terms $\mathbf{A}_{\mathbf{r}}(\mathbf{u} - \mathbf{w}_{\mathbf{r}})$ in (144) vanish. At the end of the training, the camera coordinates of the end effector corresponding to $\vec{\theta}_{\mathbf{r}}$ should coincide with $\vec{w}_{\mathbf{r}1}$ and $\vec{w}_{\mathbf{r}2}$ of the lattice node $\mathbf{r}$. The deviations of the end effector positions from $\vec{w}_{\mathbf{r}1}$ and $\vec{w}_{\mathbf{r}2}$ indicate the residual error of the output values $\vec{\theta}_{\mathbf{r}}$. These errors are depicted in Fig. 11.5 in the visual field of each camera by a corresponding line segment. The initial values of $\vec{\theta}_{\mathbf{r}}$ were chosen randomly, yet with the constraint that the end effector remains in front of the robot.

The development of the Jacobian matrices $\mathbf{A}_{\mathbf{r}}$ is illustrated in Fig. 11.6. For the purpose of illustration we assume that the robot arm is asked to perform small test movements parallel to the three edges of the work space. The desired movements if carried out correctly form a rectangular tripod. The starting positions for these test movements are the end effector positions that correspond to the joint angles $\vec{\theta}_{\mathbf{r}}$. Through the cameras we observe the test movements actually performed. Initially, because of the random assignment of the Jacobian matrices $\mathbf{A}_{\mathbf{r}}$, the test movements show no similarity whatsoever to the desired rectangular tripods. The initial values of the matrices $\mathbf{A}_{\mathbf{r}}$ were all chosen in the same way, namely, $A_{\mathbf{r}}^{ij} = \eta$ for all lattice points $\mathbf{r}$ where η is a random variable that is homogeneously distributed in the interval $[-10, 10]$.

The middle frames of Fig. 11.5 and Fig. 11.6 present the test of the 0-th order terms $\vec{\theta}_{\mathbf{r}}$ and of the Jacobian matrices $\mathbf{A}_{\mathbf{r}}$ after 2000 learning steps. At this stage the end effector positions resulting from the joint angles $\vec{\theta}_{\mathbf{r}}$ all lie within the work space (Fig. 11.5). The test movements for $\mathbf{A}_{\mathbf{r}}$ (Fig 11.6) already look approximately like rectangular tripods, except that the amplitudes of the movements are still too small. The bottom frames of Figs. 11.5 and 11.6 show the result after 6000 training instances, a stage where the positioning error has already reached its minimum; the output values $\vec{\theta}_{\mathbf{r}}$ and $\mathbf{A}_{\mathbf{r}}$ have been optimized. As desired, the end effector positions resulting from $\vec{\theta}_{\mathbf{r}}$, indicated by cross marks, now coincide with the image locations $\vec{w}_{\mathbf{r}1}$ and $\vec{w}_{\mathbf{r}2}$ of the network nodes, and the test movements for testing the Jacobian matrices are also performed as desired. Only near the base of the robot do test movements deviate slightly from the shape of a perfect rectangular tripod, an effect caused by a singularity in the transformation $\vec{\theta}(\mathbf{u})$. Because the Jacobian matrices $\mathbf{A}_{\mathbf{r}}^{0}$ represent the derivative $\vec{\theta}(\mathbf{u})$ at the locations $\mathbf{w}_{\mathbf{r}}$, some elements of $\mathbf{A}_{\mathbf{r}}$ must take on very large values. Therefore, a more precise adaptation requires an unacceptably high number of learning steps.

To demonstrate the success of the learning process we show in Fig. 11.7 the dependence of the mean positioning error on the number of trial movements. The mean positioning error at different instances is determined by an "intermediate test" after every 100 additional learning steps. During each intermediate test the robot system is presented with 1000 targets which are chosen at random within the work space. The arithmetic average of the end effector deviations from the targets provides the mean positioning error. During the intermediate tests the

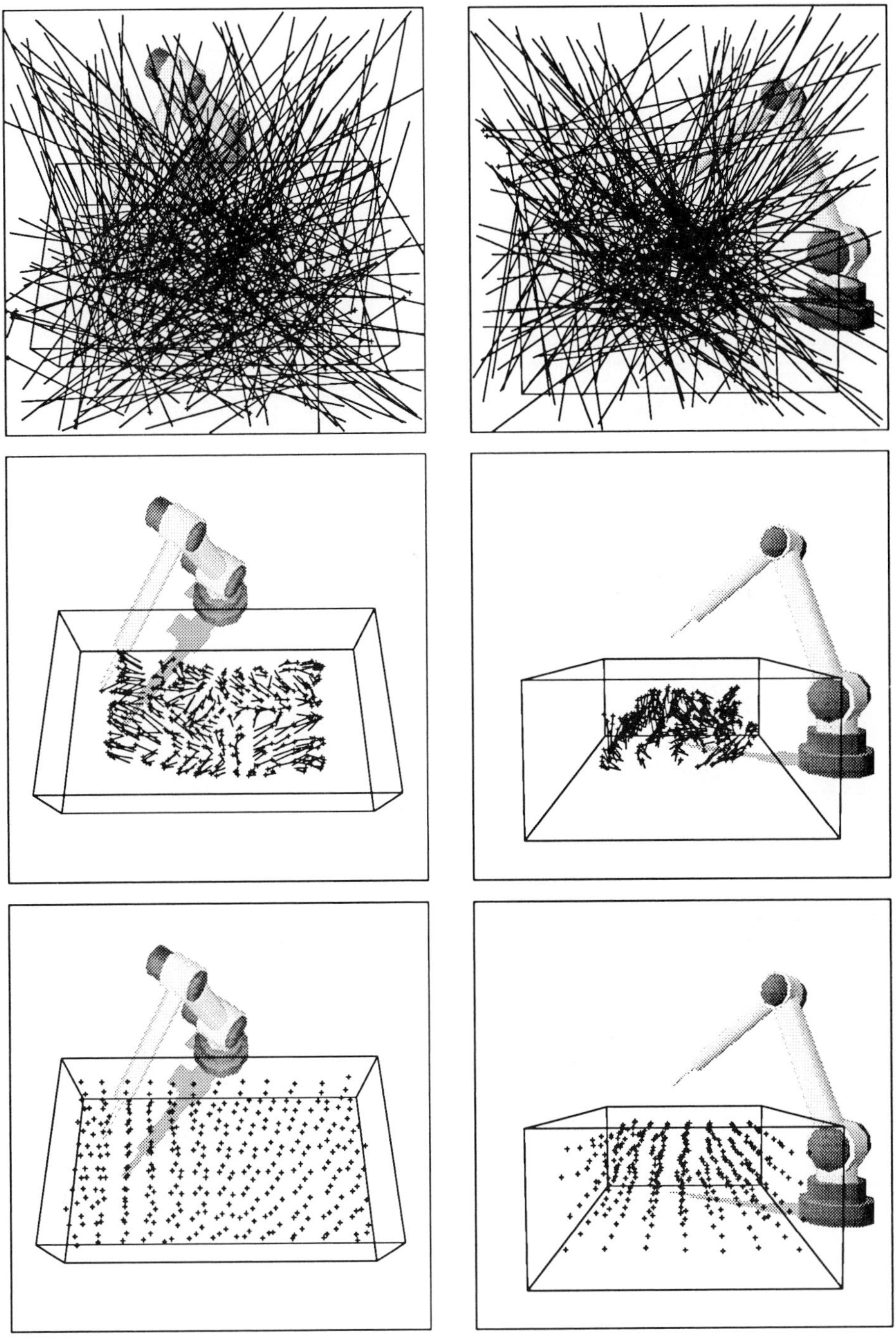

Figure 11.5 The end effector positions corresponding to $\vec{\theta}_{\mathbf{r}}$ represented by cross marks. The deviation from the desired locations $\mathbf{u} = (\vec{w}_{\mathbf{r}1}, \vec{w}_{\mathbf{r}1})$ is displayed by lines appended to the cross marks. Shown are the states at the beginning (top), after 2000 (middle), and after 6000 learning steps (bottom). Left (right) column: view through the image plane of camera 1 (camera 2).

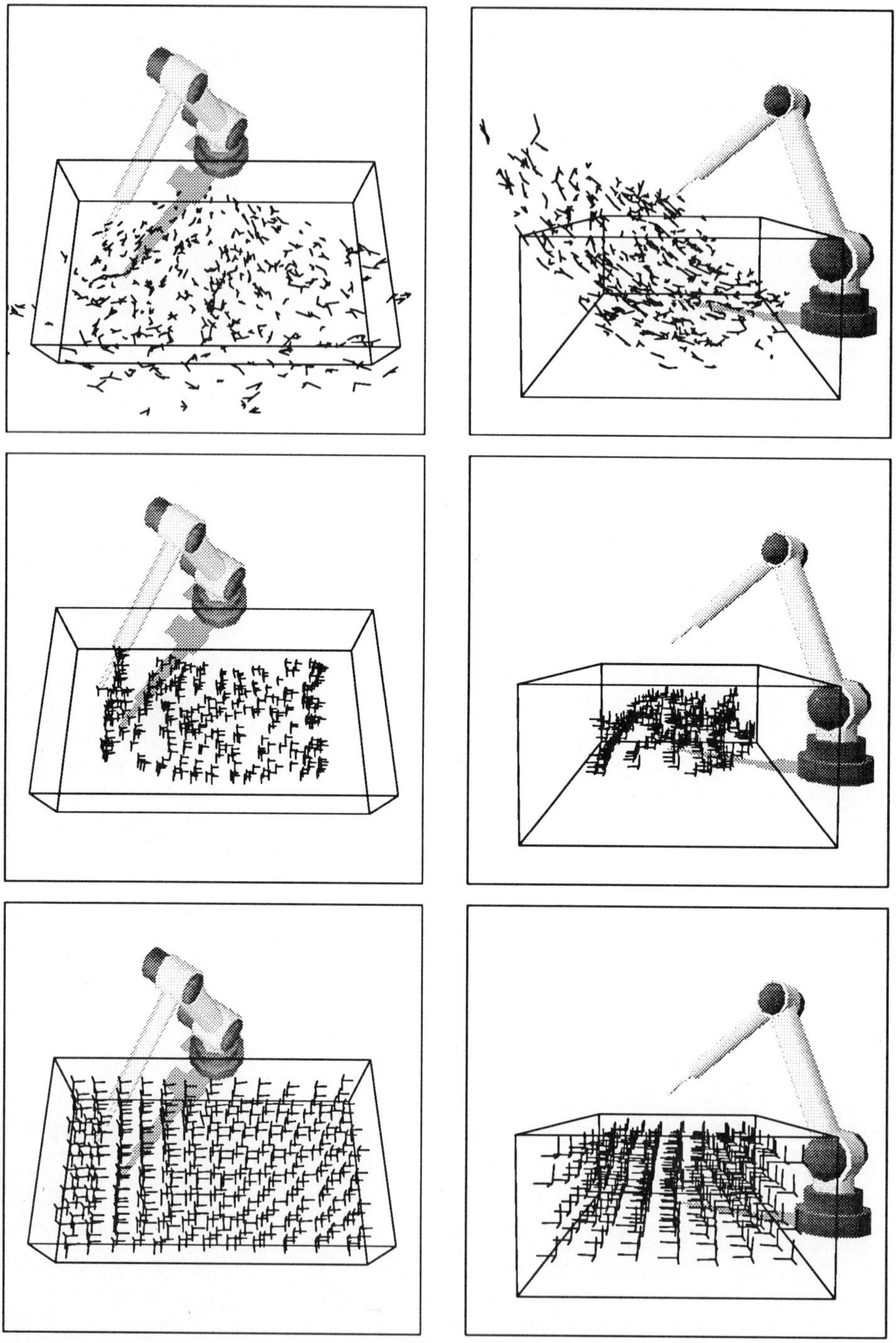

Figure 11.6 Training of the Jacobian matrices $\mathbf{A_r}$. Displayed are the result of small test movements parallel to the edges of the work space, at the beginning, after 2000, and after 6000 learning steps. Left (right) column: view through the image plane of camera 1 (camera 2).

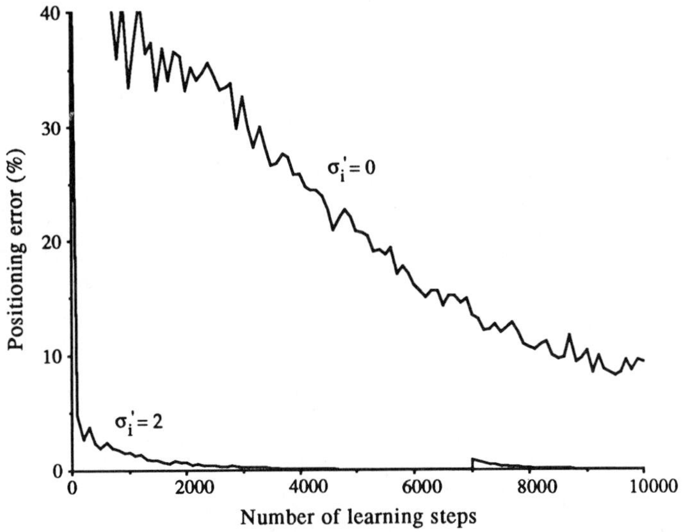

Figure 11.7 The average deviation of the end effector from the target versus the number of training steps. σ' denotes the initial range of the cooperation between neighbors. Without cooperation between neighbors ($\sigma'_i = 0$) during the learning of the output values, training progress is slow and the system does not reach an error-free final state. With cooperation between neighbors ($\sigma'_i = 2$) the desired learning of an essentially error-free final state is achieved rapidly. The residual error after 6000 learning steps is only 0.0004 length units—about 0.06% of the length of the work space. After 7000 learning steps the third arm segment of the robot was extended by 0.05 length units, about 10% of the size of the robot arm. The resulting positioning error, which was initially 0.006 length units or about 1%, decays with more adaptation steps until the previous minimum value is regained.

neural network remains untrained.

The cooperation between neighboring neural units as described by (147) plays a decisive role in achieving a fast and precise visuomotor control. To demonstrate this we show in Fig. 11.7 the positioning error from a simulation without cooperation between neighbors ($\sigma'_i = \sigma'_f = 0$ for the neighborhood function $h'_{\mathbf{rs}}$ employed in (147)). The resultung error shows that the system no longer achieves the learning goal. The positioning error remains noticeable even after 10,000 trial movements. In contrast, cooperation between neighbors (initial range of cooperation of $\sigma'_i = 2.0$) induces the error to decay rapidly to a small, residual error. After 100 trial movements the positioning error, in case of cooperation, has decayed to 0.034 length units, *i.e.*, approximately to about 5% of the length of the work space. After about 6000 learning steps the positioning error has stabilized at a value of 0.0004 length units which corresponds to about 0.06% of the length of the work space. If the work space were one meter long, the robot would be able to move to target locations within a few tenths of a millimeter.

To demonstrate the adaptative capability of the neural network algorithm, we extended the last arm segment to which the end effector is connected by 0.05 length units. This corresponds to a change of about 10% of the total length of the robot arm. Immediately after this modification, the positioning error increases since the neural net needs a few adaptation steps to be able to adjust to this new configuration. It is remarkable that immediately after the modification the positioning error is about 1%—smaller by a factor of ten than one would expect from the size of the modification. This is due to the feedback inherent in the positioning process: the second step in the positioning of the end effector, the corrective movement $\Delta\vec{\theta} = \mathbf{A}_\mathbf{r}(\mathrm{u} - \mathrm{v}_i)$, corrects the deviation of the intermediate end effector position v_i from the targeted position u, which has been increased by the modification of the robot arm. Extension of the last arm segment changes, for the most part, the target values of the zeroth order expansion terms $\vec{\theta}_\mathbf{r}$. In contrast to that, the Jacobian matrices $\mathbf{A}_\mathbf{r}$ are only affected slightly by the arm extension and, therefore, are still suitable for the execution of the corrective movement and for the correction of the error resulting from the wrong $\vec{\theta}_\mathbf{r}$. Figure 11.7 shows that after a few learning steps the neural net has completely adapted to the arm extension, and the positioning error has decreased to its previous small value.

The capability of the algorithm to adapt immediately to small changes in the robot arm adds significantly to its flexibility. For example, robots trained and controlled by the suggested algorithm could be equipped with different tools without the need for an entirely new course of training.

In the following section we will demonstrate the high degree of flexibility of the described learning algorithm in another respect. It turns out that the neural network can control a robot arm with more joints than necessary to position the end effector to any point in the three-dimensional workspace without additional modifications in the learning method. We will show how the neural network algorithm can handle such robots with "redundant degrees of freedom" which imply the difficulty that no unique relationship exists between joint angles and end effector positions.

11.5. Control of a Robot Arm with Redundant Degrees of Freedom

The triple-jointed robot that we discussed in previous sections could reach any target location within the work space by a unique set of joint angles.† Mathematically speaking, this implies that there existed a one-to-one mapping between target positions and sets of joint angles.

Nonetheless, most organisms capable of movement possess extra degrees of freedom. The human arm, for example, has four degrees of freedom: three in the shoulder joint and one in the elbow. It is indeed possible for humans to reach an object by many different arm configurations. With more than three degrees of freedom the set of joint angles is not uniquely determined by the location of the target, but rather there is a whole range of different sets of angles which will reach the target. From this range, a single set must be chosen. Such a problem is called an *ill posed* or *under-determined* problem since the constraints that must be fulfilled do not uniquely determine the solution (Bernstein 1967; Saltzman 1979; Jordan and Rosenbaum 1988).

The redundant degree of freedom in the human arm is, of course, not superfluous; it is particularly convenient when certain configurations are not possible due to additional constraints, *e.g.*, due to obstacles or when unique approaches are compulsory. A huge palette of arm configurations offers the chance to find one that works well.

In the following, however, we will not consider the implications of such constraints. We will stick to the task of positioning the end effector in a work space free of obstacles. We want to study the learning performance of the algorithm of the previous sections as it is applied to an arm with more than three degrees of freedom. Which arm configurations will the algorithm learn when it can select from many possibilities for each target?

Common methods for the control of an arm with redundant degrees of freedom eliminate the under-determination of the

†Actually there exist two sets of joint angles which lead to a given target location. They correspond to a "convex" and a "concave" configuration of the arm. By prohibiting, e.g., the concave configurations, the required set of angles becomes unique.

Figure 11.8 Simulated robot with redundant degrees of freedom. The arm has a total of five joints: one joint permitting rotation around the vertical axis and four joints about which the arm can move in the vertical plane.

control problem by selecting that joint angle configuration that minimizes a reward function in addition to reaching the target point (Kirk 1970; Hogan 1984; Nelson 1983). Psychophysical experiments show that humans also prefer arm configurations that minimize certain "costs." It has been shown (Cruse et. al. 1990) that humans prefer arm configurations using middle-range angles, *i.e.*, fully extended or tightly contracted angles are generally avoided. Such a tendency can be modelled in an algorithm by selecting from all possible arm configurations the one that minimizes a suitable reward function, such as,

$$E(\vec{\theta}) = \sum_{i=1}^{L} \left(\theta_i - \theta_i^{(0)}\right)^2 . \tag{159}$$

Here $\theta_i^{(0)}$ is a middle-ranged value for joint i. Joint angle configurations that deviate from $\theta_i^{(0)}$ increase the "costs" and are therefore less desireable.

Another form of the reward function is obtained if the arm is supposed to be as "lazy" as possible while moving, *i.e.*, the change of the joint angles of the arm should be as small as possible. This is a sensible, real-life requirement; it reduces both the wear and tear and the energy consumption.

If we denote the difference between two points that are neighbors, either in space or in camera coordinates, by $\Delta\mathbf{u}$, then the norm $\|\Delta\vec{\theta}\|$ of the difference between the joint angles which correspond to these points should be as small as possible on average. Mathematically, this constraint can be written as

$$\left\langle \sum_{i,j} \left(\frac{\Delta\theta_i}{\Delta u_j}\right)^2 \right\rangle_{\Delta\mathbf{u}} = \text{Min}. \tag{160}$$

Here $\Delta\theta_i$ denotes the change of the i-th joint angle and Δu_j denotes the difference in the j-th component of the space or camera coordinates. If we assume that the distribution of the occurring movements $\Delta\mathbf{u}$ which is averaged over in Eq. (160) is isotropic—which implies $\langle\Delta\mathbf{u}\Delta\mathbf{u}^T\rangle = \gamma\mathbf{1}$ where γ is a scalar and $\mathbf{1}$ is the identity matrix—then it can be shown that the constraint to minimize the reward function (160) is equivalent to the constraint that, for the inversion of the transformation $\mathbf{u}(\vec{\theta})$, the particular inverse $\vec{\theta}(\mathbf{u})$ must be selected from the whole range of possibilities for which the norm $\|\mathbf{A}\| = \sqrt{tr\mathbf{A}\mathbf{A}^T}$ of the Jacobian

$$\mathbf{A}(\mathbf{u}) = \frac{\partial\vec{\theta}(\mathbf{u})}{\partial\mathbf{u}} \tag{161}$$

is minimal at each location $\mathbf{u}$. It is natural then to look for the inverse that fulfills this constraint.

The Jacobian matrices $\mathbf{A}(\mathbf{u})$ of all the possible inverse transformations $\vec{\theta}(\mathbf{u})$ generate joint angle changes $\Delta\vec{\theta} = \mathbf{A}(\mathbf{u})\Delta\mathbf{u}$ for a given $\Delta\mathbf{u}$. If we denote by $\mathbf{B}(\vec{\theta})$ the Jacobian matrices of the so-called "forward transformation" $\mathbf{u}(\vec{\theta})$, which is, in contrast to its inverse transformation $\vec{\theta}(\mathbf{u})$, uniquely determined and which is often easily obtained, then it holds for every pair of corresponding $\Delta\mathbf{u}$, $\Delta\vec{\theta}$,

$$\Delta\mathbf{u} = \mathbf{B}(\vec{\theta})\Delta\vec{\theta}. \tag{162}$$

The Jacobian matrices $\mathbf{A}(\mathbf{u})$ of the inverse $\vec{\theta}(\mathbf{u})$ for which we are searching must obey the condition

$$\mathbf{B}\big(\vec{\theta}(\mathbf{u})\big)\mathbf{A}(\mathbf{u}) = \mathbf{1}.$$

A cannot be determined from this equation by inversion of **B** because in the case of redundant degrees of freedom, **B** is rectangular and, therefore, not invertible. Here we face the same situation as in Chapter 3 where we had to determine the optimal memory matrix of an associative memory. There we obtained a solution with the help of the pseudo-inverse of **B** (Albert 1972). From Chapter 3 we know that upon selecting the pseudo-inverse, the constraint to minimize the norm $\|\mathbf{A}\|$ is fulfilled simultaneously. Thus, the desired solution for **A** is

$$\mathbf{A} = \lim_{\alpha \to 0} \mathbf{B}^T \big(\mathbf{B}\mathbf{B}^T + \alpha\mathbf{1}\big)^{-1}. \tag{163}$$

Of the many possible transformations that are inverse to the transformation $\mathbf{u}(\vec{\theta})$, there is one that generates movements with minimal changes in the joint angles. If that particular transformation is called for, then the inverse $\vec{\theta}(\mathbf{u})$ whose Jacobian matrices are given by the pseudo-inverse (163) of the Jacobian matrices of $\mathbf{u}(\vec{\theta})$ yields the solution.

In robotics the precise form of the reward function is often only of minor importance. The reward function often only serves to smooth the robot arm's movements. For two adjacent target points an algorithm could select two completely different arm configurations when there are redundant degrees of freedom. By employing a reward function one ensures that adjacent target points will be assigned to similar arm configurations.

The assignment of similar joint angles to adjacent target points is, in fact, one of the main features of our learning algorithm. In contrast to other common methods, we do not have to minimize an explicitly formulated reward function. By the construction of a topographic map between input signal space and neural net it is made sure that adjacent target points always activate adjacent elements in the network. In addition, learning step (147) forces adjacent lattice nodes to adapt their output towards similar values. At the end of the learning phase the output values will vary smoothly from node to node. Both features bring about a continuous and smooth transformation from the input signal space of target points to the output space of joint angle sets. This transformation guarantees smooth and efficient movements of the arm.

11.6. Simulation Results

In Fig. 11.8 we see the robot system as simulated in the computer, now composed of five joints and, therefore, having two redundant degrees of freedom. As before the robot arm can pivot around its vertical axis, and the other joint axes are parallel to each other and parallel to the horizontal plane. The length of the arm segments were chosen as follows, beginning at the base of the robot: 0.13, 0.19, 0.19, 0.19, and 0.15 length units. The Kohonen net used in this simulation had the same size as the previous one, namely $7 \times 12 \times 4$ lattice nodes. The parameters ϵ, ϵ', σ and σ' as well as their time dependence, the location of the cameras, and the parameters describing the work space were adopted unchanged from the simulation of the triple-jointed robot arm. In connection with the five joints the vectors $\vec{\theta}_{\mathbf{r}}$ now have five components, and the matrices $\mathbf{A_r}$ are now 5×4-dimensional.

The graph in Fig. 11.9 shows the decay of the positioning error with the number of performed learning steps. As with the robot arm with only three degrees of freedom the error decays rapidly in the beginning and reaches, after only 200 learning steps, a value of 0.027 length units, which corresponds to about 4% of the length of the work space. It is noteworthy that the positioning error after 6000 learning steps reaches the same minimal value of 0.0004 length units as the triple-jointed robot, in spite of the increased number of degrees of freedom. After 7000 trial movements, we again extended the last arm segment by 10% of the length of the robot arm to test the adaptational capability of the system. As in the triple-jointed case, the positioning error initially increases but then decays again with additional adaptation steps until the previous value of 0.0004 learning steps is regained.

In order to test how well adjacent target points are reached

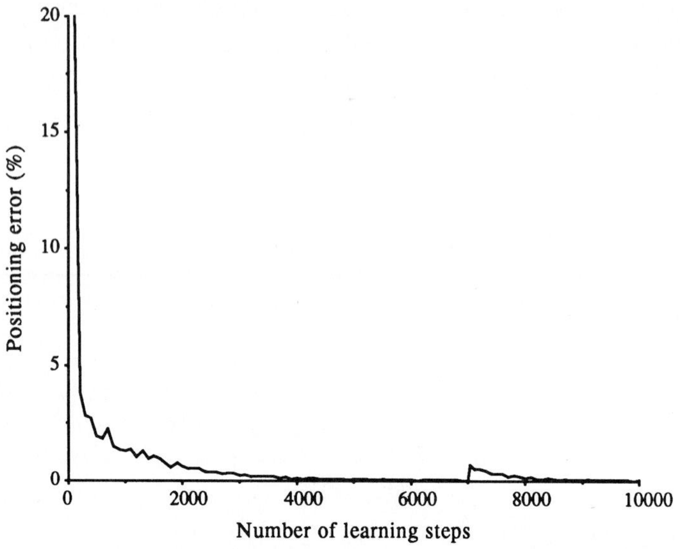

Figure 11.9 The average deviation of the end effector from the target during training for a robot system with redundant degrees of freedom. As for the robot arm with only three joints the residual error after 6000 learning steps is 0.0004 length units, *i.e.*, approximately 0.06% of the length of the work space. In order to test the adaptation capability we extended the last arm segment after 7000 learning steps by 0.05 length units. The resulting positioning error decays with additional adaptation steps until it has regained its previous value of 0.0004 after 2000 additional learning steps.

by similar arm configurations, the robot is commanded to move along a trajectory of target points. In Fig. 11.10 the arm's movement in such a test is shown by monitoring the arm's position at different times. We recognize that the robot indeed performs a smooth motion while moving its end effector along the diagonal of the work space. This demonstrates that the learning algorithm adapts to those arm configurations out of the many possible ones that lead to smooth changes in the joint angles as the arm moves. This is achieved without the explicit minimization of a reward function. The development of a topology-preserving mapping between the input signal space and the neuron lattice, and between the space of output values and the neuron lattice alone does the job (Martinetz et al. 1990b).

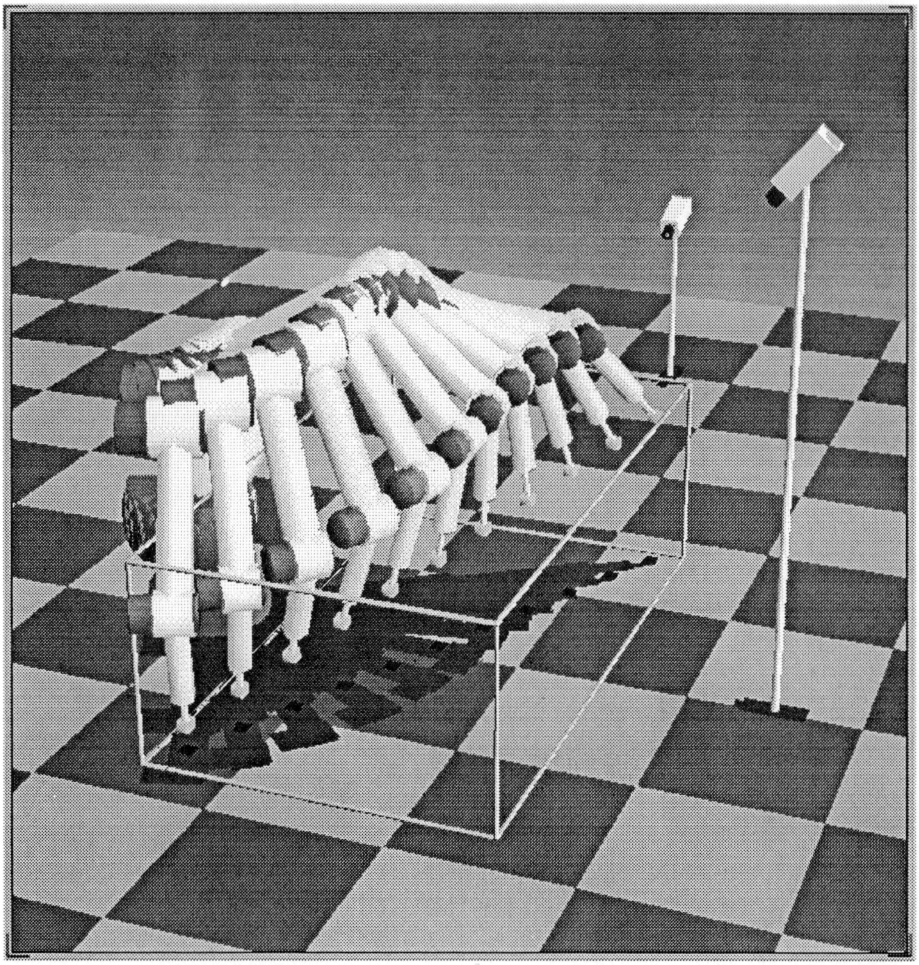

Figure 11.10 Stroboscopic rendering of a movement of the robot arm. The robot arm passes along the diagonal of the work space with its end effector. Due to the redundancy of the robot arm each point along the trajectory can be reached by an infinite number of joint angle sets. The topology-preserving feature of the algorithm forces the use of joint angles that give rise to a smooth movement.

11.7. The Neural Network as a "Look-Up Table"

The presented network for the learning of visuomotor control of arm movements can adapt to arbitrary, continuous, nonlinear input-output relations. The learning algorithm belongs to the class of *"learning by doing"* methods. The approach of the algorithm really amounts to the generation of a *look- up table.* After presentation of an input value (target position) an entry $(\vec{\theta}_s, \mathbf{A}_s)$ must be taken from a table (Kohonen net) that determines the joint angles that are needed to reach the target. The table entry, however, does not immediately deliver the required joint angles, which would correspond to the approximation of the transformation $\vec{\theta}(\mathbf{u})$ to be learned by a step function, but rather two expansion terms for the representation of $\vec{\theta}(\mathbf{u})$ up to linear order are made available. From the expansion terms the required joint angles can be determined to a much greater precision. Each table entry is responsible for only a small subregion of the input signal space; thus, an approximation of the input-output relation to be learned is obtained by a covering of the input signal space with locally valid linear mappings.

The use of Kohonen's algorithm offers the advantage of a flexible wiring between input values and the entries (network nodes) in the table (network), which depends on the input values which have already occurred. The Kohonen algorithm ensures that, in fact, all slots of the table are utilized, and by this the limited number of possible entries are optimally employed. Furthermore, the Kohonen algorithm distributes the entries in the table such that entries which are neighbors in the table are assigned to input values which are neighbors in the input space, based on a given metric. In our example we used the Euclidean metric in the camera coordinates. In order to represent the three-dimensional work space in this neighborhood-conserving way, we employed a three-dimensional "table." In addition to the Kohonen algorithm which exclusively organizes the distribution of the entries of the table, we used an algorithm for the learning of suitable entry contents. Here we used an adaptation step following the Widrow-Hoff rule. An additional cooperation between neighboring entries of the table supports the convergence of the learning algorithm, because, as a consequence of the Kohonen algorithm, neighboring table entries must take on similar contents. It even turns out that without the transfer of each learning success to neighboring entries, the table (neural net) does not converge towards the desired state.

The visuomotor control task with its input-output relation $\vec{\theta}(\mathbf{u})$ is one example among many other control tasks which can be learned by the neural network described. In a real-life implementation there is an opportunity to further abstract the notion of input and output values. Why should the image point coordinates be used explicitly as input values and why should the output values provide explicitly the angles to be set? The presented method adapts arbitrary continuous nonlinear input-output relations. Therefore, a sufficient prerequisite for the application of the learning method is the use of a continuous coding of the input and output signals. Instead of the image point coordinates that we have used so far, the voltage values provided from the cameras could be directly used as input signals for the neural net, without requiring the precise knowledge about the relation between object positions and voltage values. Correspondingly, we would not have to take care of the precise transformation from voltage impulses into rotation movements of the joint motors, or of the amplifiers, filters etc. that might be installed between the input and the output. In case of an "antropomorphic" arm, output values that describe muscle contractions could be delivered instead of joint angles. The algorithm would autonomously adapt the complicated nonlinear transformation from muscle contractions to joint angles. It is only necessary that the response of the robot arm to target points is continuous and reproducible. The coding of the input-output relation can remain unknown and also the inner workings of the robot system may be considered as a "black box." The neural network will adapt to all unknown specifications with the help of the learning algorithm and will achieve its learning goal without help from outside.

With this we conclude this chapter about the learning of one of the basic tasks in robotics, namely end effector positioning. After the robot has learned to reach objects at arbitrary locations in the work space, the next step will be to learn simple manipulations. For these manipulations in most of the cases the grasping of objects will be necessary. The grasping of objects is the next basic task that a robot must accomplish after end effector positioning, which is the reason that we consider this problem more closely in the following chapter.

12. Control of a Manipulator by a Hierarchical Network

12.1. The Robot for the New Task

In Chapter 11 we have shown how an artificial neural network can learn to position a robot arm with its gripper at a desired target. This fundamental capability is the basis of our approach to a new and more complex task in robotics: the control of coordinated grasping movements for simple objects (Martinetz and Schulten 1990).

As we reach for a can of beer or soda, we hardly ever think about the vast complexity involved in grasping an object or, correspondingly, what must be regarded in detail while driving an artificial manipulator. For one thing, the movement to be performed depends on the location of the object in the work space. The shape of the object plays a crucial role in planning a grasping movement. It must be estimated where the center of mass lies because, if there is too large a distance between the center of mass and the chosen grasping position, then undesirable torques can arise which make it difficult to hold the object steadily. The object has to be sufficiently narrow at some place to account for the limited opening of the gripper. The orientation of the object must be considered since grasping an upright object like a beverage requires a different gripper position than that which is effective for the same object on its side. Even the contour of the object must be considered so that the gripper does not slip, and so on.

These complications make us realize the difficulty in developing an overall grasping strategy, and so it should not come as a surprise that this problem forms an area of current research. So far there have been only partial solutions. One promising approach, for instance, uses potential fields of artificial charge distributions which guide the arm and the gripper along the desired trajectory towards the final position (Hwang 1988, Ritter 1990).

We restrict the discussion in this chapter to the complications surrounding the orientation and location of an object to be fetched. We consider a pliers-type end effector of the form displayed in Fig. 12.2, and we choose a relatively simple shape for the object to be grasped, namely, a cylinder. By choosing a rotationally symmetric object the problems relating to the selection of a proper grasping point are simplified, since in this case reaching for the center of the cylinder from any direction is appropriate. Aside from the position in the work space, the orientation of the cylinder is the only other factor which determines the final position of the arm and the gripper.

In Fig. 12.1 we see the model of the robot that we used in our computer simulations. Neither the position of the cameras nor the work space has changed relative to the simulation model of the previous chapter. The geometry of the present robot model, however, imitates the shape of the human arm. This configuration allows the robot always to approach presented objects from the front. By "from the front" we mean that it is possible to bring the gripper into a position between the object and the base of the robot, and from this position the gripper proceeds to grasp the object. This anthropomorphically designed form of the robot arm will later allow the robot to use a grasping strategy which corresponds to a motion that is typical for humans. When grasping an object by hand, humans usually reach from the front. Only in exceptional cases does one opt for a different strategy as might happen, for example, when impeded by an obstacle or when picking up an object from its far side. The robot arm has three degrees of freedom by which each arm configuration is uniquely determined (there is no redundancy). As before, the arm can rotate around its vertical axis (θ_1) and around the axes of the middle (θ_2) and the outer (θ_3) joints, which are parallel to each other and parallel to the horizontal plane. For the orientation of the gripper, two degrees of freedom are available. The first degree of freedom is

Figure 12.1 Model of the robot used in the simulation, the two cameras, and the work space. The robot itself is now in its geometry similar to the form of the human arm. This construction makes it always possible to drive towards objects from the front. The robot's arm has three degrees of freedom: rotation around the vertical axis plus the middle and outer joint, whose axes are parallel to each other and perpendicular to the vertical direction as in previous models. The orientation of the gripper can be modified by two degrees of freedom. The axis of the first joint is parallel to the joint axes of the middle and the outer joint of the arm. The second joint can rotate the gripper around its own symmetry axis.

given by the axis at the "wrist," which is parallel to the middle and outer joint of the arm. The second degree of freedom allows rotation around the gripper's symmetry axis.

Figure 12.2 shows a sketch of the gripper with its two joint angles β_1 and β_2 and the normal vector $\mathbf{n}$ which describes the orientation of the gripper. This vector is perpendicular to the symmetry axis and perpendicular to the flat side of the gripper.

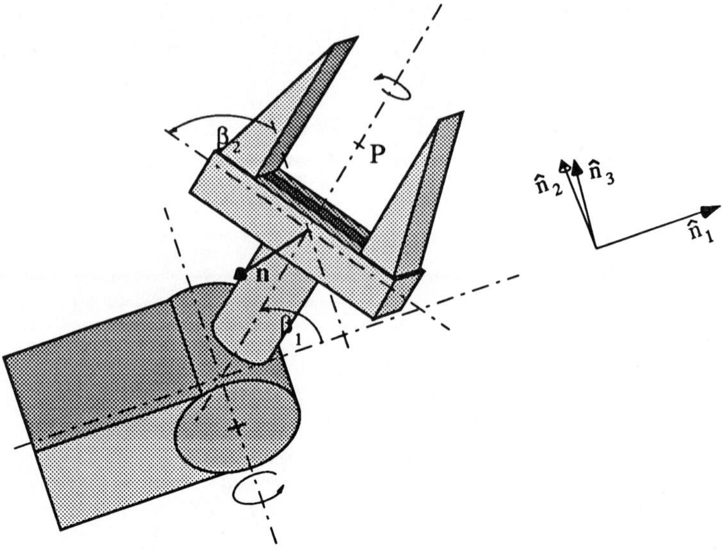

Figure 12.2 A sketch of the gripper with its two joint angles β_1 and β_2 and the normal vector **n**, which describes the orientation of the gripper. Also shown is a coordinate system which is attached to the last segment. The components n_1, n_2, and n_3 of the normal vector **n** relative to this coordinate system are given by Eq. (164). The point P denotes the center and, thereby, the location of the gripper which must be guided towards the center of the cylinder to be grasped.

The point P in Fig. 12.2 denotes the place of the gripper which must be guided towards the center of the cylinder to be grasped. Simultaneously, it is necessary to orient the normal vector n parallel to the axis of the cylinder. Therefore, this normal vector must be able to take on any orientation. This is ensured by the two joint angles β_1 and β_2. The relation between the three components of the normal vector n and the joint angles is given by

$$\begin{aligned} n_1 &= -\sin\beta_1 \cos\beta_2 \\ n_2 &= -\sin\beta_2 \\ n_3 &= \cos\beta_1 \cos\beta_2 \end{aligned} \tag{164}$$

where n_1, n_2, and n_3 are the projections of n on the coordinate system shown in Fig. 12.2, spanned by the unit vectors $\hat{n}_1$, $\hat{n}_2$, and $\hat{n}_3$. In Fig. 12.2 $\hat{n}_1$ runs parallel to the longitudinal axis of the outer segment, $\hat{n}_2$ is perpendicular to $\hat{n}_1$ and lies parallel to the x-y plane, and $\hat{n}_3$ is perpendicular to both.

That we are really able to orient n in any direction can be

recognized particularly well when we perform the transformation $\beta_1 \to -\bar{\beta}_1$ and $\beta_2 \to \bar{\beta}_2 - 90°$. Then we obtain

$$\begin{aligned} n_1 &= \sin \bar{\beta}_1 \sin \bar{\beta}_2 \\ n_2 &= \cos \bar{\beta}_2 \\ n_3 &= \cos \bar{\beta}_1 \sin \bar{\beta}_2, \end{aligned} \tag{165}$$

which corresponds to the polar representation of a three-dimensional vector n with $\bar{\beta}_1$ as the polar angle and $\bar{\beta}_2$ as the azimuthal angle.

12.2. View through Cameras

The task of the neural network is again to transform input signals, delivered by the cameras, into suitable joint angles for the arm and the gripper. In the previous chapter we assumed that an image processing system extracts the required image coordinates of the target location from the camera images. Again we do not want to be concerned with details of the image processing, and we take for granted that we have a suitable image processing system which extracts the required input data from the camera images. To be able to grasp a cylinder, the neural network needs, in addition to the information about the location of the cylinder in the work space, information about the cylinder's orientation in space. At each position in the work space, the cylinder has two additional orientational degrees of freedom which determine the angles of the configuration that is required for arm and gripper while grasping.

In what form do the cameras deliver the necessary information about the orientation of the cylinder? In Fig. 12.3 we see the bars that result from the projection of a cylinder onto the image planes of the two cameras. The bar locations in the two image planes implicitly contain the information about the location of the cylinder in space. The orientations of the bars in the image planes provide the information about the spatial orientation of the cylinder axis.

As can be seen in Fig. 12.3 we describe the location of the center of each bar by its two-dimensional coordinates in the respective image plane of each camera and combine the two coordinate pairs to a four-dimensional vector u. To describe the

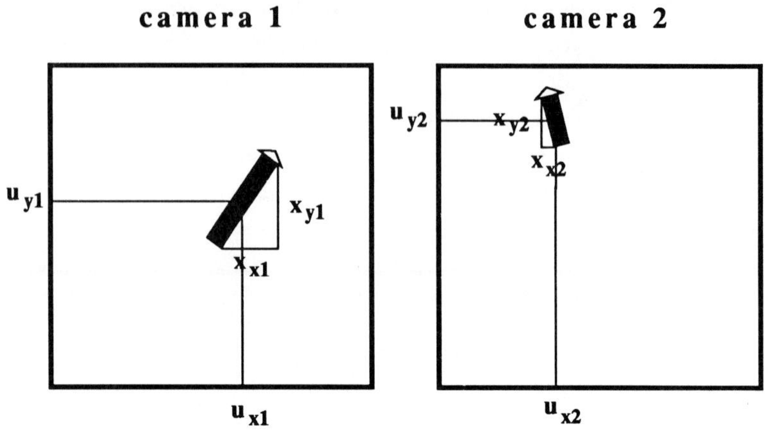

Figure 12.3 The cylinder as seen from cameras 1 and 2. One end of each bar is marked by an arrow head (see text). The position of the centers of both bars described by $(u_{x1}, u_{y1}, u_{x2}, u_{y2})$ determines the spatial position of the cylinder. The coordinate set $(x_{x1}, x_{y1}, x_{x2}, x_{y2})$ in a normalized form contains the information about the orientation of the cylinder that is needed by the neural net.

orientation of each bar we use its projection onto the x- and y-axes of each camera's image plane. To be able to determine this projection uniquely with respect to its sign, it is necessary to assign a direction to the bar in the image plane. In Fig. 12.3 a particular end of the bar is marked by an arrowhead. It does not matter which end is picked, but it must be certain that in both image planes the special end is the same actual end of the cylinder. This demands that the image processing system is able to identify the corresponding ends of both bars. This could be achieved, for example, through comparison of textures. In the case of a soda can, the image processing system must be able to find out which end of both bars corresponds, *e.g.*, to the top.

Thus, there are always two equal possibilities for selecting the special end of the bars. In our simulation, which will be described in greater detail, we choose always that end of the bar that lies "higher" in the image plane of camera 2, *i.e.*, in the coordinate system of the camera's image plane, the one located in the more positive region of the y-axis. The image processing system must then identify the corresponding end of the bar in the image plane of camera 1, and also mark it there.

The projections yield a pair of two-dimensional vectors denoted by (x_{x1}, x_{y1}) and (x_{x2}, x_{y2}) which uniquely describe both bars, including the selected direction. Combining this pair of vectors, we obtain a four-dimensional vector that contains, in addition to the orientation, information about the length of both bars. Because the information about the length of both bars which is correlated to the length of the cylinder is not relevant for the task, we normalize $(x_{x1}, x_{y1}, x_{x2}, x_{y2})$ and obtain the four-dimensional input signal x that now exclusively contains the required information on the cylinder's orientation. The two four-dimensional vectors u and x together comprise the complete information that is needed by the neural net to direct the grasping movement.

12.3. Hierarchical Arrangement of Kohonen Networks

To represent the input signals describing the location and the orientation of the cylinder, we use a network that is composed of an hierarchical arrangement of many subordinated Kohonen nets. As depicted in Fig. 12.4, the network architecture is composed of a set of two-dimensional *sub-lattices* which are arranged in a three-dimensional *super-lattice.*

To represent the input signals responsible for the spatial position, we again choose, as in the last chapter, a three-dimensional Kohonen lattice, however, providing it with two-dimensional subnets at its nodes. Each node of the three-dimensional super-lattice, *i.e.*, each sub-lattice, specializes in a small subregion of the work space during the learning process. Within each of these subregions of the work space, a topology-conserving representation of the different orientations of the cylinder emerges through the corresponding subnet.

The output values are attached to the elements of the two-dimensional sub-lattices. A hierarchically organized selection process chooses the element out of all sub-lattices whose output values will later determine the joint angles for the particular object position and orientation. The selected element should represent the spatial position of the cylinder better than all the other elements. In the selection process we can restrict ourselves to that sub-lattice of the three-dimensional super-lattice which is closest to the object position. The element of this subnet

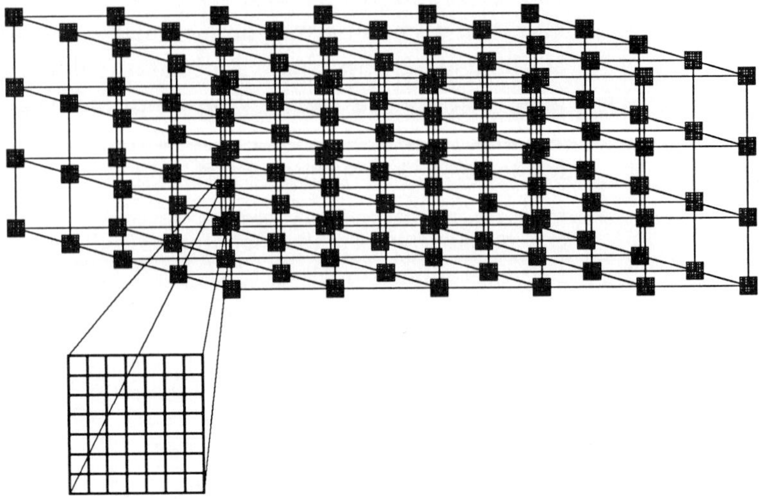

Figure 12.4 Hierarchical arrangement of Kohonen nets. A two-dimensional sub-lattice is assigned to every node of the three-dimensional super-lattice. If $\mathbf{s}$ is the subnet of the super-lattice that is closest to the cylinder, then the element $\mathbf{q}$ within $\mathbf{s}$ that best describes the orientation of the cylinder is selected to determine the output.

that is also closest to the input signal in the space of cylinder orientations will then finally determine the output values.

If we denote the position of every subnet $\mathbf{r}$ in the four-dimensional space of camera coordinates U by $\mathbf{w_r}$, then we search for the particular subnet $\mathbf{s}$ for which holds

$$\|\mathbf{u} - \mathbf{w_s}\| \leq \|\mathbf{u} - \mathbf{w_r}\|, \quad \text{for all} \quad \mathbf{r}.$$

This is followed by the selection of the neural unit within the subnet $\mathbf{s}$ which is finally to be activated. By $\mathbf{z_{sp}}$, we denote the position attached to every element $\mathbf{p}$ of the sub-lattice $\mathbf{s}$ in the space of the input signals $\mathbf{x}$ which describe the cylinder's orientation. By taking also into account the information about the cylinder's orientation, the element $\mathbf{q}$ of $\mathbf{s}$ which finally determines the output signals is defined by

$$\|\mathbf{x} - \mathbf{z_{sq}}\| \leq \|\mathbf{x} - \mathbf{z_{sp}}\|, \quad \text{for all} \quad \mathbf{p}.$$

Because of the hierarchical organization of the Kohonen nets, the time needed to search for the neural unit responsible for the output can be kept short. In our case the relevant submanifold of the whole input signal space, *i.e.*, $U \otimes X$, is five-dimensional because of the five degrees of freedom of the cylinder. If one made an unstructured assignment of this space with equal discretization points, *e.g.*, by applying a five-dimensional Kohonen net, the time needed for the selection of the element q would increase as N^5 where N is the number of elements of the Kohonen net along a single dimension. Due to the hierarchical structure of the network and, consequently, due to the hierarchically organized selection method, the search time t_{search} in our case increases only as

$$t_{search} \sim N_S^3 + N_E^2. \tag{166}$$

Here N_S^3 is the number of subnets and N_E^2 is the number of elements per subnet. The selection of the responding neuron can consequently be managed much faster, assuming $N_E \approx N_S \approx N$. Although the control task has become much more complex, the search time t_{search} does not increase faster with the number of net nodes per dimension than in the case of a robot without a gripper. The search time still increases only as N^3.

After the selection of the subnet with $\mathbf{w_s}$ closest to u and the neural unit with $\mathbf{z_{sq}}$ closest to x, adaptation steps are performed on both levels of the hierarchy of the network. These steps cause (i) a shift of all subnets in the space of camera coordinates U and (ii) an adjustment of all elements of all subnets in the space of cylinder orientations X. The shift of the subnets is accomplished by the familiar adaptation step

$$\mathbf{w_r}^{new} = \mathbf{w_r}^{old} + \epsilon \cdot h_{\mathbf{rs}}(\mathbf{u} - \mathbf{w_r}^{old}), \quad \text{for all} \quad \mathbf{r}\,. \tag{167}$$

The adjustment of the elements of the selected subnet s is also accomplished according to the Kohonen rule, which yields

$$\mathbf{z_{sp}}^{new} = \mathbf{z_{sp}}^{old} + \delta \cdot g_{\mathbf{pq}}(\mathbf{x} - \mathbf{z_{sp}}^{old}), \quad \text{for all} \quad \mathbf{p}. \tag{168}$$

Just as $h_{\mathbf{rs}}$ determined the neighborhood within the three-dimensional super-lattice, now $g_{\mathbf{pq}}$ determines the neighborhood within each two-dimensional subnet. By the adaptation step (167) we obtain a topology-conserving distribution of subnets in the input signal space U. Therefore, it is guaranteed that subnets that are neighbors in the super-lattice must represent a similar distribution of input signals x. Hence, it makes sense to extend the adaptation step for the neurons p in the selected subnet s onto all neighboring subnets r in a way that decreases with the distance from s. To do so we again use $h_{\mathbf{rs}}$ as a measure for the neighborhood within the three-dimensional super-lattice. This motivates us to replace (168) by the adaptation step

$$\mathbf{z}_{\mathbf{rp}}^{new} = \mathbf{z}_{\mathbf{rp}}^{old} + \delta \cdot h_{\mathbf{rs}} g_{\mathbf{pq}} (\mathbf{x} - \mathbf{z}_{\mathbf{sp}}^{old}), \quad \text{for all} \quad \mathbf{r}, \mathbf{p} \tag{169}$$

for all neurons $\mathbf{p}$ of all subnets $\mathbf{r}$.

A hierarchical arrangement of Kohonen nets is useful when the input channels can be combined to groups of different modality with different priority for the quality of their representation. In our case the input signals had the modalities "position" and "orientation." In selecting the best, *i.e.*, closest to $\mathbf{u}$ and $\mathbf{x}$, element of the network, the modality "position" had a higher priority because the gripper attached to the end effector has to be first placed at the object before an alignment of the gripper position makes any sense. By combining elements into groups with identical receptive fields in the space of location information, we obtain a whole set of elements that represent the location information of a cylinder equally well. Within this set, the element is selected which, in addition, provides the best information on the orientation of the cylinder.

Interestingly enough, one finds similar hierarchical structures in the visual cortex of higher animals (Hubel and Wiesel 1974; Blasdel and Salama 1986; Obermayer et al. 1990, 1991). Orientation-sensitive neurons are arranged according to a hierarchically composed topographic map in the visual cortex. Locations on the map represent "locations in the visual field" as well as the "orientation" of a bar appearing on the retina. The visual cortex can be parcelled into many small sections, each of which corresponds to one location in the visual field. Within each of these sections, each neuron is specialized for a different bar orientation, and the whole orientation spectrum of 180° is represented within each section. In this way, a connection between the sections on the visual cortex and the subnets presented in this chapter can be made. The arrangement of the sections on the visual cortex then corresponds to the arrangement of the subnets in the super-lattice.

12.4. The Output Values and the Positioning Process

The required joint angles are uniquely given by the spatial position and the orientation of the cylinder, *i.e.*, by the presentation of the target for P and the direction for n (see Fig. 12.2). The overall five degrees of freedom of the robot's arm and gripper are required in order to handle the three degrees of freedom for the spatial position plus the two degrees of freedom of the cylinder's orientation. It is not possible to decouple the arm and gripper configurations which are required for the different positions and orientations of the cylinder. Similar orientations of the cylinder at different locations in the work space require not only different configurations of the arm but also different alignments of the gripper's joints. The situation is similar when the cylinder at the same location appears with different orientations of its axis. In this case not only must the orientation of the gripper be changed, as one might at first assume, but also the arm must compensate by small corrections of its joint angles for the small shift of the gripper's center P that was caused by a change of the direction of the normal vector $\mathbf{n}$. Mathematically put, this means that the arm's joint angles $\vec{\theta} = (\theta_1, \theta_2, \theta_3)$ and the angles of the gripper $\vec{\beta} = (\beta_1, \beta_2)$ depend simultaneously on u as well as on x. If we combine all five joint angles to the vector $\vec{\phi} = (\theta_1, \theta_2, \theta_3, \beta_1, \beta_2)$, then it holds

$$\vec{\phi}(\mathbf{u},\mathbf{x}) = \begin{pmatrix} \vec{\theta}(\mathbf{u},\mathbf{x}) \\ \vec{\beta}(\mathbf{u},\mathbf{x}) \end{pmatrix}. \tag{170}$$

After presentation of the object the neural unit q within the subnet s is selected which will be responsible for determining suitable output values for setting the joint angles $\vec{\phi}$. For this purpose each element p of every subnet r, in the following denoted by rp, stores two terms, a term $\vec{\phi}_{\mathbf{rp}}$ for gross-positioning and a tensor $\mathbf{A}_{\mathbf{rp}}$ which serves to lineraly interpolate between neighboring units rp. $\vec{\phi}_{\mathbf{rp}}$ in this case is a five-dimensional vector and $\mathbf{A}_{\mathbf{rp}}$ is of dimensions 5×8. The representation of the transformation $\vec{\phi}(\mathbf{u},\mathbf{x})$ that has to be learned is achieved by covering the input signal space with locally valid linearizations of $\vec{\phi}(\mathbf{u}, \mathbf{x})$. The linearizations are done around the locations $\tilde{\mathbf{w}}_{\mathbf{rp}} = (\mathbf{w}_{\mathbf{r}}, \mathbf{z}_{\mathbf{rp}})$, where $\tilde{\mathbf{w}}_{\mathbf{rp}}$ denotes the position in the whole input signal space (the product space $U \otimes X$) connected with unit rp. If we combine both input signals u and x into $\tilde{\mathbf{u}} = (\mathbf{u}, \mathbf{x})$, then the responding neural unit sq generates as an output signal the joint angles

$$\vec{\phi}_i = \vec{\phi}_{\mathbf{sq}} + \mathbf{A}_{\mathbf{sq}}(\tilde{\mathbf{u}} - \tilde{\mathbf{w}}_{\mathbf{sq}}). \tag{171}$$

Equation (171) is of the same form as Eq. (144) for a robot arm without a gripper.

Equation (171) determines the first movement step which is followed by a corrective movement—just like in the case of the robot arm without a gripper. For this purpose it is necessary to determine the position of the arm and gripper from both camera perspectives after the first movement step. For one thing, one needs the image coordinates of the center P of the gripper in cameras 1 and 2. The pair of two-dimensional image coordinates is combined to a four-dimensional vector denoted by $\mathbf{v}_i$. Furthermore, one needs information about the orientation of the gripper that is provided by the direction of the normal vector n (see Fig. 12.2). If we imagine the normal vector n projected onto the camera image planes, then we obtain a two-dimensional vector in each camera. The orientations of both vectors describe the orientation of the gripper in camera coordinates, and they must be brought into alignment with the orientation of the two vectors (x_{x1}, x_{y1}) and (x_{x2}, x_{y2}) that describe the orientation of the cylinder. The pair of two-dimensional vectors that describe the orientation of n after the first movement step is combined to a four-dimensional vector $\mathbf{y}_i$. The absolute value of the difference $\|\mathbf{x} - \mathbf{y}_i\|$ of the vector $\mathbf{y}_i$ and the input signal x is to be minimized.

How can the projection of the normal vector n on the image planes be determined from the images of the gripper? One possibility would be to attach a mark that can easily be identified, *e.g.*, a light, on each of the two flat sides of the gripper directly opposite to each other. The difference vector from the positions of the two lights as seen from the first camera yields the projection of the normal vector n onto the image plane of camera 1. Analogously, we obtain the projection of n onto the image plane of camera 2. Both difference vectors are then combined to a four-dimensional vector and are normalized to eliminate the irrelevant information about the distance of both lamps to each other. In that way, information about the direction of the virtual normal vector or equivalently, about the orientation of the gripper, can be obtained in a very simple way from the camera pictures of the gripper.

The information about the intermediate position of the arm $\mathbf{v}_i$ and about the intermediate orientation of the gripper $\mathbf{y}_i$ (resulting from the angles $\vec{\phi}_i$ as given by (171)) are again combined into a vector $\tilde{\mathbf{v}}_i = (\mathbf{v}_i, \mathbf{y}_i)$. The residual difference $\tilde{\mathbf{u}} - \tilde{\mathbf{v}}_i$ between the target coordinates $\tilde{\mathbf{u}}$ and the intermediate coordinates $\tilde{\mathbf{v}}_i$ determines a corrective step. This step uses the Jacobian matrix of the responding neural unit $\mathbf{sq}$ and determines a correction for all five joint angles,

$$\Delta\vec{\phi} = \mathbf{A}_{\mathbf{sq}}(\tilde{\mathbf{u}} - \tilde{\mathbf{v}}_i), \tag{172}$$

by which we obtain the final joint angle configuration $\vec{\phi}_f = \vec{\phi}_i + \Delta\vec{\phi}$. The corresponding position and orientation of the gripper is again observed through the cameras and denoted by $\tilde{\mathbf{v}}_f = (\mathbf{v}_f, \mathbf{y}_f)$.

The corrective step (172) can be performed several times in succession to further reduce the positioning and orientation error to values only limited by the imperfections of the devices used in practice, *e.g.*, by the camera resolution. The corrective step, being based on feedback control, will later allow us to use a grasping strategy that is similar to the grasping strategy that humans use. The feedback process allows to move toward an object cautiously, thereby avoiding a collision with the object. In the following considerations we will confine ourselves to a single corrective step (172).

12.5. The Learning Method for the Output Values

The use of a vector $\vec{\phi}_{\mathbf{rp}}$ and of a Jacobian matrix $\mathbf{A}_{\mathbf{rp}}$ to represent the transformation $\vec{\phi}(\mathbf{u}, \mathbf{x})$ is analogous to the learning algorithm for the robot arm without a gripper in the previous chapter. This is also true for the positioning process with its two phases, gross positioning according to (171) and corrective step according to (172) (step 5 and step 6 in Section 11.2). Therefore, we can adopt the algorithm presented in Section 11.3 that we employed for the learning of the end effector positioning to improve the output values $\vec{\phi}_{\mathbf{rp}}$ and $\mathbf{A}_{\mathbf{rp}}$. Only the transformation of the learning success of one neural unit onto its neighbors will be of a different form because of the hierarchical architecture of the network.

The corrective movement (172) again serves to iteratively determine the Jacobian matrices from small changes in the joint angles in conjunction with the corresponding small changes in the camera coordinates. This makes it possible to determine an improved estimate $\mathbf{A}^*$ for $\mathbf{A}_{\mathbf{sq}}$. Combined with the step that determines an improved estimate $\vec{\phi}^*$, we obtain

$$\begin{aligned} \vec{\phi}^* &= \vec{\phi}_{\mathbf{sq}} + \delta_1 \cdot \mathbf{A}_{\mathbf{sq}}(\tilde{\mathbf{u}} - \tilde{\mathbf{v}}_i) \\ \mathbf{A}^* &= \mathbf{A}_{\mathbf{sq}} + \delta_2 \cdot \mathbf{A}_{\mathbf{sq}}(\tilde{\mathbf{u}} - \tilde{\mathbf{v}}_f)\Delta\tilde{\mathbf{v}}^T, \end{aligned} \tag{173}$$

where $\Delta\tilde{\mathbf{v}} = \tilde{\mathbf{v}}_f - \tilde{\mathbf{v}}_i$. For the adaptation step widths δ_1 and δ_2 we choose, as in Section 11.2, the optimal values $\delta_1 = 1$ and $\delta_2 = 1/\|\Delta\tilde{\mathbf{v}}\|^2$.

The new estimates $\vec{\phi}^*$, $\mathbf{A}^*$ obtained by means of Eq. (173) are used to improve the output values of the neural unit sq and its neighbors. But in the present case of a robot arm with gripper we have two hierarchies of neighborhoods, one within the subnet that is described by the neighborhood function $g'_{\mathbf{pq}}$, and the other between the subnets described by the neighborhood function $h'_{\mathbf{rs}}$. Not only the neighboring neurons p within the subnet s participate in the learning of the activated neuron sq, but also the subnets r which are neighboring in the super-lattice participate according to their distance to the subnet s. This leads to the adaptation step

$$\begin{aligned} \vec{\phi}^{\,new}_{\mathbf{rp}} &= \vec{\phi}^{\,old}_{\mathbf{rp}} + \epsilon' h'_{\mathbf{rs}} g'_{\mathbf{pq}} \left(\vec{\phi}^{\,*} - \vec{\phi}^{\,old}_{\mathbf{rp}}\right) \\ \mathbf{A}^{new}_{\mathbf{rp}} &= \mathbf{A}^{old}_{\mathbf{rp}} + \epsilon' h'_{\mathbf{rs}} g'_{\mathbf{pq}} \left(\mathbf{A}^* - \mathbf{A}^{old}_{\mathbf{rp}}\right) \end{aligned} \tag{174}$$

for the neural units of all subnets.

The learning steps (174) for the output values are of the same form as the learning step (169) for the position $\mathbf{z}_{\mathbf{rp}}$ attached to each element rp. Both affect neural units that are neighbors in the subnet and also subnets that are neighbors in the super-lattice. Instead of the input signals x, the improved estimates $\vec{\phi}^{\,*}$ and $\mathbf{A}^*$ occur in Eq. (174).

12.6. Simulation Results

In this section we describe the results of a simulation of the learning algorithm. For the computer simulation we have employed a super-lattice consisting of 4×7×2 subnets. Each of the subnets contains 3×3 neural units. The parameters that describe the work space and the position of the cameras are the same as in the previous chapter.

In total, the robot arm performed 10,000 learning steps. In Fig. 12.5 we present the development of the three-dimensional super-lattice. We again show the focal planes of cameras 1 and 2. In the left column of Fig. 12.5 we see the projection of the centers $\mathbf{w_r}$ of the receptive fields of the subnets on the focal plane of camera 1. In the same way the projections of $\mathbf{w_r}$ on the focal plane of camera 2 are depicted in the right column. In each projection, subnets which are adjacent in the super-lattice are connected by straight lines. The state of the super-lattice is shown at the beginning, after 1000, and after 10,000 learning steps. The development of the super-lattice corresponds, except for a lower number of lattice points, to the development of the three-dimensional Kohonen lattice in the previous chapter.

We illustrate the development of all the two-dimensional subnets by displaying the development of one of them. The input signals of each subnet consist of four-dimensional vectors $\mathbf{x} = (x_{x1}, x_{y1}, x_{x2}, x_{y2})$, the components of which were restricted to the interval $[-1, 1]$ through the imposed normalization. The input signals $\mathbf{x}$ are represented by the four-dimensional vectors $\mathbf{z_{rp}}$ that are assigned to the elements of each subnet. The first two components of $\mathbf{z_{rp}}$ represent the occurring bar orientations (x_{x1}, x_{y1}) as seen by camera 1, and the last two components represent the bar orientations (x_{x2}, x_{y2}) seen by camera 2. In Fig. 12.6 we show the state of the subnet in the beginning, after 1000, and after 10,000 learning steps. In the left column the first two components and in the right column the last two components of $\mathbf{z_{rp}}$ are depicted. Each of the squares in Fig. 12.6 represents the region $-1 < x_x < 1$, $-1 < x_y < 1$.

Since the edges of the presented cylinders always lie on the surface of a sphere (end-points of normalized vector $\mathbf{x}$),

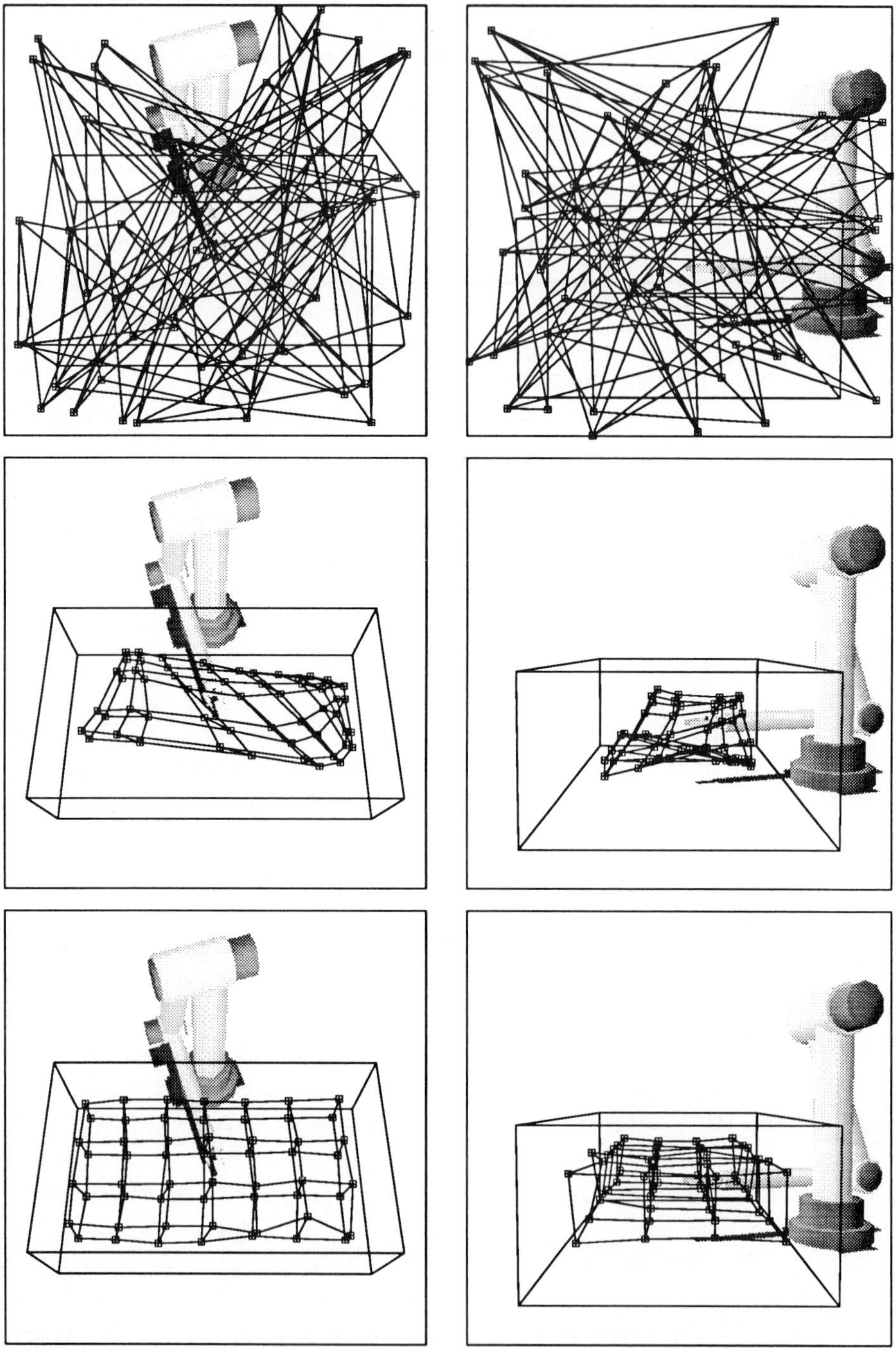

Figure 12.5 The three-dimensional super-lattice, initially (top), after 1000 (middle), and after 10,000 learning steps (bottom). The left column shows the focal plane of camera 1, and the right column shows the focal plane of camera 2. At each node of the super-lattice the corresponding subnet is schematically depicted.

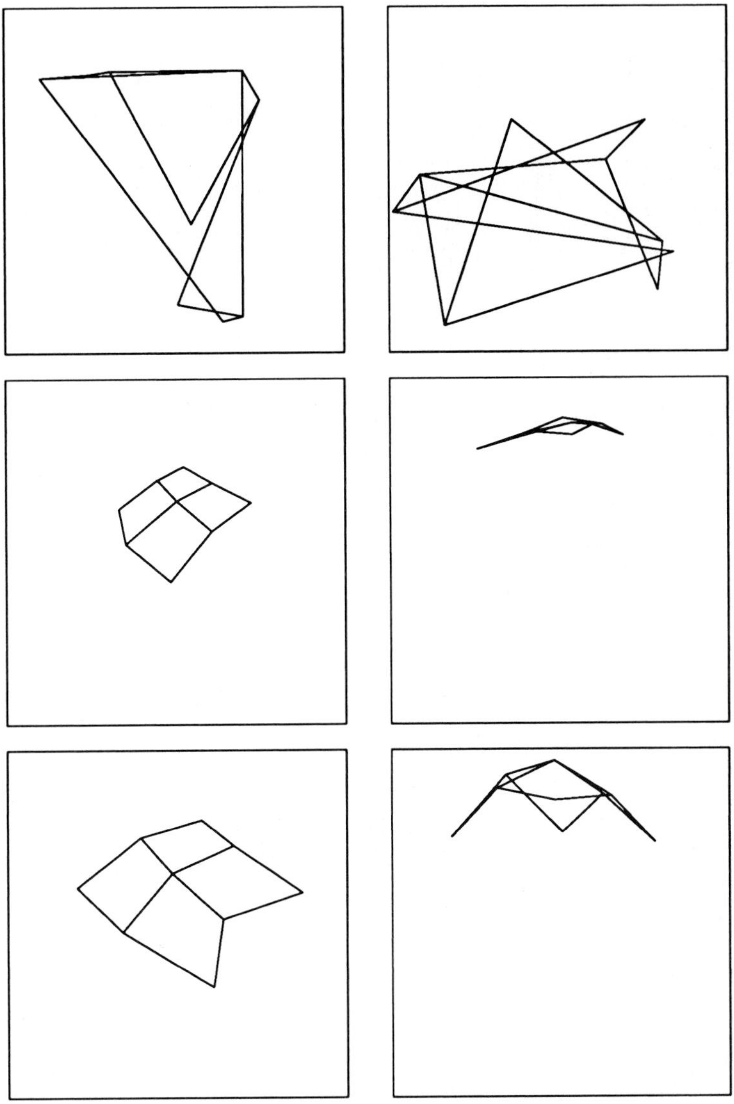

Figure 12.6 The state of a sample subnet at the beginning (top), after 1000 (middle), and after 10,000 learning steps (bottom).

it follows that the two-dimensional submanifold that is to be represented by a subnet is also spherical. Each of the two-dimensional subnets tries to adhere to the surface of the sphere. In the right column of Fig. 12.6 we see that the subnet shown lies completely in the upper half of the box. This results from our assignment of the "special" end of the bar in camera 2 to the end with the larger y-value. Hence, x_{y2} is always positive

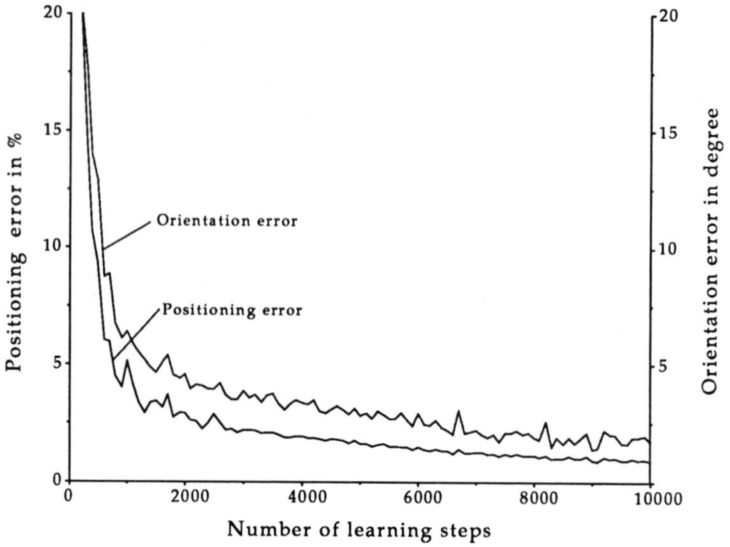

Figure 12.7 The mean positioning (in % of the length of the workspace) and orientation error (in degree) as a function of the number of learning steps. After 10,000 learning steps the positioning error is 0.004, which corresponds to about 0.6% of the length work space. The slightly larger error compared to the robot arm without a gripper in the previous chapter is due to the smaller three-dimensional main lattice. The orientation error of the gripper decreased to the small value of 1.7° after 10,000 learning steps. This value is much smaller than necessary for successful performance of the task.

and at the end of the learning, only the upper half of the sphere is covered by the subnet. The vector that describes the bar as seen by camera 1 may have almost any direction in the focal plane. Thus, in the left column of Fig. 12.6 the net at the end of the learning phase is more evenly spread out.

In the simulation just described, we assumed for all the parameters ϵ, δ, ϵ', σ, σ', ρ, and ρ' the same time dependence $x_i(x_f/x_i)^{t/t_{max}}$ with $t_{max} = 10,000$. The parameters ρ and ρ' denote the width of the Gaussians $g_{\mathbf{pq}}$ and $g'_{\mathbf{pq}}$ introduced in (169) and (174). For the initial and final values of the parameters we chose $\epsilon_i = 1$, $\epsilon_f = 0.01$, $\delta_i = 1$, $\delta_f = 0.01$, $\epsilon'_i = 0.8$, $\epsilon'_f = 0.4$, $\sigma_i = 1.5$, $\sigma_f = 0.3$, $\sigma'_i = 1$, $\sigma'_f = 0.3$, $\rho_i = 1$, $\rho_f = 0.1$, $\rho'_i = 1$, $\rho'_f = 0.3$.

In Fig. 12.7 we illustrate the learning success by presenting the positioning and orientation error as a function of the number of learning steps. The corresponding errors were determined by performing a test after every 100 trial movements. For each test we suspended the learning and monitored the performance by presenting a randomly oriented cylinder at 1000 randomly chosen locations within the work space. The mean error at that stage of learning was computed by averaging over the errors of the 1000 test movements. Two quantities were monitored: (i) the positioning error, *i.e.*, the difference between the center of the gripper P and the center of the cylinder, and (ii) the difference between the gripper orientation and the orientation of the cylinder, measured in degrees. The positioning error after 10,000 learning steps has decayed to 0.004, which corresponds to 0.6% of the length of the work space. The positioning error is slightly larger than in the previous chapter where only the end-effector positioning was learned. This results from a six-times smaller number of nodes of the three-dimensional super-lattice and, therefore, a much smaller resolution for the positioning task. Yet, a positioning error of 0.004 is still acceptable for the task. The error in orienting the gripper at the end of the learning phase measured $1.7°$. The precision in orienting the gripper is much higher than is usually necessary for grasping tasks and comparable to human performance. It is remarkable that such a precision could be achieved through subnets consisting of only nine nodes.

12.7. A Simple Grasping Strategy

We have seen that the robot system can learn orientation and positioning of a gripper in relation to a cylindrical object. However, this is not enough in order to be able to grasp the object. In addition, an adequate strategy for approaching the object is necessary. The object has to be approached such that the robot's arm and gripper do not collide with it. For that reason we have chosen, as mentioned earlier in this chapter, a robot architecture which allows the robot to always approach the object from the front (see Fig. 12.1). That means the gripper can always be positioned between the base of the robot and the object. In the following we present a grasping strategy which takes advantage of such a robot architecture.

Humans usually carry out grasping movements by first coarsely positioning the hand in front of the object and then, controlled by a feedback loop, smoothly approach and finally grasp

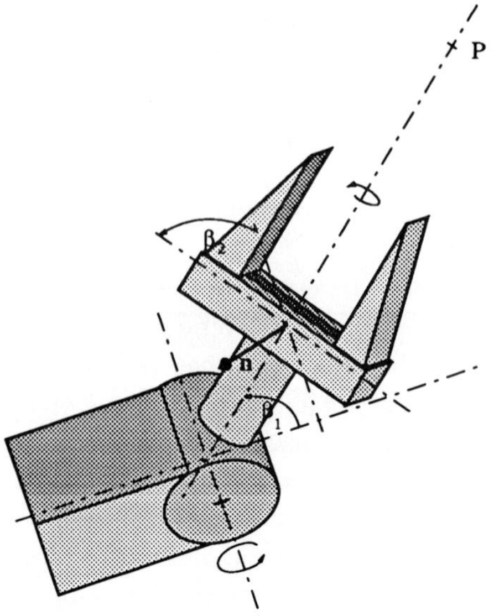

Figure 12.8 The sketch of the gripper shown in Fig. 12.2. We slide the point P, which is to be moved to the center of the cylinder by the first movement step, out along the symmetry axis of the gripper until it lies well in front of the gripper.

the object. We will choose a corresponding strategy for the robot arm. Until now the robot has tried to directly move the center of the gripper P to the center of the cylinder by means of movement step (171). However, such an approach would lead in most cases to a collision with the object. The learning algorithm has to acquire a trajectory of the manipulator which during the transition from the previous joint angles to the new ones avoids collisions. Which type of trajectory avoids collisions with the cylinder? If we assume that the gripper already has its proper orientation, then it is sufficient for the last portion of the trajectory to be arranged such that the continuation of the symmetry axis of the gripper always crosses the symmetry axis of the cylinder. To ensure this, we must modify our previous moving strategy.

For that purpose the point P which until now was placed in the center of the gripper and by design was moved to coincide with the center of the cylinder, is now slid out along the symmetry axis of the gripper to a position shown in Fig. 12.8, namely to a position in front of the gripper. The learning algorithm, by placing the point P at the center of the cylinder, positions the gripper in front of the cylinder rather than colliding with it. At the same time, during the first movement step, the gripper adjusts to its proper orientation. A feedback-guided movement follows that leads the center of the gripper smoothly and without collisions towards the center of the cylinder.†

To accomplish the latter motion we employ a corrective movement described by (172). This corrective movement, rather than having to reduce the deviation between P and the center of the cylinder, now has to reduce the remaining discrepancy between the center of the gripper and the center of the cylinder. This latter discrepancy may be relatively large, depending on how far P lies in front of the gripper. Therefore, we now have to carry out the corrective movement not just once, but several times, until the residual positioning error drops below a desired minimal value. By $\mathbf{v}'_i$ we denote the location of the center of the gripper after the first movement step (171) as seen by the cameras. This location along with the orientation $\mathbf{y}_i$ of the gripper is denoted by $\tilde{\mathbf{v}}'_i = (\mathbf{v}'_i, \mathbf{y}_i)$. We then obtain

$$\Delta\vec{\phi} = \gamma \mathbf{A}_{\mathbf{sq}}(\tilde{\mathbf{u}} - \tilde{\mathbf{v}}'_i) \tag{175}$$

for the corrective movement in approaching the object, where γ is the parameter which determines the step size.

With the first movement step, we achieve the crossing of the symmetry axis of the gripper with the symmetry axis of the cylinder. While the gripper approaches the cylinder by the corrective movements (175), these axes must remain intersected with one another. This would be guaranteed if $\mathbf{A}_{\mathbf{sq}}(\tilde{\mathbf{u}} - \tilde{\mathbf{v}}'_i)$ were exactly the required joint angle difference $\vec{\phi}(\tilde{\mathbf{u}}) - \vec{\phi}(\tilde{\mathbf{v}}'_i)$. Since this is not exactly the case, the choice of $\gamma = 1$ can lead to a significant deviation of the resulting trajectory from the desired trajectory along the line connecting the gripper center and the center of the cylinder. By choosing $\gamma \ll 1$ and, consequently, by adding a number of feedback loops (175), we force the deviation from the desired trajectory to remain small, enabling the approach towards the object to proceed smoothly and collisionless.

As an improved estimate for $\vec{\phi}_{\mathbf{sq}}$ we obtain, as before,

$$\vec{\phi}^* = \vec{\phi}_{\mathbf{sq}} + \delta_1 \cdot \mathbf{A}_{\mathbf{sq}}(\tilde{\mathbf{u}} - \tilde{\mathbf{v}}_i). \tag{176}$$

†The reader may note the similarity between the approach presented here and the observed strategy of saccadic eye movements which undershoot fovea targets as discussed in Section 9.5

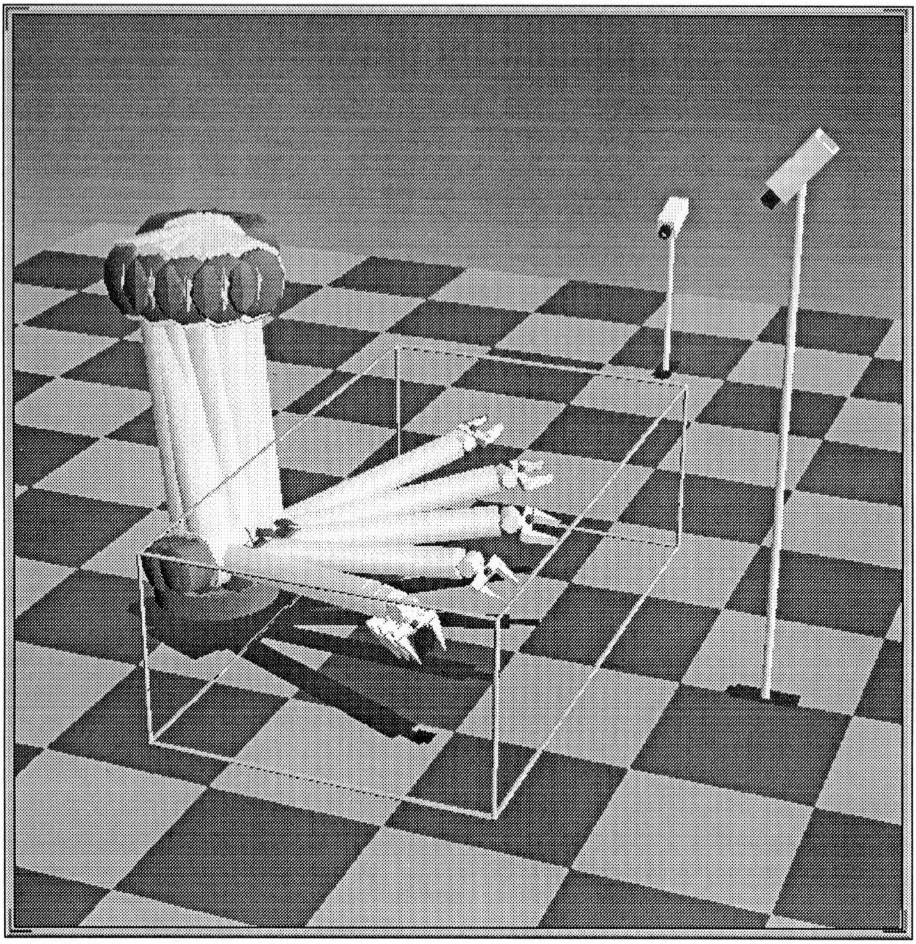

Figure 12.9 "Stroboscopic" rendering of a grasping movement of the robot. The chosen movement strategy enables the robot to approach the cylinder without collisions.

Nonetheless, the equation that determines the improved estimate for $\mathbf{A_{sq}}$ needs to be modified compared to (173) since we now employ several correction movements with step sizes $\gamma < 1$. As before we denote the position of P on the focal planes of the cameras after the first movement step by $\mathbf{v}_i$, and in combination with $\mathbf{y}_i$ we define $\tilde{\mathbf{v}}_i = (\mathbf{v}_i, \mathbf{y}_i)$. If, as before, we denote the position of P and the gripper's orientation after the first corrective movement by $\tilde{\mathbf{v}}_f$, the expression

$$\mathbf{A}^* = \delta_1 \cdot \left[\Delta\vec{\phi} - \mathbf{A_{sq}}(\tilde{\mathbf{v}}_f - \tilde{\mathbf{v}}_i)\right] \left[\tilde{\mathbf{v}}_f - \tilde{\mathbf{v}}_i\right]^T \qquad (177)$$

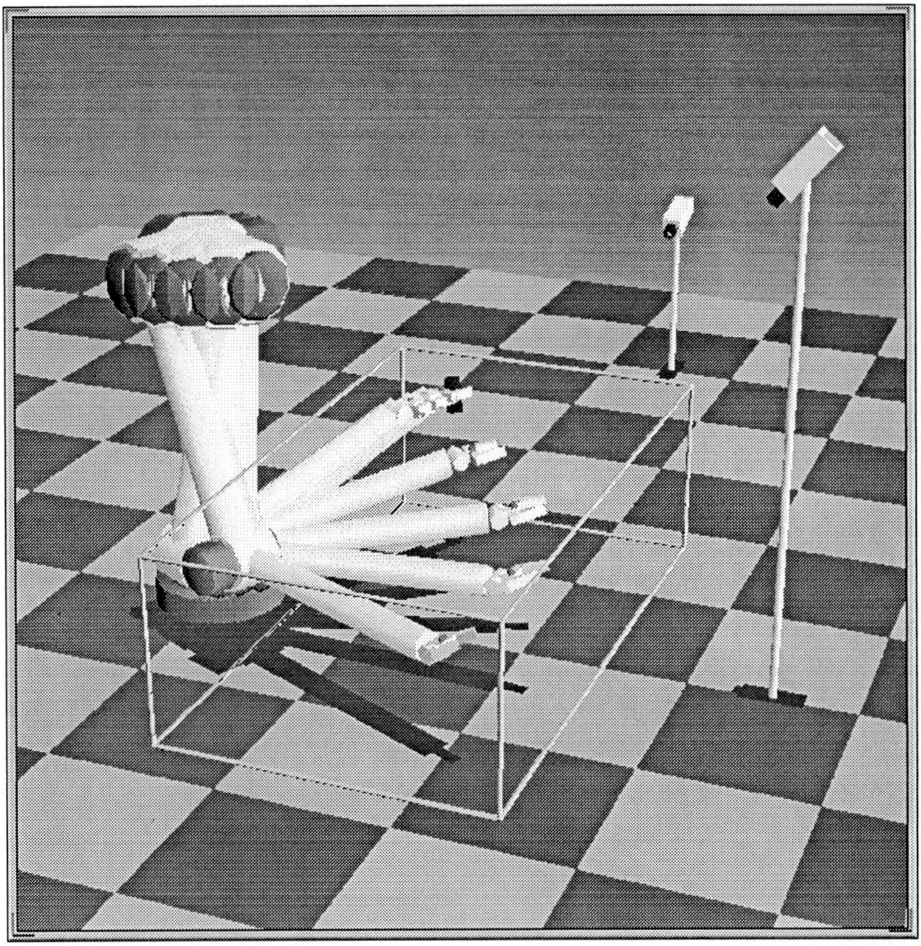

Figure 12.10 "Stroboscopic" rendering of a second grasping movement. Again the robot carries out the grasping movement successfully.

which corresponds to Eq. (153) yields in conjunction with (175)

$$\mathbf{A}^* = \delta_1 \cdot \mathbf{A}_{\mathbf{sq}} \left[\gamma(\tilde{\mathbf{u}} - \tilde{\mathbf{v}}_i') - (\tilde{\mathbf{v}}_f - \tilde{\mathbf{v}}_i)\right] \left[\tilde{\mathbf{v}}_f - \tilde{\mathbf{v}}_i\right]^T \tag{178}$$

as an improved estimate for $\mathbf{A}_{\mathbf{sq}}$. As in the earlier procedure, $\mathbf{A}^*$ is computed using only values provided by the cameras. As adaptation steps for all $\vec{\phi}_{\mathbf{rp}}$ and $\mathbf{A}_{\mathbf{rp}}$ we employ again (174).

Without major revisions we have been able to realize the described grasping strategy by our algorithm; the Jacobian matrices $\mathbf{A}_{\mathbf{rp}}$ allow us to set up the feedback loop in a natural way. The robot arm is now able to approach the cylinders that are presented within the work space without inadvertently colliding with them. To demonstrate the action of the robot arm, we show "stroboscopic" renderings of two grasping movements in Figs. 12.9 and 12.10. In every approach of the cylinder three corrective fine movements (175) were carried out after the gross positioning. For the step size γ of the fine movements, we chose $0.3 + 0.2 \cdot n$ with $n = 1, 2, 3$ as the number of the currently preformed correction step. One can see in Figs. 12.9 and 12.10 that in both cases the robot arm system accomplishes the grasping movement successfully.

We have seen that it is possible by the neural network algorithm introduced to solve not only the basic problem of end-effector positioning, but also to approach the more complex task of grasping simple objects. It turns out that less computational power and memory for controlling the robot arm are required if, as the complexity of the task rises, the network architecture becomes increasingly structured. By employing a hierarchical arrangement of Kohonen networks, the input signals for controlling the grasping movements can be represented in a natural way. In Chapter 13 we will turn to questions which arise under the *dynamic* control of robot arms.

13. Learning Ballistic Movements of a Robot Arm

13.1. Problem and Model Approach

After a sufficiently long training phase, the network described in the preceding chapters can provide the required joint angles for any desired arm position. However, setting the joints to these angles is left to the joint servo motors of the arm. Such motors achieve the target position by changing their torque in opposite direction to any angular deviation from the target joint settings. For slow movements, this is an appropriate strategy because the individual joint movements can then be regarded to good approximation as independent of one another. However, for rapid movements, the inertia of the arm segments leads to a coupling between movements of different joints. For example, the movement of an inner (proximal) joint leads to an acceleration of all outer (more distal) joints and, hence, to the occurrence of torques, which must additionally be overcome by the joint motors. Conversely, the inner joint motors must counterbalance the action of outer joint motors.

In summary, inertial, centrifugal, and gyroscopic forces occur, the interplay of which leads to a complex, nonlinear coupling of all joints. In this situation, a single motor can no longer determine its torque from the present and given joint position alone, but rather its torque must also depend on the movements of all the other joints. Thus, to achieve the desired movement, it is no longer sufficient to take into account the connection between arm position and joint angles alone, *i.e.*, the *kinematics* of the arm. The Newtonian equations of motion of the arm, *i.e.*, its *dynamics*, must be included as well. Although the Newtonian equations can be given in closed form, they become enormously complicated for multi-joint systems. A closed solution is possible only in exceptional cases, and even approximate solutions require a knowledge of the *inertia tensors* of the individual arm segments. In this case, a real-time computation of the arm torques is possible by means of recent algorithms whose computational effort grows only linearly with the number of arm joints. However, the inertia tensors required for such a computation are frequently known only imprecisely. This is due to the fact that the spatial mass distribution of the arm, which is described by these tensors, in general is very complicated for real systems. Hence, adaptive algorithms with the ability to *learn* these properties of the arm are highly desirable.

In this chapter we show how the extended Kohonen algorithm can also be applied to the problem of moving a robot arm by accounting for the arm's dynamics. We choose the task to control a three-link robot arm as introduced in Section 11.1 by means of briefly applied torque pulses at its joints in such a way as to accelerate its end effector to a prescribed velocity. During the remaining time, the arm is to move freely. The relationship between arm configuration, desired velocity, and required torque pulse is to be learned by a network again through trial movements. In contrast to the previous situation, this requires taking into account not only arm kinematics but also arm dynamics, *i.e.*, effects of inertia. Since we have shown in Chapter 12 how a network may learn to compute the transformation from visual information to joint angles, we will not consider this part of the problem here anymore and encode arm configuration directly by joint angles. As before, the arm can move its end effector freely in every spatial direction and reach any point on the working area which is now the planar surface of a table located in front of it. In the simulation, the relationship between end effector motion and joint torques is to be learned for those configurations for which the end effector is located directly above the working area. The configuration of the arm is again specified by its joint angles, expressed in vector notation by $\vec{\theta} = (\theta_1, \theta_2, \theta_3)$. The movement of the arm is effected by three torques $\mathbf{d} = (d_1, d_2, d_3)$ acting on its joint axes. Let q denote the position of the end effector in Cartesian coordinates. The equations of motion of the arm are then given by (see for example Brady et al. 1984)

$$d_i(t) = \sum_{j=1}^{3} A(\vec{\theta})_{ij}\ddot{q}_j + \sum_{j,k=1}^{3} B(\vec{\theta})_{ijk}\dot{q}_j\dot{q}_k + g_i(\vec{\theta}). \tag{179}$$

$\mathbf{A}(\vec{\theta})$ and $\mathbf{B}(\vec{\theta})$ are configuration-dependent matrices which describe the dynamical properties of the arm. The term $\mathbf{g}(\vec{\theta})$ takes the contribution of gravity into account. If the end effector is initially at rest, a briefly applied torque pulse

$$\mathbf{d}(t) = \vec{\tau} \cdot \delta(t) \tag{180}$$

thus imparts to it the velocity $\mathbf{v} = \dot{\mathbf{q}}$ satisfying

$$\vec{\tau} = \mathbf{A}(\vec{\theta})\mathbf{v}. \tag{181}$$

Here $\vec{\tau} = (\tau_1, \tau_2, \tau_3)$ denotes three torques acting on the three joints of the robot arm. In particular, the coefficients B_{ijk} and g_i do not influence the velocity attained immediately after the torque pulse (the change in $\mathbf{v}$ during the subsequent force-free motion, which is affected by B_{ijk} and g_i, is not included here). Motions generated by the brief torque pulses described by (181) are termed *ballistic movements.* Equation (181) describes a relationship between configuration $\vec{\theta}$, torque amplitude $\vec{\tau}$, and resulting end effector velocity $\mathbf{v}$ in a form similar to that of Eq.(143). Hence, the learning algorithm developed in Chapter 11 is again applicable. As before, we make use of a lattice and define a vector $\mathbf{w_r}$ and a matrix $\mathbf{A_r}$ for each lattice site $\mathbf{r}$. Just as in Chapter 11, each $\mathbf{w_r}$ specifies an arm configuration, but this time in terms of joint angles. Thus, $\mathbf{w_r}$ is now a three-component vector.

In the course of the learning phase, each lattice site $\mathbf{r}$ becomes responsible for a small subregion of the arm's configuration space, the subregion extending about the configuration defined by the joint angles $\mathbf{w_r}$. The matrix $\mathbf{A_r}$ should converge to the transformation matrix which, according to (181) connects the desired end effector velocity $\mathbf{v}$ and the required torque amplitudes $\vec{\tau}$ in this subregion.

The training phase of the robot consists again of a sequence of trial movements. For each trial, the starting configuration $\vec{\theta}$ is obtained by requiring the end effector to be at some randomly chosen position within the working area. From there, the end effector is to be moved with a prescribed velocity $\mathbf{u}$ (also chosen at random during the learning phase). On the basis of the initial configuration $\vec{\theta}$, the system selects that transformation matrix $\mathbf{A_s}$, for which $\|\mathbf{w_s} - \vec{\theta}\| = \min_{\mathbf{r}} \|\mathbf{w_r} - \vec{\theta}\|$. On the basis of the prescribed velocity $\mathbf{u}$, it then performs the movement resulting from the torque amplitude

$$\vec{\tau} = \mathbf{A_s u}. \tag{182}$$

From the end effector velocity $\mathbf{v}$ actually obtained, an improved estimate

$$\mathbf{A}^* = \mathbf{A_s} + \frac{\epsilon'}{\|\mathbf{v}\|^2}(\vec{\tau} - \mathbf{A_s v})\mathbf{v}^T \tag{183}$$

is derived for $\mathbf{A_s}$, and, taking into account the input quantity $\vec{\theta}$, the learning steps

$$\mathbf{w_r}^{(new)} = \mathbf{w_r}^{(old)} + \epsilon h_{\mathbf{rs}}(\vec{\theta} - \mathbf{w_r}^{(old)}) \tag{184}$$

$$\mathbf{A_r}^{(new)} = \mathbf{A_r}^{(old)} + h'_{\mathbf{rs}}(\mathbf{A}^* - \mathbf{A_r}^{(old)}) \tag{185}$$

are carried out for the variables $\mathbf{w_r}$, $\mathbf{A_r}$, respectively. Subsequently, the next trial movement is executed.

13.2. A Simulation

In the following simulation $h_{\mathbf{rs}}$ and $h'_{\mathbf{rs}}$ were again chosen as Gaussians, and $\sigma(t)$, $\sigma'(t)$, $\epsilon(t)$ and $\epsilon'(t)$ were all of the familiar form $x(t) = x_i \cdot (x_f/x_i)^{t/t_{max}}$.

The motion of the robot arm was simulated on a computer, using a dynamics simulation algorithm as suggested by Walker and Orin (1982). The mass distribution was assumed to consist of three unit point masses located at the middle and front joints, and at the end of the arm. Let us consider a Cartesian coordinate system whose origin is located at the base of the arm and whose xy-plane coincides with the plane of the working surface. The x and y-axes run parallel to the short and long edges of the working surface, respectively. For each trial movement, the desired velocity was chosen as a random vector with an isotropic distribution of direction and its length a random value uniformly distributed between 0 and 1.

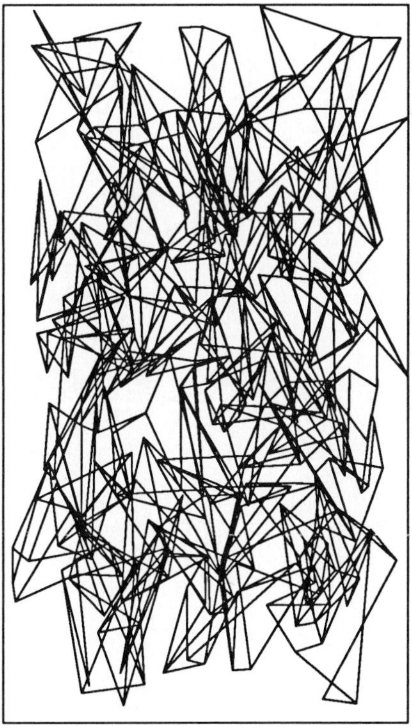

Figure 13.1a Assignment of end effector positions to lattice sites at the beginning of the simulation.

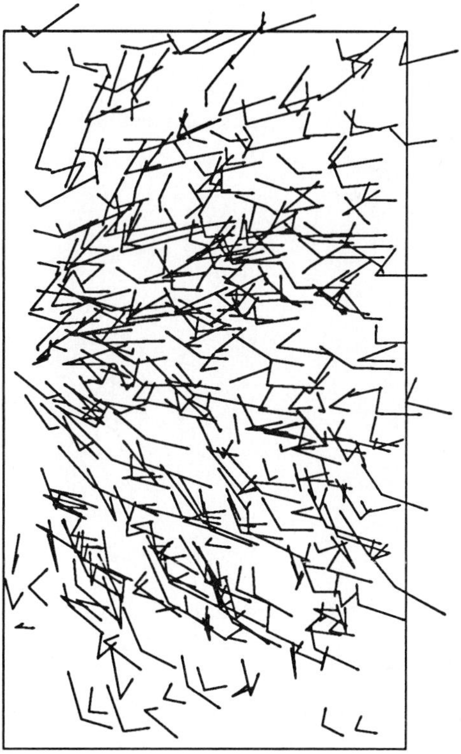

Figure 13.1b The reaction of the end effector to two test movements along the horizontal x-direction and vertical y-direction for the end effector positions of Fig. 13.1a.

The network consisted of a planar, rectangular 15×24 lattice of 360 neural units. A random initial state was generated in the following way: For each lattice site **r**, an end effector position on the working surface was selected at random, and $\mathbf{w_r}$ was set to the corresponding joint angles. For this position, the correct transformation matrix **A** was computed. The individual elements of $\mathbf{A_r}$ were then calculated from the elements of **A** by superposition of random errors according to

$$(\mathbf{A_r})_{ij} = \mathbf{A}_{ij} + \alpha \|\mathbf{A}\| \cdot \eta. \tag{186}$$

Here, $\eta \in [-1, 1]$ is a uniformly distributed random variable, and α is a parameter measuring the deviation of the initial matrices $\mathbf{A_r}$ from their correct values. The simulation data were $\alpha = 0.25$, $\epsilon_i = 0.8$, $\epsilon_f = 0.02$, $\epsilon_i' = 1$, $\epsilon_f' = 0.5$, $\sigma_i = \sigma_i' = 3$, $\sigma_f = \sigma_f' = 0.2$ and $t_{max} = 10,000$.

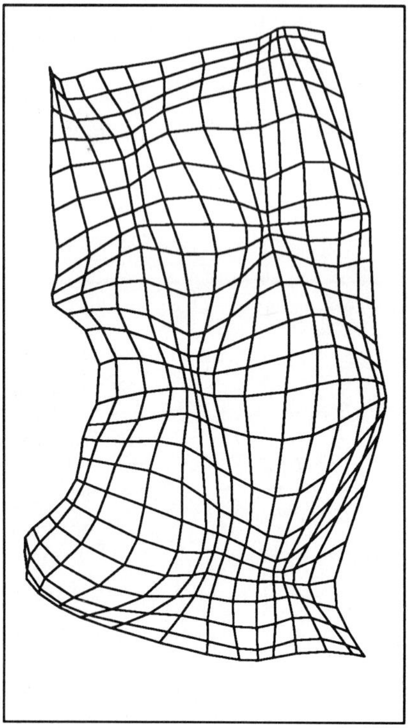

Figure 13.2a As in Fig. 13.1a, but after 500 trial movements. By this time, a recognizable order has already emerged.

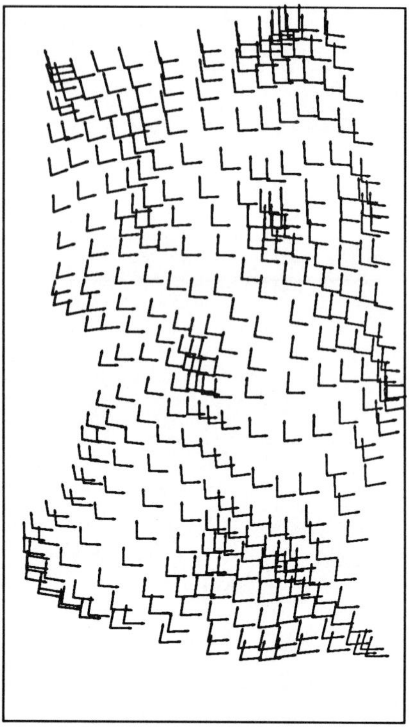

Figure 13.2b An improved agreement with the target movements is also visible in the test movements of the end effector.

The initial state of the lattice is shown in Fig. 13.1. To illustrate the correspondence between lattice sites and arm configurations, in Fig. 13.1a a perpendicular view of the working surface is shown. For each of the 360 neural units the end effector position pertaining to the arm configuration associated with that site is marked and connected in the familiar way with those other end effector locations that pertain to neighboring neural units. Since a similar illustration of the matrices $\mathbf{A_r}$ is not directly possible, in Fig. 13.1b we instead show the reaction of the end effector to test movements. For each of the end effector positions of the 360 neural units, the reaction of the end effector to two different target movements with velocities in the x- and in the y-direction is shown. Initially, these reactions only show a small correlation with the desired velocities, due to the considerable errors in the matrices $\mathbf{A_r}$ (see Fig. 13.1b). Figure 13.2 shows the state of the robot after 500 trial movements. At this stage, a recognizable, lattice-type correspondence

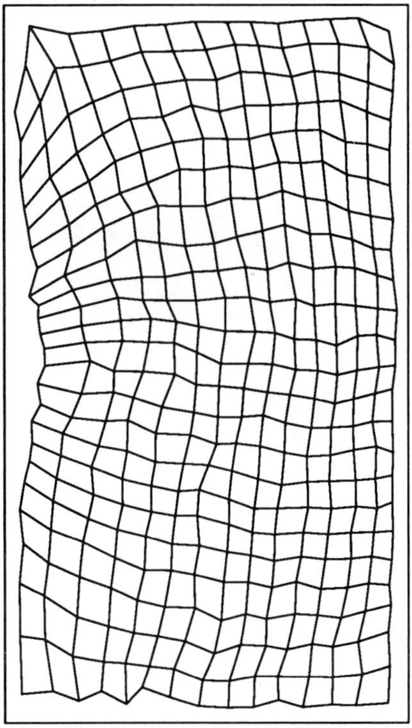

Figure 13.3a The final result after 10,000 trial movements shows the formation of a good correspondence between lattice sites and end effector positions of the working area.

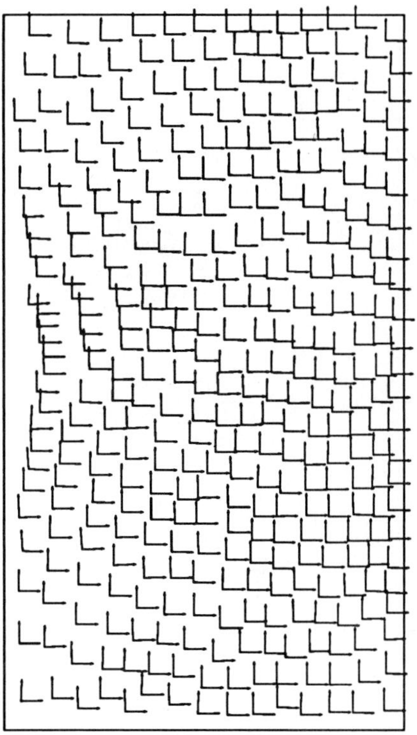

Figure 13.3b Now the corresponding test movements of the end effector agree well with the target movements.

between end effector positions and neural units has emerged, and the actual velocities resulting for the test movements point approximately in the x- and y-directions. Finally, Fig. 13.3 shows the result after 10,000 trial movements. In Fig. 13.3a, a regular mapping between lattice sites and end effector positions can be recognized in the working surface. The test movements are now carried out with good accuracy (Fig. 13.3b).

The representation chosen can only visualize the reaction to test movements that lie in the plane of the working surface. Therefore, for the developmental stages of Fig. 13.2 and Fig. 13.3, the Euclidean matrix norm $e_{\mathbf{r}} := \|\mathbf{A}_{\mathbf{r}} - \mathbf{A}^{exact}(\mathbf{w}_{\mathbf{r}})\|$ of the deviation from the exact transformation matrix is given in Fig. 13.4 for each lattice site $\mathbf{r}$ as a height above the end effector position in the working surface corresponding to $\mathbf{w}_{\mathbf{r}}$. Hence, an "error

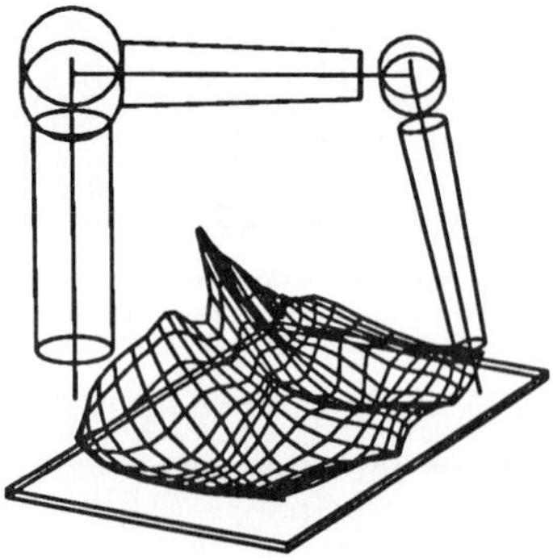

Figure 13.4a "Error surface" above the working surface after 500 trial movements. At this time, the errors are still relatively large.

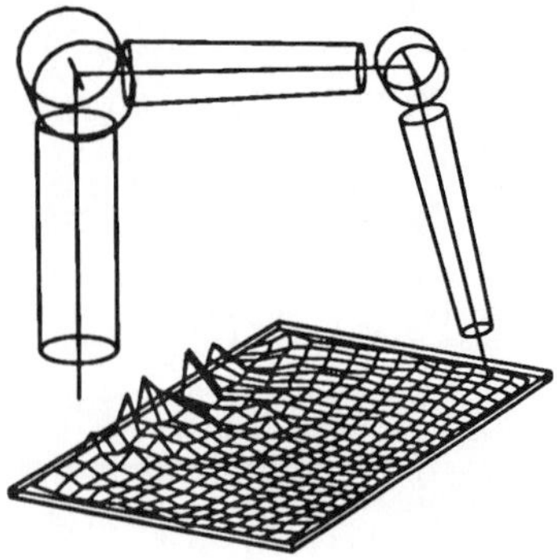

Figure 13.4b After 10,000 trial movements, no significant errors remain except for end effector positions near the base of the arm.

surface" above the working surface is created, whose height at each point is a measure of the discrepancy between desired and actual movement, averaged over all spatial directions. Figure 13.4 shows that the remaining errors are inhomogeneously distributed and are largest for those configurations in which the end effector is located near the base of the arm. This is due to the singular character of the transformation between torque amplitude and velocity for positions close to the base,[†] near which a convergence of the procedure will take a larger number of trial movements.

During our discussion of models of oculo-motor control and visuo-motor coordination in Chapters 9, 11, and 12 we repeatedly came to see the important role of neighborhood cooperation between neurons for the success of learning the output mapping. Also in the present case, neighborhood cooperation has a positive effect on the convergence of the learning algorithm. This can be illustrated by repeating the simulation as before, except that neighborhood cooperation is suppressed for the learning steps of $\mathbf{A_s}$. This is achieved by setting the parameters characterizing the range of $h'_{\mathbf{rs}}$ to values $\sigma'_i = 0$ and $\sigma'_f = 0$ (implying $h'_{\mathbf{rs}} = \delta_{\mathbf{rs}}$). Figure 13.5 illustrates the limited learning success by showing the reaction to the two test movements in the x- and y-direction. A closer inspection shows that $\mathbf{A_r}$ converges to the correct transformation only for those neural units with

[†]The singularity is analogous to the one in the transformation between joint angles and effector positions encountered in Sect. 11.4.

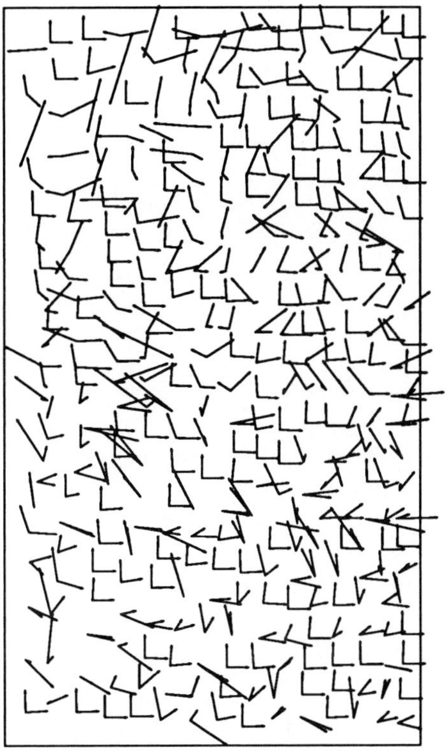

Figure 13.5 Result of the same simulation as in Fig. 13.1-13.3, obtained after 10,000 learning steps, but without lateral interaction between the array variables $\mathbf{A_r}$, *i.e.*, with $h'_{\mathbf{rs}} = \delta_{\mathbf{rs}}$. In this case, the desired convergence is only achieved for a fraction of all end effector configurations. This illustrates the important contribution of lateral interaction to a robust convergence behavior of the system.

sufficiently "good" initial random values of $\mathbf{A_r}$. The remaining units do not achieve convergence, even if further learning steps are allowed.

The essential role of neighborhood-based cooperative learning is also evident in Fig. 13.6 where we present the average error $\langle \|\mathbf{v} - \mathbf{u}\| \rangle$ between the target movement $\mathbf{u}$ and the actual movement $\mathbf{v}$ performed as a function of the number of learning steps carried out. The average was taken over all lattice points and over isotropically distributed, unit target velocities $\mathbf{u}$. The three curves correspond to three simulations with the same disordered initial state but distinct initial ranges $\sigma'_i = 0.5$, $\sigma'_i = 1.0$, and $\sigma'_i = 2.0$ for the lateral interaction $h'_{\mathbf{rs}}$. The initial state was generated according to Eq. (186) with a value $\alpha = 2$, *i.e.*, the deviations of the initial matrices from their correct values were significantly higher than in the simulations of Figs. 13.1-13.4. The remaining simulation data were chosen as before. In the case of the long-range interaction $\sigma'_i = 2$ the error decreases fastest and the system achieves a very small residual error. In the case of shorter ranges $\sigma'_i = 1$, $\sigma'_i = 0.5$, the decay of the

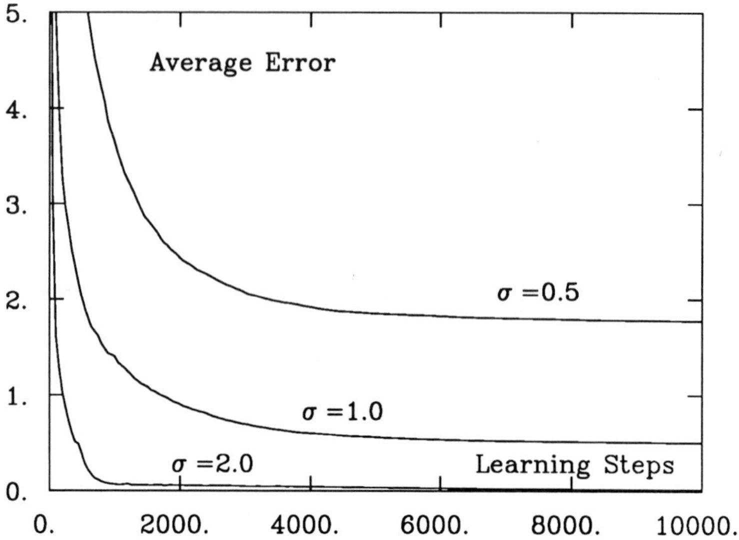

Figure 13.6 Improvement of the convergence behavior by lateral interaction between the lattice sites. For three different initial ranges σ'_i of the lateral interaction $h'_{\mathbf{rs}}$, the diagram shows the decrease, as a function of the number of learning steps, of the average error between target velocity $\mathbf{u}$ and actual velocity $\mathbf{v}$ of the robot end effector. For the two shorter ranges, a considerable error remains at the end.

error during training is slowed down and only some of the matrices $\mathbf{A_r}$ manage to converge to their correct values. The residual errors are correspondingly larger, the smaller of the two occurring for the longer of the two ranges.

The procedure described here is not restricted to the learning of ballistic movements. Another conceivable application would be to learn in this manner the relationship between joint torques and the force exerted by the end effector. This would be of interest for movements in which the end effector is guided in its motion by contact with a surface and in which the contact is to be maintained with a specified contact force ("compliant motions"). Similarly, it would be possible to learn configuration-dependent joint torques compensating for the influence of gravity on the arm, thus eliminating one of the main factors responsible for changes in the end effector velocity during force-free, ballistic phases of the motion.

This concludes our investigation of the capabilities of Kohonen's model and its extensions by means of computer simulations. In the subsequent chapters, we will take a closer look at important mathematical aspects of the model and analyze some of its properties that became evident in the simulations.

V

Mathematical Analysis of the Learning Methods

14. Mathematical Analysis of Kohonen's Model

The preceding chapters have shown the versatility of self-organizing maps for sensory processing and control by means of a series of examples. The properties of self-organizing maps that became evident in these examples will be characterized in this chapter from a more general mathematical point of view, and their relationship to other signal processing algorithms will be pointed out.

14.1. Overview

First, there is an important connection between self-organizing maps and algorithms for *adaptive data compression*. The latter algorithms are dealing with the coding of given data in a more compact form, so that later the original data can be recovered with as little error as possible. Obviously, in the interest of obtaining the highest possible "compression factor," a certain reconstruction error must be permitted. The method of *vector quantization* is a class of compression procedures leading to minimization of a prescribed measure of the reconstruction error. We will show that self-organizing maps can be regarded as a generalization of this approach. The neighborhood function modifies the error quantity to be minimized as compared to that minimized in conventional procedures.

Maps have a second important connection to the various procedures of *principal component analysis* of data. In these procedures, one seeks to describe as faithfully as possible the distribution of data points embedded in a high-dimensional space, using only a space of lower dimension. In principal component analysis, this occurs by linear projection onto a space spanned by those eigenvectors of the data distribution that belong to the largest eigenvalues of the two-point correlation matrix. Topology preserving maps offer a generalization of this linear procedure by providing a projection onto nonlinear, so-called *principal manifolds*. Projections onto principal manifolds can yield a low-dimensional image of the original data with smaller projection errors, *i.e.*, more faithful representations of the original data compared to linear procedures that use the same projection dimension.

The problems of data compression and of obtaining "good" projections onto lower-dimensional spaces are related and play an important role for numerous information processing tasks. A large part of the applicability of topology preserving maps is due to their relevance to both kinds of problems. Hence, it may not be too surprising that topology preserving maps are found in various areas of the brain.

The map formation process is adaptive and is driven by a random sequence of input signals. Mathematically, the process corresponds to an adaptively changing map that gradually evolves toward a stationary state. This leads to the question of the *convergence properties* of the process. We will investigate this question in Sections 14.6–14.9 more closely and, among other things, we will derive convergence conditions as well as expressions for the magnitude of fluctuations that occur due to the random distribution of input signals.

For this purpose we derive a *Fokker-Planck equation* describing the adaptation process and allowing a more precise discussion of the dependence of the stationary map on the input signal distribution. We can then show that, under certain conditions, the map takes on a structure which is *spatially periodic* with respect to a subset of the components of the input signal. This result is especially interesting in view of experimentally established spatial periodicities in the response behavior of many neurons belonging to cortical and noncortical areas of the brain. A well-known example of such periodicity is provided by the *ocular dominance stripes* observed in the visual cortex, along which neurons segregate into groups with preference for one eye or the other. A similar structure on a smaller scale than occular dominance stripes in the striate cortex are orientation columns, a segregation of neurons with receptive fields favouring different orientations in the visual field of an animal (Blasdel and Salama 1986).

14.2. Vector Quantization and Data Compression

An important prerequisite for any kind of information processing is the establishment of an appropriate encoding for the data under consideration. In the case of the brain, this encoding has to a large extent been determined by nature, and indeed one of the principal research questions is to decipher the coding schemes that underly brain function. In the case of artificial information processing systems, the decision for an appropriate encoding of the data is left to the designer, and a determination of which features are to play an important role and must be coded well may be very task specific. However, there are also important aspects of more general relevance. One such aspect is the average code length required for transmission of a specified amount of information. For example, one current scheme for text encoding uses 8-bit words, the so-called ASCII-characters, for individual letters. Theoretically, $2^8 = 256$ distinct characters can be encoded in this way. However, in many cases 128 characters suffice, which can be coded with only 7 bits per character. Taking into account the different frequency with which different characters occur, one can find still more efficient codes. If the characters in the sequence are statistically independent of one another, and if p_i denotes the probability for the occurrence of the ith character, then the lower limit for the most efficient code is

$$S = -\sum_i p_i \,\mathrm{ld}(p_i) \tag{187}$$

bits per character ("ld" denotes the logarithm to the base two). The quantity S is known as the so-called *Shannon information* (see for example Khinchin 1957) transmitted on the average by a single character. However, for most character sequences, the assumption of statistically independent characters does not hold. By exploiting correlations between several characters, one can find even more efficient codes. For example, in the case of language, one can encode whole words in place of individual letters, thus achieving a further compactification. Written Chinese provides an example of this strategy.

This sort of code optimization is of particular importance when large quantities of data are to be stored or transmitted. This happens particularly in image processing. The bitwise transmission of a raster image with a resolution of $1{,}000 \times 1{,}000$ pixels and 256 gray levels per pixel requires the transfer of about 1 Mbyte of data. However, in most images, adjacent pixels are strongly correlated, and significantly more efficient coding schemes than simple bitwise transmission can be found. Interestingly enough, the brain also seems to make use of such possibilities. The optic nerve contains only about 10^6 nerve fibres, whereas the retina is covered by about 10^8 light sensitive receptors (Kandel und Schwartz 1985). Hence, the optic nerve constitutes a kind of "bottleneck" for the transmission of visual information from the retina to the brain. However, before transmission occurs, the signal is subjected to an extensive preprocessing stage in the retina, involving nearly 100 different cell types and enabling a subsequent transmission of all necessary information through the optic nerve.

Hence, data compression is an equally important task for both artificial and natural information processing systems. A general approach developed for the solution of this task is the method of *vector quantization* (see, *e.g.*, Makhoul et al. 1985). This method supposes that the data are given in the form of a set of data vectors $\mathbf{v}(t)$, $t = 1, 2, 3, \ldots$ (possibly of rather high dimension). The index t numbers the individual vectors. The components of a vector $\mathbf{v}(t)$ may take binary, integer, or analogue values, corresponding for example to bits of a binary sequence, gray level values of image pixels, or amplitudes of a speech signal. "Compression" of the data occurs by approximating every data vector $\mathbf{v}(t)$ by a *reference vector* $\mathbf{w}_s$ of equal dimension. This presupposes that a fixed, finite set W of reference vectors $\mathbf{w}_s$ has been established, determined such that a "good" approximate vector $\mathbf{w}_s \in W$ can be found for every data vector that may arise. The set W of reference vectors plays the role of a *code book* assigning to each data vector $\mathbf{v}$ that reference vector $\mathbf{w}_s \in W$ for which the norm of the difference $\delta = \|\mathbf{v} - \mathbf{w}_s\|$ assumes its minimum over all code book vectors. As the new code for the data vector $\mathbf{v}$, it then suffices to specify the index s of the reference vector $\mathbf{w}_s$ that yielded the most accurate approximation. In the case of a code book with N reference vectors, this requires specification of at most ld N bits. Therefore, the smaller the code book can be chosen, the better the resulting data compression factor.† However, this gain has its price: the original data can no longer be exactly recovered from the codes s. For reconstruction of the original data vector $\mathbf{v}$ from its code s, only the reference vector $\mathbf{w}_s$ is available. This gives rise to a "reconstruction error" that is equal to the approximation error $\delta = \|\mathbf{v} - \mathbf{w}_s\|$.

Crucial for the whole procedure is the construction of a good code book W. It should contain sufficiently many appropriately distributed reference vectors to enable a good approximation to any data vector $\mathbf{v}$ by a reference vector $\mathbf{w}_s$. For a mathematical formulation of this requirement, one often considers the expectation value of the squared reconstruction error, *i.e.*, the quantity

$$E[W] = \int \|\mathbf{v} - \mathbf{w}_{s(\mathbf{v})}\|^2 P(\mathbf{v})\, d\mathbf{v}, \tag{188}$$

where $P(\mathbf{v})$ is the probability density describing the distribution of data vectors $\mathbf{v}$. $E[W]$ depends on the ensemble W of all code book vectors $\mathbf{w}_s$. A frequently appropriate requirement demands the minimization of E subject to the constraint of a fixed, prescribed number of code book vectors $\mathbf{w}_s$ (without such a constraint, E could be reduced to arbitrarily small positive values simply by increasing the number of code vectors. However, this would also entail an arbitrary reduction of the compression effect, since the effort required to specify a single value of s increases with the number N of reference vectors).

The minimization of E with respect to reference vectors $\mathbf{w}_s$ is a complicated, nonlinear optimization problem, for which in most cases no closed solutions are known. Hence, one must resort to iterative approximation methods. In Chapter 15 we will see that these approximation methods are closely related to Kohonen's map-formation algorithm. The maps provided by Kohonen's procedure can be regarded in this context as code books of a vector quantization procedure in which the topology preserving property of the maps leads to a modification of the original error quantity (188).

---

†The astute reader will notice that the probability distribution of the discrete codes s may be nonuniform. Exploiting this circumstance in the assignment of code words (shorter code words for more frequent codes), one can improve the code efficiency still further.

14.3. Self-Organizing Maps and Vector Quantization

The construction of a good code book requires the minimization of the average reconstruction error $E[\mathbf{w}]$ with respect to the reference vectors $\mathbf{w}_r$. The simplest procedure for this is gradient descent. Starting with initial values $\mathbf{w}_r(0)$, all reference vectors are changed according to

$$\mathbf{w}_r(t+1) = \mathbf{w}_r(t) - \frac{\epsilon}{2} \cdot \frac{\partial E}{\partial \mathbf{w}_r} \tag{189}$$

$$= \mathbf{w}_r(t) + \epsilon \cdot \int_{s(\mathbf{v})=r} (\mathbf{v} - \mathbf{w}_r(t)) P(\mathbf{v})\, d\mathbf{v}, \tag{190}$$

where we employed (188).

The integration condition $s(\mathbf{v}) = r$ restricts the region of integration to those v-values for which $\mathbf{w}_r$ is the most suitable reference vector ($s(\mathbf{v})$ defined through $\|\mathbf{w}_{s(\mathbf{v})} - \mathbf{v}\| = \min_{r'} \|\mathbf{w}_{r'} - \mathbf{v}\|$). For a sufficiently small step size parameter ϵ, repeated application of (190) leads to a decrease of $E[W]$ until a *local* minimum is reached. Equation (190) was first suggested by Linde, Buzo, and Gray (1980) and is known as the "LBG"-procedure. Although this procedure does not guarantee that a *global* minimum is achieved, in many important cases the *local* minimum reached provides a sufficiently good solution. If required, better *local* minima can be found by repeating the procedure with different initial values or with the help of "annealing techniques" (see, for example, Kirkpatrick et al. 1983).

However, carrying out the procedure in this form requires a knowledge of the probability distribution $P(\mathbf{v})$ of the data vectors. Usually, $P(\mathbf{v})$ is not known explicitly. This difficulty can be avoided by replacing (190) with the simpler prescription

$$\mathbf{w}_{s(\mathbf{v})}(t+1) = \mathbf{w}_{s(\mathbf{v})}(t) + \epsilon \cdot \left(\mathbf{v} - \mathbf{w}_{s(\mathbf{v})}(t)\right), \tag{191}$$

where for each step (191) a new data vector v selected at random from the (unknown) distribution is used. For sufficiently small step size ϵ, the accumulation of many individual steps (191) will lead to an approximate realization of the integration in (190) (the "step counting parameters" t of (190) and (191) of course no longer agree).

Comparison of equation (191) with the adaptation rule (70) in Kohonen's model of self-organizing maps shows that (191) represents a special case of Kohonen's algorithm which results in the limit of vanishing neighborhood cooperation (*i.e.*, $h_{rs} = \delta_{rs}$). Kohonen's algorithm can thus be understood as a generalization of a vector quantization procedure for data compression. The "synaptic strengths" $\mathbf{w_r}$ correspond to the reference vectors, the map provides the code book, and the choice of the excitation center s for an input signal $\mathbf{v}$ defines the mapping $\mathbf{v} \mapsto s(\mathbf{v})$, *i.e.*, corresponds to the *coding step* of the vector quantization procedure. The "receptive fields" F_s introduced earlier (Eq.(99)) comprise just those input signals for which the coding step leads to the same excitation center s.

The shift of a reference vector $\mathbf{w}_s$ in the LBG-procedure (190) always occurs in the direction of the center of gravity $\int_{F_\mathbf{r}} \mathbf{v} P d\mathbf{v}$ of the density distribution of the input data, but restricted to the field F_s. This leads to a distribution of reference vectors, in which each reference vector coincides with the center of gravity of the data in "its" field F_s.

The introduction of the neighborhood functions h_{rs} leads to a modification of the distribution of reference vectors compared to standard vector quantization. The average shift of a reference vector then becomes

$$\langle \Delta \mathbf{w}_r \rangle = \sum_s h_{rs} \int_{F_s} (\mathbf{v} - \mathbf{w}_s) P(\mathbf{v}) \, d\mathbf{v}, \qquad (192)$$

i.e., the shift of $\mathbf{w}_r$ now occurs in the direction of the mean center of gravity of all fields F_s, the contribution of each field being weighted by the neighborhood function h_{rs}. In a stationary state, every reference vector $\mathbf{w}_r$ therefore coincides with a weighted average density, where the weighting is taken over a neighborhood and includes contributions with relative weight h_{rs} from all neighboring fields s for which $h_{rs} \neq 0$.

This no longer leads to minimization of the reconstruction error (188), but to a minimization of a modified expression. For the case of a one-dimensional "chain" of reference vectors, each with n neighbors on both sides (*i.e.*, $h_{rs} = 1$ for $\|r - s\| \leq n$, and $h_{rs} = 0$ otherwise), one finds

$$E[W] = \int \|\mathbf{v} - \mathbf{w}_{s(\mathbf{v})}\|^r P(\mathbf{v}) \, d\mathbf{v}, \qquad (193)$$

where the exponent r now differs from the value $r = 2$ in (188) taking instead the smaller value

$$r = \frac{1}{2} + \frac{3}{2(2n+1)^2} \tag{194}$$

(Ritter 1989). This can be interpreted as implying that the inclusion of a neighborhood region in each adaptation step leads to a vector quantizer which, relative to a vector quantizer minimizing the quadratic error quantity (188), suppresses small quantization errors.

14.4. Relationship to Principal Component Analysis

Gaining deeper insights into an observed phenomenon often depends crucially on the discovery of a more effective description, involving a smaller number of variables than needed before. This has motivated the search for algorithms that could, at least to some extent, automate the generation of more effective data descriptions.

A rather general and frequent case is the availability of a number of measurements $\mathbf{v}^{(1)}, \mathbf{v}^{(2)}, \ldots$ of the parameters $\mathbf{v} = (v_1, v_2, \ldots, v_L)^T$ of an experiment. As a rule, the individual parameters v_i will not vary completely independently of one another, but rather will be correlated to a greater or lesser extent, the type of correlation being often unknown. This entails the following question: to what extent can one attribute the observed variation of the measurements to a dependence of the v_i on a smaller number of "hidden" variables $r_1, r_2, \ldots, r_D$, $D < L$? If such dependency exists, one can find L functions $f_1, \ldots, f_L$ of the hidden variables for which

$$v_i = f_i(r_1, r_2, \ldots, r_D), \quad i = 1, \ldots, L, \tag{195}$$

holds. The variables r_i enable then a more economical description of the observed phenomenon compared to the directly available measurements v_i. In particular, they are more likely to correspond to the true "degrees of freedom" that are involved and the number for which, in many cases, is smaller than the number of observed parameters v_i.

Here, one should keep in mind that the new parameters — if such a simplification is possible — are not uniquely determined. Any invertible one-to-one mapping of the r_i onto an equal number of new variables r'_i provides, a priori, an equally "good" set of parameters for a description of the variation of the original variables v_i. Mathematically, each of these different, but equivalent parametrizations can be regarded as a "coordinate system" on an abstract manifold (indeed, this manifold characterizes the system independently of any special choice of coordinates).

However, the non-uniqueness of the parameters r_i makes their general determination difficult. The procedure most frequently applied, *principal component analysis*, makes the simplifying assumption of a *linear relationship between the variables r_i and v_i*. This assumption can be viewed geometrically as the introduction of a D-dimensional "hyperplane" lying in the L-dimensional data space, the location and orientation of which are chosen such that every data point can be approximated well by a point of the hyperplane (Fig. 14.1).

This corresponds to a representation of each data point in the form

$$\mathbf{v} = \mathbf{w}^0 + \sum_{i=1}^{D} \mathbf{w}^i r_i(\mathbf{v}) + d_{\mathbf{w}}(\mathbf{v}), \tag{196}$$

where $\mathbf{w}^0, \ldots, \mathbf{w}^D \in R^L$ are $D+1$ vectors specifying the hyperplane and $r_1(\mathbf{v}), \ldots, r_D(\mathbf{v})$ are the new parameters belonging to data point $\mathbf{v}$. Since, as a rule, not all data points will be located within the hyperplane, for most data points a nonvanishing distance $d_{\mathbf{w}}(\mathbf{v})$ perpendicular to the hyperplane results (the index $\mathbf{w}$ is a reminder of the fact that this distance depends on the choice of hyperplane). The choice of hyperplane is optimal if the vectors $\mathbf{w}_i$ are determined such that the weighted mean square residual error $\langle d_{\mathbf{w}}(\mathbf{v})^2 \rangle$, where the weighting factor is the probability density $P(\mathbf{v})$ of the data, takes its smallest possible value, *i.e.*,

$$\int \|\mathbf{v} - \mathbf{w}^0 - \sum_{i=1}^{D} \mathbf{w}^i r_i(\mathbf{v})\|^2 P(\mathbf{v})\, d^L\mathbf{v} = \text{Minimum!} \tag{197}$$

One can show that the solution of this minimization problem yields

$$\mathbf{w}^0 = \int \mathbf{v} P(\mathbf{v})\, d^L\mathbf{v}, \tag{198}$$

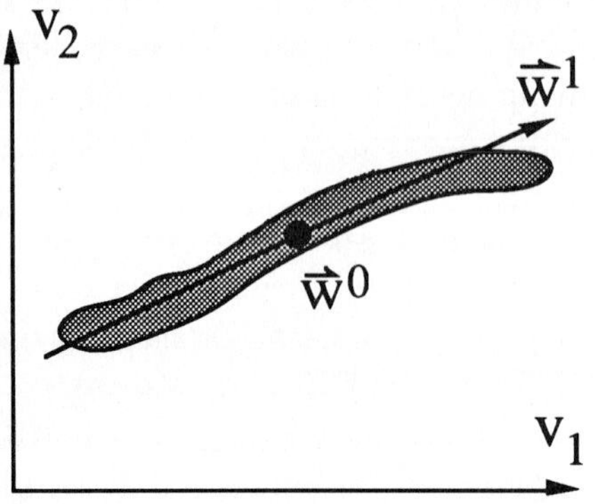

Figure 14.1 Description of a two-dimensional data distribution (shaded region) by a straight line (one-dimensional "hyperplane"). The best description of the distribution results if the line passes through the center of gravity $\mathbf{w}^0$ and is directed parallel to the "principal eigenvector" $\mathbf{w}^1$ (*i.e.*, the eigenvector with largest eigenvalue) of the correlation matrix **C**.

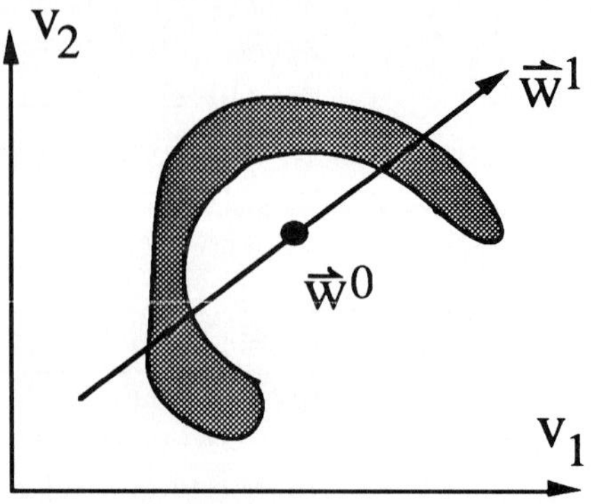

Figure 14.2 If the form of the data distribution is too "nonlinear," no straight line (lowerdimensional hyperplane) leading to a good description of the data can be found.

i.e., $\mathbf{w}^0$ coincides with the center of gravity of the data distribution, whereas the remaining vectors $\mathbf{w}^i$, $i = 1, 2 \ldots, D$, must form a basis of the eigenspace spanned by those D eigenvectors of the correlation matrix that have the largest eigenvalues

$$\mathbf{C} = \int (\mathbf{v} - \mathbf{w}^0) \otimes (\mathbf{v} - \mathbf{w}^0)^T P(\mathbf{v})\, d^L\mathbf{v} \tag{199}$$

(see for example Lawley and Maxwell 1963) when $\otimes$ denotes the tensor product of two vectors, *i.e.*, $(\mathbf{u} \otimes \mathbf{v})_{jk} = u_j v_k$. One possible special choice for the $\mathbf{w}^i$ $(i > 0)$ are the D normalized eigenvectors of C corresponding to the largest eigenvalues. In this case, the new parameters r_i turn out to be the projections of the data vectors along D "principal axes" of their distribution and are called "principal components" of the distribution:

$$r_i = \mathbf{w}^i \cdot \mathbf{v}, \quad i = 1, 2, \ldots, D. \tag{200}$$

Geometrically, this implies that the hyperplane passes through the center of gravity $\mathbf{w}^0$ of the data distribution and is spanned by the D eigenvectors or "principal axes" of the correlation matrix that have the largest eigenvalues. One can show that the orientation of the hyperplane determined in this way maximizes the variance of the perpendicular projection of the data points. The D variables r_i can thus be characterized by the property to account for (with a linear ansatz) the total data variation as much as possible . However, for the quality of such a description the adequacy of the underlying linearity assumption is crucial: the more the actual distribution of data points deviates from a hyperplane, the worse the description resulting from a projection onto the principal axes of the distribution (Fig. 14.2).

Topology-preserving maps overcome this problem by replacing the linear principal axes or hyperplanes with curved surfaces, which enable a better description of nonlinear data distributions. Here, the maps approximate so-called *principal curves* or *principal surfaces*, which represent a generalization of linear principal axes or eigenspaces. In the following section, we discuss this generalization and its relation to topology-preserving maps.

14.5. Principal Curves, Principal Surfaces and Topology Preserving Maps

Principal component analysis yields a linear description of a prescribed data distribution by a hyperplane that is characterized by the property (198), (197). This can be interpreted geometrically as a minimization of the "mean squared perpendicular distance" $\langle d_{\mathbf{w}}(\mathbf{v})^2 \rangle$ between the data points and the hyperplane. This property motivates a generalization from a hyperplane to nonlinear manifolds (Hastie and Stuetzle 1989). Let us first consider the one-dimensional case. Let $f(s)$ be a "smooth" curve in the space V parametrized by arc length. To every point $\mathbf{v} \in \mathbf{V}$ one can define then a distance $d_f(\mathbf{v})$ to the curve f. Thus, for any such curve and for any density distribution $P(\mathbf{v})$ of points in V we can define a mean squared distance D_f, given by

$$D_f = \int d_f^2(\mathbf{v}) P(\mathbf{v})\, d^L\mathbf{v}. \tag{201}$$

We call the curve f a *principal curve* of the density distribution $P(\mathbf{v})$, if D_f is extremal, *i.e.*, if the curve is stationary with respect to small, "sufficiently smooth" deformations of the curve.†

†A precise mathematical discussion requires consideration of the special situation at the curve endpoints. We will not go into this problem here. The reader interested in a more thorough discussion is refered to Hastie and Stuetzle (1989).

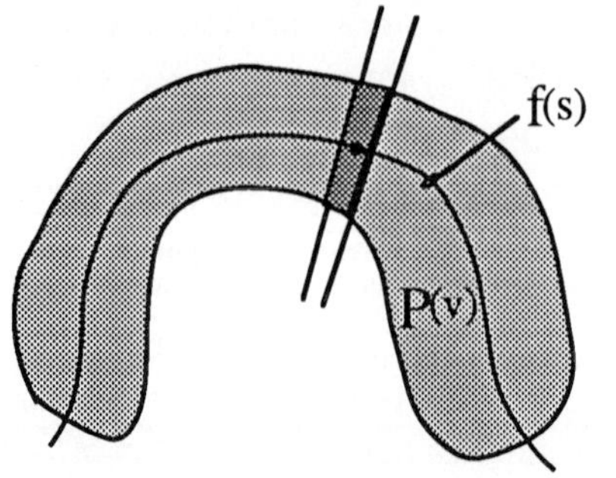

Figure 14.3 Principal curve as nonlinear generalization of the concept of principal axes of a density distribution (shaded). We consider the center of gravity of the density distribution in the region between two "infinitesimally seperated" curve normals. For a principal curve, this center of gravity must always lie on the curve itself.

Intuitively, this requirement demands that a principal curve pass "right through the middle" of its defining density distribution. For better illustration of this situation, we consider a principal curve for the two-dimensional distribution presented in Fig. 14.3. The figure demonstrates that for the principal curve the center of gravity of the density distribution enclosed by two "infinitesimally" distant normals lies on the principal curve. This property must hold, in fact, for every such pair of normals since, otherwise, the mean squared distance D_f could be decreased by a local deformation of the curve in the direction of the deviation, which would contradict the extremal property of D_f. Conversely, the extremality of D_f follows from the fact that the center of gravity of every such "normal strip" coincides with a point on the curve f.

Principal axes arise as a special case of principal curves. One has the following *theorem:* If $P(\mathbf{v})$ has zero mean and a straight line as principal curve, then this principal curve coincides with one of the principal axes of the distribution P (Hastie and Stuetzle 1989).

The generalization to *principal surfaces* and higher-dimensional *"principal manifolds"* proceeds analogously to the one-dimensional case:

Definition of a principal surface: Let $f(\mathbf{s})$ be a surface in the vector space V, *i.e.*, dim(f) = dim(V) – 1, and let $d_f(\mathbf{v})$ be the shortest distance of a point $\mathbf{v} \in V$ to the surface f. f is a principal surface corresponding to a density distribution $P(\mathbf{v})$ in V, if the "mean squared distance"

$$D_f = \int d_f^2(\mathbf{v}) P(\mathbf{v}) \, d^L\mathbf{v} \tag{202}$$

is extremal with respect to local variations of the surface.

Thus, Kohonen's algorithm can be interpreted as an approximation procedure for the computation of principal curves, surfaces,

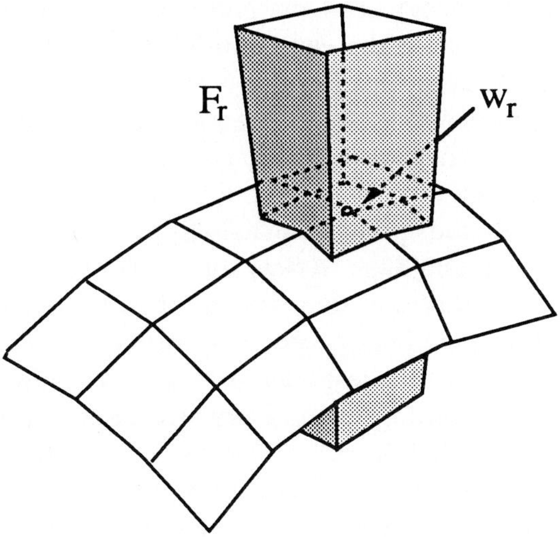

Figure 14.4 2d-Kohonen lattice as discrete approximation to a "principal surface". To each lattice point $\mathbf{w_r}$, a volume $F_\mathbf{r}$ is assigned which is bounded by planes perpendicularly bisecting the distances to the lattice neighbors. The lattice possesses the property of a principal surface, if each lattice point $\mathbf{w_r}$ coincides with the center of gravity of the part of the density distribution enclosed within the volume $F_\mathbf{r}$. This state is approximately achieved as a result of the adaptation procedure of Kohonen's algorithm.

or higher-dimensional principal manifolds. The approximation consists in the discretization of the function f defining the manifold. The discretization is implemented by means of a lattice A of corresponding dimension, where each weight vector $\mathbf{w_r}$ indicates the position of a surface point in the embedding space V. In Kohonen's algorithm, a volume region $F_\mathbf{r}$ was assigned to each point r of the surface, containing all those points v for which $\mathbf{w_r}$ is the surface point with the shortest distance (Eq.(99)). $F_\mathbf{r}$ is thus the realization of a volume region which in the continuous limit would be bounded by a "bundle of normals" of infinitesimal cross section penetrating the surface perpendicularly at the point $\mathbf{w_r}$ (Fig. 14.4). The crucial property of Kohonen's algorithm now consists in iteratively deforming the discretized surface in such a way that the center of gravity of the density distribution $P(\mathbf{v})$ contained within the volume $F_\mathbf{r}$ coincides with the surface point $\mathbf{w_r}$ for every r. But this is just the (discretized form) of the condition leading to extremality of the mean squared distance D_f and thus to the "principal surface property" of the stationary state.

As we saw in Section 14.3, however, this property results if and only if $h_{\mathbf{rs}} = \delta_{\mathbf{rs}}$ holds for the neighborhood function. Otherwise, in addition to $F_\mathbf{r}$, other volumes $F_\mathbf{s}$ contribute to the calculation of the equilibrium location of $\mathbf{w_r}$. These volumes lie in a neighborhood about $F_\mathbf{r}$ whose extension is determined by the size of the region within which $h_{\mathbf{rs}}$ differs significantly from zero. This has the effect of "broadening" the volume region over which the averaging of the probability density is performed in order to obtain the equilibrium location of the center of gravity for the determination of $\mathbf{w_r}$. This is a desirable property for the practical application of the procedure, because most of the data are not given as continuous distributions, but rather as discrete distributions of a finite number of "trials." Strictly speaking, continuous principal manifolds can no longer be defined for such discrete data. A way out of this predicament consists in "smearing out" the data to obtain a better approximation of their underlying probability distribution. The neighborhood function $h_{\mathbf{rs}}$ has just such a "smearing effect," where the amount of "smearing " can be adjusted through the range σ of the neighborhood function. The optimal choice of σ depends on the density of the available data: the principal surfaces thus obtained yield a good description of the data if the neighborhood determined by σ contains sufficiently many data points. For values of the "smearing " that are too small, the surface attempts to touch every single data point, and the desired "smooth" interpolation of the data by a principal surface is lost. In the case of a one-dimensional lattice A, we encountered this behavior (which in that context was desired) in the "traveling salesman problem" of Chapter 6: the curve obtained at the end of the simulation touched every one of the prescribed "cities." The "Peano curve" which, as discussed in Section 4.3, results for a one-dimensional lattice of an infinite number of nodes embedded in a two-dimensional space is another example. For a further discussion of this problem, see also Hastie and Stuetzle (1989).

This section can thus be summarized as follows. Kohonen's algorithm for topology-preserving maps leads to a generalization of standard principal component analysis. The mathematical background of this generalization consists of a nonlinear extension of the concept of principal axes and eigenspaces to so-called *principal curves* and *principal manifolds*. These nonlinear concepts allow one to find dimensionally reduced descriptions even for very nonlinear data distributions, and Kohonen's model can be regarded as an implementation of the required calculations in a neural network.

14.6. Learning as a Stochastic Process

Many learning systems, including Kohonen's self-organizing maps, achieve their goal by means of a sequence of finite adaptation steps. Every single adaptation step results from an "interaction" with the environment. Through these "interactions" information about the environment is obtained. To ensure that the whole sensory space V is explored a random process is employed to generate the sequence of adaptation steps. For example, in the case of sensory maps each of the sensory stimuli $\mathbf{v}$ are chosen at random.

Nevertheless, the assumption of some probability distribution $P(\mathbf{v})$ (usually unknown to the system) for the sensory stimuli frequently provides a reasonable idealization (at least in a stationary environment). The random sequence of input stimuli $\mathbf{v}$ leads to a corresponding random sequence of adaptation steps. Let us denote by $\mathbf{w}$ the ensemble of system parameters which are subject to the learning process (in our case $\mathbf{w} = (\mathbf{w}_{\mathbf{r}_1}, \mathbf{w}_{\mathbf{r}_2}, \ldots, \mathbf{w}_{\mathbf{r}_N})$ is again, as in Section 5.4, the ensemble of all synaptic strengths of a network). Each adaptation step then induces a transformation

$$\mathbf{w}^{new} = \mathbf{T}(\mathbf{w}^{old}, \mathbf{v}). \tag{203}$$

Here, $\mathbf{v}$ is a random variable with probability distribution $P(\mathbf{v})$. Equation (203) does not describe a fixed, deterministic sequence, but rather a "stochastic process." The simulation of such a process provides in each case only one of its infinitely many realizations, a so-called *"sample,"* of the process. To what extent a specific realization represents a "typical" case can only be judged by sufficiently frequent repetition of the simulation. In this way, an "ensemble" of realizations is created, by means of which typical realizations can be identified through their particularly frequent occurrence. Thus, ideally one would like to know the distribution function $\tilde{S}(\mathbf{w}, t)$ of the realizations of an ensemble of infinitely many simulation runs after t time steps, $t = 1, 2, \ldots$. An intuitive picture of $\tilde{S}(\mathbf{w}, t)$ can be given as follows: We consider the space spanned by the synaptic strengths of a network and regard each network of the ensemble as a point with position vector $\mathbf{w}$ in this space (for a network with N neurons and D synaptic strengths per neuron, this space is a $N \cdot D$-dimensional space). The ensemble can thus be regarded as a cloud of points in this space, and $\tilde{S}(\mathbf{w}, t)$ is the density distribution of the points in the cloud. Thus, after t adaptation steps, an "infinitesimal" volume element $d^N\mathbf{w}$ centered at $\mathbf{w}$ contains a fraction $\tilde{S}(\mathbf{w}, t)\, d^N\mathbf{w}$ of all ensemble members.

If $\tilde{S}(\mathbf{w}, t)$ is known, then all of the statistical properties of the stochastic process can be calculated from it. A typical question can be posed as follows: one has some function $F(\mathbf{w})$ of the synaptic strengths $\mathbf{w}$ and is interested in the average value $\langle F \rangle_t$ to be expected after t adaptation steps. This "expectation value" is then given by

$$\langle F \rangle_t = \int F(\mathbf{w})\tilde{S}(\mathbf{w}, t)\, d^N\mathbf{w}. \tag{204}$$

Hence, $\tilde{S}(\mathbf{w}, t)$ contains all information to calculate the expectation values of arbitrary functions of the system parameters $\mathbf{w}$. If, for example, one wishes to know the average value $\bar{\mathbf{w}}$ of the synaptic strengths, one chooses $F(\mathbf{w}) = \mathbf{w}$, whereas the choice $F(\mathbf{w}) = (\mathbf{w} - \bar{\mathbf{w}})^2$ yields their mean squared deviation due to the statistical sequence of adaptation steps.

By sufficiently many simulations, one can in principle generate a large ensemble and with it the approximate distribution function $\tilde{S}(\mathbf{w}, t)$. However, the required computational effort rapidly rises to an unfeasible level as the desired accuracy and the complexity of the stochastic process increase. In that case, the derivation of analytic results becomes indispensable. This will be the aim of the following sections. The technical point of departure is the derivation of a so-called *Fokker-Planck equation*, which describes the evolution of the distribution function $\tilde{S}(\mathbf{w}, t)$ in the vicinity of an equilibrium state and which is valid in the limit of small learning step size ϵ. From this we obtain a necessary and sufficient condition for convergence of the learning procedure to an asymptotic equilibrium state during the final phase of the algorithm. The condition involves an appropriate decrease of the learning step size $\epsilon(t)$. Provided the distribution $P(\mathbf{v})$ is restricted to a multidimensional box volume and is constant there, the statistical fluctuations about the asymptotic equilibrium state can be computed explicitly. From this result, one can conclude that the learning step size must be chosen inversely proportional to the number of lattice points in order that the remaining fluctuations not exceed a fixed tolerance threshold. We also investigate the ability of the algorithm to automatically use the directions of maximal signal variation as the primary map dimensions. We show that this property derives from an instability which arises when the variance of the sensory events v along a direction which is "poorly" represented by the map exceeds a critical value. The occurrence of this instability manifests itself by strong fluctuations of a characteristic wavelength. Both the critical variance and the characteristic wavelength are computed for the case of a multidimensional box volume.

14.7. Fokker-Planck Equation for the Learning Process

For the derivation of a Fokker-Planck equation that governs the stochastically driven learning process, we consider an ensemble of systems whose states $\mathbf{w}$ after t learning steps are distributed according to a distribution function $\tilde{S}(\mathbf{w}, t)$. As in Chapter 5, we assume that all systems are close to the same asymptotic equilibrium state $\bar{\mathbf{w}}$ and that the learning step size ϵ is sufficiently small so that transitions into the neighborhood of different equilibrium states can be neglected. We thus restrict our attention to the asymptotic phase of the convergence behavior which, actually, takes up the largest part of the total computing time in simulations. We obtain the new distribution $\tilde{S}(\mathbf{w}, t+1)$ after an additional learning step from the previous distribution $\tilde{S}(\mathbf{w}, t)$ by integrating over all transitions from states $\mathbf{w}'$ to states $\mathbf{w}$. Each transition contributes with a weight given by the product of the transition probability $Q(\mathbf{w}, \mathbf{w}')$ from $\mathbf{w}'$ to $\mathbf{w}$ to the probability $\tilde{S}(\mathbf{w}', t)$ of the occurrence of the state $\mathbf{w}'$ in the ensemble. Both factors were first introduced in Section 5.4. This yields

$$\begin{aligned}\tilde{S}(\mathbf{w}, t+1) &= \int d^N\mathbf{w}' \; Q(\mathbf{w}, \mathbf{w}')\tilde{S}(\mathbf{w}', t) \\ &= \sum_{\mathbf{r}} \int d^N\mathbf{w}' \int_{F_{\mathbf{r}}(\mathbf{w}')} d\mathbf{v} \; P(\mathbf{v})\delta(\mathbf{w} - \mathbf{T}(\mathbf{w}', \mathbf{v}, \epsilon))\tilde{S}(\mathbf{w}', t)\end{aligned} \tag{205}$$

where $P(\mathbf{v})$ and $\mathbf{T}(\mathbf{w}', \mathbf{v}, \epsilon)$ are defined in Section 5.4. In order to carry out the $\mathbf{w}'$-integration, which is taken over all N vector variables $\mathbf{w}'_{\mathbf{r}}$, $\mathbf{r} \in A$, we require the inverse Jacobian

$$J(\epsilon) = \left[\det \frac{\partial \mathbf{T}}{\partial \mathbf{w}}\right]^{-1}. \tag{206}$$

By assuming for the moment $\mathbf{v} \in F_{\mathbf{s}}(\mathbf{w}')$, we obtain

$$J(\epsilon) = \left[\prod_{\mathbf{r}} (1 - \epsilon h^0_{\mathbf{rs}})\right]^{-d}. \tag{207}$$

Here, d is the dimension of the input vectors $\mathbf{v}$ and we have denoted the excitatory response by $h^0_{\mathbf{rs}}$. Since $h^0_{\mathbf{rs}}$ should only depend on the difference $\mathbf{r}-\mathbf{s}$, J is independent of $\mathbf{s}$ and depends only on ϵ.
The $\mathbf{w}'$-integration yields

$$\begin{aligned}\tilde{S}(\mathbf{w}, t+1) =& J(\epsilon) \sum_{\mathbf{r}} \int \chi_{\mathbf{r}}\left(\mathbf{T}^{-1}(\mathbf{w}, \mathbf{v}, \epsilon), \mathbf{v}\right) \\ & \times P(\mathbf{v}) \tilde{S}\left(\mathbf{T}^{-1}(\mathbf{w}, \mathbf{v}, \epsilon), t\right) d\mathbf{v}.\end{aligned} \tag{208}$$

Here, $\chi_{\mathbf{r}}(\mathbf{w}, \mathbf{v})$ is the characteristic function of the region $F_{\mathbf{r}}(\mathbf{w})$, *i.e.*,

$$\chi_{\mathbf{r}}(\mathbf{w}, \mathbf{v}) = \begin{cases} 1, & \text{if } \mathbf{v} \in F_{\mathbf{r}}(\mathbf{w}); \\ 0, & \text{otherwise.} \end{cases} \tag{209}$$

$\mathbf{T}^{-1}$ denotes the inverse of the transformation $\mathbf{T}(\,.\,, \mathbf{v}, \epsilon)$. For $\mathbf{v} \in F_{\mathbf{s}}(\mathbf{w})$, $\mathbf{T}^{-1}(\mathbf{w}, \mathbf{v}, \epsilon)$ is given by

$$\left[\mathbf{T}^{-1}(\mathbf{w}, \mathbf{v}, \epsilon)\right]_{\mathbf{r}} = \mathbf{w}_{\mathbf{r}} + \epsilon h_{\mathbf{rs}}(\mathbf{w}_{\mathbf{r}} - \mathbf{v}), \tag{210}$$

where we have introduced the new function $h_{\mathbf{rs}} := h^0_{\mathbf{rs}}/(1 - \epsilon h^0_{\mathbf{rs}})$. In this section $h_{\mathbf{rs}}$ stands for a rescaled excitatory response differing from the original excitatory response $h^0_{\mathbf{rs}}$ only in order ϵ.

For $\epsilon \ll 1$ and $\mathbf{v} \in F_{\mathbf{s}}(\mathbf{w})$, we can expand $\tilde{S}(\mathbf{T}^{-1}(\mathbf{w}, \mathbf{v}, \epsilon), t)$ as

$$\begin{aligned}\tilde{S}(T^{-1}(\mathbf{w}, \mathbf{v}, \epsilon), t) =& \tilde{S}(\mathbf{w}, t) + \epsilon \sum_{\mathbf{r}m} h_{\mathbf{rs}}(\mathrm{w}_{\mathbf{r}m} - \mathrm{v}_m) \frac{\partial \tilde{S}}{\partial \mathrm{w}_{\mathbf{r}m}} + \\ & + \frac{1}{2}\epsilon^2 \sum_{\mathbf{r}m} \sum_{\mathbf{r}n} h_{\mathbf{rs}} h_{\mathbf{r}'\mathbf{s}} (\mathrm{w}_{\mathbf{r}m} - \mathrm{v}_m)(\mathrm{w}_{\mathbf{r}'n} - \mathrm{v}_n) \frac{\partial^2 \tilde{S}}{\partial \mathrm{w}_{\mathbf{r}m} \partial \mathrm{w}_{\mathbf{r}'n}} \\ & + O(\epsilon^3).\end{aligned} \tag{211}$$

Correspondingly, $J(\epsilon)$ can be expanded as

$$J(\epsilon) = 1 + \epsilon J_1 + \frac{1}{2}\epsilon^2 J_2 + \ldots, \tag{212}$$

where

$$J_1 = d \cdot \sum_{\mathbf{r}} h_{\mathbf{rs}} = d \cdot \sum_{\mathbf{r}} h_{\mathbf{r}0} \tag{213}$$

is independent of s. Substituting Eq.(211) and (212) into (208) while keeping derivatives up to second order and of these only the leading order in ϵ, we obtain

$$\begin{aligned}\frac{1}{\epsilon}\Big[\tilde{S}(\mathbf{w},t+1) - \tilde{S}(\mathbf{w},t)\Big] &= J_1 \tilde{S}(\mathbf{w},t)\\ &+ \sum_{\mathbf{s}} \int_{F_{\mathbf{s}}(\mathbf{w})} d\mathbf{v}\ P(\mathbf{v}) \sum_{\mathbf{r}m} h_{\mathbf{rs}}(\mathbf{w}_{\mathbf{r}m} - \mathbf{v}_m)\frac{\partial \tilde{S}}{\partial \mathbf{w}_{\mathbf{r}m}}\\ &+ \frac{\epsilon}{2}\sum_{\mathbf{s}} \int_{F_{\mathbf{s}}(\mathbf{w})} d\mathbf{v}\ P(\mathbf{v})\\ &\times \sum_{\mathbf{r}m}\sum_{\mathbf{r}n} h_{\mathbf{rs}} h_{\mathbf{r}'\mathbf{s}}(\mathbf{w}_{\mathbf{r}m} - \mathbf{v}_m)(\mathbf{w}_{\mathbf{r}'n} - \mathbf{v}_n)\frac{\partial^2 \tilde{S}}{\partial \mathbf{w}_{\mathbf{r}m}\partial \mathbf{w}_{\mathbf{r}'n}}.\end{aligned} \tag{214}$$

In the vicinity of the stationary state we expect $\tilde{S}(\mathbf{w},t)$ to be peaked around the asymptotic equilibrium value $\bar{\mathbf{w}}$. Therefore, we shift variables and define

$$S(\mathbf{u},t) := \tilde{S}(\bar{\mathbf{w}} + \mathbf{u}, t), \tag{215}$$

i.e., $S(\mathbf{u},t)$ is the distribution function of the deviations u from the asymptotic equilibrium value $\bar{\mathbf{w}}$. In what follows it is useful to introduce the quantities

$$\hat{P}_{\mathbf{r}}(\mathbf{w}) := \int_{F_{\mathbf{r}}(\mathbf{w})} d\mathbf{v} P(\mathbf{v}), \tag{216}$$

$$\bar{\mathbf{v}}_{\mathbf{r}} := \frac{1}{\hat{P}_{\mathbf{r}}(\mathbf{w})} \int_{F_{\mathbf{r}}(\mathbf{w})} d\mathbf{v} P(\mathbf{v})\mathbf{v}, \tag{217}$$

$$\mathrm{V}_{\mathbf{r}m}(\mathbf{w}) := \sum_{\mathbf{s}} (\mathbf{w}_{\mathbf{r}m} - \bar{\mathbf{v}}_{\mathbf{s}m}) h_{\mathbf{rs}} \hat{P}_{\mathbf{s}}(\mathbf{w}), \tag{218}$$

$$\begin{aligned}\mathrm{D}_{\mathbf{r}m\mathbf{r}'n}(\mathbf{w}) := \sum_{\mathbf{s}} h_{\mathbf{rs}} h_{\mathbf{r}'\mathbf{s}} \Big[&(\mathbf{w}_{\mathbf{r}m} - \bar{\mathbf{v}}_{\mathbf{s}m})(\mathbf{w}_{\mathbf{r}'n} - \bar{\mathbf{v}}_{\mathbf{s}n})\hat{P}_{\mathbf{s}}(\mathbf{w})\\ &+ \int_{F_{\mathbf{s}}(\mathbf{w})} (\mathbf{v}_m \mathbf{v}_n - \bar{\mathbf{v}}_{\mathbf{s}m}\bar{\mathbf{v}}_{\mathbf{s}n}) P(\mathbf{v}) d\mathbf{v}\Big].\end{aligned} \tag{219}$$

$\hat{P}_{\mathbf{r}}(\mathbf{w})$ is the probability for neuron $\mathbf{r}$ to be selected as excitation center, and $\bar{\mathbf{v}}_{\mathbf{r}}$ is the expectation value of all input signals giving rise to this case. $-V_{\mathbf{r}m}(\mathbf{w})$ can be interpreted as the expectation value for the change $\delta w_{\mathbf{r}m}$ (change of the synapse between incoming axon m and neuron $\mathbf{r}$) under an infinitesimal learning step, but normalized to $\epsilon = 1$. Correspondingly, $D_{\mathbf{r}m\mathbf{r}'n}(\mathbf{w})$ is the expectation value of the product $\delta w_{\mathbf{r}m}\delta w_{\mathbf{r}'n}$, also normalized to $\epsilon = 1$.

For sufficiently small ϵ we can evaluate the $O(\epsilon)$-term in (214) directly at $\mathbf{w} = \bar{\mathbf{w}}$ and replace $S(\mathbf{u}, t+1) - S(\mathbf{u}, t)$ by $\partial_t S(\mathbf{u}, t)$. This yields the *Fokker-Planck equation*

$$\frac{1}{\epsilon}\partial_t S(\mathbf{u},t) = J_1 S(\mathbf{u},t) + \sum_{\mathbf{r}m} V_{\mathbf{r}m}(\bar{\mathbf{w}}+\mathbf{u})\frac{\partial S(\mathbf{u},t)}{\partial u_{\mathbf{r}m}} + \frac{\epsilon}{2}\sum_{\mathbf{r}m\mathbf{r}'n} D_{\mathbf{r}m\mathbf{r}'n}(\bar{\mathbf{w}})\frac{\partial^2 S(\mathbf{u},t)}{\partial u_{\mathbf{r}m}\partial u_{\mathbf{r}'n}}. \tag{220}$$

The term with the first derivative represents a "back driving force." It vanishes for $\mathbf{u} = 0$ and must therefore be kept up to linear order in $\mathbf{u}$. This gives

$$\sum_{\mathbf{r}m} V_{\mathbf{r}m}(\bar{\mathbf{w}}+\mathbf{u})\frac{\partial S(\mathbf{u},t)}{\partial u_{\mathbf{r}m}} = -\sum_{\mathbf{r}m}\frac{\partial V_{\mathbf{r}m}}{\partial w_{\mathbf{r}m}} S + \sum_{\mathbf{r}m\mathbf{r}'n}\frac{\partial}{\partial u_{\mathbf{r}m}}\left(\frac{\partial V_{\mathbf{r}m}}{\partial w_{\mathbf{r}'n}}(\bar{\mathbf{w}})u_{\mathbf{r}'n}S\right). \tag{221}$$

In order to obtain a more convenient form of $\sum_{\mathbf{r}m} \partial V_{\mathbf{r}m}/\partial w_{\mathbf{r}m}$, we make use of

$$\begin{aligned} V_{\mathbf{r}}(\mathbf{w}) &= \sum_{\mathbf{s}} h_{\mathbf{rs}} \int_{F_{\mathbf{s}}(\mathbf{w})} d\mathbf{v} P(\mathbf{v})(\mathbf{w}_{\mathbf{r}} - \mathbf{v}) \\ &= \frac{1}{\epsilon}\int d\mathbf{v}\; P(\mathbf{v})\Big(\mathbf{w}_{\mathbf{r}} - \mathbf{T}(\mathbf{w},\mathbf{v},\epsilon)_{\mathbf{r}}\Big) \end{aligned} \tag{222}$$

and obtain

$$\sum_{\mathbf{r}m}\frac{\partial V_{\mathbf{r}m}}{\partial w_{\mathbf{r}m}} = \frac{1}{\epsilon}\int d\mathbf{v}\; P(\mathbf{v})\; \mathrm{Tr}\left(\mathbf{1} - \frac{\partial \mathbf{T}}{\partial \mathbf{w}}\right) \tag{223}$$

where Tr denotes the trace operation. The deviation of the Jacobi matrix $\partial \mathbf{T}/\partial \mathbf{w}$ from the unit matrix is of order ϵ. Hence, $\frac{\partial \mathbf{T}}{\partial \mathbf{w}} = \mathbf{1} + \epsilon \mathbf{A}$, and together with (206), one has

$$J(\epsilon) = \det(\mathbf{1} - \epsilon\mathbf{A}) + O(\epsilon^2) = 1 - \epsilon \cdot \mathrm{Tr}\;\mathbf{A} + O(\epsilon^2). \tag{224}$$

Comparison with (212) yields

$$J_1 = -\operatorname{Tr}\mathbf{A} = \frac{1}{\epsilon}\operatorname{Tr}\left(\mathbf{1} - \frac{\partial \mathbf{T}}{\partial \mathbf{w}}\right). \tag{225}$$

Substituting this into Eq. (223), we obtain the relation

$$\sum_{\mathbf{r}m} \frac{\partial \mathrm{V}_{\mathbf{r}m}}{\partial \mathrm{w}_{\mathbf{r}m}} = J_1. \tag{226}$$

This leads us to the final form of our equation for the distribution density $S(\mathbf{u}, t)$

$$\begin{aligned} \frac{1}{\epsilon}\partial_t S(\mathbf{u},t) = &\sum_{\mathbf{r}m\mathbf{r}'n} \frac{\partial}{\partial \mathrm{u}_{\mathbf{r}m}} \mathrm{B}_{\mathbf{r}m\mathbf{r}'n}\mathrm{u}_{\mathbf{r}'n} S(\mathbf{u},t) \\ &+ \frac{\epsilon}{2}\sum_{\mathbf{r}m\mathbf{r}'n} \mathrm{D}_{\mathbf{r}m\mathbf{r}'n} \frac{\partial^2 S(\mathbf{u},t)}{\partial \mathrm{u}_{\mathbf{r}m}\partial \mathrm{u}_{\mathbf{r}'n}}, \end{aligned} \tag{227}$$

where the constant matrix $\mathbf{B}$ is given by

$$\mathrm{B}_{\mathbf{r}m\mathbf{r}'n} := \left(\frac{\partial \mathrm{V}_{\mathbf{r}m}(\mathbf{w})}{\partial \mathrm{w}_{\mathbf{r}'n}}\right)_{\mathbf{w}=\bar{\mathbf{w}}}. \tag{228}$$

(227) is the desired Fokker-Planck equation for the asymptotic phase of the map formation process.

One can derive explicit expressions for the expectation value $\bar{\mathrm{u}}_{\mathbf{r}m}(t) = \langle \mathrm{u}_{\mathbf{r}m}\rangle_S$ and the correlation matrix $\mathrm{C}_{\mathbf{r}m\mathbf{s}n}(t) = \langle(\mathrm{u}_{\mathbf{r}m} - \bar{\mathrm{u}}_{\mathbf{r}m})(\mathrm{u}_{\mathbf{s}n} - \bar{\mathrm{u}}_{\mathbf{s}n})\rangle_S$ of the distribution S (see, for example, van Kampen 1981; Gardiner 1985). Defining

$$\mathbf{Y}(t) = \exp\Big(-\mathbf{B}\int_0^t \epsilon(\tau)\, d\tau\Big), \tag{229}$$

one obtains for $\bar{\mathrm{u}}(t)$, The vector with components $\bar{\mathrm{u}}_{\mathbf{r}m}$,

$$\bar{\mathrm{u}}(t) = \mathbf{Y}(t)\bar{\mathrm{u}}(0). \tag{230}$$

Here, $\bar{\mathrm{u}}(0)$ is the expectation value at $t = 0$. The quantity $\bar{\mathrm{u}}(t)$ gives the trajectory of the expectation value of the synaptic strengths and provides a good approximation for the evolution of the system in the limit of sufficiently small learning step size ϵ. For the correlation matrix $\mathrm{C}(t)$, one has (van Kampen, 1981)

$$\mathrm{C}(t) = \mathbf{Y}(t)\Big[\mathrm{C}(0) + \int_0^t \epsilon(\tau)^2 \mathbf{Y}(\tau)^{-1}\mathbf{D}(\mathbf{Y}(\tau)^{-1})^T\, d\tau\Big]\mathbf{Y}(t)^T. \tag{231}$$

If the initial distribution is δ-like, *i.e.*, if $S(\mathbf{u},0) = \prod_{\mathbf{r}m}\delta(\mathbf{u}_{\mathbf{r}m} - \mathbf{u}(0)_{\mathbf{r}m})$ and $\mathbf{C}(t)$ is positive definite, then $S(\mathbf{u},t)$, the solution of Eq. (227), is a Gaussian distribution

$$S(\mathbf{u},t) = \det(2\pi\mathbf{C})^{-1/2}\exp\left(-\frac{1}{2}(\mathbf{u}-\bar{\mathbf{u}})^T\mathbf{C}^{-1}(\mathbf{u}-\bar{\mathbf{u}})\right). \qquad (232)$$

If $\epsilon(t)$ is chosen such that the initial conditions become irrelevant in the limit $t \to \infty$, for example if ϵ = constant, the stationary solution can by obtained by substituting the asymptotic values for $\mathbf{C}$ and $\bar{\mathbf{u}}$. If $\mathbf{B}$ and $\mathbf{D}$ commute and ϵ is constant, a further simplification occurs. In this case, one can carry out the integration of (231) explicitly and obtains for the stationary distribution the Gaussian (232) with

$$\mathbf{C} = \epsilon\,(\mathbf{B}+\mathbf{B}^T)^{-1}\mathbf{D}. \qquad (233)$$

14.8. Convergence Condition on Sequences of Learning Step Sizes

The goal of the algorithm is convergence to an asymptotic equilibrium state $\bar{\mathbf{w}}$. In order for this to occur with probability one for every member of the ensemble, the sequence of learning step sizes $\epsilon(t)$ must decrease sufficiently slowly with the number t of learning steps, so that both the variance of the distribution function and the average $\bar{\mathbf{u}}(t)$ of its deviation $\bar{\mathbf{w}}$ vanish in the limit $t \to \infty$. In the following, we derive a necessary and sufficient condition for this.

From (231), one has (van Kampen 1981)

$$\dot{\mathbf{C}} = -\epsilon(t)\left(\mathbf{B}\mathbf{C} + \mathbf{C}\mathbf{B}^T\right) + \epsilon(t)^2\mathbf{D}. \qquad (234)$$

Hence, one obtains for the time derivative of the Euclidean matrix norm $\|\mathbf{C}\|^2 := \sum_{\mathbf{r}m\mathbf{r}'n} \mathbf{C}^2_{\mathbf{r}m\mathbf{r}'n}$

$$\frac{1}{2}\partial_t\|\mathbf{C}\|^2 = -\epsilon(t)\ \mathrm{Tr}\ \mathbf{C}(\mathbf{B}+\mathbf{B}^T)\mathbf{C} + \epsilon(t)^2\ \mathrm{Tr}\ \mathbf{D}\mathbf{C}. \qquad (235)$$

In the following, we require that $\mathbf{C}$ remains bounded if $\epsilon(t)$ is constant and the initial correlation matrix $\mathbf{C}(\mathbf{0})$ is sufficiently small, but otherwise arbitrarily chosen. This is a stability requirement on the equilibrium state $\bar{\mathbf{w}}$. Since $\mathbf{C}$ and $\mathbf{D}$ are both symmetric and nonnegative, one has $\mathrm{Tr}\,\mathbf{DC} \geq 0$. Hence, by the stability requirement, $(\mathbf{B} + \mathbf{B}^T)$ must be positive. Thus, there exist constants $\beta > 0$ and $\gamma > 0$ such that

$$\mathrm{Tr}\,\mathbf{C}\big[\mathbf{B}(\bar{\mathbf{w}}) + \mathbf{B}(\bar{\mathbf{w}})^T\big]\mathbf{C} > \beta\|\mathbf{C}\|^2/2, \tag{236}$$

and, hence,

$$\partial_t\|\mathbf{C}\|^2 \leq -\epsilon(t)\beta\|\mathbf{C}\|^2 + \epsilon(t)^2\gamma. \tag{237}$$

Integration yields the inequality

$$\|\mathbf{C}(t)\|^2 \leq \gamma \int_0^t \epsilon(t')^2 \exp\Big(-\beta \int_{t'}^t \epsilon(t'')\, dt''\Big)\, dt'. \tag{238}$$

Every positive function $\epsilon(t)$ for which the RHS of (238) vanishes asymptotically guarantees the desired convergence of C to zero. In the appendix at the end of this chapter, it is shown that this condition is equivalent to the requirement $\lim_{t\to\infty} \epsilon(t) = 0$, together with

$$\lim_{t\to\infty} \int_0^t \epsilon(t')\, dt' = \infty. \tag{239}$$

With $\lim_{t\to\infty} \mathbf{C}(t) = 0$, this also guarantees $\lim_{t\to\infty} \bar{\mathbf{u}}(t) = 0$ and, hence, convergence to the equilibrium average $\bar{\mathbf{w}}$ with probability one. This criterion cannot be weakened: because of Eq.(234), $\lim_{t\to\infty} \epsilon(t) = 0$ is necessary for the asymptotic vanishing of the variance, and according to (229) and (230), condition (239) is required for $\lim_{t\to\infty} \bar{\mathbf{u}}(t) = 0$. Hence, for convergence to an asymptotic equilibrium state $\bar{\mathbf{w}}$ satisfying the stability requirement, we have shown the following:

> Let $\epsilon(t) > 0$ for all sufficiently small t so that the Markov process (70) can be described by the Fokker-Planck equation (227) in the neighborhood of an equilibrium state. Then the two conditions
>
> $$\lim_{t\to\infty} \int_0^t \epsilon(t')\, dt' = \infty, \tag{240}$$
>
> $$\lim_{t\to\infty} \epsilon(t) = 0 \tag{241}$$
>
> together are necessary and sufficient for the convergence to $\bar{\mathbf{w}}$ of any initial state lying sufficiently close to $\bar{\mathbf{w}}$.

The demand (240) is identical to the first convergence condition of Cottrell and Fort (1986) for a closely related process. Their second condition, the requirement $\int_0^\infty \epsilon(t)^2\, dt < \infty$, is overly strict in the present case and has been replaced by the weaker condition (241). In particular, (240) and (241) are satisfied for all functions $\epsilon(t) \propto t^{-\alpha}$ with $0 < \alpha \leq 1$. In contrast, the conditions of Cottrell and Forts require $1/2 < \alpha \leq 1$. For $\alpha > 1$ or exponential vanishing of $\epsilon(t)$, (240) is no longer satisfied, and a nonvanishing residual deviation remains even in the limit $t \rightarrow \infty$. Nevertheless, (230) and (231) show that the residual error $\bar{\mathrm{u}}$ of the average becomes exponentially small with increasing $\int_0^\infty \epsilon(t)\, dt$. For $\int_0^t \epsilon(t')\, dt' \gg 1$, the main contributions to the residual error come from the equilibrium fluctuations of the correlation matrix **C**. Hence this error is of order ϵ. Thus, in practical applications, aside from a small residual $\epsilon(t)$, the condition, $\int \epsilon(t) dt \gg 1$ is sufficient, and the precise behavior of $\epsilon(t)$ is of little importance as long as the decrease is monotonic.

14.9. Uniform Signal Density Restricted to a Rectangular Box

In the following sections we consider a Kohonen net which is a two-dimensional lattice A with a three-dimensional input space V. The probability density $P(\mathbf{v})$, $\mathbf{v} \in V$ is assumed to be uniform and restricted to the region of a rectangular box. We also assume that the learning step size ϵ varies sufficiently slowly with the number of learning steps such that at any time t the density $S(\mathbf{u}, t)$ may be replaced by its stationary value for fixed ϵ. Since the input vectors $\mathbf{v}$ are drawn from a volume of dimension three, *i.e.*, larger than the dimension two of the Kohonen net, the Markov process will attempt to project onto the Kohonen net those two directions along which the distribution has its largest variance. In this way, the resulting map is a two-dimensional projection reproducing the higher-dimensional region V as faithfully as possible. Figure 14.5 illustrates this for a three-dimensional rectangular box V of size $40\times40\times10$ and a 40×40-lattice A. Figure 14.5a shows the resulting map again as an "imbedding" in the box V. Since the box is relatively flat, the map is basically a simple projection onto the subspace that is aligned with the two longest sides of the rectangular box.

For nonvanishing ϵ, the learning steps cause continual fluctuations about an average "equilibrium map." These fluctuations appear in Fig. 14.5a as shallow "bumps" and as weak tangential distortions of the lattice. These "bumps"are destortions which will be described quantitatively in this section.

If inputs in case of a d-dimensional input space scatter too much along some or all of the additional $d-2$ dimensions not represented by a two-dimensional Kohonen net, then for many vectors v the restriction of the projection to a reproduction of the two principal directions of V would be unsatisfactory. In this case, the simple projection just described loses its stability and changes into a more complicated equilibrium map. Usually, this new map possesses a lower symmetry and corresponds to an imbedding of the lattice A in V that is strongly folded in the direction of the additional dimensions. This property, known as "automatic choice of feature dimensions," (Kohonen 1984a) is apparent in Fig. 14.5b. In comparison to Fig. 14.5a, the height of the box was increased from 10 to 14 units. The symmetric projection is now no longer stable, and the corresponding imbedding seeks a new configuration. This new configuration breaks the symmetry of the probability distribution $P(\mathbf{v})$ in order to enable a better reproduction of the vertical variation of v by means of an appropriate folding. In the following, we will show that this change to a new equilibrium state arises at a critical value $2s^*$ of the height of the box and that, approaching that value from below, the maps exhibit increasing equilibrium fluctuations of a typical wavelength λ^*. Both values s^* and λ^* will be calculated in the following.

In the mapping of a multidimensional box volume (dimension d) onto a two-dimensional neural net A, each of the $d-2$ "height dimensions" contributes in the same manner and independently of the other dimensions to the instability and to the equilibrium fluctuations. Hence, there is no loss of generality if we consider a three-dimensional box V. We choose for A a square lattice of N×N points† and for V the volume $0 \leq x, y \leq N$, $-s \leq z \leq s$. This yields $P(\mathbf{v}) = [2sN^2]^{-1}$ as a homogeneous distribution. In order to avoid boundary effects, we assume periodic boundary conditions along the x- and y-directions. From symmetry considerations, we expect that for sufficiently small s the assignment $\bar{\mathbf{w}}_\mathbf{r} = \mathbf{r}$, $\mathbf{r} = m\mathbf{e}_x + n\mathbf{e}_y$ represents the average for $\tilde{S}(\mathbf{w}, t \to \infty)$. In this case, the state

†Note that the number of lattice points is now N^2 instead of N.

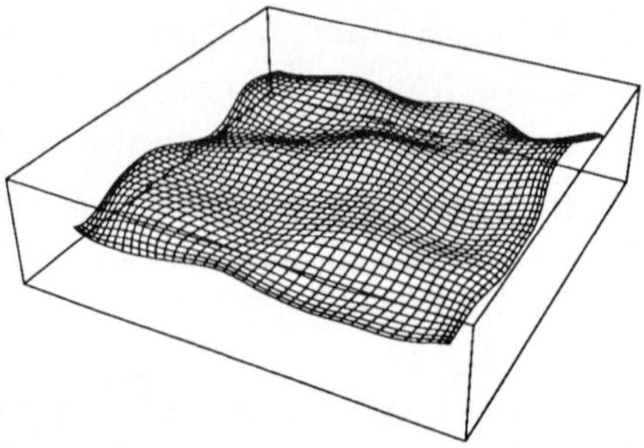

Figure 14.5a "Snapshot" of a Monte Carlo simulation for a 40 × 40-Kohonen net A and a 40 × 40 × 10 units large rectangular box representing the input space V. Due to the sufficiently small box height (10 units), the resulting mapping is essentially a projection perpendicular to the two principal (long) directions of the box. Fluctuations about the equilibrium value due to the statistical sequence of learning steps are evident as shallow "bumps."

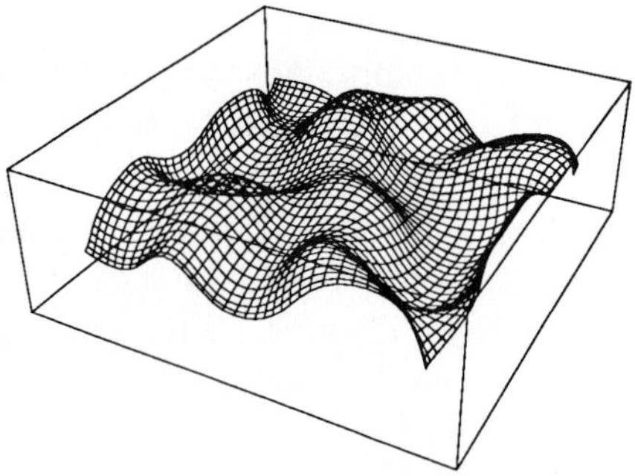

Figure 14.5b The same simulation as in Fig. 14.5a, but for a box height of 14 units. In this case, the state of the net in Fig. 14.5a is no longer stable and a less symmetric configuration emerges. The resulting imbedding achieves a better reproduction of the vertical direction of the map by means of folds extending along this direction.

$\bar{\mathbf{w}}$ is stable up to equilibrium fluctuations. The equilibrium fluctuations can be computed from Eq. (232).

In the following, let $S(\mathbf{u}) = \lim_{t\to\infty} S(\mathbf{u}, t)$ be the stationary distribution of the deviations $\mathbf{u} = \mathbf{w} - \bar{\mathbf{w}}$ from the average value (let ϵ be constant). Due to translational invariance , both $\mathrm{D}_{\mathbf{r}m\mathbf{r}'n}$ and $\mathrm{B}_{\mathbf{r}m\mathbf{r}'n}$ depend only on the difference $\mathbf{r} - \mathbf{r}'$ and on n and m. Hence, we can decouple Eq. (227) if we express $S(\mathbf{u})$ in terms of Fourier amplitudes

$$\hat{\mathbf{u}}_{\mathbf{k}} = \frac{1}{N} \sum_{\mathbf{r}} e^{i\mathbf{k}\cdot\mathbf{r}} \mathbf{u}_{\mathbf{r}}. \tag{242}$$

In fact, the individual amplitudes are distributed independently of one another, *i.e.*, one can express

$$S(\mathbf{u}) = \prod_{\mathbf{k}} \hat{S}_{\mathbf{k}}(\hat{\mathbf{u}}_{\mathbf{k}}), \tag{243}$$

and obtains a set of mutually independent, stationary Fokker-Planck equations for the distributions $\hat{S}_{\mathbf{k}}$ of the individual modes

$$\sum_{mn} \hat{\mathrm{B}}(\mathbf{k})_{mn} \frac{\partial}{\partial \mathrm{u}_m} \mathrm{u}_n \hat{S}_{\mathbf{k}}(\mathbf{u}) + \frac{\epsilon}{2} \sum_{mn} \hat{\mathrm{D}}(\mathbf{k})_{mn} \frac{\partial^2}{\partial \mathrm{u}_m \partial \mathrm{u}_n} \hat{S}_{\mathbf{k}}(\mathbf{u}) = 0. \tag{244}$$

Here, $\hat{\mathbf{D}}(\mathbf{k})$ and $\hat{\mathbf{B}}(\mathbf{k})$ are the d×d matrices

$$\begin{aligned}\hat{\mathbf{D}}(\mathbf{k}) &= \sum_{\mathbf{r}} e^{i\mathbf{k}(\mathbf{r}-\mathbf{r}')}\mathbf{D}_{\mathbf{r}\mathbf{r}'} \\ &= \frac{1}{N^2}\left[(\nabla_k \hat{h}(\mathbf{k}))(\nabla_k \hat{h}(\mathbf{k}))^T + \mathbf{M}\ \hat{h}(\mathbf{k})^2\right]\end{aligned} \tag{245}$$

and

$$\hat{\mathbf{B}}(\mathbf{k}) = \frac{\hat{h}(\mathbf{0})}{N^2}\left[\mathbf{1} - \frac{\hat{h}(\mathbf{k})}{\hat{h}(\mathbf{0})}\hat{\mathbf{a}}(\mathbf{k})\right] - \frac{1}{N^2}\left(i\nabla_k \hat{h}(\mathbf{k})\right)\hat{\mathbf{b}}(\mathbf{k})^T. \tag{246}$$

For a more compact notation, we defined $\mathbf{k} := (k_x, k_y, 0)^T$. $\mathbf{M}$ is given by

$$\mathbf{M} = \frac{1}{2s}\int_{F_{\mathbf{r}}(\bar{\mathbf{w}})} d\mathbf{v}\ (\mathbf{v}\mathbf{v}^T - \bar{\mathbf{v}}_{\mathbf{r}}\bar{\mathbf{v}}_{\mathbf{r}}{}^T) = \begin{pmatrix} 1/12 & 0 & 0 \\ 0 & 1/12 & 0 \\ 0 & 0 & s^2/3 \end{pmatrix}, \tag{247}$$

i.e., $\mathbf{M}$ is the correlation matrix of the distribution $\hat{P}(\mathbf{v})$ restricted to one of the regions $F_{\mathbf{r}}(\bar{\mathbf{w}})$. Since all of the $F_{\mathbf{r}}(\bar{\mathbf{w}})$ are equal and since $\hat{P}(\mathbf{v})$ is constant, $\mathbf{M}$ is independent of the choice of $\mathbf{r}$. The function $\hat{h}(\mathbf{k})$ is the discrete Fourier transform of the neighborhood function $h_{\mathbf{rs}}$, *i.e.*,

$$\hat{h}(\mathbf{k}) = \sum_{\mathbf{r}} e^{i\mathbf{k}\cdot\mathbf{r}} h_{\mathbf{r}\mathbf{0}}. \tag{248}$$

The matrix $\hat{\mathbf{a}}(\mathbf{k})$ and the vector $\hat{\mathbf{b}}(\mathbf{k})$ are the Fourier transforms of the functions

$$\mathbf{a}_{\mathbf{r}\mathbf{r}'} := \left.\frac{\partial \bar{\mathbf{v}}_{\mathbf{r}}(\mathbf{w})}{\partial \mathbf{w}_{\mathbf{r}'}}\right|_{\bar{\mathbf{w}}}, \tag{249}$$

$$\mathbf{b}_{\mathbf{r}\mathbf{r}'} := \left.\frac{1}{\hat{P}_{\mathbf{r}}}\frac{\partial \hat{P}_{\mathbf{r}}(\mathbf{w})}{\partial \mathbf{w}_{\mathbf{r}'}}\right|_{\bar{\mathbf{w}}}. \tag{250}$$

respectively. The quantities $\hat{\mathbf{a}}$ and $\hat{\mathbf{b}}$ depend only on the geometry of the vectors $\mathbf{w}_{\mathbf{r}}$ in the equilibrium state, but not on the excitatory response h. The matrix $\hat{\mathbf{a}}$ describes the shift of the center of gravity of a region $F_{\mathbf{r}}$ under an infinitesimal change of the equilibrium state, and $\hat{\mathbf{b}}$ describes essentially the corresponding volume change of $F_{\mathbf{r}}$. In the present case, $F_{\mathbf{r}}(\mathbf{w})$ is the volume that is enclosed by the four planes perpendicularly bisecting the distances $\mathbf{w}_{\mathbf{r}} - \mathbf{w}_{\mathbf{r}'}$ ($\mathbf{r}'$ are the nearest lattice neighbors of $\mathbf{r}$)

together with the two planes $z = \pm s$. For this geometry and after some calculation, one obtains

$$\mathbf{a}_{\mathbf{rr}'} = \delta_{\mathbf{rr}'}\begin{pmatrix} 2/3 & 0 & 0 \\ 0 & 2/3 & 0 \\ 0 & 0 & 4s^2/3 \end{pmatrix} - \begin{pmatrix} -1/4 & 0 & 0 \\ 0 & 1/12 & 0 \\ 0 & 0 & s^2/3 \end{pmatrix} \cdot (\delta_{\mathbf{r}+\mathbf{e}_x,\mathbf{r}'} + \delta_{\mathbf{r}-\mathbf{e}_x,\mathbf{r}'}) - \begin{pmatrix} 1/12 & 0 & 0 \\ 0 & -1/4 & 0 \\ 0 & 0 & s^2/3 \end{pmatrix} \cdot (\delta_{\mathbf{r}+\mathbf{e}_y,\mathbf{r}'} + \delta_{\mathbf{r}-\mathbf{e}_y,\mathbf{r}'}) \tag{251}$$

and

$$\mathbf{b}_{\mathbf{rr}'} = \frac{1}{2} \sum_{\mathbf{n}=\pm\mathbf{e}_x,\mathbf{e}_y} \mathbf{n}\ (\delta_{\mathbf{r}+\mathbf{n},\mathbf{r}'} - \delta_{\mathbf{rr}'}). \tag{252}$$

The corresponding Fourier transforms are then

$$\begin{aligned} \hat{\mathbf{a}}(\mathbf{k}) = & \frac{1}{6}(4 + 3\cos k_x - \cos k_y)\mathbf{e}_x\mathbf{e}_x^T \\ & + \frac{1}{6}(4 - \cos k_x + 3\cos k_y)\mathbf{e}_y\mathbf{e}_y^T \\ & + \frac{2s^2}{3}(2 - \cos k_x - \cos k_y)\mathbf{e}_z\mathbf{e}_z^T, \end{aligned} \tag{253}$$

$$\hat{\mathbf{b}}(\mathbf{k}) = -i \cdot (\mathbf{e}_x \sin k_x + \mathbf{e}_y \sin k_y). \tag{254}$$

With this, we can discuss the behavior of the system in the vicinity of the state $\bar{\mathbf{w}}$. We can see from $\lim_{k\to 0} \hat{\mathbf{b}}(\mathbf{k}) = 0$ and $\lim_{k\to 0} \hat{\mathbf{a}}_{mn}(\mathbf{k}) = \delta_{mn}(1 - \delta_{m,3})$ that, in the limit of small wavenumbers, for deviations of $\bar{\mathbf{w}}$ along the x- and y-directions the restoring force vanishes, which is consistent with the two vanishing eigenvalues of $\hat{\mathbf{B}}(\mathbf{k})$ in this limit. Hence, long-wavelength fluctuations of these modes can become very large. In contrast, the restoring force to displacements along the z-direction is always nonvanishing even at $\mathbf{k} = 0$.

However, displacements in the z-direction are subject to a different instability. Since $\hat{\mathbf{a}}_{33}(\mathbf{k}) \propto s^2$, $\hat{\mathbf{B}}(\mathbf{k})$ according to (246) can develop a negative eigenvalue for these modes, if s becomes too large. Hence, some or all of these modes can become unstable if s exceeds a critical value s^*. If the variance of $P(\mathbf{v})$ along the "transverse" dimensions is too large, this causes the system to assume a new equilibrium state which as a rule breaks the symmetry of the distribution $P(\mathbf{v})$. A precursor to this symmetry breaking is an increase of fluctuations of a characteristic wavelength λ^*.

For a more detailed analysis and calculation of λ^* and s^* we now turn to the two cases of long- and short-range interactions (neighborhood functions) $h_{\mathbf{rs}}$.

14.9.1. Long-Range Interaction

We consider as the interaction a Gaussian

$$h_{\mathbf{rr}'} = \sum_{\mathbf{s}} \delta_{\mathbf{r}+\mathbf{s},\mathbf{r}'} \exp\left(-\frac{s^2}{2\sigma^2}\right) \tag{255}$$

with range σ, where we require $1 \ll \sigma \ll N$. In this case, we can replace the discrete Fourier series to a good approximation by the continuous transform and obtain

$$\hat{h}(\mathbf{k}) = 2\pi\sigma^2 \exp(-\sigma^2 k^2/2). \tag{256}$$

Substitution of (256) into (245) yields

$$\hat{\mathbf{D}}(\mathbf{k}) = \frac{4\pi^2\sigma^4}{N^2}\left[\mathbf{k}\mathbf{k}^T\sigma^4 + \mathbf{M}\right]\exp(-k^2\sigma^2). \tag{257}$$

The nonvanishing elements of $\hat{\mathbf{B}}(\mathbf{k})$ are

$$\hat{\mathbf{B}}_{11} = \frac{2\pi\sigma^2}{N^2}\left[1 - \frac{1}{6}(4 + 3\cos k_x - 6k_x\sigma^2 \sin k_x - \cos k_y)\cdot e^{-\frac{1}{2}k^2\sigma^2}\right], \tag{258}$$

$$\hat{\mathbf{B}}_{22} = \frac{2\pi\sigma^2}{N^2}\left[1 - \frac{1}{6}(4 - \cos k_x - 6k_y\sigma^2 \sin k_y + 3\cos k_y)\cdot e^{-\frac{1}{2}k^2\sigma^2}\right], \tag{259}$$

$$\hat{\mathbf{B}}_{33} = \frac{2\pi\sigma^2}{N^2}\left[1 - \frac{2s^2}{3}(2 - \cos k_x - \cos k_y)\exp(-k^2\sigma^2/2)\right], \tag{260}$$

$$\hat{\mathbf{B}}_{12} = \frac{2\pi\sigma^4}{N^2}\cdot k_x \sin k_y \cdot \exp(-k^2\sigma^2/2), \tag{261}$$

$$\hat{\mathbf{B}}_{21} = \frac{2\pi\sigma^4}{N^2}\cdot k_y \sin k_x \cdot \exp(-k^2\sigma^2/2). \tag{262}$$

In order to simplify these expressions, we use the fact that for $\sigma \gg 1$ either $e^{-\sigma^2 k^2}$ is very small or k_x and k_y admit an expansion of the angular functions. Neglecting as well the k^2-terms compared to $k^2\sigma^2$-terms, we obtain for $\hat{\mathbf{B}}$ the simpler form

$$\hat{\mathbf{B}}(\mathbf{k}) \approx \frac{2\pi\sigma^2}{N^2}\left[1 - \left(1 - \sigma^2\mathbf{k}\mathbf{k}^T + \frac{s^2k^2}{3}\mathbf{e}_z\mathbf{e}_z^T\right)\exp\left(-k^2\sigma^2/2\right)\right]. \tag{263}$$

In this approximation, $\hat{\mathbf{B}}(\mathbf{k})$ and $\hat{\mathbf{D}}(\mathbf{k})$ commute with each other and, in fact, possess the same eigenvectors, *i.e.*, $\vec{\xi}_3 = \mathbf{e}_z$, $\vec{\xi}_2 = \mathbf{k}$ and the vector $\vec{\xi}_1 = \mathbf{k}^\perp$ perpendicular to both of these. The corresponding eigenvalues λ_n^B and λ_n^D for $\hat{\mathbf{B}}(\mathbf{k})$ and $\hat{\mathbf{D}}(\mathbf{k})$ are

$$\begin{aligned}\lambda_1^B(\mathbf{k}) &= \frac{2\pi\sigma^2}{N^2}\left(1 - e^{-k^2\sigma^2/2}\right);\\ \lambda_1^D(\mathbf{k}) &= \frac{\pi^2\sigma^4}{3N^2}e^{-k^2\sigma^2};\end{aligned} \tag{264}$$

$$\begin{aligned}\lambda_2^B(\mathbf{k}) &= \frac{2\pi\sigma^2}{N^2}\left(1 - (1 - k^2\sigma^2)e^{-k^2\sigma^2/2}\right);\\ \lambda_2^D(\mathbf{k}) &= \frac{\pi^2\sigma^4}{3N^2}(12k^2\sigma^4 + 1)e^{-k^2\sigma^2};\end{aligned} \tag{265}$$

$$\begin{aligned}\lambda_3^B(\mathbf{k}) &= \frac{2\pi\sigma^2}{N^2}\left(1 - \frac{s^2k^2}{3}e^{-k^2\sigma^2/2}\right);\\ \lambda_3^D(\mathbf{k}) &= \frac{4\pi^2\sigma^4}{3N^2}\ s^2e^{-k^2\sigma^2}.\end{aligned} \tag{266}$$

$\hat{\mathbf{B}}$ gives the strength of the "drift term" driving the expectation value of the distribution toward the equilibrium average. Hence, by (264) and (265), the system exhibits more "stiffness" against displacements along the $\vec{\xi}_2$-mode and, thus, parallel to k than against displacements along the $\vec{\xi}_1$-mode and, thus, perpendicular to k. For wavelengths large compared to the range σ of $h_{\mathbf{rs}}$, we have asymptotically $\lambda_2^B(\mathbf{k}) = 3\lambda_1^B(\mathbf{k}) = O(k^2)$, *i.e.*, the $\vec{\xi}_2$-mode is three times stiffer as the $\vec{\xi}_1$-mode, and both "stiffnesses" vanish in the limit $\mathbf{k} \to 0$. However, this does not hold for the $\vec{\xi}_3$-mode, which owes its stability to sufficiently small values of s. If s becomes too large, then $\lambda_3^B(\mathbf{k})$ can become negative for a whole band of k-values. The corresponding modes $\vec{\xi}_3(\mathbf{k})$ then become unstable, the chosen state $\bar{\mathbf{w}}$ no longer represents the average equilibrium value, and the system seeks a new equilibrium. This can be seen even more clearly from the fluctuations of the corresponding mode amplitudes u_n. From (233) follows

$$\langle u_n(\mathbf{k})^2\rangle = \frac{\epsilon\lambda_n^D(\mathbf{k})}{2\lambda_n^B(\mathbf{k})}, \quad n = 1, 2, 3. \tag{267}$$

All other correlations vanish. We thus obtain

$$\langle u_1(\mathbf{k})^2\rangle = \epsilon\pi\sigma^2\frac{\exp(-k^2\sigma^2)}{12(1 - \exp(-k^2\sigma^2/2))}, \tag{268}$$

$$\langle u_2(\mathbf{k})^2 \rangle = \epsilon\pi\sigma^2 \frac{(12k^2\sigma^4 + 1)\exp(-k^2\sigma^2)}{12 - 12(1 - k^2\sigma^2)\exp(-k^2\sigma^2/2)}, \quad (269)$$

$$\langle u_3(\mathbf{k})^2 \rangle = \epsilon\pi\sigma^2 \frac{s^2\exp(-k^2\sigma^2)}{3 - s^2k^2\exp(-k^2\sigma^2/2)}. \quad (270)$$

For the fluctuations of u_1 and u_2, the deviation of $\mathbf{w_r}$ from the equilibrium $\bar{\mathbf{w}}_\mathbf{r}$ lies along one of the two principal directions of the map. In the map, these fluctuations affect the image locations $\mathbf{r}$ of the region $F_\mathbf{r}$ and, therefore, are called "longitudinal" in what follows. From (268) and (269), we see that these fluctuations for wavelengths shorter than σ are practically absent. Hence, the main contribution to statistical distortions of the map comes from fluctuations of long wavelength, whose amplitudes are subject to a $1/k^2$-singularity. For an estimate of the influence of these fluctuations, we expand (268) for the lowest possible wavenumber $k = 2\pi/N$, where we assume $k\sigma = 2\pi\sigma/N << 1$. This yields

$$\langle u_1^2 \rangle^{1/2} \approx N\sqrt{\epsilon/24\pi} \approx 0.12N\epsilon^{1/2}. \quad (271)$$

In order for this not to exceed a fixed, prescribed number of lattice constants, ϵ must be chosen inversely proportional to the number N^2 of lattice points of A. For practical applications, these distortions, which are smooth and distributed over large distances, are not disturbing, since one is often mainly interested in the correct, two-dimensional reproduction of the neighborhood relationships in the original higher-dimensional space V. Therefore, for many applications, a significantly larger learning step size ϵ is allowable even in the final phase of the algorithm.

The u_3-mode describes the deviation of each $\mathbf{w_r}$ along the direction perpendicular to the local imbedding plane of A in V. According to (270), its amplitude remains bounded, in contrast to u_1 and u_2, even at $\mathbf{k} = 0$, but, as mentioned previously, its stability depends crucially on s. Instability occurs for s-values for which the denominator of (270) no longer is positive for all k-values. This is the case for $s > s^* = \sigma\sqrt{3e/2} \approx 2.02\ \sigma$. For $s = s^*$, the wavelength of the marginally unstable mode is $\lambda^* = \sigma\pi\sqrt{2} \approx 4.44\ \sigma$. A mapping is hence stable if and only if the variance of $P(\mathbf{v})$ transverse to the imbedding plane does not exceed a maximal value that is proportional to the range σ of $h_{\mathbf{rs}}$. If necessary, the algorithm enforces this condition by an appropriate folding of the imbedding. By the choice of σ, one can control what variance will be tolerated before folds occur. If s approaches the limiting value s^* from below, the system exhibits fluctuations which grow as the difference to s^* becomes smaller, and which are particularly evident in the vicinity of the wavelength λ^*. The fluctuations, in case of further increasing s, lead to a destabilization of the symmetric equilibrium distribution above s^*.

14.9.2. Short-Range Interaction

We consider now the short-range limit, in which $h_{\mathbf{rs}}$ extends only as far as the nearest neighbors, *i.e.*,

$$h_{\mathbf{rs}} = \delta_{\mathbf{rs}} + \sum_{\mathbf{n}=\pm\mathbf{e}_x,\mathbf{e}_y} \delta_{\mathbf{r+n,s}}. \tag{272}$$

In this case holds

$$\hat{h}(\mathbf{k}) = 1 + 2\cos k_x + 2\cos k_y. \tag{273}$$

For the representative case $k_y = 0,\ k := k_x$, one has

$$\langle u_1(\mathbf{k})^2 \rangle = \frac{\epsilon \cdot (3 + 2\cos k)^2}{4(1 - \cos k)(9 - 2\cos k)}, \tag{274}$$

$$\langle u_2(\mathbf{k})^2 \rangle = \frac{\epsilon \cdot (44\sin^2 k + 12\cos k + 13)}{12(1 - \cos k)(11 + 6\cos k)}, \tag{275}$$

$$\langle u_3(\mathbf{k})^2 \rangle = \frac{\epsilon s^2 \cdot (1 + 2\kappa)^2}{2(4s^2\kappa^2 - 6s^2\kappa + 15 - 4s^2)}, \tag{276}$$

with $\kappa := \cos k_x + \cos k_y$. Expression (276) also holds for $k_y \neq 0$. There is again a $1/k^2$-singularity of the longitudinal fluctuations. As before, $\hat{\mathbf{B}}_{11}(\mathbf{k}) > \hat{\mathbf{B}}_{22}(\mathbf{k})$, *i.e.*, the restoring force for displacements in the direction of k is again higher than for displacements perpendicular to it. Due to $\hat{\mathbf{D}}_{11}(\mathbf{k}) = \hat{\mathbf{D}}_{22}(\mathbf{k})$, this behavior arises also for the smaller fluctuations of the "stiffer" mode. By considerations similar to those of section 14.9.1, one has $\langle u_1(\mathbf{k})^2 \rangle_{max}^{1/2} \approx 0.2\epsilon^{1/2}N$. Hence, the limitation of the fluctuations to a fixed number of lattice constants requires $\epsilon \propto 1/N^2$. The critical limit for the occurrence of the transverse instability becomes $s^* = \sqrt{12/5} = 1.549$, and the corresponding first unstable modes belong to $\kappa^* = 3/4$. For $k_y = 0$, this corresponds to the relatively small wavelength of 3.45 lattice constants, *i.e.*, again as in the long wavelength case, a wavelength of the order of the range of $h_{\mathbf{rs}}$.

14.9.3. Comparison with Monte-Carlo Simulations

In this section, we compare the analytical results obtained in Sections 14.9.1 and 14.9.2 with data from Monte-Carlo simulations of the Markov process (70) for the cases of long-range (Eq.(255)) and short-range (Eq.(272)) excitatory response $h_{\mathbf{rs}}$.

In the first simulation, we use a square 32×32-lattice (*i.e.*, $N = 32$) with the short-range excitatory response (272) and constant learning step size $\epsilon = 0.01$. Beginning with the equilibrium state $\bar{\mathbf{w}}_{\mathbf{r}} = m\mathbf{e}_x + n\mathbf{e}_y,\ m, n = 1, 2, \ldots, 32$, 20,000 "snapshots" of the Markov process described by (70) were generated in intervals of 2,000 Markov steps for the evaluation of the correlation function $\langle u_n(\mathbf{k})^2 \rangle$. For the ensemble of states obtained in this manner, the correlation function $f_n(\mathbf{k}) := \langle u_n(\mathbf{k})^2 \rangle^{1/2},\quad n = 1, 2, 3$ was evaluated at the discrete wave vectors $\mathbf{k} = \mathbf{e}_x \cdot 2\pi l/N$, $l = 1, \ldots, 32$. The data points, thus obtained for the "hard" mode u_1 and the "soft" mode u_2, are presented for $s = 10^{-4}$ in Fig. 14.6 and Fig. 14.7. Also shown are the predictions on the basis of (274) and (275). Obviously, the analytical description agrees very well with the simulation data. Figure 14.8 shows the dependence of the transverse fluctuations (in units of s) on the height $2s$ of the box for parameter values $s = 10^{-4}$, $s = 1.3$, and $s = 1.5$. The transverse fluctuations are described by the correlation function $f_3(\mathbf{k})$ and were obtained through simulations and from Eq. (276). For $s = 10^{-4}$, *i.e.*, essentially a very flat, two-dimensional box, the fluctuations decrease monotonically with wavelength. As s approaches the critical value s^*, the fluctuations of the modes near $k^* = 0.58\pi$ increase markedly. At $s = 1.5$, *i.e.*, just below $s^* \approx 1.54$, the fluctuations already take up a significant fraction of the box volume height and, thus, indicate the incipient instability. For all three parameter values, the agreement between the theoretical graphs and simulation data is very good.

A similar Monte-Carlo simulation for the long-range excitatory response is difficult to perform because of the considerably higher computational effort. Therefore, for this case we have carried out a simulation for a one-dimensional lattice consisting of $N = 128$ points. The box volume is replaced by a rectangular strip of length N and vertical extension $2s$. The learning step size was again $\epsilon = 0.01$. In this case, we generated an ensemble of states consisting of $10,000$ "snapshots" at intervals of 1000 Markov steps. The derivations of the preceding Section are eas-

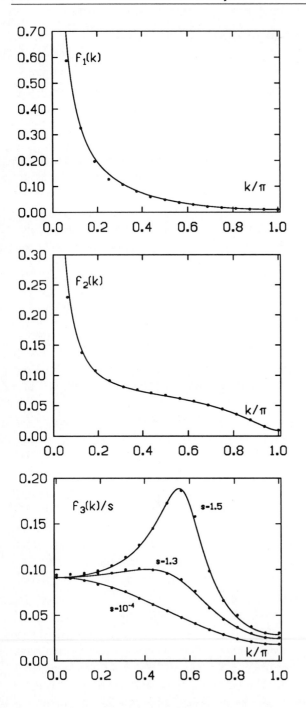

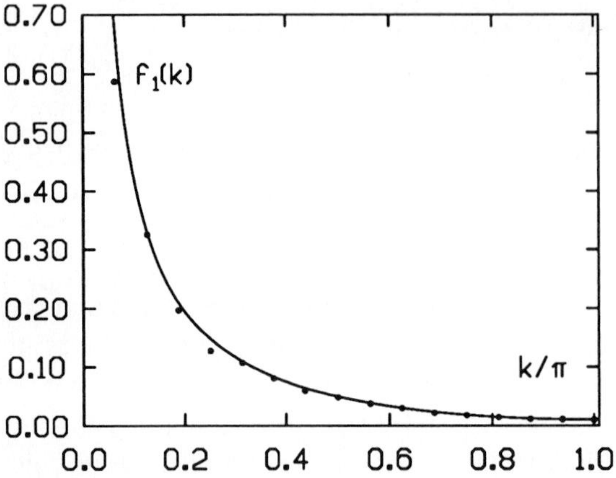

Figure 14.6 Dependence of the fluctuations of the "soft" mode u_1 for a short-range excitatory response of Eq. (272) on the wavenumber k. The data points are from a Monte-Carlo simulation of the Markov process (70) with fixed $\epsilon = 0.01$ and $s = 10^{-4}$. Superimposed is the dependence according to Eq.(274).

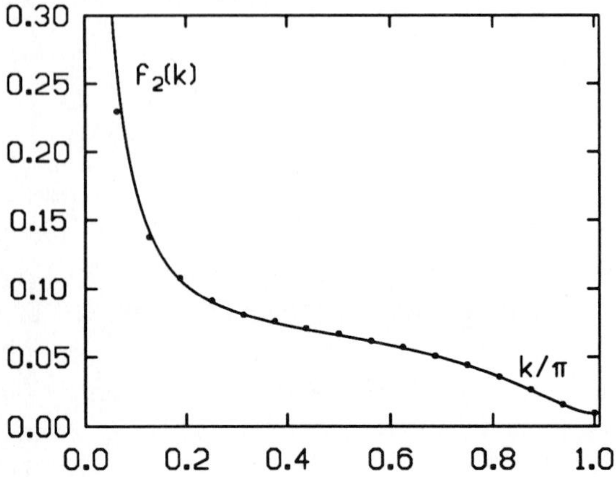

Figure 14.7 Fluctuations of the "hard" mode u_2, obtained from the same simulation as in Fig.14.6 (analytic result according to Eq.(275)). For small wavenumbers, the fluctuations are smaller than for u_1.

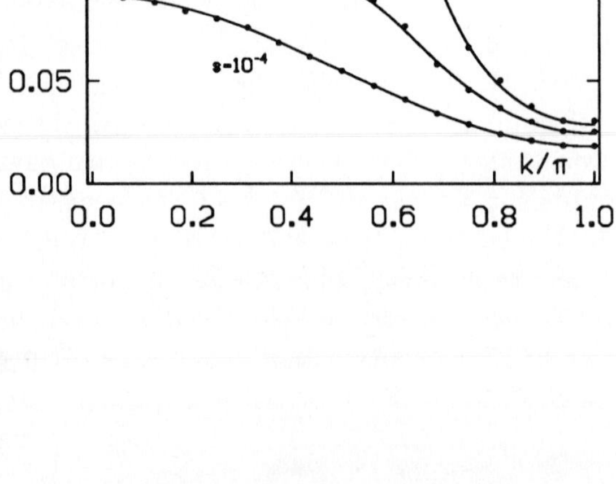

Figure 14.8 Fluctuations of the "transverse" mode u_3 (analytic results according to Eq. (276)) for three different values of the height parameter s: for $s = 10^{-4}$, *i.e.*, an essentially two-dimensional probability distribution, there are only small transverse fluctuations. For $s = 1.3$, the fluctuations begin to show a broad maximum near $k = 0.58\pi$. This is quite evident for $s = 1.5$, *i.e.*, just below s^*.

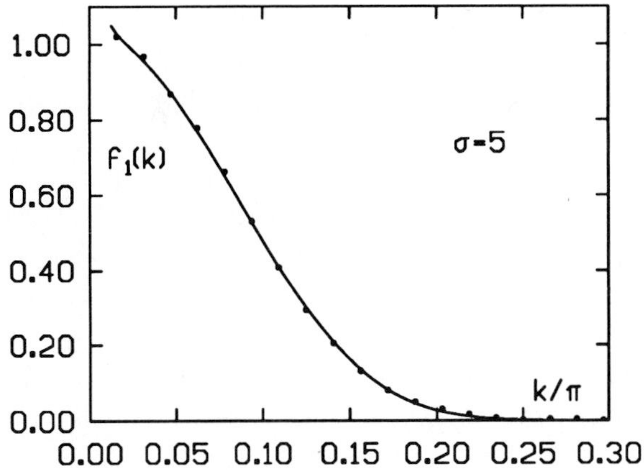

Figure 14.9 Dependence of the longitudinal fluctuations on the wavenumber k for a Gaussian excitatory response (255) with $\sigma = 5$. The data points pertain to a Monte-Carlo simulation of a chain with $N = 128$ points. Superimposed is the theoretical graph according to Eq.(277). The exponential fall-off at large wavenumbers is correctly reproduced by the data.

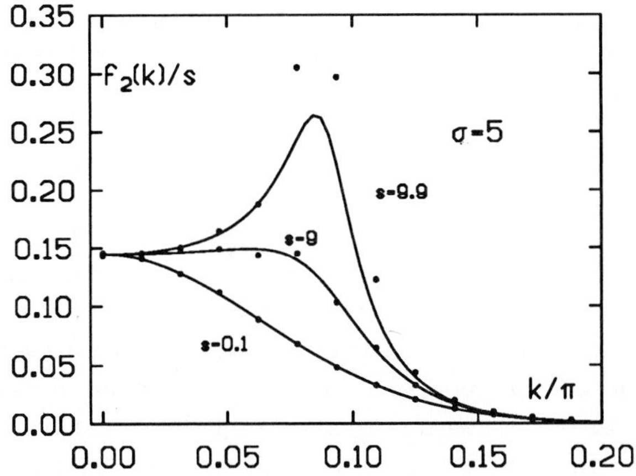

Figure 14.10 The corresponding transversale fluctuations for three different values of s (analytical results according to Eq.(278)). In comparison to Fig. 14.8, the critical value is now $s^* \approx 10.1$, and the fluctuations show an exponential fall-off for larger k-values. The maximum, related to the transverse instability, is shifted in comparison to Fig. 14.8 toward lower k-values.

ily adapted to the present situation and yield for the equilibrium fluctuations of the longitudinal (u_1) and transverse (u_2) modes (here the only ones):

$$\langle u_1(\mathbf{k})^2 \rangle = \frac{\epsilon\sigma\sqrt{2\pi}(12k^2\sigma^4 + 1)\exp(-k^2\sigma^2)}{12(2 - [1 + \cos k - 2\sigma^2 k \sin k]\exp(-k^2\sigma^2/2))}, \tag{277}$$

$$\langle u_2(\mathbf{k})^2 \rangle = \frac{\epsilon\sigma\sqrt{2\pi}s^2 \exp(-k^2\sigma^2)}{6 - 4s^2(1 - \cos k)\exp(-k^2\sigma^2/2)}. \tag{278}$$

These expressions are, up to an additional factor of $(\sigma\sqrt{2\pi})^{-1}$, identical to the results (268) and (270) for the two-dimensional lattice in the limit $k \to 0$. In particular, for s^* and λ^* we obtain the same values as before. Figure 14.9 and Fig. 14.10 show a comparison of the shape of the theoretical correlation functions according to (277) and (278) with the data from a Monte-Carlo simulation at $\sigma = 5$. Figure 14.9 shows the data points of the simulation for the longitudinal fluctuations $f_1(k)$ and $s = 0.1$. The expected exponential fall off for $k^2\sigma^2 > 1$ is reproduced well. On the other hand, the expected $1/k$-singularity for $f_1(k)$ is not visible, since the very small k-values required are possible only for considerably longer chains. Figure 14.10 shows the transverse fluctuations $f_2(k)$ for the three cases $s = 0.1$, *i.e.*, essentially a one-dimensional input vector distribution, $s = 9.0$ (still significantly below the critical value $s^* \approx 2.02\sigma \approx 10.1$), and $s = 9.9$ which is just below s^*. The main differences between the present case and the short-range case presented in Fig. 14.8 turn out to be the shift of the instability (maximum of $f_2(k)$) to shorter wavenumbers and the exponential fall-off of the fluctuations for $k\sigma >> 1$.

14.10. Interpretation of Results

In this section, we summarize the results of the preceding sections 14.8–14.9 and interpret them in terms of biological maps.

The situation analysed in Section 14.8 can be regarded as the simplest possible "scenario" in which a "dimensionality conflict" arises between the manifold of input signals (3-dimensional rectangular box) and the topology of the map (two-dimensional surface). The quantity determining the "strength" of the "conflict" is the height dimension $2s$ of the box volume. For small values of s, the variation of the input signal along the vertical dimension is hardly noticeable, and the structure of the resulting map is not affected by this part of the input signal variation. In this case the map corresponds geometrically to a vertical projection of the box onto a horizontal plane.

However, as shown by our analysis, this map only remains stable as long as $s \leq s^* = \sigma\sqrt{3e/2}$ is satisfied. In this stability region, the components w_{r3} of all weight vectors fluctuate about their common average value zero, and the size of the fluctuations decreases with the square root of the adaptation step size. The "stability threshold" s^* *can be interpreted essentially as that distance in the space of input signals which corresponds to the range of the neighborhood function h_{rs} in the lattice.* For $s > s^*$, a map with periodic "distortions" develops. Mathematically, these "distortions" stem from those components w_{r3} the average values of which are no longer spatially constant above the stability threshold, but rather vary with position $\mathbf{r}$ in the map. This variation exhibits a periodic pattern and begins to makes itself felt even below the threshold s^* by an increase of wavelike fluctuations about the equilibrium value $w_{\mathbf{r}3} = 0$. Here, contributions from fluctuations of wavelength $\lambda^* = \sigma\pi\sqrt{2}$ dominate, that is, *the scale of the dominant wavelengths is also determined by the range of the neighborhood function.*

In the context of a pattern processing task, the x- and y-coordinate would have the interpretation of two "primary" features, characterized by large variations. In contrast, the z-coordinate would correspond to a "secondary" feature with less strongly evident variation. As long as $s < s^*$, the system converges to a topographic map of the two "primary" features alone, and the "secondary" feature remains completely invisible in the map. As soon as the variation of the "secondary" feature exceeds the threshold value given by s^*, a map is created in which the "secondary" feature is also visible. This happens in such a way that the components of the weight vector $\mathbf{w_r}$ become position dependent in the direction of the "secondary" feature. If one represents the values $w_{\mathbf{r}3}$ of these components by gray levels, one finds an irregular pattern consisting of black and white stripes, as shown in Fig. 14.11.

Interestingly enough, in the brain one finds a whole series of two-dimensional arrangements of neurons whose response properties are distributed in qualitatively similar spatial patterns. The best-known examples of this are the "ocular dominance stripes," an irregular pattern of stripes containing neurons that prefer either the left or the right eye as their input, as well as the "orientation columns," along which neurons reacting to stimulation of the retina by brightness edges of the same orientation are grouped. In both cases, the response behavior of the neurons is described (to a first approximation) by three "stimulus variables," and there is a "dimensionality conflict" for the distribution of these parameters on the two-dimensional visual cortex: in addition to the two "primary" stimulus variables "retinal position" (x- and y-coordinates), the relative weight of the input of both eyes is a "secondary" feature in the case of the ocular dominance stripes. On the other hand, in the orientation stripes, the "secondary" feature is the orientation of the brightness edge, and each neuron — in addition to its specialization to a particular retinal position — will respond well to a small range of edge orientations only. Several models

Figure 14.11 Topographic map with periodic structure of stripes. The input signals came from a three-dimensional feature space $0 \leq x, y \leq 40$, $-4 \leq z \leq 4$. The map was generated by Kohonen's algorithm on a 40×40-lattice ($\sigma = 1.4$, 10^4 steps). The height (z-dimension) plays the role of the "secondary" feature, whose distribution in the map is represented by gray levels. The resulting pattern qualitatively resembles the pattern of *ocular dominance stripes* observed in the visual cortex, into which cells with a preference for the same eye become segregated, or of *orientation columns* in the striate cortex separating cells with receptive fields of different orientation.

for the description of such spatial patterns of neural stimulus variables have been suggested in the past. The papers of von der Malsburg (1979, 1982), Willshaw and von der Malsburg (1976), Takeuchi and Amari (1979), as well as Miller et al. (1989) represent some selected contributions to this area. In particular, the ability of Kohonen's model to generate such striped patterns was noticed very early by Kohonen himself in computer simulations (Kohonen 1982a). However, until recently this important property of the model received only little attention by other researchers. The derivation given here augments the earlier simulation results by means of a mathematical analysis that can serve as a point of departure for the mathematical treatment of more realistic versions of Kohonen's model. It shows that stripe formation can be regarded as an instability against wavelike "distortions" resulting from a 'dimensionality conflict" between input signals and the neuron layer.

14.11. Appendix

In this appendix, we show that for every positive function $\epsilon(t)$ the conditions

$$\lim_{t\to\infty}\int_0^t \epsilon(\tau)\,d\tau = \infty \qquad\qquad (i)$$
$$\lim_{t\to\infty}\epsilon(t) = 0$$

and

$$\lim_{t\to\infty}\int_0^t \epsilon(t')^2 \exp\Big(-\beta\int_{t'}^t \epsilon(t'')\,dt''\Big)\,dt' = 0. \qquad (ii)$$

are equivalent for arbitrary $\beta > 0$.

Proof: $(ii) \to (i)$ is obvious for $\epsilon > 0$; $(i) \to (ii)$:

Choose $\delta > 0$ arbitrarily small and $a > 0$ such that $\epsilon(t) < \beta\delta$ holds for all $t > a$. Let $\epsilon_{max} := \max_t \epsilon(t)$. Then a $b > a$ can be chosen such that $\exp(-\beta\int_a^t \epsilon(\tau)\,d\tau) < \beta\delta/\epsilon_{max}$ holds for all $t > b$. It then follows for all $t > b$ that:

$$\begin{aligned}
&\int_0^t \epsilon(t')^2 \exp\Big(-\beta\int_{t'}^t \epsilon(t'')\,dt''\Big)\,dt' = \\
=&\frac{1}{\beta}\Big(\int_0^a + \int_a^t\Big)\Big[\epsilon(t')\frac{\partial}{\partial t'}\exp\Big(-\beta\int_{t'}^t \epsilon(t'')\,dt''\Big)\Big]\,dt' \\
\le&\frac{\epsilon_{max}}{\beta}\Big[\exp\Big(-\beta\int_{t'}^t \epsilon(t'')\,dt''\Big)\Big]_{t'=0}^{t'=a} + \delta\cdot\Big[\exp\Big(-\beta\int_{t'}^t \epsilon(t'')\,dt''\Big)\Big]_{t'=a}^{t'=t} \\
\le&\frac{\epsilon_{max}}{\beta}\cdot\frac{2\beta\delta}{\epsilon_{max}} + \delta = 3\delta.
\end{aligned}$$

Since δ may be chosen arbitrarily small, (ii) must hold.

15. Local Linear Mappings

In the treatment of robot control tasks, we have seen that often the use of matrices, *i.e.*, linear mappings, as output values provides a useful extension of output learning maps. In the simulation of visuomotor coordination, the network learned the transformation between the visual image of the target point and the joint angles for the required arm position. Each neuron represented this nonlinear transformation for a neighborhood of a grid point. To this end, it had a matrix available that gave the linear part of the expansion of the transformation about the relevant grid point. In this way, the required transformation was approximated by an adaptive superposition of many linear mappings, each one valid only locally. Compared to the use of fixed output values, this yields a considerably higher accuracy with the same number of neurons.

Another interesting possibility was demonstrated for ballistic movements in Chapter 13. There, an output quantity (torque amplitude), varying as a function of further parameters (components of the target velocity), was assigned by means of an array to each input signal (arm position) which describes a linear relationship between torque amplitudes and velocity components. Such linear relationship represented by a matrix eliminates the necessity of representing the further parameters (*e.g.*, velocities) in the map as well, and, hence, the dimension of the space to be projected onto the lattice can be significantly reduced.

A precondition for such a strategy is a splitting of the input variables $v_1, v_2, \ldots, v_d$ into two (not necessarily disjoint) sets $\{v'_1, v'_2, \ldots, v'_a\}$ and $\{v''_1, v''_2, \ldots, v''_b\}$ such that

$$\{v_1, \ldots, v_d\} = \{v'_1, \ldots, v'_a\} \cup \{v''_1, \ldots, v''_b\},$$

and such that that output quantities $\mathbf{f}$ locally depend only linearly on one of the sets, *i.e.*,

$$\mathbf{f} = \mathbf{A}(\mathbf{v}')\mathbf{v}''. \tag{279}$$

Here, we have put $\mathbf{v}' := (v'_1, \ldots, v'_a)$, $\mathbf{v}'' := (v''_1, \ldots, v''_b)$. All those parameters not represented in the map themselves are included in $\mathbf{v}''$.

Such a splitting is possible in many cases. For example, in Chapter 11 the vector $\mathbf{v}'$ consisted of the coordinates $\mathbf{u}$ of the target point in the two camera fields of view. The vector $\mathbf{f}$ was the change of the joint angle under a small shift $\mathbf{v}''$ of the location of the end effector in the camera fields of view. In Chapter 13, $\mathbf{v}'$ stood for the joint angles of the arm, $\mathbf{f}$ was the torque amplitude in the joints, and $\mathbf{v}''$ was the resulting velocity to which the end effector was accelerated under the action of $\mathbf{f}$.

15.1. The Learning Algorithm for Local Linear Mappings

In this section we formulate the general version of the learning algorithm already derived for the special discussed in Chapters 11, 12, and 13.

We assume as before that the only available information is a sequence of n-tuples $(\mathbf{v}', \mathbf{v}'', \mathbf{f})$ satisfying (279). These are created during the learning phase by the reaction of the system to, *e.g.*, pseudo-randomly selected targets. In visuomotor coordination (Chapter 11), for example, $\mathbf{v}'$ was the position in the field of view of the target point and $\mathbf{v}''$ and $\mathbf{f}$ were the changes of the position in the field of view of the end effector and the joint angles during fine positioning. In the ballistic movements of Chapter 13, the $\mathbf{v}'$ were the arm joint angles, and $\mathbf{v}''$ was the velocity of the end effector due to an acceleration with torque amplitudes $\mathbf{f}$.

The task of the network is to learn the matrix $\mathbf{A}(\mathbf{v}')$ of Eq. (279) for each $\mathbf{v}'$. As was shown in Chapter 11, this can occur by means of a linear error correction rule. Together with the principle of neighborhood cooperation in Kohonen's original model, this leads to the following learning algorithm:

1. Register the next input signal $(\mathbf{v}', \mathbf{v}'', \mathbf{f})$.
2. Determine the lattice site $\mathbf{s} := \phi_{\mathbf{w}}(\mathbf{v}')$, assigned to $\mathbf{v}'$ in the map.
3. Compute an improved estimate $\mathbf{A}^*$ for the linear mapping $\mathbf{A}_{\mathbf{s}}^{old}$ of the chosen lattice site s

$$\mathbf{A}^* = \mathbf{A}_{\mathbf{s}}^{old} + \delta \cdot \left(\mathbf{f} - \mathbf{A}_{\mathbf{s}}^{old}\mathbf{v}''\right)(\mathbf{v}'')^T \tag{280}$$

4. Carry out a learning step

$$\mathbf{A}_{\mathbf{r}}^{new} = \mathbf{A}_{\mathbf{r}}^{old} + \epsilon h_{\mathbf{rs}}\left(\mathbf{A}^* - \mathbf{A}_{\mathbf{r}}^{old}\right) \tag{281}$$

for the assignment of linear mappings $\mathbf{A}_{\mathbf{r}}$.

5. Carry out a learning step

$$\mathbf{w}_{\mathbf{r}}^{new} = \mathbf{w}_{\mathbf{r}}^{old} + \epsilon' h'_{\mathbf{rs}}\left(\mathbf{v}' - \mathbf{w}_{\mathbf{r}}^{old}\right) \tag{282}$$

for the synaptic strengths $\mathbf{w}_{\mathbf{r}}$, and continue with Step 1

We encountered this algorithm in its application to the control of a robot arm by means of computer simulations. In the following, we analyze the algorithm mathematically in more detail. We are mainly interested in the question of convergence of the linear mappings $\mathbf{A}_{\mathbf{r}}$ to their correct values. For this, we first discuss the convergence behavior of the matrices $\mathbf{A}_{\mathbf{r}}$ in the absence of the lateral interaction, *i.e.*, for $h_{\mathbf{rs}} = \delta_{\mathbf{rs}}$. Building on this, we then investigate the important influence of lateral interaction.

15.2. Convergence Behavior without Lateral Interaction

Without lateral interaction, each lattice site learns its linear mapping isolated from all the others. We can then consider the evolution of the matrix of a single lattice site in our treatment of convergence. We further assume that the correspondence between lattice sites and values $\mathbf{v}'$ given by the vectors $\mathbf{w}_{\mathbf{r}}$ has already formed and no longer changes significantly in the course of the learning phase. To each vector $\mathbf{v}'$ is assigned a fixed lattice site s and thus a matrix $\mathbf{A}_{\mathbf{s}}$. We emphasize this in the following by writing $\mathbf{A}(\mathbf{v}', t)$ instead of $\mathbf{A}_{\mathbf{s}}$, where t gives the number of learning steps after which lattice site s was chosen in step 2 of the algorithm. With $h_{\mathbf{rs}} = \delta_{\mathbf{rs}}$ and equations (280) and (281), one then has

$$\mathbf{A}(\mathbf{v}', t+1) = \mathbf{A}(\mathbf{v}', t) + \delta \cdot \big(\mathbf{A}(\mathbf{v}') - \mathbf{A}(\mathbf{v}', t)\big)\mathbf{v}''(\mathbf{v}'')^T \qquad (283)$$

Here, we have absorbed the product $\epsilon \cdot \delta$ into the single constant δ. Denoting by $\mathbf{D}(\mathbf{v}', t) := \mathbf{A}(\mathbf{v}', t) - \mathbf{A}(\mathbf{v}')$ the deviation from the exact matrix $\mathbf{A}(\mathbf{v}')$, we obtain for the change of the Euclidean matrix norm $\|\mathbf{D}\| = (\mathrm{Tr}\ \mathbf{D}^T\mathbf{D})^{1/2}$ during one step (283)

$$\begin{aligned}\Delta\|\mathbf{D}\|^2 =& 2\mathrm{Tr}\ \mathbf{D}^T\Delta\mathbf{D} + \mathrm{Tr}\ \Delta\mathbf{D}^T\Delta\mathbf{D} \\ =& -\delta(2 - \delta\|\mathbf{v}''\|^2)\|\mathbf{D}\mathbf{v}''\|^2\end{aligned} \qquad (284)$$

If $0 < \delta < 2/\|\mathbf{v}''\|^2$, the norms $\|\mathbf{D}(\mathbf{v}', t)\|$ thus constitute a monotonically decreasing sequence. For a nonsingular correlation matrix $\langle \mathbf{v}''(\mathbf{v}'')^T \rangle$, this guarantees the convergence $\lim_{t\to\infty} \mathbf{A}(\mathbf{v}', t) = \mathbf{A}(\mathbf{v}')$.[†]

The preceding treatment of convergence assumes that the correlation matrix $\langle \mathbf{v}''(\mathbf{v}'')^T \rangle$ is independent of $\mathbf{A}(\mathbf{v}', t)$. However, this is often not satisfied because the values of $\mathbf{v}''$ are generated by the system itself, *i.e.*, the system tries to learn *from its own reactions.* At each learning step, the system receives a *target* $\mathbf{v}''_{targ}$ for $\mathbf{v}''$. For ballistic movements, this is the target velocity of the end effector, in visuomotor coordination, it is the residual difference between achieved and prescribed end effector position in the two camera fields of view after coarse positioning. In order to reach the target, the system determines its output quantity $\mathbf{f}$ by (279), but instead of the correct matrix $\mathbf{A}(\mathbf{v}')$ it uses the matrix $\mathbf{A}(\mathbf{v}', t)$ which deviates more or less from $\mathbf{A}(\mathbf{v}')$. Thus,

$$\mathbf{f} = \mathbf{A}(\mathbf{v}', t)\mathbf{v}''_{targ}. \qquad (285)$$

By (279), this leads to

$$\mathbf{v}'' = \mathbf{A}(\mathbf{v}')^{-1}\mathbf{A}(\mathbf{v}', t)\mathbf{v}''_{targ}. \qquad (286)$$

Hence, a nonsingular correlation matrix $\langle \mathbf{v}''_{targ}(\mathbf{v}''_{targ})^T \rangle$ of the target is not enough to guarantee convergence, because if $\mathbf{A}(\mathbf{v}', t)$ evolves "unfavorably" during learning, $\langle \mathbf{v}''(\mathbf{v}'')^T \rangle$ can still become singular, and the learning process can get stuck. This was

[†]For singular $\langle \mathbf{v}''(\mathbf{v}'')^T \rangle$ $\mathbf{D}$ can converge to a nonvanishing value from the null-space $\langle \mathbf{v}''(\mathbf{v}'')^T \rangle$, but even in this case the mean squared error Tr $\mathbf{D}\langle \mathbf{v}''(\mathbf{v}'')^T \rangle \mathbf{D}^T$ goes to zero.

the reason why in Chapter 11 and 13 we obtained convergence only for a fraction of the lattice sites without neigborhood cooperation between the neurons (see Figs. 11.7 and 13.5). We now analyse this behavior mathematically in more detail.

We neglect the slight variation of $\mathbf{v}'$ within the "parcels" of the particular lattice site s chosen and thus write $\mathbf{v}$ in place of $\mathbf{v}''$ and $\mathbf{A}(t)$ or $\mathbf{A}$ in place of $\mathbf{A}(t, \mathbf{v}')$ or $\mathbf{A}(\mathbf{v}')$, respectively. In order to investigate convergence, we consider the matrix $\mathbf{B}(t) = \mathbf{A}^{-1}\mathbf{A}(t) - \mathbf{1}$. We obtain for the change $\Delta\mathbf{B} := \mathbf{B}(t+1) - \mathbf{B}(t)$ of $\mathbf{B}$ under a learning step the expression

$$\Delta\mathbf{B} = -\delta \cdot \mathbf{B}\big(\mathbf{1} + \mathbf{B}\big)\mathbf{u}\mathbf{u}^T\big(\mathbf{1} + \mathbf{B}\big)^T. \tag{287}$$

Similar to (284), the change of $\|\mathbf{B}\|^2$ under a learning step (283) becomes

$$\Delta\|\mathbf{B}\|^2 = -\delta\big(2 - \delta\|\mathbf{v}\|^2\big)\|\mathbf{B}(\mathbf{1} + \mathbf{B})\mathbf{u}\|^2. \tag{288}$$

Hence, a monotonically decreasing sequence again arises for $\|\mathbf{B}(t)\|$, provided $0 < \delta < 2/\|\mathbf{v}\|^2$ holds. Maximization of the decrease per learning step occurs by means of the choice $\delta = 1/\|\mathbf{v}\|^2$. If δ is to be chosen independently of $\mathbf{v}$, then the condition $0 < \delta < 2/\alpha(1 + \|\mathbf{B}(0)\|)^2$ with $\alpha = \sup\|\mathbf{u}\|^2$ is sufficient for $\Delta\|\mathbf{B}\|^2 < 0$. Every possible stationary value for $\|\mathbf{B}(t)\|$ requires $\mathbf{B}^2 = -\mathbf{B}$. Since for $\|\mathbf{B}(0)\| < 1$ solutions $\mathbf{B} \neq 0$ with $\mathbf{B}^2 = -\mathbf{B}$ can no longer be reached, we obtain the convergence statement

> For $\|\mathbf{B}(0)\| < 1$ and $0 < \delta < 2/\|\mathbf{v}\|^2$ holds $\lim_{t\to\infty}\mathbf{B}(t) = 0$, *i.e.*, $\lim_{t\to\infty}\mathbf{A}(t) = \mathbf{A}$.

However, the condition $\mathbf{B}^2 = -\mathbf{B}$ has, in contrast to the previous situation described by (284), in addition to $\mathbf{B} = 0$ a whole manifold M of undesired stationary solutions. As we will show, a subset of M possesses an attractive neighborhood. Hence, there are initial values with the property $\|\mathbf{B}(0)\| > 1$ that evolve toward M under the learning rule and thus do not lead to the desired limit $\mathbf{A}$. For such initial values, the learning procedure converges to the wrong value.

This behavior can be illustrated well if one restricts to the one-dimensional case. In this case, u and B are scalar quantities, and (287) simplifies to

$$\dot{B} = -\delta \cdot B \cdot (B + 1)^2 u^2. \tag{289}$$

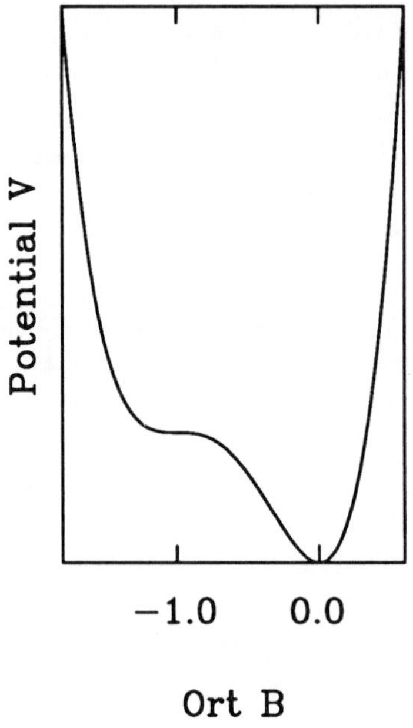

Figure 15.1 The shape of the potential $V(B)$. The absolute minimum lies at $B = 0$, which corresponds to the correctly learned matrix. The "force" acting at the position $B = -1$ on B also vanishes. Hence, for an unfavorable initial value, B gets "stuck" on this plateau.

For sufficiently small learning step lengths δ, one can neglect statistical fluctuations due to the random variables u and replace u^2 by its average. Without loss of generality, we assume $\langle u^2 \rangle = 1$. This yields

$$\dot{B} = -\delta \cdot B \cdot (B+1)^2. \tag{290}$$

We can interpret B as the position coordinate of a mass point in a viscous medium, *e.g.*, a small, not too heavy sphere in a jar of honey. The equation of motion for viscous motion is

$$\frac{m}{\gamma}\ddot{B} + \dot{B} = -\frac{d}{dB}V(B). \tag{291}$$

Here $V(B)$ is a potential in which the sphere moves. In the case of a small mass m and large viscosity γ, *i.e.*, $m/\gamma \ll 1$, the acceleration term with $\ddot{B}$ can be neglected, and the velocity $\dot{B}$ is proportional to the force $-V'(B)$. Equation (291) goes over to (290) in this limit for

$$V(B) = \frac{1}{4}B^4 + \frac{2}{3}B^3 + \frac{1}{2}B^2. \tag{292}$$

Figure 15.1 presents the shape of $V(B)$. The global minimum lies at $B = 0$, the value to be learned. The finite attractive neighborhood of this minimum extends from $B > -1$ to $B =$

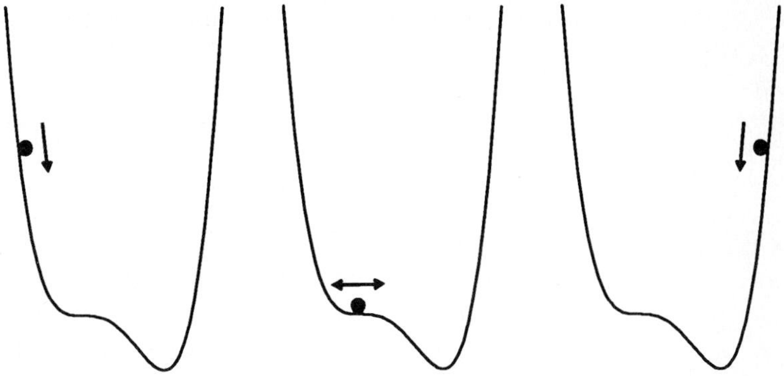

Figure 15.2 An illustration of the convergence behavior of B. The sphere with initial value less than -1 (left) will get stuck on the plateau at $B = -1$ (middle). Any sphere to the right of the plateau will roll as desired into the global minimum at $B = 0$ (right).

∞. Any initial value of B within this interval converges to the desired value during the learning process described by (290). The condition $\|\mathbf{B}(0)\| < 1$ assumed in the above convergence statement thus implies that we are located within the basin of attraction of the minimum at $B = 0$. In the one-dimensional case, the submanifold M of "false" stationary solutions consists of just the isolated point $B = -1$. Figure 15.2 shows that the attractive region of M is given by the interval $]-\infty, -1]$. Since the motion in the potential surface $V(B)$ is "infinitely" viscous, any initial value within the interval $]-\infty, -1]$ is pushed towards the point M and gets stuck there. However, an arbitrarily small disturbance in the positive direction suffices for leaving M in favor of the desired minimum $B = 0$. In higher dimensions, one has in addition undesired stationary solutions which are no longer unstable, and in this case M even has points where a small perturbation no longer leaves M. We show this in the remainder of this section.

We now resume the discussion of the general case. M consists of all matrices $\mathbf{B} \neq 0$ satisfying the condition $\|\mathbf{B}(\mathbf{B}+\mathbf{1})\| = 0$. Hence, we can take the quantity $d(\mathbf{B}) = \|\mathbf{B}(\mathbf{B}+\mathbf{1})\|^2 = \mathrm{Tr}\,\mathbf{B}(\mathbf{B}+\mathbf{1})(\mathbf{B}+\mathbf{1})^T\mathbf{B}^T$ as a measure of the distance from $\mathbf{B}$ to M. If δ is small enough to justify neglect of the terms of quadratic order, the learning step (283) leads to the change

$$\begin{aligned}\Delta d(\mathbf{B}) = & -2\delta \mathrm{Tr}\ \mathbf{B}(\mathbf{1}+\mathbf{B}) \\ & \times \left[\mathbf{B}\mathbf{u}\mathbf{u}^T(\mathbf{1}+\mathbf{B})^T + \mathbf{u}\mathbf{u}^T(\mathbf{1}+\mathbf{B})^T(\mathbf{1}+\mathbf{B})\right] \\ & \times (\mathbf{1}+\mathbf{B})^T\mathbf{B}^T.\end{aligned} \tag{293}$$

This expression is not particularly accessible to further manipulation. Hence, we restrict ourselves as above to the case in which (293) can be averaged over the target vector $\mathbf{u}$. This is consistent with the assumption of small learning step lengths δ. We further assume for $\mathbf{u}$ an isotropic distribution independently in each component, so that (perhaps after appropriate rescaling) $\langle \mathbf{u}\mathbf{u}^T \rangle = \mathbf{1}$ holds. This leads to

$$\begin{aligned}\langle \Delta d(\mathbf{B}) \rangle = & -2\delta \cdot \mathrm{Tr}\ \mathbf{B}(\mathbf{1}+\mathbf{B})\big(\mathbf{1} + 2\mathbf{B} + \mathbf{B}^T + \mathbf{B}\mathbf{B}^T + \mathbf{B}^T\mathbf{B}\big) \\ & \times (\mathbf{1}+\mathbf{B})^T\mathbf{B}^T \\ = & -2\delta \cdot \mathrm{Tr}\ \mathbf{B}(\mathbf{1}+\mathbf{B})\big(\mathbf{1} + \frac{3}{2}\mathbf{B} + \frac{3}{2}\mathbf{B}^T + \mathbf{B}\mathbf{B}^T + \mathbf{B}^T\mathbf{B}\big) \\ & \times (\mathbf{1}+\mathbf{B})^T\mathbf{B}^T \\ = & -2\delta \cdot \mathrm{Tr}\ \mathbf{B}(\mathbf{1}+\mathbf{B})\mathbf{H}(\mathbf{B})(\mathbf{1}+\mathbf{B})^T\mathbf{B}^T,\end{aligned} \tag{294}$$

where the matrix $\mathbf{H}(\mathbf{B})$ is defined by

$$\mathbf{H}(\mathbf{B}) = \mathbf{1} + \frac{3}{2}\mathbf{B} + \frac{3}{2}\mathbf{B}^T + \mathbf{B}\mathbf{B}^T + \mathbf{B}^T\mathbf{B}. \tag{295}$$

For all regions of M for which $\mathbf{H}$ is strictly positive, one has $\langle \Delta d(\mathbf{B}) \rangle < 0$. Thus, any point $\mathbf{B}$ located sufficiently close to such a region is drawn farther toward M on the average. A condition for this to occur results from the following

Theorem 1. Let $\mathbf{B}_0 := \sum_{i=1,n} \mathbf{p}_i\mathbf{q}_i^T$, where $\mathbf{p}_i, \mathbf{q}_i$ are $2n$ vectors, whose scalar products satisfy the conditions

$$\mathbf{p}_i \cdot \mathbf{p}_j = 0, \quad \mathbf{q}_i \cdot \mathbf{q}_j = 0, \quad (i \neq j);$$

together with $\|\mathbf{p}_i\| \cdot \|\mathbf{q}_i\| \geq 3/2$, $i = 1, \ldots, n$. For every $\mathbf{B}$ sufficiently close to $\mathbf{B}_0$, one then has $\langle \Delta d(\mathbf{B}) \rangle < 0$.
Proof: For $i = 1, \ldots, n$, define

$$\begin{aligned}\alpha_i := & \|\mathbf{q}_i\|; \\ \beta_i := & \frac{3}{2\|\mathbf{q}_i\|} \leq \|\mathbf{p}_i\|; \\ \mathbf{w}_i := & \alpha_i\mathbf{p}_i + \beta_i\mathbf{q}_i;\end{aligned}$$

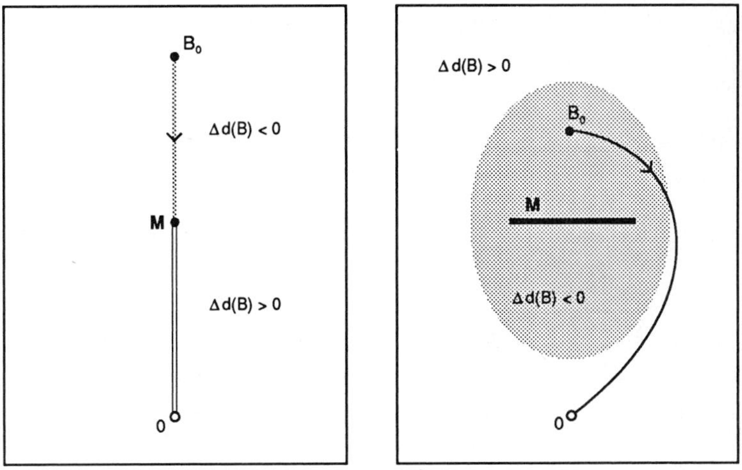

Figure 15.3 Difference between the one-dimensional and the multidimensional case. *Left:* In the one-dimensional case, the desired solution $\mathbf{B} = 0$ cannot be reached if the undesired fixed point M separates the initial value $\mathbf{B}_0$ from the origin. *Right:* In the multidimensional case, on the other hand, it is possible to avoid the manifold M of undesired fixed points. It may even be possible to reach the desired solution $\mathbf{B} = 0$ if the initial value $\mathbf{B}_0$ lies in the (shaded) neigborhood of M within which $d(\mathbf{B})$, the distance to M, is everywhere decreasing.

This yields

$$\mathbf{H}(\mathbf{B}_0) = \mathbf{1} + \sum_{i=1..n} \mathbf{w}_i \mathbf{w}_i^T + \sum_{i=1..n} (\|\mathbf{p}_i\|^2 - \beta_i^2)\mathbf{q}_i \mathbf{q}_i^T. \tag{296}$$

Therefore, $\mathbf{H}(\mathbf{B}_0)$ is strictly positive. Since $\mathbf{H}$ depends continuously on its argument, this holds throughout a whole neighborhood of $\mathbf{B}_0$ and implies $\langle d(\mathbf{B})\rangle < 0$ there.

This deserves two remarks. First, there are matrices $\mathbf{B}_0$ for which the above theorem holds, but which are located so far from the manifold M, *i.e.*, for which $\|\mathbf{B}_0(\mathbf{1} + \mathbf{B}_0)\|$ is so large, that the matrices are attracted to the desired solution $\mathbf{B} = 0$ before reaching M. For these initial values, the above theorem does not necessarily imply convergence to M, since the learning steps (283) might induce the system to leave the neighborhood of the initial value within which this property exists, even if they decrease $\|\mathbf{B}(\mathbf{1} + \mathbf{B})\|$ on the average. This is shown in Fig. 15.3 on the right. A sufficient condition for $\mathbf{B}_0 \in M$ is for example $\mathbf{p}_i \cdot \mathbf{q}_j = -\delta_{ij}$.

Secondly, M possesses points for which $\langle \Delta d(\mathbf{B})\rangle < 0$ can not even be guaranteed within an entire neighborhood. Near these points, it is no longer possible to guarantee convergence to M. An example of such a point is $\mathbf{B} = -\mathbf{1}$. As we have seen, in the one-dimensional case M consists only of this one point.

Thus, we have shown that under the learning rule (283) $\mathbf{A}(t)$ converges to the desired value $\mathbf{A}$, provided the initial value $\mathbf{A}(0)$ is not "too badly" chosen. The basin of attraction for the desired $\mathbf{A}$ contains the region $\|\mathbf{A}^{-1}\mathbf{A}(0) - \mathbf{1}\| < 1$. Moreover, there is a whole manifold of undesired fixed points which can be reached for bad initial values. This unfortunate property led in Chapters 11 and 13 to poor results in the computer simulations whenever there was no neighborhood cooperation between the neurons. With sufficient neighborhood cooperation between the neurons, on the other hand, convergence to the desired state occured. In the following, we show how this improvement through neighborhood cooperation arises.

15.3. Improvement of Convergence through Neighborhood Cooperation

We now investigate the effects of neighborhood cooperation due to the lateral interaction $h_{\mathbf{rs}}$. A significant consequence of neighborhood cooperation is that none of the adaptation steps is restricted to the particular lattice site s, but rather all of the adjacent lattice sites participate in the adaptation step as well. The degree of participation decreases according to $h_{\mathbf{rs}}$ with increasing distance from s. In the following, we will show that this offers at least two advantages. First, the effective rate of convergence is improved, and secondly the robustness of the system with respect to unfavorable initial values of the linear mappings $\mathbf{A}_\mathbf{r}$ is increased. Even for initial values for which in the absence of lateral interaction, not all the mappings $\mathbf{A}_\mathbf{r}$ would converge as desired, convergence of all $\mathbf{A}_\mathbf{r}$ to the correct matrices is ensured in the presence of lateral interaction.

To make the following investigation feasible, we make a few additional simplifying assumptions. First, we suppose that the adaptation of the synaptic strengths $\mathbf{w}_\mathbf{r}$ is already finished and has attained an asymptotic distribution such that each lattice site is selected in step 2 of the algorithm with the same probability. As shown in Chapter 5, it is just this (approximate) creation of such a state which forms an essential property of the algorithm. Secondly, we restrict ourselves to the case in which the correct mapping $\mathbf{A}(\mathbf{v}')$ is independent of $\mathbf{v}'$ and thus the same for every lattice site. This assumption will not significantly influence the results in all cases where the change in $\mathbf{A}(\mathbf{v}')$ is small over the range of the function $h_{\mathbf{rs}}$. We further suppose that the step lengths δ are small enough to allow one to neglect terms of quadratic and higher order. Under these assumptions, we can summarize steps 1–4 for the matrices $\mathbf{B_r} = \mathbf{A}(\mathbf{w_r})^{-1}\mathbf{A_r}(t) - \mathbf{1}$ as follows:

1. Choose $\mathbf{s} = \phi_{\mathbf{w}}(\mathbf{v}')$.
2. Set

$$\mathbf{B}^* = \mathbf{B_s}(t) + \Delta_L\big(\mathbf{B_s}(t)\big), \tag{297}$$

   where $\Delta_L\big(\mathbf{B_s}(t)\big) = -\delta\mathbf{B_s}(t)(\mathbf{1}+\mathbf{B_s}(t))\mathbf{u}\mathbf{u}^T(\mathbf{1}+\mathbf{B_s}(t))^T$ is the change of $\mathbf{B_s}(t)$ under the learning rule (283).
3. Improve the matrices $\mathbf{B_r}(t)$ according to

$$\mathbf{B_r}(t+1) = \mathbf{B_r}(t) + \epsilon h_{\mathbf{rs}}\big(\mathbf{B}^* - \mathbf{B_r}(t)\big), \tag{298}$$

   and begin again at step 1.

With (297) and (298), we obtain for the average time rate of change $\dot{\mathbf{B}}_\mathbf{r}$ of the matrix $\mathbf{B_r}$ in the presence of additional neighborhood cooperation

$$\dot{\mathbf{B}}_\mathbf{r} = \sum_\mathbf{s} h_{\mathbf{rs}}(\mathbf{B_s} - \mathbf{B_r}) - \delta \cdot \sum_\mathbf{s} h_{\mathbf{rs}}\mathbf{B_s}(\mathbf{B_s}+\mathbf{1})(\mathbf{B_s}+\mathbf{1})^T. \tag{299}$$

Here, we have again replaced $\mathbf{u}\mathbf{u}^T$ by its mean, and we have assumed as before $\langle \mathbf{u}\mathbf{u}^T\rangle = \mathbf{1}$. A multiplicative factor ϵ/N has been normalized to unity by an appropriate scaling of the time constant.

We decompose the summation over all lattice points $\mathbf{s}$ into sums over nearest neighbors of $\mathbf{r}$, next nearest neighbors, etc. This yields the expression

$$\begin{aligned}\dot{\mathbf{B}}_\mathbf{r} =& h\sum_{\langle \mathbf{s}\rangle}(\mathbf{B_s}-\mathbf{B_r}) + h^2\sum_{\langle\langle \mathbf{s}\rangle\rangle}(\mathbf{B_s}-\mathbf{B_r}) + \ldots \\ &- \delta\cdot\mathbf{B_r}(\mathbf{B_r}+\mathbf{1})(\mathbf{B_r}+\mathbf{1})^T \\ &- \delta\cdot h\sum_{\langle \mathbf{s}\rangle}\mathbf{B_s}(\mathbf{B_s}+\mathbf{1})(\mathbf{B_s}+\mathbf{1})^T + \ldots\,,\end{aligned} \tag{300}$$

where $\langle \mathbf{s}\rangle$ is to be understood as a summation over nearest neighbors and $\langle\langle \mathbf{s}\rangle\rangle$ as a sum over next nearest neighbors. The factor h is the fall-off of the Gaussian $h_{\mathbf{rs}}$ from the center of the excitation s to the nearest lattice points, *i.e.*, $h = \exp(-1/2\sigma^2)$. The fall-off up to the next nearest neighbors then has the value h^2 etc.

Three cases can be discussed on the basis of Eq. (300). First, the limit $h \approx 1$ and $\delta \ll h$. This corresponds to a very-long-range neighborhood interaction and (relative to this) a negligible length δ of the improvement step, as present at the beginning of the learning phase. For this extreme case, we can again give a potential for the viscous motion $\dot{\mathbf{B}}_{\mathbf{r}}$, namely

$$V = \frac{h}{4}\sum_{\mathbf{r}}\sum_{\langle\mathbf{s}\rangle}(\mathbf{B_s} - \mathbf{B_r})^2 + \frac{h^2}{4}\sum_{\mathbf{r}}\sum_{\langle\langle\mathbf{s}\rangle\rangle}(\mathbf{B_s} - \mathbf{B_r})^2 + \dots, \qquad (301)$$

which corresponds to the simple situation of coupled springs with spring constants depending on the lattice spacing. In this potential, the matrices $\mathbf{B_r}$ try to take the same value at every lattice site. This is important in the initial phase of learning, because "deviants" in the initial values are "tamed" by all other neighbors, and each $\mathbf{B_r}$ settles down to an average over all initial values. This average need not lie at the desired $\mathbf{B_r} = 0$; this can be seen from the fact that the above potential is translationally invariant, and thus every value for $\mathbf{B_r}$ which is equal at all lattice sites minimizes V. Hence, we need an additional term favoring $\mathbf{B_r} = 0$.

We obtain the opposite case at the end of the learning phase, when $h \ll \delta$. The neighborhood interaction then falls off very rapidly and in the extreme case is negligible compared to the learning step length δ. Evidently, the time rate of change $\dot{\mathbf{B}}_{\mathbf{r}}$ in this approximation is given by the expression

$$\dot{\mathbf{B}}_{\mathbf{r}} = -\delta \cdot \mathbf{B_r}(\mathbf{B_r} + \mathbf{1})(\mathbf{B_r} + \mathbf{1})^T, \qquad (302)$$

which we have already discussed thoroughly. By itself, this expression produced unsatisfactory convergence of the system as a whole, to the degree that initial values could lie in the wrong region of attraction. However, now neighborhood cooperation can pull the values of all $\mathbf{B_r}$ into the potential well at $\mathbf{B_r} = 0$ before entering the final phase of the learning process, which allows it to be completed successfully. The manner in which this occurs is shown by consideration of the intermediate learning phase.

The intermediate learning phase is characterized as a state lying between the two previous extreme cases, *i.e.*, a state for

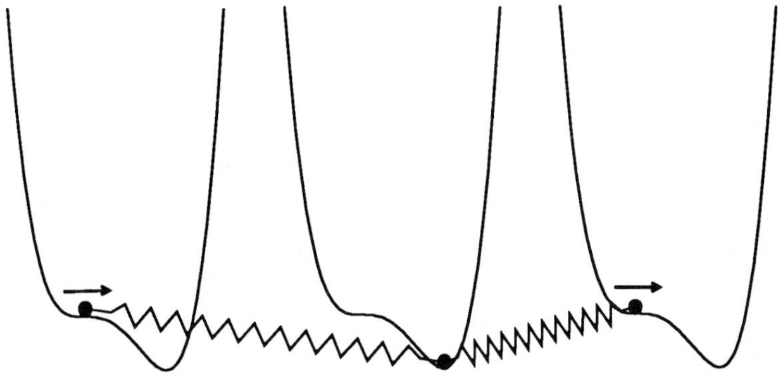

Figure 15.4 An illustration of the convergence behavior of B in the presence of additional coupling by means of springs. The spheres that are "stuck" on the plateau (left and right) are pulled or pushed into the potential well at $B = 0$ by the springs from the adjacent sphere (middle) and are thus able to assume the desired position in the global minimum.

which $h \approx \delta$ and $h, \delta \ll 1$ hold simultaneously. If we neglect the terms of quadratic and higher order in these factors in (300), one obtains

$$\dot{\mathbf{B}}_{\mathbf{r}} = h \sum_{\langle \mathbf{s} \rangle} (\mathbf{B}_{\mathbf{s}} - \mathbf{B}_{\mathbf{r}}) - \delta \cdot \mathbf{B}_{\mathbf{r}}(\mathbf{B}_{\mathbf{r}} + \mathbf{1})(\mathbf{B}_{\mathbf{r}} + \mathbf{1})^T. \tag{303}$$

15.3.1. One-Dimensional Case

If we again discuss this approximation for the one-dimensional case, a very interesting situation occurs. Here, it is again possible to state a potential for $\dot{B} = -dV/dB$, namely

$$V = \frac{h}{4} \sum_{\mathbf{r}} \sum_{\langle \mathbf{s} \rangle} (B_{\mathbf{s}} - B_{\mathbf{r}})^2 + \delta \sum_{\mathbf{r}} \Big(\frac{1}{4} B_{\mathbf{r}}^4 + \frac{2}{3} B_{\mathbf{r}}^3 + \frac{1}{2} B_{\mathbf{r}}^2 \Big). \tag{304}$$

Our "spheres in honey" again move in the potential whose shape is shown in Fig. 15.1, but now the "spheres" of each lattice site are coupled via springs to the nearest neighbors. In contrast to the potential (301), one now has the necessary additional term favoring the desired value $B_{\mathbf{r}} = 0$. Figure 15.4 presents this new situation.

"Spheres" that are stuck on the undesired plateau at $B_{\mathbf{r}} = -1$ can now be "pulled" or "pushed" off the plateaus by a neighbor located inside the well at $B_{\mathbf{r}} = 0$.

In principle, the system as a whole can still of course remain stuck outside the desired state. For example, this is the case when all initial values without exception lie in the interval $[-\infty, -1]$. All matrices then converge simultaneously to the value $B_{\mathbf{r}} = -1$, and the coupling via springs may even accelerate this convergence. However, this situation becomes more and more unlikely as the number N of lattice points increases: The probability of such an occurrence decreases exponentially like α^N, where $\alpha < 1$ gives the probability that the initial value of $B_{\mathbf{r}}$ lies to the left of the plateau $B_{\mathbf{r}} = -1$.

15.3.2. Multi-Dimensional Case

For the further investigation of convergence properties in the multidimensional case, we consider the quantity

$$S(t) := \sum_{\mathbf{r}} \|\mathbf{B}_{\mathbf{r}}(t)\|. \tag{305}$$

For each iteration 1–3, one has

$$\begin{aligned}
\Delta\|\mathbf{B}_{\mathbf{r}}(t)\|^2 &= 2\mathrm{Tr}\ \Delta\mathbf{B}_{\mathbf{r}}(t)\mathbf{B}_{\mathbf{r}}(t)^T \\
&= 2h_{\mathbf{rs}}\mathrm{Tr}\ \left[\left(\mathbf{B}^* - \mathbf{B}_{\mathbf{r}}(t)\right)\mathbf{B}_{\mathbf{r}}(t)^T\right] \\
&\leq 2h_{\mathbf{rs}}\left(\|\mathbf{B}^*\| - \|\mathbf{B}_{\mathbf{r}}(t)\|\right)\|\mathbf{B}_{\mathbf{r}}(t)\| \\
&= 2h_{\mathbf{rs}}\left(\Delta_L\|\mathbf{B}_{\mathbf{s}}(t)\| + \|\mathbf{B}_{\mathbf{s}}(t)\| - \|\mathbf{B}_{\mathbf{r}}(t)\|\right)\|\mathbf{B}_{\mathbf{r}}(t)\|,
\end{aligned} \tag{306}$$

where we have written $\|\mathbf{B}^*\| - \|\mathbf{B}_{\mathbf{s}}(t)\| =: \Delta_L\|\mathbf{B}_{\mathbf{s}}(t)\|$. Inequality (306) yields

$$\Delta\|\mathbf{B}_{\mathbf{r}}(t)\| \leq h_{\mathbf{rs}}\left(\Delta_L\|\mathbf{B}_{\mathbf{s}}(t)\| + \|\mathbf{B}_{\mathbf{s}}(t)\| - \|\mathbf{B}_{\mathbf{r}}(t)\|\right), \tag{307}$$

where we recall that $\Delta_L\|\mathbf{B}_{\mathbf{s}}(t)\|$ also depends on the target vector $\mathbf{u}$, which as before is assumed to be a random variable with $\langle \mathbf{u}\mathbf{u}^T\rangle = \mathbf{1}$. For the change of the quantity $S(t)$ with an iteration step, averaged over $\mathbf{u}$ and lattice sites $\mathbf{s}$ by taking into account the symmetry of $h_{\mathbf{rs}}$ and equation (307), one obtains

$$\begin{aligned}
\langle \Delta S(t)\rangle_{\mathbf{s},\mathbf{u}} &\leq \frac{1}{N}\sum_{\mathbf{r},\mathbf{s}} h_{\mathbf{rs}}\left(\|\mathbf{B}_{\mathbf{s}}(t)\| - \|\mathbf{B}_{\mathbf{r}}(t)\| + \Delta_L\|\mathbf{B}_{\mathbf{s}}(t)\|\right) \\
&= \frac{h}{N}\sum_{\mathbf{s}}\langle \Delta_L\|\mathbf{B}_{\mathbf{s}}(t)\|\rangle_{\mathbf{u}} \leq 0,
\end{aligned} \tag{308}$$

where N is the number of lattice sites, and $h = \sum_{\mathbf{r}} h_{\mathbf{rs}}$. If we ignore boundary effects, h is independent of $\mathbf{s}$. Without lateral interaction, *i.e.*, $h_{\mathbf{rs}} = \delta_{\mathbf{rs}}$, we would have obtained (308) with $h = 1$. Hence, because of lateral interaction, the convergence rate is raised by a factor of h. Since h is a measure for the size of the neighborhood region participating in a learning step, this region should be chosen as large as possible consistent with the requirement of small variations of $\mathbf{A_r}$ and $\mathbf{B_r}$.

This result concerning the convergence rate is still quite general, since we have not yet used special properties of the learning rule for $\Delta_L\mathbf{B}$. This will done in the remainder of this section, where we will show that lateral interaction leads to an effective enlargement of the attraction region about the desired fixed point of the learning rule (283), thus raising the robustness of the algorithm against poorly chosen initial values.
To this end, we first show two lemmas.
Lemma 1: Let $h_{\mathbf{rs}}$ be nonnegative, symmetric with respect to commutation of r and s and nonvanishing at least for all nearest neighbor pairs r and s of the lattice. Let $Q(t) := \sum_{\mathbf{r}} \|\mathbf{B_r}(t)\|^2$. Then the mean change $\langle \Delta Q \rangle$ per learning step vanishes only if all norms $\|\mathbf{B_r}(t)\|$ are equal.
Proof: From (306) and $\Delta_L\|\mathbf{B_s}(t)\| \leq 0$, we obtain

$$\Delta Q \leq 2\sum_{\mathbf{r}} h_{\mathbf{rs}} \left(\|\mathbf{B_s}(t)\| - \|\mathbf{B_r}(t)\|\right) \|\mathbf{B_r}(t)\|. \tag{309}$$

Averaging over s and taking into account the symmetry of $h_{\mathbf{rs}}$ yields

$$\langle \Delta Q \rangle_{\mathbf{s}} \leq -\frac{1}{N} \sum_{\mathbf{r,s}} h_{\mathbf{rs}} \left(\|\mathbf{B_s}(t)\| - \|\mathbf{B_r}(t)\|\right)^2. \tag{310}$$

Together with $h_{\mathbf{rs}} > 0$ for all nearest-neighbor pairs r, s, this proves the claim.

With respect to convergence to the desired fixed point $\mathbf{B} = 0$, all matrices $\mathbf{B_r}(t)$ share the same fate: either all of them converge to $\mathbf{B} = 0$, or else all of them tend to the manifold M of undesired fixed points. However, as soon as the mean of the $\|\mathbf{B_r}(t)\|$ of the lattice gets below the value unity, at least some of the $\|\mathbf{B_r}(t)\|$ must converge to $\mathbf{B} = 0$ by (308) and Theorem 1. But this induces the convergence of all the others to $\mathbf{B} = 0$, no matter how bad their initial values may have been. Without lateral interaction, *i.e.*, $h_{\mathbf{rs}} = \delta_{\mathbf{rs}}$, one does not have this result. In this case (310) does not imply a restriction on the norms $\|\mathbf{B_r}(t)\|$, and Lemma 1 no longer applies. Hence, lateral interaction enables those lattice sites with good initial values to extend the zone of convergence about the desired fixed point for all the other lattice sites. As a consequence, even if a considerable portion of the lattice sites has poor initial values, the common convergence of all matrices $\mathbf{B_r}(t)$ to the desired fixed point cannot be prevented.

It is even possible to improve the bound for the mean norm $\|\mathbf{B_r}(t)\|$ below which convergence is guaranteed. For this, we prove

Lemma 2: For sufficiently small step sizes δ, the expectation value $\langle d(\mathbf{B}(t))\rangle_{\mathbf{u}}$ of the function $d(\mathbf{B}) = \|\mathbf{B}(\mathbf{B}+\mathbf{1})\|^2$ obeying Eq. (294) satisfies the inequality

$$\langle d(\mathbf{B}(t))\rangle_{\mathbf{u}} \geq d(\mathbf{B}(0)) \cdot \exp(-2\delta\lambda t). \tag{311}$$

Here, λ is a constant upper bound for the matrix $\mathbf{H}$ of (295) over the complete time evolution, which is equivalent to

$$\lambda \geq \sup_{\mathbf{B}(t)} \|\mathbf{H}(\mathbf{B}(t))\|. \tag{312}$$

(Such an upper bound can always be determined, since $\|\mathbf{H}\|$ is bounded by some polynomial in $\|\mathbf{B}\|$, which itself is bounded).

Proof: From (294) and Tr $\mathbf{AB} \leq \|\mathbf{A}\| \cdot \|\mathbf{B}\|$ one has

$$\frac{\langle \Delta d(\mathbf{B})\rangle_{\mathbf{u}}}{d(\mathbf{B})} \geq -2\delta\|\mathbf{H}(\mathbf{B})\| \geq -2\delta\lambda. \tag{313}$$

For sufficiently small δ, we can replace (313) by

$$\langle \Delta \ln d(\mathbf{B})\rangle_{\mathbf{u}} \geq -2\delta\lambda. \tag{314}$$

This yields

$$\begin{aligned}\langle d(\mathbf{B}(t))\rangle_{\mathbf{u}} &\geq \exp\big(\langle \ln(d(\mathbf{B}(t))\rangle_{\mathbf{u}}\big) \\ &\geq d(\mathbf{B}(0)) \cdot \exp(-2\delta\lambda t),\end{aligned} \tag{315}$$

which proves the claim.

One thus has

$$\begin{aligned}\langle \Delta_L \|\mathbf{B_s}(t)\|\rangle_{\mathbf{u}} &= \frac{1}{2}\langle \Delta_L \|\mathbf{B_s}(t)\|^2\rangle_{\mathbf{u}} / \|\mathbf{B_s}(t)\| \\ &= -\frac{\delta}{2}\langle \|\mathbf{B_s}(t)(\mathbf{B_s}(t)+\mathbf{1})\mathbf{u}\|^2\rangle_{\mathbf{u}} / \|\mathbf{B_s}(t)\| \\ &= -\frac{\delta}{2} d(\mathbf{B_s}(t)) / \|\mathbf{B_s}(t)\|.\end{aligned} \tag{316}$$

Equations (309), (316) and Lemma 2 yield

$$\begin{aligned}\langle \Delta S(t)\rangle_{\mathbf{s},\mathbf{u}} &\leq -\frac{h\delta}{2N}\sum_{\mathbf{s}} \frac{d(\mathbf{B_s}(t))}{\|\mathbf{B_s}(t)\|} \\ &\leq -\frac{h\delta e^{-2\delta\lambda t}}{2N}\sum_{\mathbf{r}} \frac{d(\mathbf{B_r}(0))}{\|\mathbf{B_r}(t)\|}.\end{aligned} \tag{317}$$

This shows that $\|\mathbf{B_r}(t)\|$ decreases on the average. Hence the replacement of the denominator $\|\mathbf{B_r}(t)\|$ with $\|\mathbf{B_r}(0)\|$ should not destroy the inequality. It then follows that

$$\langle \Delta S(t)\rangle_{\mathbf{s},\mathbf{u}} \le -\frac{h\delta e^{-2\delta\lambda t}}{2N}\sum_{\mathbf{r}}\frac{d(\mathbf{B_r}(0))}{\|\mathbf{B_r}(0)\|}. \tag{318}$$

Integration of this equation gives the final result

$$\lim_{t\to\infty}\langle S(t)\rangle_{\mathbf{s},\mathbf{u}} \le S(0) - \frac{h}{2\lambda}D_0, \tag{319}$$

with

$$\begin{aligned} D_0 &= -\frac{1}{2N}\sum_{\mathbf{r}}\frac{d(\mathbf{B_r}(0))}{\|\mathbf{B_r}(0)\|} \\ &= -\frac{1}{N\delta}\sum_{\mathbf{r}}\langle\Delta_L\|\mathbf{B_r}(0)\|\rangle_{\mathbf{u}}. \end{aligned} \tag{320}$$

The quantity described by $-D_0$ can be interpreted as the average initial change of $\|\mathbf{B}\|$ of a lattice site due to the learning rule (283), but with respect to $\delta = 1$.

Equation (320) shows that on the average each $\|\mathbf{B_r}(0)\|$ is shifted by at least $hD_0/2N\lambda$ towards the desired fixed point $\mathbf{B} = 0$. The bound of unity given above for the critical value of the mean norm $\|\mathbf{B_r}(t)\|$ leading to global convergence rises by this shift, which is proportional to the strength of the lateral interaction.

This concludes our theoretical discussion of the properties of the learning algorithm.

Bibliography

Albert A (1972) *Regression and the Moore-Penrose Pseudoinverse.* Academic Press, New York.

Albus JS (1971) "A Theory of Cerebellar Function." *Math. Biosci.*, **10**:25–61.

Amit DJ, Gutfreund H, Sompolinsky H (1985) "Spin-Glass Models of Neural Networks." *Phys. Rev.*, **A32**:1007–1018.

Amit DJ, Gutfreund H, Sompolinsky H (1985) "Storing Infinite Number of Patterns in a Spin-Glass Model of Neural Networks." *Phys. Rev. Lett.*, **55**:1530–1533.

Amit DJ, Gutfreund H, Sompolinsky H (1987) "Information Storage in Neural Networks with Low Level of Activity." *Phys. Rev.*, **A35**:2293–2303.

Anderson JA (1968) "A Memory Model Using Spatial Correlation Functions." *Kybernetik*, **5**:113–119.

Anderson JA (1970) "Two Models for Memory Organization." *Math. Biosci.*, **8**:137–160.

Anderson JA, Silverstein JW, Ritz SA, Jones RS (1977) "Distinctive Features, Categorical Perception and Probability Learning: Some Applications of a Neural Model." *Psych. Rev.*, **84**:413–451.

Angeniol B, de la Croix Vaubois G, le Texier JY (1988) "Self-Organizing Feature Maps and the Traveling Salesman Problem." *Neural Networks*, **1**:289-293.

Arbib MA (1981) "Perceptual Structures and Distributed Motor Control." *Handbook of Physiology: The Nervous System II, Motor Control*, VB Brooks (ed.), 1449–1480. Bethesda, Md.

Arbib MA, Amari SI (1985) "Sensori-Motor Transformations in the Brain [with a Critique of the Tensor Theory of Cerebellum]." *J. Theor. Biol.*, **112**:123–155.

Ballard DH (1986) "Cortical Connections and Parallel Processing: Structure and Function." *Behav. & Brain Sci.*, **9**:67–91.

Barto AG, Sutton SR (1981) "Goal Seeking Components for Adaptive Intelligence: An Initial Assessment." AFWAL-TR-81-1070, Avionics Laboratory, Air Force Wright Aeronautical Laboratories, Wright-Patterson AFB, Ohio 45433.

Barto AG, Sutton SR, Anderson CW (1983) "Neuron-Like Adaptive Elements That Can Solve Difficult Learning Control Problems." *IEEE SMC*, **13**:834–846.

Baum EB (1986) "Intractable Computations without Local Minima." *Phys. Rev. Lett.*, **57**:2764–2767.

Becker W, Fuchs AF (1969) "Further Properties of the Human Saccadic System: Eye Movements and Correction Saccades with and without Visual Fixation Points." *Vis. Res.*, **9**:1247–1258.

Bernstein N (1967) *The Coordination and Regulation of Movements.* Pergamon, London.

Bertsch H, Dengler J (1987) Klassifizierung und Segmentierung medizinischer Bilder mit Hilfe der selbstlernenden topologischen Karte, E Paulus (ed.), 9.DAGM-Symposium Mustererkennung, 166–170, Springer Informatik Fachberichte 149, Berlin, Heidelberg.

Blasdel GG, Salama G (1986) "Voltage-Sensitive Dyes Reveal a Modular Organization in Monkey Striate Cortex." *Nature*, **321**:579–585.

Block HD (1962) "The Perceptron: A Model for Brain Functioning." *Rev. of Mod. Phys.*, **34**:123–135.

Bounds DG (1987) "New Optimization Methods from Physics and Biology." *Nature*, **329**:215–219.

Bradburn DS (1989) "Reducing Transmission Error Effects Using a Self-Organizing Network." *IJCNN-89*, **II**:531–538. Washington, D.C.

Brady M, Hollerbach JM, Johnson TL, Lozano-Perez T, Mason MT (1984) *Robot Motion: Planning and Control.* MIT Press, Cambridge, Mass.

Brooks RA (1983) "Solving the Find-Path Problem by Good Representation of Free Space." *IEEE SMC*, **13**:190–197.

Brooks VB (1981) "The Nervous System: Motor Control." *Handbook of Physiology*, American Physiological Society, Bethesda, Md.

Buhmann J, Schulten K (1987) "Noise-Driven Temporal Association in Neural Networks." *Europhy. Lett.*, **4**(10):1205–1209.

Buhmann J, Divko R, Schulten K (1989) "Associative Memory with High Information Content." *Phys. Rev.*, **A39**:2689–2692.

Caianiello ER (1961) "Outline of a Theory of Thought and Thinking Machines." *J. Theor. Bio.*, **1**:204–235.

Campenot RB (1977) "Local Control of Neurite Development by Nerve Growth Factor." *PNAS*, **74**:4516–4519.

Cohen M, Grossberg S (1983) "Absolute Stability of Global Pattern Formation and Parallel Memory Storage by Competitive Neural Networks." *IEEE SMC*, **13**: 815–826.

Cotrell M, Fort JC (1986) "A Stochastic Model of Retinotopy: A Self-Organizing Process." *Bio. Cybern.*, **53**:405–411.

Cragg BG, Temperley HNV (1954) "The Organization of Neurones: A Cooperative Analogy." *EEG and Clin. Neurophy.*, **6**: 85–92.

Cragg BG, Temperley HNV (1955) "The Analogy with Ferromagnetic Hysteresis." *Brain*, (78)**II**:304–316.

Creutzfeld OD (1983) *Cortex Cerebri.* Springer, Berlin.

Cruse H, Wischmeyer E, Brüwer M, Brockfeld P and Dress A (1990) "On the Cost Functions for the Control of Human Arm Movements." *Bio. Cybern.*, **62**:519–528.

Derrida B, Gardner E, Zippelius A (1987) "An Exactly Soluble Asymmetric Neural Network Model." *Europhys. Lett.*, **4**:167–173.

Durbin R, Willshaw D (1987) "An Analogue Approach to the Travelling Salesman Problem Using an Elastic Net Method." *Nature*, **326**:689–691.

Edelman GM (1978) "Group Selection and Phasic Reentrant Signalling: A Theory of Higher Brain Function." *The Mindful Brain*, GM Edelman and VB Mountcastle (eds.), 51–100. MIT Press, Cambridge, Mass.

Fox J (1984) "The Brain's Dynamic Way of Keeping in Touch." *Science*, **225**:820–821.

Gardiner CW (1985) *Handbook of Stochastic Methods* (2nd Ed.). Springer, New York.

Gardner E (1988) "The Space of Interactions in Neural Network Models." *J. Phys.*, **A21**:257–270.

Gardner E, Derrida B (1988) "Optimal Storage Properties of Neural Network Models." *J. Phys.*, **A21**:271–284.

Garey MR, Johnson DS (1979) *Computers and Intractability: A Guide to the Theory of NP-Completeness.* Freeman, New York.

Ginsburg H, Opper S (1969) *Piaget's Theory of Intellectual Development.* Prentice Hall, Englewood Cliffs, N.J.

Golgi C (1903) *Opera Omnia*, **I**, **II**. U Hoepli, Milan.

Grossberg S (1976a) "On the Development of Feature Detectors in the Visual Cortex with Applications to Learning and Reaction-Diffusion Systems." *Bio. Cybern.*, **21**:145–159.

Grossberg S (1976b) "Adaptive Pattern Classification and Universal Recoding: I. Parallel Development and Coding of Neural Feature Detectors." *Bio. Cybern.*, **23**:121–134.

Grossberg S (1978) "Competition, Decision and Consensus." *J. Math. Anal. Appl.*, **66**:470–493.

Grossberg S, Kuperstein M (1986) *Neural Dynamics of Adaptive Sensory-Motor Control.* North Holland, Amsterdam.

Gutfreund H, Mezard M (1987) "Processing Temporal Sequences." *Neural Networks*, preprint.

Harris WA (1986) "Learned Topography: The Eye Instructs the Ear." *TINS*, March, 97–99.

Hastie T, Stuetzle W (1989) "Principal Curves." *J. Am. Stat. Assn.*, **84**:502–516.

Hebb D (1949) *Organization of Behavior.* Wiley, New York.

Held R, Hein A (1963) "Movement-Produced Stimulation in the Development of Visually Guided Behaviour." *J. Comp. Physiol. Psy.*, **56**:872–876

Henson DB (1977) "Corrective Saccades: Effects of Altering Visual Feedback." *Vis. Res.*, **17**:63–67.

Hillis WD (1985) *The Connection Machine.* MIT Press, Cambridge, Mass.

Hogan N (1984) "An Organizing Principle for a Class of Voluntary Movements." *J. Neurosci.*, **4**:2745–2754.

Hopfield JJ (1982) "Neural Networks and Physical Systems with Emergent Collective Computational Abilities." *PNAS USA*, **79**:2554–2558.

Hopfield JJ (1984) "Neurons with Graded Response Have Collective Computational Properties Like Those of Two-State Neurons." *PNAS USA*, **81**:3088–3092.

Hubel DH, Wiesel TN (1974) "Sequence Regularity and Geometry of Orientation Columns in the Monkey Striate Cortex." *J. Comp. Neurol.*, **158**:267–294.

Hubel DH, Wiesel TN, Stryker PN (1978) "Anatomical Demonstration of Orientation Columns in Macaque Monkey." *J. Comp. Neurol.*, **177**:361–380.

Hwang YK (1988) "Robot Path Planning Using Potential Field Representation." Thesis, Univ. of Illinois, Urbana-Champaign.

Jenkins WM, Merzenich MM, Ochs MT (1984) "Behaviorally Controlled Differential Use of Restricted Hand Surfaces Induces Changes in the Cortical Representation of the Hand in Area 3b of Adult Owl Monkeys." *Soc. Neurosci. Abstr.*, **10**:665.

Jordan MI, Rosenbaum DA (1988) "Action." *Foundation of Cognitive Science*, MI Posner (ed.). MIT Press, Cambridge, Mass.

Kaas JH, Nelson RJ, Sur M, Lin CS, Merzenich MM (1979) "Multiple Representations of the Body within the Primary Somatosensory Cortex of Primates." *Science*, **204**:521–523.

Kaas JH, Merzenich MM, Killackey HP (1983) "The Reorganization of Somatosensory Cortex Following Peripheral Nerve Damage in Adult and Developing Mammals." *Ann. Rev. Neurosci.*, **6**:325–56.

van Kampen NG (1981) *Stochastic Processes in Physics and Chemistry.* North Holland, Amsterdam.

Kandel ER, Schwartz JH (1982) "Molecular Biology of Learning: Modulation of Transmitter Release." *Science*, **218**:433–443.

Kandel ER, Schwartz JH (1985) *Principles of Neural Science* (2nd Ed.). Elsevier, New York.

Kawato M, Furukawa K, Suzuki R (1987) "A Hierarchical Neural-Network Model for Control and Learning of Voluntary Movement." *Bio. Cybern.*, **57**:169–185.

Kelso SR, Ganong AH, Brown TH (1986) "Hebbian Synapses in Hippocampus." *PNAS USA*, **83**:5326–5330.

Khinchin A.I. *Mathematical Foundations of Information Theory.* Dover, New York.

Kirk DE (1970) *Optimal Control Theory.* Prentice Hall, Englewood Cliffs, N.J.

Kirkpatrick S, Gelatt CD, Vecchi MP (1983) "Optimization by Simulated Annealing." *Science*, **220**:671–680.

Kirkpatrick S (1984) "Optimization by Simulated Annealing: Quantitative Studies." *J. Stat. Phys.*, **34**:975–986.

King AJ, Hutchings ME, Moore DR, Blakemore C (1988) "Developmental Plasticity in the Visual and Auditory Representations in the Mammalian Superior Colliculus." *Nature*, **332**:73–76.

Knudsen EI, du Lac S, Esterly SD (1987) "Computational Maps in the Brain." *Ann. Rev. Neurosci.*, **10**:41–65.

Kohonen T (1972) "Correlation Matrix Memories." *IEEE*, **C21**:353–359.

Kohonen T (1982a) "Self-Organized Formation of Topologically Correct Feature Maps." *Bio. Cybern.*, **43**:59–69.

Kohonen T (1982b) "Analysis of a Simple Self-Organizing Process." *Bio. Cybern.*, **44**:135–140.

Kohonen T (1982c) "Clustering, Taxonomy and Topological Maps of Patterns." *Proc. 6th Int. Conf. on Pattern Recognition*, Munich, 114–128.

Kohonen T (1984a) "Self-Organization and Associative Memory." *Springer Series in Information Sciences* 8, Heidelberg.

Kohonen T, Mäkisara K, Saramäki T (1984b) "Phonotopic maps—Insightful Representation of Phonological Features for Speech Recognition." *Proc. 7th Int. Conf. on Pattern Recognition*, Montreal, 182–185.

Kohonen T (1986) "Learning Vector Quantization for Pattern Recognition." Report TKK-F-A601, Helsinki University of Technology.

Korn A (1982) Bildverarbeitung durch das visuelle System. Fachberichte Messen, Steuern, Regeln 8, Springer-Verlag, Heidelberg.

Kuperstein M (1987) "Adaptive Visual-Motor Coordination in Multijoint Robots Using Parallel Architecture." *Proc. IEEE Int. Conf. Automat. Robotics*, 1595–1602, Raleigh N.C.

Kuperstein M (1988) "Neural Model of Adaptive Hand-Eye Coordination for Single Postures." *Science*, **239**:1308–1311.

Lawley DN, Maxwell AE (1963) *Factor Analysis as a Statistical Method.* Butterworths, London.

Lee C, Rohrer WH, Sparks DL (1988) "Population Coding of Saccadic Eye Movements by Neurons in the Superior Colliculus." *Nature*, **332**:357–360.

Lemon R (1988) "The Output Map of the Primate Motor Cortex: Trends." *Neural Sci.*, **11**:501–506.

Lin S, Kernighan BW (1973) "An Effective Heuristic for the Travelling Salesman Problem." *Optimization Research*, **21**:498–516.

Linde Y, Buzo A, Gray RM (1980) "An Algorithm for Vector Quantizer Design." *IEEE Trans. Comm.*, **28**:84–95.

Little WA (1974) "The Existence of Persistent States in the Brain." *Math. Biosci.*, **19**:101–120.

Little WA, Shaw GL (1975) "A Statistical Theory of Short and Long Term Memory." *Behav. Bio.*, **14**:115–133.

Luttrell SP (1989) "Self-Organization: A Derivation from First Principles of a Class of Learning Algorithms." *Proc. IJCNN 89*, **II**:495–498, Washington, D.C.

Makhoul J, Roucos S, Gish H (1985) "Vector Quantization in Speech Coding." *Proc. IEEE.* **73**:1551–1588.

von der Malsburg C (1973) "Self-Organization of Orientation Sensitive Cells in the Striate Cortex." *Kybernetik*, **14**:85–100.

von der Malsburg C, Willshaw DJ, (1977) "How to Label Nerve Cells So That They Can Interconnect in an Ordered Fashion." *Proc. Nat. Acad. Sci. USA*, **74**:5176–5178.

von der Malsburg C (1979) "Development of Ocularity Domains and Growth Behavior of Axon Terminals." *Bio. Cybern.*, **32**:49–62.

von der Malsburg C (1982) "Outline of a Theory for the Ontogenesis of Iso-Orientation Domains in Visual Cortex." *Bio. Cybern.*, **45**:49–56.

Marks KM, Goser KF (1987) "AI Concepts for VLSI Process Modelling and Monitoring." Preprint.

Marr D (1969) "A Theory of Cerebellar Cortex." *J. Physiol.*, **202**:437–470.

Martinetz T, Ritter H, Schulten K (1988) "Kohonen's Self-Organizing Map for Modeling the Formation of the Auditory Cortex of a Bat." *SGAICO Proc. Connectionism in Perspective*, 403–412, Zürich.

Martinetz T, Ritter H, Schulten K (1989) "3D-Neural Net for Learning Visuomotor-Coordination of a Robot Arm." *IJCNN-89, Conf. Proc.*, **II**:351–356, Washington,.

Martinetz T, Ritter H, Schulten K (1990a) "Three-dimensional Neural Net for Learning Visuomotor-Coordination of a Robot Arm." *IEEE Trans. on Neur. Net.*, **1**(1):131–136.

Martinetz T, Ritter H, Schulten K (1990b) "Learning of Visuomotor Coordination of a Robot Arm with Redundant Degrees of Freedom." *ICNC-90 Proc. Int. Conf. on Parallel Processing; Neur. Sys. and Comp.*, Düsseldorf, 431–434, R, Eckmiller G, Hartmann, and G Hauske (eds.), North-Holland, Amsterdam; and in *ISRAM-90 Proc. Third Int. Symp. Robot. and Mfg., Vancouver, B.C.* , 521–526.

Martinetz T, Schulten K (1990) "Hierarchical Neural Net for Learning Control of a Robot's Arm and Gripper." *IJCNN-90 Conf. Proc., San Diego 1990*, **III**:747–752.

McCulloch WS, Pitts W (1943) "A Logical Calculus of the Ideas Immanent in Nervous Activity." *Bull. Math. Biophys.* **5**:115–133.

Merzenich MM, Knight PL, Roth GL (1975) . *J. Neurophysiol.*, **38**:231.

Miller KD, Keller JB, Stryker MP (1989) "Ocular Dominance Column Development: Analysis and Simulation." *Science*, **245**:605–615.

Miller WT (1989) "Real-Time Application of Neural Networks for Sensor-Based Control of Robots with Vision." *IEEE Trans. Sys., Man, and Cybern.*, **19**(4):825-831.

Minsky M, Papert S (1969) *Perceptrons.* MIT Press, Cambridge, Mass.

Mountcastle VB (1978) "An Organizing Principle for Cerebral Function: The Unit Module and the Distributed System." *The Mindful Brain*, GM Edelman and VB Mountcastle (eds.), 7–50. MIT Press, Cambridge, Mass.

Murphy JT, Kwan HC, MacKay WA, Wong YC (1977) "Spatial Organization of Precentral Cortex in Awake Primates. III. Input-Output Coupling." *J. Neurophysiol.*, **41**:1132–1139.

Nelson W (1983) "Physical Principles for Economies of Skilled Movements." *Biol. Cybern.*, **46**:135–147

Obermayer K, Ritter H, Schulten K (1989) "Large-Scale Simulation of a Self-Organizing Neural Network: Formation of a Somatotopic Map." *Parallel Processing in Neural Systems and Computers*, Eckmiller et al. (eds.), 71–74, North Holland, Amsterdam.

Obermayer K., Ritter H., Schulten K. (1990a) "Large-Scale Simulations of Self-Organizing Neural Networks on Parallel Computers: Application to

Biological Modelling." *Parallel Computing*, **14**:381–404.

Obermayer K, Ritter H, Schulten K (1990b) "A Neural Network Model for the Formation of Topographic Maps in the CNS: Development of Receptive Fields." *IJCNN-90 Conf. Proc.*, **II**:423–429. San Diego.

Obermayer K, Ritter H, Schulten K (1990c) "A Principle for the Formation of the Spatial Structure of Cortical Feature Maps." *Proc. Nat. Acad. Sci. USA*, **87**:8345–8349.

Obermayer K, Blasdel GG, Schulten K (1991) "A Neural Network Model for the Formation and for the Spatial Structure of Retinotopic Maps, Orientation- and Ocular-Dominance Columns." *ICANN-91*, Helsinki, June 1991.

Overton KJ, Arbib MA (1982) "The Branch Arrow Model of the Formation of Retino-Tectal Connections." *Bio. Cybern.*, **45**:157–175

Palm G (1980) "On Associative Memory." *Bio. Cybern.*, **36**:19-31.

Palm G (1981) "On the Storage Capacity of an Associative Memory with Randomly Distributed Storage Elements." *Bio. Cybern.* **39**:125–127.

Pearson JC, Finkel LH, Edelman GM (1987) "Plasticity in the Organization of Adult Cerebral Maps: A Computer Simulation Based on Neuronal Group Selection." *J. Neurosci.*, **12**:4209–4223.

Pellionisz A, Llinas R (1979) "Brain Modelling by Tensor Network Theory and Computer Simulation. The Cerebellum: Distributed Processor for Predictive Coordination." *Neurosci.*, **4**:323–348.

Ramón y Cajal S (1955) Histologie du Systeme Nerveux. II., C.S.I.C., Madrid.

Rauschecker JP, Singer W (1981) "The Effects of Early Visual Experience on the Cat's Visual Cortex and Their Possible Explanation by Hebb-Synapses." *J. Physiol.*, **310**:215–239.

Ritter H, Schulten K (1986a) "On the Stationary State of Kohonen's Self-Organizing Sensory Mapping." *Bio. Cybern.*, **54**:99–106.

Ritter H, Schulten K (1986b) "Topology Conserving Mappings for Learning Motor Tasks." *Neural Networks for Computing*, JS Denker (ed.) *AIP Conf Proc.*, **151**:376–380, Snowbird, Utah.

Ritter H, Schulten K (1987) "Extending Kohonen's Self-Organizing Mapping Algorithm to Learn Ballistic Movements." *Neural Computers,* R Eckmiller and E von der Malsburg (eds.), Springer, Heidelberg, 393–406.

Ritter H, Schulten K (1988) "Kohonen's Self-Organizing Maps: Exploring their Computational Capabilities." *IEEE ICNN 88 Conf.*, **I**:109–116, San Diego.

Ritter H, Schulten K (1989) "Convergence Properties of Kohonen's Topology Conserving Maps: Fluctuations, Stability, and Dimension Selection." *Bio. Cybern.*, **60**:59–71.

Ritter H, Martinetz T, Schulten K (1989a) "Topology Conserving Maps for Learning Visuomotor-Coordination." *Neural Networks*, **2**:159–168.

Ritter H, Martinetz T, Schulten K (1989b) "Topology Conserving Maps for Motor Control." *Neural Networks, from Models to Applications*, (L Personnaz and G Dreyfus (eds.), I.D.S.E.T. Paris, 579–591.

Ritter H, Martinetz T, Schulten K (1989c) Ein Gehirn für Roboter—Wie neuronale Netzwerke Roboter steuern können. MC-Mikrocomputerzeitschrift, Franzis-Verlag München, Feb. 1989.

Ritter H (1989) "Asymptotic Level Density for a Class of Vector Quantization Processes." *Internal Report A9*, Helsinki Univ. of Technology. IEEE Trans. on Neural Networks, Jan. 1991.

Ritter H, Kohonen T (1989) "Self-Organizing Semantic Maps." *Bio. Cybern.*, **61**:241–254.

Ritter H, Kohonen T (1990) "Learning 'Semantotopic Maps' from Context." *IJCNN-90, Conf. Proc.*, 1990, **I**:23–26 Washington, D.C.

Ritter H. (1990) "Motor Learning by 'Charge' Placement with Self-Organizing Maps." *Neural Networks for Sensory and Motor Systems*, R Eckmiller (ed.), Elsevier, Amsterdam.

Robinson DA (1973) "Models of the Saccadic Eye Movement Control System." *Kybernetik*, **14**:71–83.

Rosenblatt F (1958) "The Perceptron: A Probabilistic Model for Information Storage and Organization in the Brain." *Psych. Rev.*, **65**:386–408.

Rosenblatt F (1961) *Principles of Neurodynamics: Perceptrons and the Theory of Brain Mechanisms.* Spartan Books, Washington, D.C.

Rubner J, Schulten K (1990) "A Self-Organizing Network for Complete Feature Extraction." *Bio. Cybern.*, **62**:193–199.

Rumelhart DE, McClelland JL (1984) *Parallel Distributed Processing.* MIT Press, Cambridge, Mass.

Rumelhart DE, Hinton GE, Williams RJ (1986) "Learning Representations by Back-Propagating Errors." *Nature*, **323**:533–536.

Saltzman EL (1979) "Levels of Sensorimotor Representation." *J. Math. Psy.*, **20**:91–163.

Schwartz EL (1980) "Computational Anatomy and Functional Architecture of Striate Cortex: A Spatial Mapping Approach to Perceptual Coding." *Vision Res.*, **20**:645–669.

Sejnowski T, Rosenberg CR (1987) "Parallel Networks That Learn to Pronounce English Text." *Complex Systems*, **1**:145–168.

Sparks DL, Nelson JS (1987) "Sensory and Motor Maps in the Mammalian Superior Colliculus." *TINS*, **10**:312–317.

Steinbuch K (1961) "Die Lernmatrix." *Kybernetik*, **1**:36–45.

Suga N, Jen PH (1976) "Disproportionate Tonotopic Representation for Processing CF–FM Sonar Signals in the Mustache Bat Auditory Cortex". *Science*, **194**:542–544.

Suga N, O'Neill WE (1979) "Neural Axis Representing Target Range in the Auditory Cortex of the Mustache Bat." *Science*, **206**:351–353.

Takeuchi A, Amari S (1979) "Formation of Topographic Maps and Columnar Microstructures." *Bio. Cybern.*, **35**:63–72.

Taylor WK (1956) "Electrical Simulation of Some Nervous System Functional Activities." *Information Theory*, C Cherry (ed.), 314–328, Butterworths, London.

Walker MW, Orin DE (1982) "Efficient Dynamic Computer Simulation of Robotic Mechanisms." *J. Dyn. Sys., Meas., and Cont.*, **104**:205–211.

Werbos P (1974) "Beyond Regression: New Tools for Prediction and Analysis in the Behavioral Sciences." Ph.D. thesis, Harvard Univ. Committee on Applied Mathematics.

Widrow B, Hoff ME (1960) "Adaptive Switching Circuits." *WESCON Conv. Rec.*, **IV**:96–104.

Willshaw DJ, Buneman OP, Longuet-Higgins HC (1969) "Non-Holographic Associative Memory." *Nature* **222**:960–962.

Willshaw DJ, von der Malsburg C (1976) "How Patterned Neural Connections Can Be Set up by Self-Organization." *Proc. R. Soc. London*, **B194**:431–445.

Willshaw DJ, von der Malsburg C (1979) "A Marker Induction Mechanism for the Establishment of Ordered Neural Mappings: Its Application to the Retinotectal Problem." *Proc. R. Soc. London*, **B287**:203–243.

Woolsey CN, Harlow HF (1958) *Biological and Biochemical Basis of Behavior.* Univ. of Wisconsin Press, Madison, 63–81.

Wurtz RH, Goldberg ME, Robinson DL (1986) Neuronale Grundlagen der visuellen Aufmerksamkeit. Wahrnehmung und visuelles System, Spektrum der Wissenschaft, Heidelberg, 58–66.

Zipser D, Andersen RA (1988) "A Back-Propagation Programmed Network That Simulates Response Properties of a Subset of Posterior Parietal Neurons." *Nature*, **331**:679–683.

Index